OTHER VOLUMES IN THE STAR WISDOM SERIES

Cosmology Reborn

Star Wisdom, vol 1
With Monthly Ephemerides and Commentary for 2019

Saturn - Mary - Sophia

Star Wisdom, vol 2
With Monthly Ephemerides and Commentary for 2020

As Above, So Below

Star Wisdom, vol 3
With Monthly Ephemerides and Commentary for 2021

Cosmic Communion

Star Wisdom, vol 4
With Monthly Ephemerides and Commentary for 2022

The Turning Point

Star Wisdom, Volume 5
2023

EDITOR
Joel Matthew Park

ADVISORY BOARD

Brian Gray ~ Claudia McLaren Lainson ~ Robert Powell, PhD
Lacquanna Paul ~ Robert Schiappacasse

Lindisfarne Books

LINDISFARNE BOOKS

an imprint of Steinerbooks/Anthroposophic Press, Inc.

402 Union Street, No. 58, Hudson, NY 12534

www.steinerbooks.org

With grateful acknowledgment to Peter Treadgold (1943–2005), who wrote the Astrofire program (available from the Sophia Foundation), with which the ephemeris pages in *Star Wisdom* are computed each year.

ISBN: 978-1-58420-893-8

Printed in the United States of America

CONTENTS

ASTROSOPHY

The Sophia Foundation was founded and exists to help usher in the new age of Sophia and the corresponding Sophianic culture, the Rose of the World, prophesied by Daniel Andreev and other spiritual teachers. Part of the work of the Sophia Foundation is the cultivation of a new star wisdom, *Astro–Sophia* (*astrosophy*), now arising in our time in response to the descent of Sophia, who is the bearer of Divine Wisdom, just as Christ (the Logos, or the Lamb) is the bearer of Divine Love. Like the star wisdom of antiquity, astrosophy is sidereal, which means "of the stars." Astrosophy, inspired by Divine Sophia, descending from stellar heights, directs our consciousness toward the glory and majesty of the starry heavens, to encompass the entire celestial sphere of our cosmos and, beyond this, to the galactic realm—the realm that Daniel Andreev referred to as "the heights of our universe"—from which Sophia is descending on her path of approach into our cosmos. Sophia draws our attention not only to the star mysteries of the heights, but also to the cosmic mysteries connected with Christ's deeds of redemption wrought two thousand years ago. To penetrate these mysteries is the purpose of the annual volumes of *Star Wisdom*.

For information about Astrosophy/Choreocosmos/Cosmic Dance
workshops
Contact the Sophia Foundation:
4500 19th Street, #369, Boulder, CO 80304.
Phone: (303) 242-5388; sophia@sophiafoundation.org;
www.sophiafoundation.org

PREFACE

Robert Powell, PhD

This is the fifth volume of the annual *Star Wisdom* (formerly *Journal for Star Wisdom*), intended to help all people interested in the new star wisdom of astrosophy and in the cosmic dimension of Christianity, which began with the Star of the Magi. The calendar comprises an ephemeris page for each month of the year, computed with the help of Peter Treadgold's *Astrofire* computer program, with a monthly commentary by Joel Matthew Park. The monthly commentary relates the geocentric and heliocentric planetary movements to events in the life of Jesus Christ.

Jesus Christ united the levels of the earthly personality (*geocentric* = Earth-centered) and the higher self (*heliocentric* = Sun-centered) insofar as he was the most highly evolved earthly personality (Jesus) embodying the higher self (Christ) of all existence, the Divine "I AM." To see the life of Jesus Christ in relation to the world of stars opens the door to a profound experience of the cosmos, giving rise to a new star wisdom (astrosophy) that is the Spiritual Science of Cosmic Christianity.

Star Wisdom is scientific, resting on a solid mathematical–astronomical foundation and a secure chronology of the life of Jesus Christ, while it is also spiritual, aspiring to the higher dimension of existence, expressed outwardly in the world of stars. The scientific and the spiritual come together in the sidereal zodiac that originated with the Babylonians and was used by the three magi who beheld the star of Bethlehem and came to pay homage to Jesus a few months after his birth.

In continuity of spirit with the origins of Cosmic Christianity with the three magi, the sidereal zodiac is the frame of reference used for the computation of the geocentric and heliocentric planetary movements that are commented upon in the light of the life of Jesus Christ in *Star Wisdom*.

Thus, all zodiacal longitudes indicated in the text and presented in the following calendar are in terms of the sidereal zodiac, which needs to be distinguished from the tropical zodiac widely used in contemporary astrology in the West. The tropical zodiac was introduced into astrology in the middle of the second century AD by the Greek astronomer Claudius Ptolemy. Prior to this, the sidereal zodiac was used. Such was the influence of Ptolemy on the Western astrological tradition that the tropical zodiac replaced the sidereal zodiac used by the Babylonians, Egyptians, and early Greek astrologers. Yet the astrological tradition in India was not influenced by Ptolemy, and so the sidereal zodiac is still used to this day by Hindu astrologers.

The sidereal zodiac originated with the Babylonians in the sixth to fifth centuries BC and was defined by them in relation to certain bright stars. For example, Aldebaran ("the Bull's Eye") is located in the middle of the sidereal sign–constellation of the Bull at 15° Taurus, while Antares ("the Scorpion's heart") is in the middle of the sidereal sign–constellation of the Scorpion at 15° Scorpio. The sidereal signs, each 30° long, coincide closely with the twelve astronomical zodiacal constellations of the same name, whereas the signs of the tropical zodiac—since they are defined in relation to the vernal point—now have little or no relationship to the corresponding zodiacal constellations. This is because the vernal point, the zodiacal location of the Sun on March 20–21, shifts slowly backward through the sidereal zodiac at a rate of 1° every seventy-two years ("the precession of the equinoxes"). When Ptolemy introduced the tropical zodiac into astrology, there was a nearly exact coincidence between the tropical and the sidereal zodiac, as the vernal point, which is defined as 0° Aries in the tropical zodiac, was at 1° Aries in the sidereal zodiac in the middle of the second century AD. Thus, there was only 1° difference between the two zodiacs. Thus, it made hardly any difference to Ptolemy or his contemporaries to use the tropical zodiac instead of the sidereal zodiac. Now, however—the vernal point having shifted back from 1° Aries to 5° Pisces owing to precession—there is a 25° difference, and thus there is virtually no correspondence between the two. Without going into further detail concerning the complex issue of the zodiac (as shown in the *Hermetic Astrology* trilogy), the sidereal zodiac is the zodiac used by the three magi, who were the last representatives of the true star wisdom of antiquity. For this reason, the sidereal zodiac is used throughout the texts in *Star Wisdom*.

Readers interested in exploring the scientific (astronomical and chronological) foundations of Cosmic Christianity are referred to the works listed here under "Literature." The *Chronicle of the Living Christ: Foundations of Cosmic Christianity* (listed on the following page) is an indispensable reference source (abbreviated *Chron.*) for *Star Wisdom*. The chronology of the life of Jesus Christ rests upon Robert Powell's research into the description of Christ's daily life by Anne Catherine Emmerich in her three-volume work, *The Visions of Anne Catherine Emmerich* (abbreviated *ACE*).

Further details concerning *Star Wisdom* and how to work with it on a daily basis may be found in the general introduction to the *Christian Star Calendar*. The general introduction explains all the features of *Star Wisdom*. The new edition, published in 2003, includes sections on the megastars (stars of great luminosity) and on the 36 decans (10° subdivisions of the twelve signs of the zodiac) in relation to their planetary rulers and to the extra-zodiacal constellations, or the constellations above or below the circle of the twelve constellations–signs of the zodiac.

Further material on the decans, including examples of historical personalities born in the various decans, as well as a wealth of other material on the signs of the sidereal zodiac, can be found in *Cosmic Dances of the Zodiac* (listed below). Also foundational is *History of the Zodiac*, published by Sophia Academic Press (listed under "Works by Robert Powell").

LITERATURE

(See also "References" section)

General Introduction to the Christian Star Calendar: A Key to Understanding, 2nd ed. Palo Alto, CA: Sophia Foundation, 2003.

Bento, William, Robert Schiappacasse, and David Tresemer, *Signs in the Heavens: A Message for our Time*. Boulder: StarHouse, 2000.

Emmerich, Anne Catherine, *The Visions of Anne Catherine Emmerich* (new edition, with material by Robert Powell). Kettering, OH: Angelico Press, 2015.

Paul, Lacquanna, and Robert Powell, *Cosmic Dances of the Planets*. San Rafael, CA: Sophia Foundation Press, 2007.

———, *Cosmic Dances of the Zodiac*. San Rafael, CA: Sophia Foundation Press, 2007.

Smith, Edward R., *The Burning Bush: Rudolf Steiner, Anthroposophy, and the Holy Scriptures* (3rd ed.). Great Barrington, MA: SteinerBooks, 2020.

Steiner, Rudolf, *Astronomy and Astrology: Finding a Relationship to the Cosmos*. London: Rudolf Steiner Press, 2009.

Sucher, Willi, *Cosmic Christianity and the Changing Countenance of Cosmology*. Great Barrington, MA: SteinerBooks, 1993. *Isis Sophia* and other works by Willi Sucher are available from the Astrosophy Research Center, PO Box 13, Meadow Vista, CA 95722.

Tidball, Charles S., and Robert Powell, *Jesus, Lazarus, and the Messiah: Unveiling Three Christian Mysteries*. Great Barrington, MA: SteinerBooks, 2005. This book offers a penetrating study of the Christ mysteries against the background of *Chronicle of the Living Christ* and contains two chapters by Robert Powell on the Apostle John and John the Evangelist (Lazarus).

Tresemer, David (with Robert Schiappacasse), *Star Wisdom and Rudolf Steiner: A Life Seen Through the Oracle of the Solar Cross*. Great Barrington, MA: SteinerBooks, 2007.

WORKS ON ASTROSOPHY BY ROBERT POWELL, PHD

Starcrafts (formerly Astro Communication Services, or ACS):
History of the Houses (1997)
History of the Planets (1989)
The Zodiac: A Historical Survey (1984)
www.acspublications.com
www.astrocom.com
Business Address:
Starcrafts Publishing
334 Calef Hwy.
Epping, NH 03042
Phone: 603-734-4300
Fax: 603-734-4311
Contact maria@starcraftseast.com

SteinerBooks:

Orders: (703) 661-1594; www.steinerbooks.org
By email: service@steinerbooks.org

The Astrological Revolution: Unveiling the Science of the Stars as a Science of Reincarnation and Karma, coauthor Kevin Dann (Great Barrington, MA: SteinerBooks, 2010). After reestablishing the sidereal zodiac as a basis for astrology that penetrates the mystery of the stars' relationship to human destiny, the reader is invited to discover the astrological significance of the totality of the vast sphere of stars surrounding the Earth. This book points to the astrological significance of the entire celestial sphere, including all the stars and constellations beyond the twelve zodiacal signs. This discovery is revealed by the study of megastars, illustrating how they show up in an extraordinary way in Christ's healing miracles by aligning with the Sun at the time of those events. This book offers a spiritual, yet scientific, path toward a new relationship to the stars.

Christian Hermetic Astrology: The Star of the Magi and the Life of Christ (Hudson, NY: Anthroposophic Press, 1998). Twenty-five discourses set in the "Temple of the Sun," where Hermes and his pupils gather to meditate on the Birth, the Miracles, and the Passion of Jesus Christ. The discourses offer a series of meditative contemplations on the deeds of Christ in relation to the mysteries of the cosmos. They are an expression of the age-old hermetic mystery wisdom of the ancient Egyptian sage, Hermes Trismegistus. This book offers a meditative approach to the cosmic correspondences between major events in the life of Christ and the heavenly configurations at that time 2,000 years ago.

Chronicle of the Living Christ: Foundations of Cosmic Christianity (Hudson, NY: Anthroposophic Press, 1996). An account of the life of Christ, day by day, throughout most of the 3½ years of his ministry, including the horoscopes of conception, birth, and death of Jesus, Mary, and John the Baptist, together with a wealth of material relating to the new star wisdom focused on the life of Christ. This work provides the chronological basis for *Christian Hermetic Astrology* and *Star Wisdom.*

Elijah Come Again: A Prophet for our Time: A Scientific Approach to Reincarnation (Great Barrington, MA: SteinerBooks, 2009). By way of horoscope comparisons from conception–birth–death in one incarnation to conception–birth–death in the next, this work establishes scientifically two basic astrosophical research findings. These are: the importance 1) of the sidereal zodiac and 2) of the heliocentric positions of the planets. Also, for the first time, the identity of the "saintly nun" is revealed, of whom Rudolf Steiner spoke in a conversation with Marie von Sivers about tracing Novalis's karmic background. The focus throughout the book is on the Elijah individuality in his various incarnations, and is based solidly on Rudolf Steiner's indications. It also can be read as a karmic biography by anyone who chooses to omit the astrosophical material.

Star Wisdom (Great Barrington, MA: Lindisfarne Books, 2019–); *Journal for Star Wisdom* (Lindisfarne Books, 2010–2018), edited by Joel Matthew Park, Robert Powell, and others engaged in astrosophic research. A guide to the correspondences of Christ in the stellar and etheric worlds. Includes articles of interest, a complete geocentric and heliocentric sidereal ephemeris, and an aspectarian. According to Rudolf Steiner, every step taken by Christ during his ministry between the baptism in the Jordan and the resurrection was in harmony with, and an expression of, the cosmos. The journal is concerned with these heavenly correspondences during the life of Christ. It is intended to help provide a foundation for Cosmic Christianity, the cosmic dimension of Christianity. It is this dimension that has been missing from Christianity in its 2,000-year history. A starting point is to contemplate the movements of the Sun, Moon, and planets against the background of the zodiacal constellations (sidereal signs) today in relation to corresponding stellar events during the life of Christ. This opens the possibility of attuning to the life of Christ in the etheric cosmos in a living way.

Sophia Foundation Press and Sophia Academic Press Publications

Books available from Amazon.com
JamesWetmore@mac.com
www.logosophia.com

History of the Zodiac (San Rafael, CA: Sophia Academic Press, 2007). Book version of Robert Powell's PhD thesis, *The History of the Zodiac*. This penetrating study restores the sidereal zodiac to its rightful place as the original zodiac, tracing it back to fifth-century-BC Babylonians. Available in paperback and hardcover.

Hermetic Astrology: Volume 1, Astrology and Reincarnation (San Rafael, CA: Sophia Foundation Press, 2007). This book seeks to give the ancient science of the stars a scientific basis. This new foundation for astrology based on research into reincarnation and karma (destiny) is the primary focus. It includes numerous reincarnation examples, the study of which reveals the existence of certain astrological "laws" of reincarnation, on the basis of which it is evident that the ancient sidereal zodiac is the authentic astrological zodiac, and that the heliocentric movements of the planets are of great significance. Foundational for the new star wisdom of astrosophy.

Hermetic Astrology: Volume 2, Astrological Biography (San Rafael, CA: Sophia Foundation Press, 2007). Concerned with karmic relationships and the unfolding of destiny in seven-year periods through one's life. The seven-year rhythm underlies the human being's astrological biography, which can be studied in relation to the movements of the Sun, Moon, and planets around the sidereal zodiac between conception and birth. The "rule of Hermes" is used to determine the moment of conception.

Sign of the Son of Man in the Heavens: Sophia and the New Star Wisdom (San Rafael, CA: Sophia Foundation Press, 2008). Revised and expanded with new material, this edition deals with a new wisdom of stars in the light of Divine Sophia. It was intended as a help in our time, as we were called on to be extremely wakeful up to the end of the Maya calendar in 2012.

Cosmic Dances of the Zodiac (San Rafael, CA: Sophia Foundation Press, 2007), coauthor Lacquanna Paul. Study material describing the twelve signs of the zodiac and their forms and gestures in cosmic dance, with diagrams. Includes a wealth of information on the twelve signs and the 36 decans (the subdivision of the signs into decans, or 10° sectors, corresponding to constellations above and below the zodiac).

Cosmic Dances of the Planets (San Rafael, CA: Sophia Foundation Press, 2007), coauthor Lacquanna Paul. Study material describing the seven classical planets and their forms and gestures in cosmic dance, with diagrams, including much information on the planets.

American Federation of Astrologers (AFA) Publications (currently not in print)

www.astrologers.com

The Sidereal Zodiac, coauthor Peter Treadgold (Tempe, AZ: AFA, 1985). A *History of the Zodiac* (sidereal, tropical, Hindu, astronomical) and a formal definition of the sidereal zodiac with the star Aldebaran ("the Bull's Eye") at 15° Taurus. This is an abbreviated version of *History of the Zodiac*.

Rudolf Steiner College Press Publications

9200 Fair Oaks Blvd., Fair Oaks, CA 95628

The Christ Mystery: Reflections on the Second Coming (Fair Oaks, CA: Rudolf Steiner College Press, 1999). The fruit of many years of reflecting on the Second Coming and its cosmological aspects. Looks at the approaching trial of humanity and the challenges of living in apocalyptic times, against the background of "great signs in the heavens."

The Sophia Foundation

4500 19th Street, #369, Boulder, CO 80304; distributes many of the books listed here and other works by Robert Powell.
Tel: (303) 242-5388
sophia@sophiafoundation.org
www.sophiafoundation.org

Computer program for charts and ephemerides, with grateful acknowledgment to Peter Treadgold, who wrote the computer program *Astrofire* (with research module, star catalog of over 4,000 stars, and database of birth and death charts of historical personalities), capable of printing geocentric and heliocentric–hermetic sidereal charts and ephemerides throughout history. The hermetic charts, based on the astronomical system of the Danish astronomer Tycho Brahe, are called "Tychonic" charts in the program. This program can:

- compute birth charts in a large variety of systems (tropical, sidereal, geocentric, heliocentric, hermetic);
- calculate conception charts using the hermetic rule, in turn applying it for correction of the birth time;
- produce charts for the period between conception and birth;
- print out an "astrological biography" for the whole of lifework with the geocentric, heliocentric (and even lemniscatory) planetary system;
- work with the sidereal zodiac according to the definition of your choice (Babylonian sidereal,

Indian sidereal, unequal-division astronomical, etc.);
- work with planetary aspects with orbs of your choice.

The program includes eight house systems and a variety of chart formats. The program also includes an ephemeris program with a search facility. The geocentric–heliocentric sidereal ephemeris pages in the annual volumes of *Star Wisdom* are produced by the software program *Astrofire*, which is compatible with Microsoft Windows.

Those interested in obtaining the *Astrofire* program should contact:

The Sophia Foundation
4500 19th Street, #369
Boulder, CO 80304
Tel: (303) 242-5388
sophia@sophiafoundation.org
www.sophiafoundation.org

Birth of Kaspar Hauser - Geocentric
At Durlach, Latitude 49N0'0", Longitude 8E29'0"
Date: Tuesday, 29/SEP/1812, Gregorian
Time: 10:30:0, Local Time
Sidereal Time 11: 2: 3, Vernal Point 7 ♓ 52'23", House System: Placidus
Zodiac: Sidereal SVP, Aspect set: Major Variable Orbed

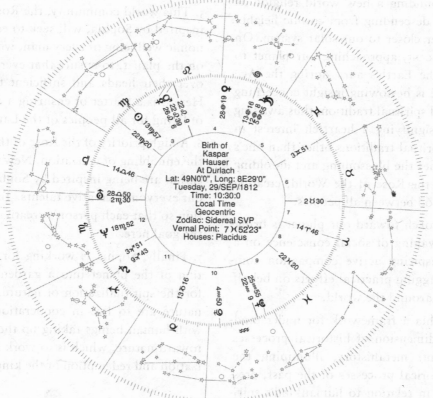

Birth of
Kaspar
Hauser
At Durlach
Lat: 49N0'0", Long: 8E29'0"
Tuesday, 29/SEP/1812
Time: 10:30:0
Local Time
Geocentric
Zodiac: Sidereal SVP
Vernal Point: 7 ♓ 52'23"
Houses: Placidus

A horoscope generated by the Astrofire *program*

THE SEVEN IDEALS OF THE ROSE OF THE WORLD

Robert Powell, PhD

In gratitude to Daniel Andreev (1906–1959), the Russian prophet of the Rose of the World as the coming world culture, inspired by Sophia—a culture based on Love and Wisdom.

Daniel and Alla Andreev (1959)

The Rose of the World is arising through the approach of Divine Sophia toward the Earth. Her approach is calling forth the following basic qualities or attributes of the new world culture that She is creating and inspiring:

1. First and foremost: *interreligion*. For Sophia all true religious and spiritual traditions are different layers of spiritual reality, which She seeks to weave together as petals of the Rose of the World. Sophia is not founding a new world religion as She approaches, descending from cosmic heights, and drawing ever closer to our solar system. On Her path of descent, approaching our planet to incarnate into the Earth's aura during the Age of Aquarius, She is bestowing insight concerning each religion and spiritual tradition, thus awaking interreligiosity, signifying a heartfelt interest in religious and spiritual traditions other than one's own. This signifies the blossoming and unfolding of the petals of the Rose of the World, creating brother–sisterhood between all peoples.

2. Sophia's approach toward our planet is bringing about an awaking of social conscience on a global scale, inspiring active compassion combined with unflagging practical efforts on behalf of social justice around the world.

3. Through Sophia a framework for understanding the higher dimension of historical processes is coming about: metahistory, illumining the meaning of historical processes of the past, present, and future in relation to humankind's spiritual evolution. This entails glimpses into the mystical consciousness of humanity such as may be found in the book of Revelation.

4. On the national sociopolitical level, Sophia's inspiration is working to transform the state into a community. The community of Italy, the community of France, etc., is the ideal for the future, rather than the political entity of the state representing (or misrepresenting) the people. And on the global scale Sophia is seeking to bring about the unification of the planet as a world community through bringing the different country communities into a harmonious relationship with one another on a religious, cultural, and economic level.

5. This world community, the Rose of the World, inspired by Sophia, will seek to establish the economic wellbeing of every man, woman, and child on the planet, to ensure that everyone has a roof over their heads and sufficient food to live on. Here it is a matter of ensuring a decent standard of living for all peoples of the Earth.

6. A high priority of the Rose of the World will be the ennobling of education. New methods of education are being inspired by Sophia to help bring out everyone's creative talents. To ennoble education so that each person's creativity can unfold is the goal here.

7. Finally, Sophia is working for the transformation of the planet into a garden and, moreover, for the spiritualization of nature. Humanity and nature are to live in cooperation and harmony, with human beings taking up their responsibility toward nature, which is to work for the spiritualization and redemption of the kingdoms of nature.

EDITORIAL FOREWORD: THE TURNING POINT
Joel Matthew Park

Dear Readers,

This year we commemorate the 100-year anniversary of the Christmas Conference, during which "The Foundation Stone Meditation" was laid in the hearts of the newly re-founded General Anthroposophical Society. The title of this year's edition of *Star Wisdom* is taken from the fourth stanza of "The Foundation Stone Meditation":

> At the Turning Point of Time,
> The Spirit Light of the world
> Entered the stream of earthly existence
> Darkness of night
> Had held its sway;
> Day radiant Light
> Poured into human souls;
> Light that gives warmth
> To simple shepherd's hearts,
> Light that enlightens
> The wise heads of kings.
> O, Light Divine!
> O, Sun of Christ!
> Warm Thou our hearts,
> Enlighten Thou our heads
> That good may become
> What from our hearts we would found
> And from our heads direct
> With single purpose.

Whereas in the context of the Meditation, the "Turning Point of Time" refers specifically to the Mystery of Golgotha, the theme of a turning point can lead in many different directions, depending on its interpretation. For example, in Krisztina Cseri's offering for this volume, "Rudolf Steiner and the Christmas Conference: Astrological Aspects of the Laying of the Foundation Stone, Part III," she points to the first year of life after conception (nine months' gestation and the first three months after birth) as a "turning point" from one incarnation to another. We might consider the giving of "The

Foundation Stone Meditation" itself as a turning point in human evolution—and along with it, the second coming of Christ, the most significant spiritual event of our time. Each of the articles in the present volume revolves around this theme of the turning point in its own particular way, each one highlighting a particular nuance of the multivalent role of the turning point in both macro- and microcosmic evolution.

For my part, I intend to highlight the year 2023 as a turning point from a more metahistorical and metapolitical direction, and build a bridge from this to some of the other perspectives developed in the subsequent articles.

For the past year or so, I have been familiarizing myself with the generational theory of William Strauss and Neil Howe as laid out in their prescient work, *The Fourth Turning: An American Prophecy* (New York: Broadway Books, 1997). While this is a mainstream text (i.e., neither spiritually nor esoterically oriented), it is nonetheless interpreting history from an *archetypal* point of view. As far as I can tell, this has allowed the authors to make an exceptionally clear-sighted description of historical processes, inasmuch as they have recognized that history is the dream of humanity, and not an event able to be analyzed with the rational consciousness as, for example, a physical law might be.

The position that the authors hold throughout this work revolves around the idea that, for millennia, human civilizations recognized the seasonal nature and cyclical unfolding of human culture. This recognition was integrated into the sacred and religious ceremonies that marked the "turning points of time." Generally speaking, this unfolding of culture in four "seasons" took place over the course of a century—a cultural springtime, during which stability and regularity were the keynotes, succeeded by a summertime, during which new impulses and innovations would arise. This was then followed by an autumn, during which the established order become overly complex and overburdened due to the demands of the new innovations. And finally, a cultural winter would bring death and destruction. The extreme disorder of the cultural winter would demand a reestablishment of order and stability, which would start the whole cycle over again with a new cultural springtime.

Strauss and Howe refer to the seasons as "Turnings": the First Turning, springtime, they refer to as a "High"; the Second Turning, summer, as an "Awakening"; the Third Turning, autumn, as an "Unraveling"; and the Fourth Turning, winter, as a "Crisis."

Now, whereas these seasons were present in traditional civilizations, they never became extreme owing to an active recognition and honoring of their cyclicality. From my point of view (not that of Strauss and Howe), human beings were, up until relatively recently, still embedded in active perception of the spiritual world. The rhythm of cultural seasonality was recognized because human civilization was seen to be the body of higher spiritual beings (e.g., folk spirits, or archangels, and time spirits, or archai). Even when this active perception and participation ceased (around the time of the Mystery of Golgotha), for some time the traditions of the past were still adhered to as the cultural memory of a more spiritually vibrant time.

As of the dawn of the modern age in the fifteenth to sixteenth centuries, the human spirit became completely liberated from any concrete attachment to a prevailing natural-spiritual hierarchy. The free individuality—alone in the cosmos—began to assert itself. During this time period—for the first time in human history—ideas of progress (especially and specifically linear progress) and self-determination entered strongly into the social consciousness. These ideas had been impossible until the liberated individual came into being.

Now, as Strauss and Howe point out in the early parts of The Fourth Turning, paradoxically (but perhaps not unexpectedly), the more humanity attempts to detach itself from seasonal historical cycles, the more exaggerated and accelerated these cycles seem to become. Linear progress is a complete illusion, a mechanized ahrimanic fabrication born out of a luciferic striving for self-realization independent of the wholeness of reality. The spiritual beings who hold sway in "rhythms of worlds, bestowing grace" will not abide being ignored and fought against with the non-reality of the straight line—that is, not without dire consequences for humanity.[1]

However, the rise of the idea of linear progress and the liberated individual took place first and foremost in European countries, which had the buffer of centuries of traditional recognition of the spiritual cycles. While the four seasons of a century became noticeably more rapid and more intense, the lingering traditions kept them in check to some degree.

However, over the course of the eighteenth century, all of this was to change. In The Fourth Turning, Strauss and Howe present the following hypothesis:

Imagine a scenario in which most of history's "noise" is suppressed. Imagine a single large society that has never had a powerful neighbor and that, for centuries, has remained relatively isolated from foreign interference. Imagine that this society was born modern on a near-empty continent, with no time-honored traditions to restrain its open-ended development. Imagine, finally, that this thoroughly modern society has acquired a reputation for pursuing linear progress, and for suppressing the cycles of nature, unequaled by any other people on earth. From what you know about the saeculum, wouldn't you suppose that its history is governed by a cycle of astonishing regularity? Indeed, you would. But of course, this society is no hypothesis. This society is America. (p. 42)

The United States of America—the "Great Experiment"—is therefore a kind of Galápagos Island, where rather than the concentrated specialization of plant and animal species we experience

---

1 Many of Steiner's lectures during World War I present a fuller description of this, in particular the lecture cycle The Fall of the Spirits of Darkness.

the concentrated exaggeration and acceleration of cultural cycles at the hands of undiluted linearism.

Strauss and Howe note that the single historical cycle, or "saeculum," has, since the founding of the United States, sped up from being a century in length to being approximately eighty years. Each saeculum is made up of four seasons of approximately twenty years each (alluded to above, but here described in their own words from *The Fourth Turning*):

- The *First Turning* is a *High*, an upbeat era of strengthening institutions and weakening individualism, when a new civic order implants and the old values regime decays.

- The *Second Turning* is an *Awakening*, a passionate era of spiritual upheaval, when the civic order comes under attack from a new values regime.

- The *Third Turning* is an *Unraveling*, a downcast era of strengthening individualism and weakening institutions, when the old civic order decays and the new values regime implants.

- The *Fourth Turning* is a *Crisis*, a decisive era of secular upheaval, when the values regime propels the replacement of the old civic order with a new one. (p. 3)

One might wonder, how and why exactly do these seasons arise? For Strauss and Howe, they arise through a kind of generation psychology, archetypes that express themselves through generations in an organic unfolding. Let's begin with a Fourth Turning. The children who grow up during a Crisis tend to be extremely overprotected and required to obey all kinds of rules without question for the sake of preserving the social order. Strauss and Howe characterize this type of generation under the archetypal image of "Artist." The most recent "Artist" generation (other than those currently being born) were the so-called Silent Generation, born between the mid-1920s and mid-1940s. When Artists grow up, they tend to react against their overprotective and rule-heavy upbringing by letting their children run free. The children born during an Awakening, therefore, tend to be hardened

by experience early on in life, growing into alienated youth and rugged, pragmatic leaders as adults. Their archetypal image is that of the "Nomad." The most recent Nomad generation is Generation X, born between the mid-'60s and the mid-'80s. The other two archetypes—who play off of each other in a similar way to the Artists and Nomads—are the Prophets (our Baby Boomers, born between the mid-'40s and mid-'60s), and Heroes (our Millennials and Gen-Z, born between the mid-1980s and the early 2000s). Strauss and Howe give a summary of these four generations:

- A *Prophet* generation grows up as increasingly indulged post-Crisis children, comes of age as the narcissistic young crusaders of an Awakening, cultivates principle as moralistic mid-lifers, and emerges as wise elders guiding the next Crisis.

- A *Nomad* generation grows up as under-protected children during an Awakening, comes of age as the alienated young adults of a post-Awakening world, mellows into pragmatic midlife leaders during a Crisis, and ages into tough post-Crisis elders.

- A *Hero* generation grows up as increasingly protected post-Awakening children, comes of age as the heroic young team-workers of a Crisis, demonstrates hubris as energetic mid-lifers, and emerges as powerful elders attacked by the next Awakening

- An *Artist* generation grows up as overprotected children during a Crisis, comes of age as the sensitive young adults of a post-Crisis world, breaks free as indecisive midlife leaders during an Awakening, and ages into empathic post-Awakening elders. (p. 84)

These archetypes can be found in all kinds of modern day pop cultural representations (*Star Wars* and *Harry Potter* are the most accessible examples in my estimation). But they go far back into the spiritual history of humanity, and perhaps are a kind of Divine Name (YHVH). As Strauss and Howe elaborate:

1. THE HOLY PEERS OF MOSES.
   As young adults, they awakened their people to the spirit of God. Rejecting worldly privilege, they defied the authority of Pharaoh's Egypt. Later in life, they led the Hebrews on a miracle-filled journey across the Red Sea and through the wilderness to the threshold of Canaan, the Promised Land.

2. THE WORSHIPPERS OF THE GOLDEN CALF.
   It was for the sins of these wanderers and "men of little faith" that God punished the Hebrews with extra trials and tribulations. They were too young to join Moses' challenge against the Pharaoh, yet old enough to remember the enticing fleshpots of Egypt.

3. THE DUTIFUL SOLDIER PEERS OF JOSHUA.
   Born after the Exodus, they came of age waging victorious battles and were thereafter anointed for leadership by the patriarch Moses. As they entered Canaan (none older was allowed to do so), their unity and martial discipline enabled them to conquer the natives and bring substance to Moses' dreams.

4. THE ORIGINAL GENERATION OF JUDGES.
   Overshadowed by Joshua's battles, these "inheritor" youths were reminded by the dying Joshua that they enjoyed "land for which ye did not labor, and cities which ye built not." Their exercise of power was marked by political fragmentation, cultural sophistication, and anxiety about the future. (p. 85)

It is the dynamic interplay between each of these generation archetypes that gives rise to the different seasons. In turn, it is the interplay between each generation and the season in which it comes of age that gives shape to its archetypal form. The brief description I offer here does not do justice to what is elaborated more fully by Strauss and Howe in the text, but for our purposes it will have to suffice.

Now, the United States of America has been through three Crises, or Fourth Turnings, since her birth and is now in the midst of the fourth of her Fourth Turnings (perhaps the Crisis of Crises?).

Her first Fourth Turning centered on the American Revolution, which lasted from the 1760s through the 1780s. The second Fourth Turning culminated eighty years later with the Civil War, which ended in 1865. The third Fourth Turning began with the Great Depression in 1929 and lasted some twenty years. As American cultural linearism increasingly colonized the entire developed world over the course of the twentieth century, we could say that it is now not only the United States who is a victim of the exaggerated and rapid saecular cycle; it is the whole world that is affected. Strauss and Howe wrote this work in the late 1990s. They had hoped for it to be a useful guide for readers to prepare for the Crisis they foresaw, warning that it would befall humanity around 2005 to '25. Notice that each of the previous three Crises culminated in a significant military encounter.

The more I read *The Fourth Turning,* the more I wondered about any astrological underpinning for these cycles. To begin with, I noticed four features that were consistent across each of the time periods listed (1760s–'80s, 1840–'60s, 1920s–'40s). First of all, Pluto was in a cardinal sign during all three—Capricorn, Aries, and Cancer respectively. Second, Neptune was aligned with a 180° axis; she either moved from Leo into Virgo (American Revolution and World War II), or from Aquarius into Pisces (Civil War). Third, Uranus traveled through one quadrant of the starry heavens—from mid-Pisces through mid-Gemini. And finally, a Great Conjunction of Saturn and Jupiter occurred at some point during the Crisis: 1782, 1861, and 1940. To be sure, a Neptunian cycle is approximately 165 years; half of this is 82½ years. A Plutonic cycle is about three times as long at 248 years; a Uranian cycle is about 84 years; and four Great Conjunctions occur during 79½ years. Clearly, at this time period of history, *all* of the rhythms of the outermost planets are coinciding in such a way as to facilitate the saecular rhythm in question.

It is also notable that Uranus was discovered during the first American Crisis, on March 13, 1781; Neptune was discovered at the start of the second American Crisis, on September 23, 1846;

and Pluto was discovered at the start of the third American Crisis, February 18, 1930.

For the year 2023, heliocentric Pluto will journey from 3°-4° Capricorn. The last time it was in this position was between February 1775 and February 1776. Neptune will journey from 29° Aquarius to 1° Pisces; the last time she did so was between March 1857 and March 1858. Uranus will journey from 22° to 26° Aries; he last traveled this path between December 1938 and December 1939. And finally, heliocentric Jupiter will move from 46° advanced from Saturn to 67° advanced; this was their degree of separation between June 1943 and November 1944 during the previous Crisis.

Note that Neptune's position throughout 2023 will be exactly opposite that of February 1775 to February 1776, as well as December 1939 though January 1941 (29° Leo to 1° Virgo). Note that the Revolutionary War began on April 19, 1775, and World War II began on September 1, 1939. Every single planet in our solar system beyond the asteroid belt will this year be remembering not just a previous Fourth Turning, but specifically the time period of a Fourth Turning, during which a large-scale active war was taking place. Not only this, but if we consider Uranus, Neptune, and Pluto in particular, we can see that this year each one will be remembering the exact moment of the *outbreak* of the Revolutionary War and World War II. Pluto remembers his position at the outbreak of the Revolutionary War in mid-March (3°26' Capricorn); Neptune is opposite her position during that same time period in history early March (29°59' Leo); and Uranus conjoins his position at the time of the outbreak of World War II at the end of July (24°47' Aries). Neptune already opposed her position at the outbreak of World War II at the end of August, 2022 (28°50' Leo). We are therefore in the midst of the turning point of the 4th Turning—when the crisis that has been simmering for about a decade begins to boil over, a time of intense conflict that may last for up to eight years.

From my research, it would seem that it is Neptune's rhythm in particular that is married to the cultural "change of seasons," the advent of another

Turning. When we look at the events of the previous three turnings through the lens of Neptune's position, we begin to see a regular pathway along which events unfold.

The first step is the catalyst that triggers the series of events that will eventually end in conflict. This occurs when Neptune is between 7° and 8° Aquarius or Leo. At the time of the American Revolution, it was the passage of the Stamp Act on March 22, 1765, and the subsequent formation of the Sons of Liberty. At the time leading up to the Civil War, it was the beginning of the California Gold Rush on January 24, 1848, and the Ratification of the Treaty of Guadalupe, which ended the Mexican-American War on May 19, 1848. After that, Neptune reached 7°45' Leo on Black Tuesday, October 29, 1929, at the start of the Great Depression.

The second step of the Fourth Turning involves the formation of groups that, to begin with, are merely opposed but, as the Crisis continues to unfold, become increasingly mutually exclusive, to the extent that each feels the existence of the other to be a threat to its *own* existence. Neptune, during these time periods, is between 14° and 21° Leo or Aquarius. During the American Revolution, this centered on the Boston Massacre on March 5, 1770. At the time of the Civil War, it centered on the passage of the Kansas-Nebraska Act on May 30, 1854, which immediately led to the formation of the Republican Party. This also set off the prolonged period of "Bleeding Kansas," a series of violent confrontations centered on slavery, which led to the start of the Civil War. During World War II, it centered on the rise of Adolf Hitler to Chancellor on January 30, 1933, and the more-or-less simultaneous inauguration of Franklin D. Roosevelt to the Presidency on March 4, 1933.

The third step is the escalation of conflict that occurs when Neptune is between 25° and 27° Leo or Aquarius. During the American Revolution, this centered on the Boston Tea Party, December 16, 1773; prior to the Civil War, it was the *Dred Scott v. Sandford* Supreme Court decision on March 6, 1857; and prior to World War II, it was the annexation of Austria on March 13, 1938.

The fourth step usually sees the outbreak of an all-out war, and/or the emergence of a leading figure who guides people through the Crisis. Neptune is between 28° Leo or Aquarius, and 1° Virgo or Pisces during this time. In the American Revolution, this involved the First Continental Congress meeting on September 5, 1774, and the outbreak of the Revolutionary War on April 19, 1775. During the Civil War, it saw the start of the Panic of 1857 on September 12, and the emergence of Abraham Lincoln as the voice of the Republican Party, with his "A House Divided" speech on June 16, 1858, and the subsequent Lincoln-Douglas debates, which lasted until October 15. Neptune was at these positions at the outbreak of World War II on September 1, 1939, and the election of Winston Churchill to Prime Minister on May 10, 1940. Neptune has been in this range since June 2022, and will remain there until August 2023—we are now in the midst of this fourth stage of the Crisis.

Looking back over the first of the stages of our current Crisis, Neptune was between 7° and 8° Aquarius at the end of 2012 and the beginning of 2013. We can mark this time as the beginning of the Crisis; certain events that during the time period may have seemed of little significance set off the chain of events leading to the upheaval we now experience. Note that around this time, both Vladimir Putin and Barack Obama were reelected to the Presidency of their respective countries; Xi Jinping began his term as the President of the PRC; Pope Benedict XVI stepped down and was succeeded by Pope Francis. This was also the period of the rise of Big Tech and the passage of the Smith-Mundt Modernization Act. It saw the emergence of Edward Snowden as whistle-blower and Glenn Greenwald as his advocate, and the active persecution of Julian Assange, which began with his taking refuge in the Ecuadorian Embassy in 2012. We could characterize this as the start of the time period of total cooperation between Big Tech/Bid Data and the intelligence agencies of the United States to actively track as much information as possible about the citizenry; and to weaponize the Corporate Media (both social

and otherwise) with the intent of shaping narratives, influencing opinions, and squashing dissent (increasingly through blatant censorship, but preferably through convincing the populace to do so on their behalf—i.e., "cancel culture" via an endless stream of echo-chamber propaganda).

On the other hand, the start of 2013 also saw the Global Health Summit in Beijing, China, January 26 to 27, sponsored by the Rockefeller Foundation, the United Nations, and the World Health Organization. The white paper "Dreaming the Future of Health in the next 100 Years" was one result of this event. It was also in early 2013 that the phrase "Fourth Industrial Revolution" was first coined. Over the course of the past decade, it has become clear that the purpose of mass tracking, as well as propagandizing, was meant to go hand in hand with the establishment of transhumanist and technocratic agendas on the part of a cabal of unelected, wealthy, self-proclaimed experts. Issues of environmental, economic, and social justice, as well as health security (and therefore dissemination of information), have all become too complex to be managed by democratic institutions (to say nothing of sovereign individuals!). Only centralization (i.e., enforced consensus) and technological advancement can solve the great problems facing humanity. To be sure, however, the dire solutions at hand—food scarcity, fuel scarcity, digital currency, health tracking, social credit, limited travel—will apply only to the masses, while the self-appointed experts get to enjoy an ever-higher standard of living.

A unique aspect of this first phase of the modern Crisis is pointed to in a warning given by Strauss and Howe in *The Fourth Turning*:

In linear time, there would be no turnings, just segments along one directional path of progress. Each twenty-year segment would produce more of everything produced by the prior segment. On a chart, every cell in any given row would read just like the one before, except with a higher multiplier. The 2020s would be a mere extrapolation of the 1990s, with more cable channels and Web pages and senior benefits and corporate free agents—plus more handgun murders, media violence, cultural splintering, political cynicism, youth alienation, partisan meanness, and distance between rich and poor. There would be no apogee, no levelling, no correction. Eventually, America would veer totally out of control along some bizarre centrifugal path.

In cyclical time, a society always evolves. Usually, the circle is a spiral of progress, sometimes a spiral of decline. Always, people strive to mend the errors of the past, to correct the excesses of the present, to seek a future that provides whatever feels most in need. Thus can civilization endure and thrive. (pp.104–05)

These incredibly prescient words were written in 1997! But they are a perfect description of what set the tone for the entirety of this Crisis: an attempt like never before to master the course of human development, forcing it to become completely linear, dissociated from its essentially and originally cyclic/spiral movement. This was the gamble of Ahriman during the first phase (late 2012 through 2016 or so). The attempt was made to pretend as though the Crisis had already occurred (it hadn't), and thereby move directly from an Unraveling to a High, like skipping directly from 1929 to 1948 with no intervening Great Depression and World War; at the same time, this was attempted in the spirit of a period of Awakening, akin to the late '60s through the 80s. Ironically, this global attempt at conflict avoidance (to begin with) merely prolonged the malaise and ennui that is typical of an Unraveling, and was certainly the hallmark of the '90s and early 2000s. In fact, in trying to skip over the Crisis completely, what resulted was a culture that was—and to some degree still insists on being—eternally Unraveling (i.e., eternally dissatisfied) and eternally facing greater degrees of over-complexity.

If a child develops a fever, there is something within his or her that needs to be overcome. If the parent artificially suppresses the fever in order to "make the child feel better," generally speaking what is imbalanced in the child will only get worse, even while the outer symptoms are temporarily removed. Eventually, the fever breaks through with ever more veracity than before; the

child risks dying of the infection that has been allowed to fester and would have been taken care of by the presence of the fever. The longer the fever is avoided, the harder the work becomes and the more lethal the illness.

This is precisely analogous to the modern Fourth Turning, our modern Crisis. The fever needs to burn itself out—only then can we truly leave behind the perpetual Unravelling and enter into the possibility for a new High and eventual Awakening. As Strauss and Howe point out:

"Something happened to America at that time," recalled U.S. senator Daniel Inouye on V-J Day in 1995, the last of the fifty-year commemoratives of World War II. "I'm not wise enough to know what it was. But it was the strange, strange power that our founding fathers experienced in those early, uncertain days. Let's call it the Spirit of America, a spirit that united and galvanized our people."...

In the climactic years between Pearl Harbor and V-J Day, arguments were forgotten, ideals energized, and creaky institutions resuscitated for urgent new purposes. At home or in the military, teamwork and discipline were unusually strong. Anybody who doubted or complained or bent the rules drew the wrath of fellow soldiers, coworkers, or neighbors. People looked on their elected representatives as moral exemplars.... Energized by visionary leadership and hopeful followership, America attained a stunning triumph.

With the people thus united, that era established a powerful new civic order replete with new public institutions, economic arrangements, political alliances, and global treaties, many of which have lasted to this day. That era also produced a grim acceptance of destruction as a necessary concomitant to human progress.... Indeed, while this beloved Spirit of America resonates with warm reminiscences from a distance of half a century, it was also a time of blunt, cruel, even lethal forms of social change.

Today's elder veterans recall that era fondly but selectively: They would like to restore its unity and selflessness, but without the carnage. Yet how? The only way they can see is a *way back*, what Bob Dole calls a "bridge" to a better past—an America stripped of the family damage, cultural decay, and loss of civic purpose that has settled in over the intervening five decades. Such a task feels hopeless because it is.

Like nature, history is full of processes that cannot happen in reverse. Just as the laws of entropy do not allow a bird to fly backward, or droplets to regroup at the top of a waterfall, history has no rewind button. Like the seasons of nature, it moves only forward. Saecular entropy cannot be reversed. An Unraveling cannot lead back to an Awakening, or forward to a High, without a Crisis in between.

The Spirit of America comes once a saeculum, only through what the ancients called *ekpyrosis,* nature's fiery moment of death and discontinuity…. A Fourth Turning is a solstice era of maximum darkness, in which the puppy of social order is still falling, but the demand for order is now rising. (pp. 254–55)

In the second phase of our modern Crisis, the *ekpyrosis* finally began to present itself. This second phase, to which I referred as the formation of sides, lasted from approximately 2016 through 2019. Surely, this was one of the most divisive time periods in American history, and perhaps each of my readers can easily bring to their mind's eye the two sides who find it impossible to reconcile—who each find the other an existential threat to its own way of life, increasingly absolutely exclusive of each other. The third stage, the escalation of the conflict, revolved around Covid-19—and this was the time when the fever broke through stronger than ever, when the *ekpyrosis* finally won the upper hand over the entropy of linear progress and the fantasy of conflict avoidance. This disease at once significantly altered the prior division (which might be reduced down to "are you more afraid of the globalists or the nationalists?"), as well as *increased* the sharpness of the divide. This new division revolved much more on the axis of individual sovereignty. Do I consider myself and other people responsible for making health decisions? Or do I trust self-appointed experts to make increasingly draconian decisions on the behalf of all?

Slowly, perhaps, we begin to realize that the essence of the modern Crisis is not so simple as red vs. blue or right vs. left. It has much more in common with prior Crises than that. In each one, we can find a group of self-appointed elites who wish to subjugate a population they see as "lower." This becomes increasingly the case with each succeeding Crisis. In the first Crisis, it was the British Empire who wished to subjugate the Thirteen Colonies. The Colonies thirsted for Liberty, to become sovereign individuals. However, the Liberty they established was incomplete. What was overlooked during the solution to the first Crisis rose up and demanded to be reconciled in the second. Here, the elite group was made up of the slave owners, the slaves the ones suffering subjugation. They thirsted not only for Liberty, but primarily for Equality—equal rights for all. Here we see that the disdain of the elite class for those they perceive as lower deepens, to the point that the lower class is not even recognized as being fully human.

It escalates to the next level in the third Crisis, in which one particular group of human beings (Nazis, self-styled Aryans) consider themselves to be the "master race," the greatest of human beings, and with scientific precision wish to eradicate, enslave, and experiment upon the inferior (Jews, people of color, the developmentally challenged, etc.). Theirs becomes a global yearning rather than just a national one. The fraternal gesture of the Allies toward the nations suffering under Nazism went hand in hand with Fraternity arising in the economic sphere at the most basic of levels—i.e., the time period after the Great Depression saw the rise of the modern global economy, in which each part is integral to the whole. Of course, the victory and resolution of both Nazism and the Great Depression left blind spots just as great as that after the American Revolution. Indeed, the worship of science, technology, and eugenics only became more deeply embedded into our modern culture, and the global economy only remained Fraternal inasmuch as it was universally interwoven—the true gesture of fraternity, of mutuality and friendship, is yet a long distance away. But we would be prudent to adopt something more akin to the American System of Economics that Roosevelt employed in the New Deal, rather than "you will own nothing, and be happy" and central bank digital currencies!

So, now we come to the fourth of the Fourth Turnings, the Crisis of Crises in the modern age. The self-appointed elite now consider themselves not only a master race, but in some sense beyond human—if not now, then soon enough, once the singularity occurs and the human being can meld with a machine and transcend death.[2] Those who are not part of this self-appointed elite are most certainly seen as less-than-human, and are considered only so much fodder (inasmuch as it consists primarily of the lower classes) and entertainment (inasmuch as they both enjoy and benefit from pitting us against each other on issues of race, religion, environment, health, gender, etc.) for narcissistic sociopaths. It is the sovereign individual—first and foremost—who must find him or herself, alone perhaps in the face of all friends and family, and stand in quiet opposition to the waves of divisive cynicism that are parroted by every corporate media talking head and social media influencer.[3] The modern war is an asymmetrical one. It does not, thus far, take place primarily with guns and missiles; rather, it involves competing narratives and destructive substances.[4]

Not only this, but we can consider the forces working against us as a combination of those that came before, an unholy blend of what held sway in British imperialists, Southern slave owners, and Nazi eugenicists. We are facing the possibility of the outbreak of a combination of the wars that came before—a global war (akin to World War II) that presents itself as a civil war within each country to set itself free from an imperial choke hold (akin to both the Civil War and Revolutionary War). It is only the search for a threefold social order that can carry us through, and that is primarily with the image of the sovereign individuality before us. There can be no equality in the rights sphere or fraternity in the economic sphere if there are no sovereign individuals any longer. We must understand clearly that it is not a battle for the rights of sovereign nations against globalist technocracy, but rather a fight to preserve and strengthen the sovereign individuals who make up nations the world over—otherwise, the resolution to this crisis will only lead us back to the stale old nationalism of the early twentieth century.

Unfortunately, we are only just now beginning the climax of the Crisis. For the entirety of the Revolutionary War, from 1775 to 1783, Neptune was between 30° Leo and 18° Virgo. The Civil War did not end until Neptune reached 15° Pisces. And World War II ended when Neptune was at 12° Virgo. This would indicate that the current conflict—one that in a sense we are only just entering into—will last until between 2028 and '31. Perhaps the so-called Western brotherhoods understand that the time for the implementation of technocratic goals has an expiration date around 2030: this would explain the Agenda 2030 of the U.N., and its supporting program, 2030Vision, from the World Economic Forum (and, of course, the partners of both organizations, such as the Bill and Melinda Gates Foundation, the World Health Organization, the World Bank, Wellcome Trust, Amazon, Google, Facebook, Microsoft, BlackRock, etc.).

The good news is that there is an inevitable resolution and restructuring that occurs during the First Turning, the High that follows in the wake of every Crisis. The gesture of Neptune points to this, as well. During the American Revolution, Neptune was between 12° Virgo and 5° Libra, from the ratification of the Articles of Confederation in 1881, to the Constitution in 1787, and to the Bill of Rights in 1791. During the Civil War era, Neptune was between 10° Pisces and 7° Aries from the time of the Emancipation Proclamation in 1863, to the 13th, 14th, and 15th Amendments in 1865, 1868,

---

2   One might look to the work of Dr. Yuval Noah Harari as representative of this worldview.

3   See, for example, Mattias Desmet, *The Psychology of Totalitarianism*.

4   The summary of the choice that stands before us is succinctly presented in multiple languages on the following website: https://www.revolution-2030.info. See in particular the sections on "Tri-Art," "Parousia 2030," and "2030 Agenda."

and 1870, culminating in the Civil Rights Act of 1875. Finally, in the aftermath of World War II, from the time of the end of the war in 1945 through the Treaty of Rome and the establishment of the EEC in 1957, Neptune was between 12° Virgo and 7° Libra (the number of transnational agreements that came about during the reconstruction is too long to list; one point of note is that many of the transnational institutions that have become the inverse of their original intention find their origin during this time period).

In our own age, this points to a time of new possibilities arising between 2027 and 2039. As anthroposophists, we would be prudent to keep this in mind. The opposing forces are primed and ready to fill the void that will open during those twelve years with the aims of the Great Reset and the Fourth Industrial Revolution. We need to keep our eyes on that time period as a time when the world might be particularly receptive to the message of the threefold social order, since, by the end of the 2020s, the level of disorganization might become so great that a solution as radical as social threefolding might have a place at the table. It is not enough to take solace in the fact that a High inevitably follows a Crisis. There is peace and there is *Peace*. We do not want the peace of antichrist, of technocratic stability. We want the true peace of Freedom, Equality, and Fraternity. The gesture of history points to the fact that whatever social order is "locked in" during the High remains virtually unchangeable for the next sixty years—until the next Crisis comes to remind us of everything that escaped our notice eighty years earlier.

After spending a good deal of time with the ideas presented in *The Fourth Turning*, I came upon Steffen Hartmann's wonderful work *The Michael Prophecy and the Years 2012–2033: Rudolf Steiner and the Culmination of Anthroposophy*, the second chapter of which I have republished in the present volume. Toward the end of his life, Steiner prophesied that at the end of the second millennium, many anthroposophists incarnated during the early twentieth century (himself included!) would return; he emphasized that the

two streams of the Michael school—the Aristotelians and the Platonists—would have to work together at the time to rescue humanity from the catastrophe that would befall humanity at the end of the second millennium.

Typically, in anthroposophic circles, it is considered that Rudolf Steiner's warning went unheeded—that the Aristotelians and Platonists did not find each other or work together as intended, and that neither the culmination of Anthroposophy nor the catastrophe took place, etc. This is because the year 2000 came and went with scant evidence of any fulfilment of the prophecy. Now, Steffen Hartmann makes a very convincing case for the idea that when Steiner refers to the end of the second millennium, he means the end of the second millennium after the Mystery of Golgotha—i.e., 2033. There is a precedent for his doing so, as he states in the *Calendar of the Soul,* which was published in the year 1879 after the Mystery of Golgotha (i.e., 1912). Steffen Hartmann was musing this as far back as 2014. He predicted that sometime during the twenty-one years leading up to 2033 (between 2012 and 2033), the predicted catastrophe would befall humanity and require the Michaelites to work together to pass through it. Now, the Michaelites are first and foremost seekers after Truth. They are free thinkers and ethical individualists. It is clear to me that Hartmann was correct in his prediction that the global response to Covid-19 is the catastrophe, and that the Michaelites are most certainly coming together to rise up against tyranny in the name of the free individuality.

It was remarkable for me that Hartmann had come to a very similar time period for the crisis as I had done (2013–2031), yet he approached it from a completely different orientation. Hartmann chose this twenty-one-year period owing to its resonance with similar periods in prior centuries. Kaspar Hauser was born in 1812 and died in 1833; Anthroposophy was born in 1912, and Adolf Hitler came to power in 1933. It is interesting to think of these time periods as somehow related to the presence of Christ in the etheric.[5] Why these four centuries?

_____

5   See Robert Powell's article "The 33⅓–year

Steiner indicated that a crucifixion event occurred for Christ in the etheric over the course of the nineteenth century. In Camphill, there is an understanding that the life and death of Kaspar Hauser was reflective of this sacrifice of Christ. On the other hand, Robert Powell has taken the perspective that each century after the life of Christ can be considered as analogous to one year in the life of the human being. In this sense, the year 2133 corresponds to the age of 21, the incarnation of the "I" in the human biography. The unfolding of the "I" takes place over the course of ages twenty-one to forty-two for human beings; this corresponds to the years AD 2133 to 4233, at the heart of the period Steiner referred to as the Age of Light (1899–4399). From this perspective, we might see 2133 as the "end of the beginning" of Christ's second coming.

This "beginning" period, therefore, takes place during a time in history analogous to the ages eighteen to twenty-one in the human biography. Some significant astrological milestones take place during these years. One is the return of the node at age 18.61. This would correspond to the year 1861 + 33 = 1894, the year that Rudolf Steiner published *The Philosophy of Freedom*. Another is the end of the metonic cycle at age nineteen. This corresponds to the year 1900 + 33 = 1933, the year that Steiner pointed to specifically as the time when individuals would begin to become aware of Christ in the etheric. And finally, there is the age 19.86, which is the rhythm of the alignments of Jupiter and Saturn. This would correspond to 1986 + 33 = 2019. This is very close to the actual conjunction of Jupiter and Saturn that took place at the end of 2020 (corresponding to the age 19.87).[6]

We can also look at the rhythm of the Fourth Turning in reference to conjunctions of Jupiter and Saturn. A Great Conjunction took place in Sagittarius in 1782; another took place in Leo in 1861; and another took place in Aries in 1940. We can see that significant events took place seven years before each of these conjunctions—the outbreak of the Revolutionary War in 1775; the formation of the Republican Party in 1854; and the rise of Adolf Hitler in 1933. This once again points to the year 2013 as a significant time period in our current Crisis.[7]

The Great Conjunction that occurred (geocentrically) on December 21, 2020, also holds a special position between two other significant cosmic events: the so-called Great American Solar Eclipses. These are the first total solar eclipses whose paths of totality go all the way across the United States since 1918. The occurrence of these two eclipses at the heart of the Fourth Turning opens up the possibility for a high degree of volatility, disorder, yet also great spiritual potential during this time. The first Great American Solar Eclipse took place on August 21, 2017. Three years and four months later, the conjunction of Jupiter and Saturn took place. We now look forward to the companion event, three years and four months *after* the Great Conjunction, the total solar eclipse of April 8, 2024. Leading up to this second total solar eclipse in 2024 is one that we will experience this year: on October 14, 2023, an annular solar eclipse will be visible in the United States of America, from Oregon to Texas.

This eclipse remembers the Sun's position (25° Virgo) during the "Miracle of the Sun," the culmination of the visions of Our Lady of Fatima on October 13, 1917. The next day, on October 14, 1917, Steiner gave his lecture "The Battle between Michael and the 'Dragon,'" the central

---

rhythm," as well as my article "The Sacrifices of Jesus and Christ, Part II," in the present issue. We can think of the time period between the union of the Jesus children in AD 12 and the Mystery of Golgotha in 33 being recalled at different levels in the nineteenth through twenty-second centuries (1812–33, 1912–33, 2012–33, and 2112–33).

6 It is also quite close to the time period I pointed to as representing a resurrection of Anthroposophy in my article "The Cosmic Communion of Fish" in the *Journal for Star Wisdom 2018* (p. 74).

---

7 I will also remind the reader of my article "First Steps toward a Grail Timeline" from *Cosmology Reborn: Star Wisdom* vol 1, in which I indicated that between April 28, 2013 and September 13, 2022, we are both facing the forces of antichrist as well as reliving events from the time of Parzival. This corresponds to the first period of the Fourth Turning, from its inception to the turning point we now approach (p. 81).

lecture in his incredible series *The Fall of the Spirits of Darkness*. This eclipse also falls almost exactly one hundred years after the final lecture in the series *The Four Seasons and the Archangels*, "The Working Together of the Archangels," October 13, 1923.

There is much more that could be indicated regarding these three solar eclipses, which will become the theme of next year's edition of *Star Wisdom*. For now—in addition to holding "The Foundation Stone Meditation" strongly in our hearts over the course of the coming year—we are being reminded by this eclipse to turn ourselves to Mary-Sophia in the form of Our Lady of Fatima;

and to Archangel Michael. I encourage the reader to make the content of the Fatima visions and the two lecture cycles mentioned their inner work for 2023, to ready ourselves to cross the abyss of the turning point.

Once again, I wish to extend my heartfelt gratitude to each of my contributors, to the advisory board, and to those at SteinerBooks who have lent a hand in making this publication possible. Your work is very much appreciated.

"In Christ, Death becomes Life"

"Every earthly condition during a certain period of time is to be explained as a weaving and interplay of those forces that come into flower and those that die away, those that belong to the rising and those that belong to the falling line—sunrise and sunset—and in between, the zenith at noon, where the two forces unite and become one.

Seen from one's horizon, a person beholds the stars in the sky, rising in the east and climbing ever higher until they reach their highest point in the south. From then onward, they sink until they set in the west. And though the stars disappear from sight in the west, one must nevertheless say to oneself: The real place of setting lies in the south and coincides with the zenith, just as the true place of rising is in the north and coincides with the nadir.

Rising starts from the nadir. Through that, a circular motion is described that can be divided into two halves by a vertical line running south to north. In the part containing the eastern point, the rising forces are active. In the part containing the western point, the sinking forces are present. The eastern and western points cut the semicircle through the center. They are the two points in which, for our physical eye, vision of the forces begins and ends. They are one's horizon."

—RUDOLF STEINER, *Freemasonry and Ritual Work*, p. 387

RUDOLF STEINER'S MICHAEL PROPHECY AND THE YEARS 2012 TO 2033

Steffen Hartmann

This article was published originally as chapter 2 in The Michael Prophecy and the Years 2012–2033: Rudolf Steiner and the Culmination of Anthroposophy, *by Steffen Hartmann (Forest Row, UK: Temple Lodge, 2020). It appears here courtesy of the publisher.*

"Because it is written above us in supersensible script: Be aware that you will return before the end of the twentieth century and at the end of this twentieth century, which you have prepared! Become aware then how that which you have prepared can unfold!"

—RUDOLF STEINER, July 28, 1924[1]

"I have indicated how those individuals who are fully engaged in the anthroposophical movement will return at the end of the century, and that others will then join them, because it will be decided at that time whether earth civilization will be redeemed, or lost."

—RUDOLF STEINER, August 3, 1924[2]

"The very worst danger would be to align ourselves with anthroposophical trends that only lead to further decay and more illusions, instead of orienting ourselves to the advancing world-ego of Christ.... Vacillating disunity should lead to reflection within the work of spiritual science. Then it can be understood why Rudolf Steiner, looking forward to the turn of the century, said on September 16, 1924, something that was astonishingly relevant: that 'for the salvation of the earth, what anthroposophists can accomplish will be decisive for the salvation of the essential being of the earth.'"[3]

"This should not sound as if any one group has a monopoly on the Michael prophecy alluded to in Rudolf Steiner's concluding Karma lectures. Certainly, it is something crucial that should be looked at clearly and with quiet earnestness. But no place or group should relate this too much solely to themselves. That would contradict the overarching human approach associated with the work of the Michael Christ impulse."[4]

—ANTON KIMPFLER

Much has been said and written about Rudolf Steiner's Michael prophecy. That is, about the fact that Steiner's students, coworkers, and friends from the beginning of the twentieth century would incarnate again at the end of the twentieth century—after a very condensed period of life after death. For me, even as a teenager the question arose: Are these things only talked about and thought about amongst anthroposophists, or are we serious about the karmic consequences of life? And if so, how does that work? How can we fruitfully pick up the karmic context and connections where they were at the beginning of the twentieth century? This question is especially pressing seen against the background of the tragic events that took place in the Anthroposophical Society itself after Steiner's death, and in the apocalyptic course of the twentieth century in general, including two world wars, the Holocaust, the nuclear destruction of cities in Japan, the Cold War, and the like.

In 1998, Thomas Meyer published a courageous novel, entitled *Der Unverbrüchliche Vertrag* (The Unbreakable Contract), in which some of Rudolf Steiner's reincarnated students are featured as characters. Opinions vary as to the literary and/or spiritual substance of this novel marking the new millennium, but his book certainly represents a remarkable advance toward taking the topic of the Michael prophecy seriously in our time. But again, the question arose for me: Does the question about

1 Steiner, *Karmic Relationships,* vol. 3.
2 Ibid.
3 Kimpfler, *Okkulte Umweltfragen.*
4 Kimpfler, *Wege,* 6/2013.

the return of the early anthroposophists remain more or less merely a literary issue for important representatives of the anthroposophical movement, without penetrating into our actual lives? That would be more than tragic!

Recently, the voices claiming that the "leading anthroposophists" have not reincarnated at all have increased. For example, in 2013 Peter Selg wrote:

> ...despite reports to the contrary, the truly pioneering and leading anthroposophists in the various spheres of life are not incarnated at the moment...we should, I think, also see that we are not a movement bursting forth on a large scale, with brilliant capacities, and that the so-called culmination at the end of the twentieth Century has definitely not occurred.[5]

In my view, these words cannot simply be left unchallenged. One can ask from a purely scientific, logical perspective how Peter Selg arrives at such an absolute and overall negative judgement? Would it not be more accurate to say, "I myself cannot ascertain that any reincarnated 'leading anthroposophists' have returned?" Or even, "...according to my perceptions and judgement, the culmination of anthroposophy has not occurred."

In a similarly absolutist way, in his book *May Human Beings Hear It!...*, Sergei O. Prokofieff wrote in 2002,

> ...full of loyalty and devotion to Rudolf Steiner and his spiritual task, all five individualities of the founding Executive Council continue to live and work in the spiritual world. With this *common* task they will one day come back to earth to continue the teacher's cause here *together*.

Here, too, one must add that the members of the founding Executive Council: Marie Steiner, Ita Wegman, Elisabeth Vreede, Albert Steffen, and Guenther Wachsmuth—that is, their immortal individualities—are of course active in the spiritual world and are thus accessible there; but who is to say that they do not also live and work here

and now, in new physical bodies and life circumstances? Where does this absolutist judgement come from? This would be in blatant contradiction to Rudolf Steiner's Karma lectures of 1924.

Is it possible that the expectations associated with the Michael prophecy are just too high or even one-sided? Is the situation perhaps even more complicated and complex? Namely, the possibility that the respective individuals are certainly here again on earth, but the culmination of anthroposophy has not succeeded to the extent to which Rudolf Steiner intended it? (With respect to the question of success, one must certainly agree with Peter Selg.)

And is it not possible that, despite the many failures of the Anthroposophical Society in the twentieth century, students of Michael have nevertheless continued their efforts undaunted, and in many cases completely independently of the Anthroposophical Society, and therefore also not in the direct view of Sergei Prokofieff and Peter Selg?

When Selg speaks of "brilliant geniuses" (who may indeed be missing), I can say only that the referenced reincarnated anthroposophists are not geniuses. It is not necessarily in their karma to be geniuses. Geniuses are likely to be luciferically inspired, even "possessed" people, as Rudolf Steiner explained in Munich on January 9, 1912 (CW 130). In the past, such brilliant people have promoted and advanced humanity in all areas of life—but the age of geniuses is likely over. Today, it is more important to focus on new forms of community building, at least for the students of Michael.

In addition, the irregular kamaloka of the reincarnated anthroposophists was far too short to expect them to be all-knowing, esoteric supermen (as tends to be the case in Thomas Meyer's above-mentioned novel). In addition, the current world conditions have become far too confusing, chaotic, dramatic and ahrimanic all at the same time for today's anthroposophists to be effective in such a globally and externally successful manner.

This renewed and active anthroposophy, as well as the people who have enlivened it and carry it within themselves, are at first glance much more modest, pure and more heartfelt than some might think. One can recognize Rudolf Steiner's

---

5 Selg, *Das Wesen und die Zukunft der Anthroposophischen Gesellschaft.* Cf. also, Selg and Desaules (eds.), *The Anthroposophical Society: The Understanding and Continued Activity of the Christmas Conference.*

reincarnated students by their love and kindness in the quest for knowledge; their desire for honest and open community building, without power structures and pseudo-esoteric claims. They have an irrepressible yearning for freedom and an unsentimental love for Rudolf Steiner, which goes hand in hand with intellectual independence. This is also due to the fact that they are often silent about the "loud" and supposedly important anthroposophical controversies.

However, I have decided not to remain silent any longer about Rudolf Steiner's Michael prophecy and its present-day reality. As a person who, since his youth, has carried within himself karmic memories from the time of Steiner, and who has struggled with these experiences for many years, keeping silent, while repeatedly examining them, I would quite simply like to say that these original anthroposophists have not remained in the spiritual world. Rather, the pioneering anthroposophists have reincarnated in waves, distributed over several generations, beginning in 1950. Perhaps not all of them—who could judge that?—but indeed very many.

In my view, this is neither a sensation nor a matter of speculation. Everyone who lived at that time in Rudolf Steiner's environment carries the consciousness deeply inscribed in his or her heart that the best efforts at that time were not sufficient, that no one's abilities were sufficient—everyone probably failed at least once in the presence of Steiner. So, there is no reason whatsoever for any arrogance, or any inner or even outer pretension on the part of said returned anthroposophists. You can recognize them by this quality as well.

One might ask: And what good is your karmic insight to us? Anthroposophical insights are true above all because they are also fruitful. Yes, that is exactly what I would like to demonstrate with this book of essays. For what perhaps the above commentators have not considered from all angles is the question of what it means that all Michael students live and work in the era of freedom. And nowadays freedom also means that I can lose, deny or redirect my own karmic path, or also consciously take hold of it, and ever more consciously and creatively

work with my own karma. By this I mean to say that there is a struggle occurring in precisely those souls that quickly incarnated again in the twentieth century—which incidentally also applies to many Holocaust victims, and is therefore by no means a "privilege" of the anthroposophists.[6]

The manner in which we view the Michael prophecy and the years ahead until the year 2033 remains critical. We can gather courage from this Michaelic perspective; we can rekindle strength in ourselves every single day, precisely because the situation is so dire, so precarious and so much is at stake for our globalized humanity of the twenty-first century.

I would like to express another thought for people to entertain without the need for special karmic experiences or clairvoyant abilities: During the Cold War, up to the 1980s, the fate of all humanity was hanging by a thread due to the threat of nuclear war. With the reunification of Germany in 1989, some things could be turned around so that the worst threats were eliminated. It is as obvious, as it is also difficult, for many people to imagine that in such a time of trials for humanity, the leading individualities—such as Rudolf Steiner and Christian Rosenkreutz—might remain in the spiritual world and wait for better times and conditions to incarnate, but instead would participate and help precisely there, where everything is at stake, day in and day out. They would not only be concerned with the interests of an institution called the Anthroposophical Society that revolves around itself, but would help in connection with world events on a wider scale.

To be an initiate, to be a servant of Christ and a spiritual master in our time, need not entail standing in the spotlight and being a driving force in the world; one may not appear as a "genius" or notably successful to the public, but may be acting to help ensure, simply and humbly, that the connection to the spiritual world does not completely cease in our time.

When Saul persecuted the early Christians, he was a committed believer in the coming of the

---

6 See, for example, Yonassan Gershom's *Beyond the Ashes: Cases of Reincarnation from the Holocaust.*

Messiah. It was unthinkable for Saul that the Messiah had already lived on the earth for quite some time, and had died wretchedly on a cross. No, he became "Paul" through the immediate experience of Christ's presence! Only through this dramatic experience—not through a thought or general judgement, or dogma—was he empowered to proclaim the living Christ and spread Christianity over far reaches of the world.

In 2010, Judith von Halle expressed very openly in her book *Krise und Chance* (Crisis and Opportunity),

> ...that according to my observation Rudolf Steiner's prophecies have come true. As is the case with the culmination of anthroposophy, which Rudolf Steiner spoke of, that is another story.... But I think it is an excellent opportunity for many people from Rudolf Steiner's circle to come together again in the Anthroposophical Society, and nowhere else; this also follows from Rudolf Steiner's words, because if anthroposophy is to be brought to culmination, then it would make little sense for the people concerned to reincarnate themselves in completely different contexts...

She openly and courageously touched upon our taboo topic. I can agree with her generally when she writes:

> Our Society therefore consists of individuals who come to life with a "backpack" and realize that they still have almost the same things in their luggage: similar abilities and inabilities that have not been worked upon enough. Let every person examine him or herself, and for themselves—before doing so with others—whether it is possible that certain peculiarities that emerge in us, particularly with reference to anthroposophical community building, might not be exaggerations of a trait from past incarnations in the Society of Rudolf Steiner's time, that has yet to be overcome. One could say that such a self-examination for the purpose of successful community building is possibly just the bitter and painful work called for to finish tasks of Kamaloka, of the purification of our past life, but here on earth. Yet this is certainly to be understood as a deed of love to us from the

spiritual world, to be understood as an opportunity—something short of bringing anthroposophy directly to its culmination, as Rudolf Steiner had hoped—but nevertheless an opportunity, to at least struggle with tasks that should have taken place after the Karma lectures, after Rudolf Steiner's death.

Perhaps it must be added that the people incarnated today can—even must—become assisting angels to help one another if things are to continue fruitfully.[7] Not only the knowledge of how to work with karma has been put into our hands, but also the power to form future karma; this lives today in the freedom of the human heart. Through disinterest, dogmatism, arrogance, petty quarrelling and the like, the human destiny of the Michael School on earth can be paralyzed and destroyed. There is an entire army of demons working precisely toward this end.

In other words, how things will continue is up to us, each and every incarnated anthroposophist. There is no point whatsoever in waiting actively or passively for future initiates, or even Rudolf Steiner disciples alone, to reincarnate.

Johannes Greiner wrote in the journal *Der Europäer* (Oct. 2013):

> Of course, it's not about finding out who you were in previous lives and then resting comfortably in possible praise, or making outrageous demands and the like. From the knowledge of the past, one can discern one's own tasks and above all become aware of one's own shadow. Usually, the greatest obstacle to present-day work consists in the habits arising out of a past life. To recognize and transform one's own shadow is far more important than to point out errors of perception in other striving people! If much of the anthroposophical movement over the last ninety years has suspiciously been reminiscent of pharaonic behavior, of Catholic pomp and papal claim to absolute authority, of inquisitorial denunciation of marginal groups, Arab contextualization or pharisaic doctrinalism, this is certainly mostly due to the old tired

---

7   See also my essay in *Das Goetheanum,* "The School for Spiritual Science of Tomorrow Begins Today," Aug. 13, 2011.

habits we have just characterized. Just because we are now able to think Rudolf Steiner's thoughts, doesn't mean that we suddenly become other people! And yet we must become other people!

And yet we must become other people; herein lie the meaning and fruitfulness of karmic vision that we become other people—freer, more spiritually aware, more social, more loving, and more creative. Rudolf Steiner also called it "putting karma in order"—and even the angels can learn something from this. Here we encounter the power of Christ presently in the etheric realm, in the realm in which networks of destiny weave between and among people. There we can silently and yet clearly hear HIS word: "Behold, I make everything new" (Rev. 21:5).

It is an experience of the heart: Today many things between people can be seen and healed much more directly and quickly, more openly and freely than ever before in human history. But of course, the opposite is also true: divisiveness, vehement clashes, getting entangled in conflicts with each other, or a complete absence of relationship. Where the new light of Christ shines, there are also dark shadows.

Anton Kimpfler is one of the few anthroposophists who has truly lived and struggled with the Michael prophecy and its manifold consequences in the second half of the twentieth century. This can already be seen in his journal *Auf Pftngsten Zu* (Toward Pentecost) published in 1985/86. This moving journal contains an entry every day for an entire year. On June 13, 1985, for example, he wrote:

I don't have the slightest conceit at all about the past, because I must reacquire everything anew. Spiritual productivity cannot be explained by the conditions of my current life. But experiences can be made here that the heavens need. What Rudolf Steiner was able to bring down in his time would no longer be possible today. And yet it has to be won anew, otherwise we will never be able to keep it. The most dangerous thing would to get distracted or lost in petty administrative activities.

And on July 20 ,1985, we find the following note:

If anthroposophists had sorted out their karma, the world would certainly not have gotten so confused. The events mentioned in this short diary alone prove that failure was and is present. Now we have to accomplish with strangers what most of our fellow men have failed to do. Everything becomes wider and more human, more beautiful, but also more difficult.

Finally, in Kimpfler's words on March 16, 1986, speaking more generally but nevertheless very certainly about every person's striving for knowledge on the anthroposophical path:

At a certain point, where we develop our own powers, our esoteric efforts become unfruitful if we do not enter the social sphere with them. Only if we learn to pass on the powers we've acquired will they remain good.

And at the end of this journal—which is basically a shining testimonial to the reality and the daily difficulties of the Michael prophecy in the last third of the twentieth century—Anton Kimpfler writes thus as he looks back on the twentieth century as a whole:

The first quarter of the century: Collaboration with the spiritual world. Second quarter: Uprising of the opposing gods. Third quarter: The new is beginning to emerge in people. The end of the century: "These mighty events all come together." (May 12, 1986)

In this sense, the end of the century was marked by an almost incomprehensible polyphony of events: There was (and still is) an interaction of "collaboration with the spiritual world" (1900–1925), with the "uprising of the opposing gods" (1925–1950) and the emergence of the new in humanity (1950–1975). According to Kimpfler, from 1975 to 2000 we have had a "coming together of these mighty events."

Rudolf Steiner's calendar impulses of 1912 respectively 1879

At this point I would like to refer to another important context that once again sheds a completely new light on the past, namely Rudolf Steiner's calendar impulse of 1912—which brought an impulse containing nothing less than a new era. Steiner wrote on the cover of his 1912 calendar: "1879, after the birth of the 'I.'" That is, he was concerned with a calendar that began with the Mystery of Golgotha, that is, beginning in the year 33 AD of the "normal" reckoning.

Anton Kimpfler has also repeatedly pointed out these connections and their consequences for us today. For example, in *Wege* (1/2012):

> According to Rudolf Steiner, this should be the beginning of the actual new era. That is why the publication of the anthroposophical *Calendar of the Soul* in 1912 stated: 1879, after the birth of the "I" (on earth). This inspires perhaps a more hopeful consideration: So, we're only up to 1979 in 2012. And the end of the century will still be in progress up to 2033. This may mean that, through Christ over a period of 33 years, we have another chance to take up something that was previously not fruitful enough—also with regard to the realization of new or reemerging impulses of anthroposophically aligned personalities. In any case, since 1933, to the extent that we have been able to live in the experience of Christ's return in the etheric, everything that can accompany the further unfolding of the Christ power on earth has become yet more meaningful. Essentially, the etheric is the world of time and its rhythms.

From this perspective, the question of the culmination of anthroposophy at the end of the twentieth century appears to us in a new light. Two thousand years after the Mystery of Golgotha is, then, the year 2033—according to the "normal" calendar—meaning that we still have the real millennium ahead of us!

The final twenty-one years up to this point in time are extremely important and decisive (i.e., the years 2012 to 2033) according to Rudolf Steiner's calendar, 1979 to 2000.

It is clear to me that the reality of the Michael prophecy has entered a new phase beginning in 2012. Something changed in the spiritual atmosphere of the earth around the year 2012 (or 1979). Since we are still very close to this pivotal moment, we do not yet have the conceptual distance required to say much about it yet. It seems noticeable to me, however, that since that time the students of Michael have been able to encounter one another more directly in the earthly world and to recognize each other in their true essence. The unconditional intention/impulse to work together—despite all karmic difficulties and challenges—can be perceived individually as well as in their collective tone. (It goes without saying that it is precisely this impulse of unredeemed karmic patterns in so many of us that does not want to yield to the call for change.)

The "veil" that consciously separates us from the spiritual Michael school, into which we dive every night during sleep, has become even thinner and more transparent than before. This presents a great opportunity! Michael is closer than ever. However, he leaves us free, waiting upon our initiative.

Of course, in this etheric Michael school there is no central office that could issue any directives, nor any other formal criteria for participation in this event. Only the presence of mind, cognitive ability and moral integrity of each individual are decisive as to what degree each individual is able to participate in this school. In my essay "Wege zum *Geist*" (Paths to the spirit) from 2012, I tried to express the nature of Michael:

> The work of the time-spirit reveals itself only in a power of judgement marked by *presence of mind*. This type of judgement must be flexible; indeed, it must strive for constant balance in order to be able to grasp the full, living reality. What is Michaelic cannot be rigidly derived out of the past. A fixed judgement may be correct, but truth in the sense of the Christ only arises where judgement also becomes fruitful and opens out into the future. (John 14:6: "I am the way, the truth and the life.") Human discernment is itself a world process. The way I discern things contributes to the shaping of reality. Thus, our own perspective on knowledge—through self-knowledge, in the social sphere, but also regarding historical events—is a thing each of us will be called to answer for individually in the presence of the prevailing spirit of the age.

The Michaelic power of discernment characterized here necessitates that we pass through the individual karmic eye of the needle, and not once, but repeatedly. In the presence of Michael, knowledge and life, thinking and will are inseparable. "The eye of the needle must be traversed in order to achieve a new sun-like quality. This shines in a creative way and gives us new courage for the future. Discernment masters this transition only through a Michaelic gesture of will. This also includes a sacrifice of merely intellectual forces. The path to deeper heart forces leads through and beyond the suffering of an individual feeling of powerlessness" (*Wege zum Geist*, as above).

The year AD 2012 occurs within a great and meaningful rhythm: 1812–1912–2012. Kaspar Hauser is born on Michaelmas in 1812. (He is murdered in 1833.) In 1910/11 and 1912, Rudolf Steiner begins proclaiming the coming return of Christ in the etheric, and in doing so decisively prepares the entire course of the twentieth century (Adolf Hitler comes to power in 1933). And in 2012 we can perhaps speak cautiously of a new dawning of the spiritual Michael school.

What is particularly moving about Kaspar Hauser is the purity of his unspoiled sensory experience (pure perception) and the purity and sincerity of his soul being.

One hundred years after the birth of Kaspar Hauser, a new direct revelation of Christ comes to mankind through Rudolf Steiner. And another hundred years later, in 2012, new openness and flexibility of cooperation between Michael, Vidar,[8]

---

8 Vidar is the great silent spirit of the North (mentioned in the Norse mythology, *The Edda*). Through the power of silence, he keeps the future open. Vidar places his shoe in the mouth of the Fenris Wolf, so that the wolf cannot swallow everything up. Vidar works in the background with Michael, the leading spirit of the Age who shows the path to the spirit and pathways to Christ. But people must *tread* these paths themselves. Here, Vidar is present to intercede for us over and over again, if only we will steadfastly resist the dark adversarial powers. Only thus will we not be pulled down the vortex of our undoing. But also, new things come into the world through Vidar, mostly in inconspicuous ways. See Are Thoresen, *Encountering Vidar* and *Travels on the Northern Path of Initiation: Vidar and Baldur, the Three Elemental Realms and the Inner and Outer Etheric Worlds.*

and Christ and the disciples of Michael and Christ on earth seems possible to me.

In addition to what we can learn from Kaspar Hauser—pure perception and a pure soul being—two more abilities must be developed in accordance with the demands of our time: Firstly, pure thinking, which leads us into living imaginations, expressive inspirations and freeing intuitions. And secondly, basically inseparable from this, a deeper experience and recognition of destiny, which is ultimately only possible in community with other people and in interaction and encounter with others.

In between lies the impulse from 1912 to approach Christ in the etheric and to learn to live and work together with Him. The Second Coming of Christ began exactly 1,900 years after the Mystery of Golgotha. At that time (in 1933) the anthroposophical movement was greatly weakened by quarrels and divisions and a National Socialist opposing movement was able, with Adolf Hitler at the helm, to seduce all of Central Europe and ultimately unleash World War II.

Greatest vigilance is called for as we approach the year 2033! This text was composed out of concern for the mark of the times. I am not interested in personal ambitions; I am concerned with a serious examination of the current Michael school and the burning tasks of all students of Michael. I want to encourage a much deeper human connection in all those people who can relate to what is being said here to their inner being, to their hearts. The fact that in speaking and writing about these things the individual reveals a certain one-sidedness is not bad at all; it is essential that we learn to complement one another fruitfully. Then, what may seem impossible can take place! Awakened faith can move mountains.

Vidar, the silent spirit of the North, keeps access to the future constantly open. Michael encourages us when we courageously take free initiative. And Christ is present as the healer of destiny, when we open our etheric hearts to Him.

THE 33 1/3-YEAR RHYTHM

Robert Powell, PhD

Let us consider the following words of Rudolf Steiner:

Since the Mystery of Golgotha took place, many people can proclaim the name of Christ, and from the twentieth century on there will be a constantly increasing number of people who can communicate the knowledge of the Christ being given in spiritual science. Twice already, Christ has been crucified: the first time physically in the physical world at the beginning of our era, and a second time in the nineteenth century spiritually.... One could say that humanity experienced the resurrection of the Christ being's body then; from the twentieth century on, it will experience the resurrection of Christ consciousness....

This is what can be said about the relationship of the Mystery of Golgotha, which took place at the beginning of our era and the Mystery of Golgotha as it can be understood today. Let us make these feelings our own, recognizing that it is the only way we can become true spiritual scientists. From time to time other revelations will come our way, to which we must keep an open mind.[1]

Here Steiner clearly says that other revelations will come, and that we can assume he had in mind further revelations of Christ in the etheric realm. For example, he himself had proclaimed such a Christ event for the end of the twentieth century:

Just as on the physical plane in Palestine, at the beginning of our era, an event occurred in which the most important part was taken by Christ himself—an event that has its significance for the whole of humanity—so, in the course of the twentieth century, toward the end of the twentieth century, a significant event will again take place, not in the physical world but in the world we usually call the world of the etheric.[2]

The central purpose of my research into the Christ Mystery is to penetrate to the true significance of these words, and in earlier publications I present research showing fairly conclusively that the event prophesied by Steiner evidently took place in 1999, a little before or after September 3 to 5, referring to this event as "a repetition of the Mystery of Golgotha in the etheric in September 1999." This event was heralded by the great European eclipse of August 11, 1999. The question naturally arises: What led me to understand the Christ event prophesied by Rudolf Steiner as a "repetition of the Mystery of Golgotha in the etheric in September 1999"?

As it is a matter of the return of Christ in his etheric body, it is possible to approach this question by considering the rhythm of Christ's etheric body. This rhythm is 33⅓ years, the length of the life of Christ Jesus, which lasted exactly 33⅓ years from his birth shortly before midnight on December 6, 2 BC (−1) to his resurrection at sunrise on April 5, AD 33. One can rightly ask: How is it possible to know with certainty that this birth date is accurate?

I was able to determine the birth date from Anne Catherine Emmerich's visions, as I have described in my book *Chronicle of the Living Christ*. She communicated the day of the week and the date in the Hebrew calendar of various events in the life of Christ. Mathematically, through probability theory, I and two other mathematicians investigated the dates she communicated. We discovered (independent of each other) that the probability of these weekdays coinciding by chance with the

---

1 Steiner, *Approaching the Mystery of Golgotha*, pp. 29–30.

2 Steiner, *From Jesus to Christ*, p. 46.

right dates in the Hebrew calendar is 1:435 billion.[3] One does not need to be a mathematician to see that it would have been impossible for Anne Catherine Emmerich to have simply made up the dates. In other words, her dates are authentic.

When she says that Jesus was born around midnight on the twelfth day of the Hebrew month of Kislev, the evening after the Sabbath, then this date in all probability is accurate—in other words, Jesus was born at midnight Saturday/Sunday, the twelfth day of Kislev. This date in the Hebrew calendar corresponds to Saturday/Sunday, December 6/7, 2 BC (–1). From this point in time until the resurrection (April 5, 33) is exactly 33⅓ years (minus 1½ days).

There is a communication made by Rudolf Steiner that confirms this period of 33⅓ years:

> All things in historic evolution arise transfigured after thirty-three years, as from a grave, by virtue of a power connected with the holiest of all redemptions: the Mystery of Golgotha.[4]
>
> Then, when such a seed that has been laid ripens, it works further. A "thought seed" ripens through one generation of 33 years to become a "deed seed." Once ripened, it works further in the unfolding of history through 66 years. One can recognize the intensity of an impulse that someone implants into the historical process also in its effect through three generations, through a whole century.[5]

A whole century is one hundred years, equal to 3 x 33⅓ years. Here Steiner's indication of 33⅓

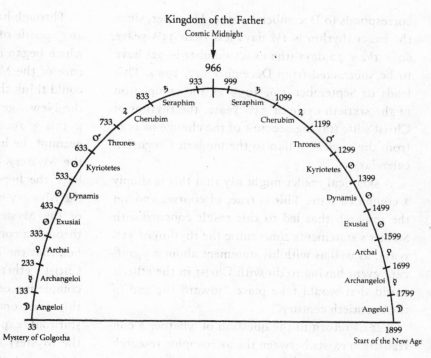

Diagram labels (left arm, top to bottom): 966 Cosmic Midnight (Kingdom of the Father) · 933 Seraphim · 999 Seraphim · 833 Cherubim · 733 Cherubim · 633 Thrones · 533 Kyriotetes · 433 Dynamis · 333 Exusiai · 233 Archai · 133 Archangeloi · 33 Angeloi — Mystery of Golgotha

Right arm, top to bottom): 1099 Seraphim · 1199 Cherubim · 1299 Thrones · 1399 Kyriotetes · 1499 Dynamis · 1599 Exusiai · 1699 Archai · 1799 Archangeloi · 1899 Angeloi — Start of the New Age

years is confirmed. In the lecture, for the sake of brevity, he simply says "33 years"—that this rhythm works further in the unfolding of history.

The reader can imagine how encouraging it was to discover that the statement by the clairvoyant Anne Catherine Emmerich regarding Jesus' birth date was confirmed in this (indirect) way by Rudolf Steiner. In this way, I arrived at certainty with respect to the truth of this 33⅓-year rhythm and that one can follow the rhythm of 33⅓ years through history. This is all the more exciting, since Steiner speaks of a "new astrology" in this connection: "This is the key, my dear friends, for reading the new astrology, in which attention is directed to the stars that shine within the historical evolution of humanity itself."[6]

It was a special joy to be able to confirm the discovery of the 33⅓-year rhythm as the basis for a new star wisdom, emerging as the "crown" of astrosophic research. The next step was then to follow this rhythm through history (see diagram above). In this way the dates September 3–5, 1999 emerge as the sixtieth return of the dates April 3–5, 33, of the Mystery of Golgotha. For 60 x 33⅓ = 2,000, added on to December 6, 2 BC (–1)

---

3   Powell, *Chronicle of the Living Christ*, p. 455. In the English edition this figure is given incorrectly as 1:53 trillion, which has been corrected to 1:435 billion in the German and Italian editions.

4   Steiner, *Et Incarnatus Est: The Time Cycle in Historic Events*, Dec. 23, 1917.

5   Steiner, *Mysterienwahrheiten und Weihnachtsimpulse* (Mystery truths and the Christmas impulses), Dec. 26, 1917.

6   Steiner, *Et Incarnatus Est: The Time Cycle in Historic Events*, Dec. 23, 1917.

corresponds to December 6, 1999. However, since the exact rhythm is 1½ days less than 33⅓ years, 60 x 1½ = 90 days (the exact number is 92) have to be subtracted from December 6/7, 1999. This leads to September 5/6, 1999 as the completion of the sixtieth cycle of 33⅓ years, the rhythm of Christ's life (taking account of the change in 1582 from the ancient Julian to the modern Gregorian calendar).

A skeptical reader might say that this is simply a computed date. This is true, of course, and yet the research that led to this result concurs with Steiner's statements concerning the rhythm of 33⅓ years, as well as with his statement about a significant event having to do with Christ in the etheric world that would take place "toward the end of the twentieth century."

Let us return to the question of whether a contradiction exists between the astrosophic research presented here and Steiner's communication concerning "the second crucifixion of Christ"—a crucifixion in the etheric world in the nineteenth century. First, let us consider the date September 3–5, 1999, which can be considered a cosmic memory of the Mystery of Golgotha (April 3–5, 33). How might this be understood?

Like all the events in the life of Christ Jesus, the Mystery of Golgotha was inscribed into Christ's etheric body as the crowning of this life. This etheric body is a *time body*, whose rhythm is 33⅓ years. Each time this rhythm is completed, the Mystery of Golgotha lights up as a cosmic memory in Christ's etheric body—at the completion of the fifty-seventh cycle, for example, in 1899. Around this time Steiner inwardly experienced the Mystery of Golgotha:

During the period when my statements about Christianity seemed to contradict my later comments, a conscious knowledge of real Christianity began to dawn within me. Around the turn of the century, this seed of knowledge continued to develop.... I stood spiritually before the Mystery of Golgotha in a deep and solemn celebration of knowledge.[7]

7   Steiner, *Autobiography: Chapters in the Course of My Life, 1861–1907*, p. 188.

Through his Christ experience, Steiner became an "apostle of the Etheric Christ." The New Age, which began in 1899, began with Steiner's experience of the Mystery of Golgotha. Of course, one could think that he perhaps arrived at the start of the New Age simply by way of computation (57 x 33⅓ = 1900). However, according to his own account, he had a genuine spiritual experience of the Mystery of Golgotha. One could, therefore, have the hypothesis that Steiner's experience of the Mystery of Golgotha was a "cosmic memory" of the Mystery of Golgotha, bestowed on him through a connection with Christ's etheric body— i.e., that the Mystery of Golgotha shone forth in Christ's etheric body at that time (1899) and the completion of a cycle of the 33⅓-year rhythm. In this case, one could ask this question: Was this spiritual experience of the cosmic memory of the Mystery of Golgotha in contradiction to his description of "the second crucifixion of Christ," a nineteenth-century crucifixion in the etheric world? By the same token, the events connected with World War II could be viewed also as "a kind of crucifixion" for the Etheric Christ, a perspective that in no way contradicts that there was a *"second crucifixion of Christ"* in the nineteenth century.

Steiner spoke about this second crucifixion on May 2, 1913 in London. On February 8, 1913, three months earlier, he commented on this in the Esoteric School in Berlin:

What is new and what will now gradually be revealed to humanity is a recollection, or repetition, of what St Paul experienced at Damascus. He saw the etheric body of Christ. The reason this will now become visible to us derives from the fact that a new Mystery of Golgotha has, as it were, taken place in the etheric world. What took place here in the physical world at the crucifixion, as a result of the hatred of uncomprehending humanity, has now been repeated on the etheric level, owing to the hatred of human beings who have entered the etheric world as materialists after death.

Let's visualize again how, at the Mystery of Golgotha, a cross of dead wood was erected, on which the body of Christ hung. Then let us visualize the wood of that cross in the etheric world as green—sprouting and living wood that has been turned to charcoal by the flames of hatred and on which seven blossoming roses appear, representing Christ's sevenfold nature. Here we have the picture of the second Mystery of Golgotha, which has now taken place in the etheric world. Through this dying—this second death of Christ—we have gained the possibility of seeing the etheric body of Christ. The densification, the dead part of Christ's etheric body, will be seen by human beings.... The Rose Cross is a symbol for the second death of Christ in the nineteenth century, the death of the etheric body caused by the army of materialists. The result of this is that Christ can now be seen in the twentieth century, as I have often described to you, namely, in the etheric body.[8]

Here, Steiner explains that the Rose Cross is the real sign of the Mystery of Golgotha in the etheric world, just as the Cross (without Roses) was the true symbol of the Mystery of Golgotha two thousand years ago. It is clearly evident that Steiner's spiritual science stands under the sign of the Rose Cross. Isn't this a confirmation that Steiner became an apostle of the Etheric Christ in 1899?

In my research into the Christ Mystery, I have described the incarnation, stage by stage, of Christ in his etheric body.[9] The years 1899, 1933, 1966, and 1999 are the main stages—the points of culmination—of this gradual incarnation beginning with the onset of the New Age in 1899. Couldn't it be—just as we considered Steiner's experience in 1899 under the hypothesis formulated earlier—that, at each of these culminating points, the Mystery of Golgotha shone forth as a cosmic memory from Christ's etheric body? Would this be in accordance with Steiner's prophecy of a continually progressing revelation of Christ in the etheric world? If this is correct, it would signify the following in relation to the series of dates coinciding with the start and end of each 33⅓-year cycle:

1899—the initiation of Rudolf Steiner through the cosmic memory of the Mystery of Golgotha, through the entrance of the Etheric Christ into the Earth's etheric aura, coming from the Moon sphere, whereby Rudolf Steiner became an apostle of the Etheric Christ (comparable to St. Paul who became an apostle through his experience of the Etheric Christ).

1933—the completion of the first cycle of the activity of Christ in the Earth's etheric aura—a time above all of Christ's activity on the level of thinking (the birth of Anthroposophy or spiritual science through Rudolf Steiner). Here it is interesting to consider that if Rudolf Steiner had lived further, he would have been seventy-two years old in 1933, corresponding to the cosmic archetype of seventy-two years for human life indicated by the retrograde movement of the vernal point through one degree of the zodiac.

1966—the completion of the second cycle of the activity of Christ in the Earth's etheric aura—a time, above all, of Christ's activity on the level of feeling (birth of the worldwide impulse of community).

1999—the completion of the third cycle of the activity of Christ in the Earth's etheric aura—a time, above all, of Christ's activity on the level of the will (birth of the worldwide impulse to protect and care for the environment and also to penetrate the mystery of destiny expressed in human biography).

2033—the completion of the fourth cycle of the activity of Christ in the Earth's etheric aura—a time, above all, of Christ's activity on the level of the human self ("I"), as expressed in St. Paul's words: "Not I, but Christ in me," an answer to the forces of the antichrist manifesting in the world with particular strength since September 11, 2001.

With respect to the period from 1966 to 1999, there are two sides to the will. First, our destiny unfolds on the level of the will:

When we begin to think along these lines, we become aware of the immense intricacy and

---

8 Steiner, *Concerning the History and Content of the Higher Degrees of the Esoteric School, 1904–1914,* pp. 369–370.

9 Powell, *The Christ Mystery: Reflections on the Second Coming.*

deep significance in the workings of our destiny or karma. And this all goes on in the domain of the human kingdom. All that thus happens to us is deep in the unconscious life. Until the moment when a decisive event approaches us, it lies in the unconscious. All this takes place as though it were subject to Laws of Nature....

One learns to pose the question of freedom in the true way only after becoming aware of this. Read my *Philosophy of Spiritual Activity* and see how much importance I attach to the point that one should not ask about freedom of the will. The will lies deep, deep down in the unconscious, and it is nonsense to ask about freedom of the will. It is only freedom of thoughts that we can speak about. I drew the line very clearly in my *Philosophy of Spiritual Activity*. One must become free in one's thoughts, and the free thoughts must give the impulse to the will—there one is free.[10]

The will is "deep down in the unconscious," and it is there that our destiny impulse plays itself out. This is one side of the will. Now, before we consider the other side of the will, let's look again at Rudolf Steiner's comments concerning the significant Christ event in the etheric world "toward the end of the twentieth century." That event is characterized by Steiner as Christ becoming the *Lord of Karma*:

Just as on the physical plane in Palestine, at the beginning of our era, an event occurred in which the most important part was taken by Christ himself—an event which has its significance for the whole of humanity—so in the course of the twentieth century, toward the end of the twentieth century, a significant event will again take place, not in the physical world, but in the realm we usually call the world of the etheric. And this event will have as fundamental a significance for the evolution of humanity as the event of Palestine had at the beginning of our era. Just as we must say that for Christ himself the event of Golgotha had the significance that with this very event a God died, a God overcame death—we will speak later concerning the way this is to be understood; the deed had

not happened before and it is an accomplished fact which will not happen again—so an event of profound significance will take place in the etheric world. And the occurrence of this event, an event connected with the Christ himself, will make it possible for human beings to learn to see the Christ, to look upon him. What is this event? It consists in the fact that a certain office in the cosmos, connected with the evolution of humanity in the twentieth century, passes over in a heightened form to the Christ. Occult clairvoyant research tells us that in our epoch Christ becomes the Lord of Karma for human evolution. This event marks the beginning of something that we find intimated also in the New Testament: He will come again to separate or to bring about the crisis for the living and the dead. Only, according to occult research, this is not to be understood as though it were a single event for all time which takes place on the physical plane. It is connected with the whole future evolution of humanity. And whereas Christianity and Christian evolution were hitherto a kind of preparation, we now have the significant fact that Christ becomes the Lord of Karma, so that in the future it will rest with him to decide what our karmic account is, how our credit and debit in life are related.[11]

In the context of the preceding stage-by-stage description of the incarnation of Christ in his etheric body (taking this as a hypothesis), wouldn't 1999 as the culmination since 1899 of the third cycle of 33⅓ years be on the level of the *will*? Is it conceivable that, at this point in time, Christ assumed the office of Lord of Karma? In other words, could 1999 have been the beginning of this Christ event in the etheric "connected with the whole future evolution of humanity"—the event of Christ becoming the Lord of Karma? How is it with regard to the other side of this Christ event?

The other side of this Christ event has to do with the side of the human will that is connected with nature. It is a fact that, through the will, human beings stand in a direct relationship with nature. We breathe in the air; we drink water; we take our food from the world of nature, and it is

---

10 Steiner, *Karmic Relationships*, vol. 1, Feb. 17, 1924, pp. 39–42.

11 Steiner, *From Jesus to Christ*, pp. 46–47.

transformed in our digestive system, which is connected with our will. The "inner side" of the will is the bearer of our destiny. The "outer side" of the will is directly related to nature. Therefore, the other side of the Christ event in the etheric world at the end of the twentieth century has to do with nature. In Steiner's words:

When one understands the Mystery of Golgotha, that is the only thing that enables us to experience the whole of nature morally. If one then gazes up at the clouds and sees lightning flashing from them, one will then be able to behold Christ in his etheric form—with the "clouds"—that is, with the elements. He will appear in spirit form. This vision will one day appear to every human being, be it sooner or be it later; only the Father knows the day and the hour—as it says in the Gospel.[12]

Here, Steiner quotes the words from the Gospel: "Of that day and hour no one knows, not even the Angels in heaven, nor the Son, but only the Father" (Matt. 24:36). Related to the individual: "The day and the hour is known to the Father alone for every individual, but for each the time will arrive."[13]

Related to the Earth and the whole of humanity, the words from the Gospel applied at the time when Christ spoke these words. Now, however, since Steiner became an apostle of the Etheric Christ, for the first time in history something of this mystery—the "greatest mystery of our time" in Steiner's words—has been revealed. For example, he clearly indicates 1933 in connection with Christ's return in the etheric world,[14] and often referred to 1899 as the start of the New Age, which can be seen in connection with the onset of the new activity of Christ in the etheric realm.

What exactly is the relationship between 1899 and 1933? The year 1933 (33⅓ years after 1899) marked the end of the first period of Christ's

activity in his etheric body in the Earth's etheric aura. The 33⅓-year rhythm of Christ's etheric body proceeds further, culminating in 1966 and again in 1999. There are also other rhythms having to do with Christ's renewed activity in our time: the rhythm of Christ's astral body of 29½-years (the rhythm of Saturn) and the twelve-year rhythm of Christ's Self, or "I" (the rhythm of Jupiter).

In this article, it is a matter of delving more deeply into Steiner's reference to "the second crucifixion of Christ"—a crucifixion in the etheric world during the nineteenth century. To conclude our considerations regarding this reference, I would like to point to the second crucifixion in the light of Christ's descent through the planetary spheres, which is also a descent through the ranks of the spiritual hierarchies (see figure on page 33). According to this descent, Christ in his etheric body was in the Moon sphere during the nineteenth century. As indicated by Rudolf Steiner, this is the sphere of the angels. He speaks of "the dying of Christ-consciousness in the sphere of the angels in the nineteenth century." In this sense, one can understand Steiner's words about the "second crucifixion" (having to do with the "black sphere of materialism") as applying primarily to the Moon sphere. The reason is that the seeds of earthly materialism—carried across the threshold of death into the spiritual world by departing souls—are increasingly causing darkness. The Moon sphere is the first planetary sphere that the soul enters after crossing the threshold of death. Negative impulses are left behind in this realm when the soul ascends further on the journey through the planetary spheres. We can understand how, during the nineteenth century, Christ in his etheric body passed through the Moon sphere at the last stage of his descent from cosmic realms to the Earth. We can perhaps grasp how Christ passed through the Moon sphere on his path of descent in his etheric body, meeting there the "black sphere of materialism." We can imagine that he took up much of the "black sphere of materialism" into his own being in the spirit of transforming evil into good.

---

12 Steiner, *Concerning the History and Content of the Higher Degrees of the Esoteric School, 1904–1914*, p. 395.

13 Ibid., 395, footnote 2.

14 Steiner, *The True Nature of the Second Coming*, Jan. 25, 1910; here, Steiner indicates the importance of the years 1933, 1935, and 1937.

One important thing clearly emerges here if one asks: Why didn't the second crucifixion occur before the nineteenth century, as the black sphere of materialism was—since the *sixteenth century*—beginning to be formed *at that time* through the seeds of earthly materialism? Why did the second crucifixion not take place in the sixteenth, seventeenth, and eighteenth centuries? The simple reason is that the black sphere of materialism formed primarily in the *Moon sphere*, and Christ on his path of descent through the planetary spheres in his etheric body did not enter this sphere until the nineteenth century, whereas during the sixteenth, seventeenth, and eighteenth centuries, Christ was descending through the spheres of Sun, Venus, and Mercury.[15]

A deeper understanding of the second crucifixion is made possible by cognizing, in the light of Astrosophy, the descending path of Christ though the spheres of the planets—that is, through the ranks of the spiritual hierarchies, passing through the sphere of the angels, the Moon sphere, during the nineteenth century as the last stage of descent prior to entering the Earth's etheric aura in 1899, denoting the onset of the New Age. Thus, Astrosophy sheds light on Cosmic Christianity.

By grasping the connection here of Christ's descent through the Moon sphere with the rise in materialism during the nineteenth century, we gain new insight into the second crucifixion in the etheric world. Here it is a matter of showing that the seeming contradiction with Steiner's statement concerning "the second crucifixion of Christ"—a crucifixion in the etheric world in the nineteenth century—only seems apparent.

The real purpose of this work is to penetrate more deeply into the significance of Steiner's words by exploring the "greatest mystery of our time," the mystery of Christ's return in the etheric, the Christ Mystery in the twentieth and twenty-first centuries. It is my hope that the reader will sense the activity of conscience—the working together of head and heart—as the underlying orientation of the research into the Christ Mystery presented here.

_____
15 Ibid.

Let's summarize the foregoing from a different perspective. At the moment of death, the human being, dwelling in the etheric body, beholds a panorama of images of the experiences undergone during the course of life between birth and death, for these images are inscribed in the etheric body. Many people who have "died" (or been at the brink of death) and returned to life describe that experience of seeing a panoramic vision of their life's experiences.

For our considerations, the important point is that the etheric body belongs to the temporal realm, whereas the physical body belongs to the spatial realm and exists in three-dimensional space, and it is a time body in which the human biography is recorded. At the moment of death, the entire biography—from the moment of birth to the moment of death—is vividly experienced. The moment of death is actually a *birth*—a birth into a higher realm. And the moment of the resurrection on Easter Sunday morning was also a moment of birth—the birth of the Risen One. The biography of the Risen One extends from the birth in Bethlehem to the moment of resurrection. The etheric body of Christ contained all the experiences from the moment of birth in Bethlehem to the resurrection, comprising a time span of 33⅓ years. At the death of a human being, the etheric body generally dissolves back into the cosmos, but in the case of Christ his etheric body did not dissolve but was preserved. Moreover, it has been—and continues to be—active, unfolding its activity rhythmically every 33⅓ years. Since the Mystery of Golgotha, therefore, the 33⅓-year rhythm has played a role in the cosmic order, just as the planets have always done. It is a new cosmic rhythm in addition to those of the planets, such as Jupiter's twelve-year rhythm and the 29½-year rhythm of Saturn. However, in contrast to the planetary rhythms—specified in terms of cosmic space by their passage against the background of the zodiacal constellations, so that a planet's rhythm is determined by the time period that elapses between its conjunction with a given fixed star until its return to conjunction with the same fixed star—the 33⅓-year rhythm is a purely temporal rhythm, specified by the duration of the life of Jesus Christ.

Since the commencement of the New Age on September 10, 1899, the 33⅓-year rhythm has begun to play a much more significant role than it did previously. This has to do with the second coming of Christ. For, whereas the first coming was an event on the physical plane, the second coming is taking place on the etheric plane of existence, in the realm of life forces. It is especially Christ's etheric body that is active in this case.

Following the Mystery of Golgotha in the year 33, the etheric body of Christ expanded slowly out into cosmic realms, attaining its greatest expansion in 966, which denoted a point of transition. It began a slow path of return of Christ's etheric body back toward Earth. With the end of the fifty-sixth 33⅓-year cycle on September 10, 1899, denoting the close of *Kali Yuga*, there began the reentry of Christ's etheric body into the Earth's etheric aura, which attained a certain level of completion 33⅓ years later, on January 8, 1933. Here, the New Age (Satya Yuga, or "Age of Light") was born, whereby 1899 can be likened to the *dawn* and 1933 to the *sunrise* of the New Age. It was precisely during this period that Rudolf Steiner's teaching activity unfolded from 1900 to 1925. He described Anthroposophy (spiritual science)

as preparing the way for the second coming, the approaching advent of which he dated to 1933. In lectures from around 1910 and in the following years, he proclaimed the advent of Christ's second coming as the greatest event of the twentieth century. Steiner acted as a kind of John the Baptist, proclaiming the approaching second coming, just as John the Baptist had prepared the way for the first coming nineteen centuries earlier.

At the first coming, the life of Jesus Christ lasted 33⅓ years, of which the last 3½ years were most important—the ministry, from the baptism to the Mystery of Golgotha. In contrast, the second coming is an event relating primarily to the etheric world and, in accordance with the 33⅓-year rhythm, will last for 2,500 years—or seventy-five 33⅓-year cycles—from September 10, 1899, to May 22, 4399. During these 2,500 years, the most important rhythm is the 33⅓-year cycle of Christ's etheric body, and a comprehension of this rhythm offers the possibility of attuning to this etheric body. It is the renewed presence of this etheric body in the Earth's etheric aura that has given birth to the New Age, thus opening up the possibility of a new communion with Christ.

"When the Christ impulse entered the evolution of humanity as we know it, one result was that the chaotic forces of the sibyls were thrust back for a time, as when a stream disappears below ground and reappears later on. These forces were indeed to reappear in another form—a form purified by the Christ impulse.... Yes, a time is coming when the old astrology will live again in a new form, a Christ-filled form, and then if one can practice it properly so that it becomes permeated with the Christ impulse, one may venture to look up to the stars and question them about their spiritual script."

—RUDOLF STEINER (*Christ and the Spiritual World and the Search for the Holy Grail*, pp. 94, 122)

CLASSICS IN ASTROSOPHY: ASTRONOMIA NOVA

Robert Powell, PhD & Willi Sucher

EDITORIAL FOREWORD TO MERCURY STAR JOURNAL, EASTER 1977

Robert A. Powell, PhD

It is now just over 400 years since the birth of Johannes Kepler, that outstanding spirit who contributed so much to the development of modern civilization. Willi Sucher commemorated the 400th anniversary of Kepler's birth (1571) with his study of the life and destiny of the great astronomer published in 1972.[1] Likewise, this issue of the *Mercury Star Journal* is dedicated to Johannes Kepler as a tribute to his contribution to human evolution, and also to his colleague, Tycho Brahe, the "Phoenix of astronomers."[2] In acknowledgement of his debt to Tycho Brahe, we can imagine Kepler giving utterance to Newton's famous words: "If I have seen further it is by standing on ye shoulders of Giants."[3]

Kepler and Brahe typify the fifth cultural epoch or period of civilization, the age of the Consciousness Soul, which they helped to inaugurate. On the one hand, in Tycho Brahe there is exemplified the concern of modern man with exact observation, and on the other hand the penetrating depth of insight shown by Johannes Kepler is indicative of the immense deepening of consciousness that took place in the transition from the fourth to the fifth period of civilization. Of this transition a leading science historian has written, "The Copernican Revolution was a revolution in ideas, a transformation in man's conception of the universe and of his own relation to it. Again and again, this episode in the history of Renaissance thought has been proclaimed an epochal turning point in the intellectual development of Western humanity."[4]

The "Astronomia Nova," which became introduced into the stream of civilization through the concerted efforts of Copernicus, Brahe, Kepler, Galileo and Newton, was an integral part of the birth of the new civilization, the fifth since the destruction of Atlantis. But now, in the twentieth century, there is a no less profound revolution taking place—one that belongs to the "Sun stream" of evolution—i.e., the evolution in which, through successive stages, the Christ Impulse penetrates the course of history. With the twentieth century humankind entered the fifth Age (or, to use the Hindu terminology, *Yuga*) of the Christ Impulse since the Golden Age or Krita Yuga, when Christ worked directly upon humankind from the Sun. The new Christ proclamation is taking place, and it is essentially a revelation of the cosmic nature of Christ.

An integral part of the birth of the fifth Age (of the Sun stream) is a new astronomy, one that can serve the proclamation of the cosmic Christ. "The new perspective needed, above all by astronomy, is one requiring the re-inclusion of *man* in the scheme of things when cosmic movements are being studied."[5] Johannes Kepler already had such a reformation in mind when he conceived of an astrology that would be a science, far removed from the prophecies of soothsayers.

[Kepler's] interest in astrology was that of a theoretician and he wanted to reform it in the same way as astronomy. He thus writes to Maestlin on March 15, 1598: "I am a Lutheran astrologer, throwing out the chaff and keeping the grain." His reform is at once simple and surprising. He wants to make astrology a natural science like the rest, or rather a practical or applied branch of the sciences of Nature.[6]

1 Sucher, *Textbook Letters*, pp. 1–65.
2 Kepler, *Tabula Rudolphinae*, title page.
3 Isaac Newton in a letter to Robert Hooke, dated Feb. 5, 1675/6.
4 Kuhn, *The Copernican Revolution*, p. 1.
5 Steiner, *Mystery of the Universe*, p. 98.
6 G. Simon, "Kepler's Astrology: The Direction of a Reform," *Vistas in Astronomy* 18 (1975), p. 440.

ASTRONOMIA NOVA I:
JULIAN THE APOSTATE AND
THE BIRTH OF COSMIC CHRISTIANITY[7]

Robert A. Powell, PhD

"...inward perception must lead to a new astronomy, to an astronomy inwardly perceived." —RUDOLF STEINER, Jan. 1, 1921

Initiation as a factor in human evolution is scarcely conceived of in modern western culture. Yet as recently as AD 362 a remarkable individual, Emperor Julian—the heretic or Apostate—endeavoured to re-found the Roman Empire on the basis of the initiation principle. He became Emperor late in 361, at the age of twenty-nine, and began forthwith to reestablish Hellenism, the Greek religion. Julian the Apostate exercised in person the function of the Pagan priesthood, dedicating a temple to the Sun within his palace at Constantinople, where, it is said, he made sacrifices to the Sun, Moon and stars. Julian himself had been initiated by a Pagan priest, Maximus of Ephesus, when he was about twenty years old, and later, in 355, he had sought out the high priest of the Eleusinian Mysteries at Athens. Not quite seven years later, early in 362, the impact of Julian's far-reaching plans for reintroducing Hellenism into the Roman culture began to be felt. The priesthood was to lead his reformation; they were to direct the people toward the wisdom of the Gods. In a letter to one of his pontiffs he wrote:

None are to be raised to the priesthood but those of the most worth in each city. In the choice no regard shall be had to birth or riches. The essential qualities only shall be sought for, which are the love of God and of humankind. We shall know that he whom we design to choose loves the Gods, if he imprints the same love on all who surround him. He loves humankind if he endeavors to do good to all; if he gives cheerfully even out of his indigence. A priest ought to serve the Gods as one continually in the presence and under the eyes of them, who penetrate the inmost heart.... The one study that is suitable is philosophy...that philosophy that lays it down as a principle that there are Gods; that they take care of human affairs; that they are neither malevolent, nor jealous, nor subject to those passions that the poets, to their own dishonor, have attributed to them.[8]

Julian was overtaken by fate, however. At his birth his mother, Basilina, had dreamt the dream of Achilles. Her prophetic dream became fulfilled in Julian's thirty-third year, when, after an indecisive battle with the Persians at Malanga, near the banks of the Tigris (in modern Turkey), he was mortally wounded by a javelin. "Like Achilles, Julian was bound to succumb prematurely on the field of battle, struck by the javelin of a coward. The dream of Basilina was therefore prophetic."[9]

Julian's mission was doomed to failure; for his plan to reinstate the Greek Mysteries actually lay counter to the course of evolution envisaged by the Hierarchies themselves. Julian's Hellenism, as with Gnosticism, was the last flicker in post-Christian culture of the primeval wisdom of the Gods, the spiritual Hierarchies, which through the mediation of Initiates had flowed into pre-Christian cultural life as the guiding principle behind civilization. With the accomplishment of the Mystery of Golgotha in AD 33 a new era began, one when humanity was no longer to be directed by the Gods but rather, through the birth of divinity within, civilization was destined to become guided by humanity itself. In AD 33

---

7 This article is written in response to a request from a reader of the journal for a report on the talk "Neomenia and Easter" given at the Neomenia (Grail) Festival held at Shalesbrook on 3-4 April 1976. After the talk Richard Zienko read the Foundation Stone mantra (cf. Steiner, *The Christmas Conference*, pp. 289–297) referred to in the article. The article is an elaboration of the content of the talk with special reference to the destiny of Julian the Apostate. For the historical background and mathematical-astronomical aspect of cosmic science referred to in the article, the series "Foundations of Cosmic Science" printed in vol. 2 (1976) of the *MSJ*, should be consulted.

8 De la Blétérie, *Vie de l'empereur Julien*, pp. 166–67.
9 Bidez, *La Vie de l'empereur Julien*, p. 10 (tr. rev.).

THE TURNING POINT: STAR WISDOM, VOLUME 5

the Aeon of Man commenced, superseding the Aeons of the Gods! Since the first Easter, in the year 33, any individual has the possibility of raising himself toward "Godhead," or rather "Manhood," by connecting himself with the Impulse proceeding from the Mystery of Golgotha. At the same time, the Doors to the Mysteries became closed—although here and there (as with Maximus of Ephesus for example) the practice of initiation continued. Julian was one of the last to find his way into the old Mysteries, but the Door was closed firmly upon him and his grand design. For it was the will of the Hierarchies that no more should their guiding wisdom flow into the world, but that man should be left to find himself, for each human being to become truly human through receiving what streams from Golgotha.

This dramatic transition in world destiny is reflected in the tragic destiny of Julian the Apostate, who was unable to perceive that Christianity had to supervene Hellenism. The magnificence and glory of the old Mystery Wisdom blinded him to a certain extent to the perception of the new principle making its way, childlike, into world evolution. Thomas Taylor wrote in the introduction to his translation of Julian's "Oration to the Sun": "[Julian was induced] to worship the Grecian deities: took down the contemptible ensign [the Cross] of his predecessor [Constantius], and raised in its stead the majestic Roman eagle; and everywhere endeavored to restore a religion that is coeval with the universe."[10]

Yet, by the fourth century AD, the age of the Eagle, symbolizing ancient clairvoyance, had finished; gradually, since the beginning of the Christian Era, human civilization has been receiving a new spiritual Impulse, not from the Initiates of the ancient Mysteries, but from the

Cross—looked at not in a physical sense, but in the sense of the spiritual Event symbolized by the Cross. The renunciation of the old for the sake of the new was something to which Julian could not bring himself. It is apparent that within him there existed a schism between the heavenly wisdom of the past (represented by the Eagle), to which he had access through his initiation, and what he could perceive in the way of life of the "Galileans" (as he called the Christians), who followed the path of the Cross. In the letter to his pontiff (see above), he wrote (concerning his Pagan priesthood), "Let them be careful to instruct the people in the obligation of giving alms; for it is scandalous that the Galileans should support their own poor and ours."

He could see that the Christians lived out of the Spirit, yet he could not connect this with the knowledge he had gained of the Spirit through initiation. In him there was exemplified a split between cosmic wisdom, inspired by the spiritual Hierarchies, and the spirituality of Christianity, belonging to earthly life. Julian lived at a time when, indeed, cosmos and earth were parted asunder. An ever-widening gulf was growing between the world of the hierarchies (i.e., the cosmos) and the earthly realm into which Christ had been born through the Event of Golgotha. This tragic note of world destiny sounded on within the soul of Julian after he had passed back into spiritual realms. As an Initiate, he knew the reality of the life of the soul beyond death, a life in cosmic spheres of existence. His dying words were: "What does it mean to weep for a prince who is going to be reunited to heaven and the stars?"

The elaboration of Julian's destiny continued on into the higher cosmic realms, the planetary spheres beyond the earth, and a decisive step was taken by this individuality when he decided to unite himself with the stream of Christianity, whose unfolding life he could perceive taking its course on the earth below. After the passage of nearly four-and-a-half centuries, he returned again to earthly life. Although the historical dates are not available, it is probable, based on cosmic-scientific research, that this individuality

10 *Two Orations of the Emperor Julian*, trans. T. Taylor (London, 1793) p. viii. In all fairness to Julian, it was against the form of Christianity it had become under Constantine (the State Religion of the Roman Empire) that he fought. "Julian the Apostate—who was no Christian, but for all that a deeply religious man—could not accept what Christianity had become under Constantine" (Steiner, *The Festivals and Their Meaning*, Mar. 27, 1921; tr. rev.).

reincarnated in France on or about New Year's Day in the year 804.

[Editor's Note: Robert Powell achieved karmic clairvoyance at the start of the year 1977, at the age of thirty. In the following decade, he began to elaborate what he came to call "rules of karma and reincarnation." He noticed that there seems to be certain resonances for an individuality between the death horoscope of an earlier incarnation, and the birth horoscope of a subsequent incarnation. Based on the limited research he was able to do, he noticed a resonance involving Saturn and Sun (the "first rule") and heliocentric Mercury and Venus (the "second rule"). It would seem, in this portion of the article, that Powell is referring to what he later came to call "rules of karma and reincarnation." He seems to employ them to make an educated guess at the birth date of Herzeloyde (the reincarnated Julian the Apostate), whose historical birth date is unknown.

However, the date he arrives at is incorrect for two reasons. First, he estimates the time period when Herzeloyde would be born based on the research of Werner Greub. Powell came to realize that Werner Greub is correct in terms of the geography of the Grail story, but not the time period. For example, Greub made the assumption that the Great Conjunction in Cancer on May 12, 848, marked the healing of Anfortas. However, if we take it for granted that Kyot, Parzival's uncle (who is still living at the time of the events of the story of Parzival) was the historical figure of St. Guilhem de Toulouse, this date does not work, as St. Guilhem died between 812 and 814. (See my article "First Steps toward a Grail Timeline," in Cosmology Reborn: Star Wisdom, *vol. 1). Therefore, Powell's guess that Herzeloyde was born in 804 is impossible; in fact, this is probably closer to the time she died of a broken heart at Parzival's departure.*

The second reason has to do with the "rules" of karma and reincarnation themselves. Over the course of the past six years, I have been working on a careful analysis of 194 reincarnation examples to see if there are consistent resonances from the death horoscope of one incarnation to the birth horoscope of a subsequent incarnation. It would seem that Robert's first "rule" applies about forty-six percent of the time, while the second "rule" applies about sixty percent of the time. It seems that these "rules" do not necessarily stand on the strongest empirical basis and, therefore, the attempt to ascertain potential birth or death dates based off of them is imprudent.

This, of course, is not to say that there is no connection between the starry heavens and the reincarnating human being, but it may be that a scientific approach to discerning and describing this connection would, on the one hand, be more phenomenological and less empirical and, on the other hand, more individual and less universal—i.e., one might be able to ascertain "rules" or resonances from individual life to individual life that are expressive of a specific individuality, but not discern more-or-less universally applicable "rules" in the fashion of the above.—JMP]

The karma research of Rudolf Steiner indicates that Julian was reborn as the historical personality upon whom the figure of Herzeloyde in Wolfram von Eschenbach's *Parzival* is based.[11] In Book 11 of *Parzival* Wolfram writes:

She was like the sunlight and made for love. Wealth and virtue that woman had, and of joys more than too much, for she had surpassed the limits of desire. Her heart was turned to the knowledge of the good, and hence she won the favor of the world. The life of Lady Herzeloyde the Queen won praise, and her virtue was declared most admirable. Queen over three countries was she: over Waleis and Anjou, and she wore the crown of Norgals in her capital of Kingrivals. Her husband was so dear to her: she could countenance it without envy.[12]

In this life during the ninth century [*Editor's Note—again, as Rudolf Steiner indicated to W. J. Stein, the time of the Parzival story is that of Charlemagne, from the turn of the eighth to ninth centuries—JMP*], incarnated in one of the royal families living in a region in the neighborhood of present-day Strasbourg and Colmar (according to

---

11 Steiner, *Karmic Relationships*, vol 4, pp. 80–98.
12 Wolfram von Eschenbach, *Parzival*, p. 58.

Werner Greub's research),[13] the individuality of the former Emperor and Initiate of the Greek Mysteries united with the stream of esoteric Christianity, Grail Christianity. Indeed, Queen Herzeloyde played a prominent role in the destiny of the Grail Events; for it was she who was the mother of Parzival, spiritual leader of the Grail movement. The husband she loved so dearly, Gahmuret, died in battle shortly after Parzival was conceived. Later she herself died of a broken heart after Parzival, while still a young lad, left her, seeking to become a knight at the court of King Arthur. As no historical dates are known for Herzeloyde, there is a degree of uncertainty about the date of her death, but on the basis of cosmic-scientific research it can be traced, in all probability, to the year 839, around December 4.[14] Although the soul of Herzeloyde passed into the spiritual world full of grief,[15] she was able to look down up on the earth and witness the deeds of her beloved son, "a very high messenger of Christ,"[16] in his [eighth- to] ninth-century incarnation as the spiritual leader of the stream of esoteric Christianity.

Having made a living connection with spiritual Christianity in an incarnation withdrawn from the attention of the world, the individuality of Julian-Herzeloyde prepared in higher realms over many centuries for an incarnation during which he would work once more as a prominent figure in world history. Some seven hundred years elapsed from the death of Herzeloyde to the subsequent birth of this individual as the Danish astronomer Tycho Brahe. He was born "on December 14, 1546, at the family seat of Knudstrup, in Scania or Skate, the most southern province of the Scandinavian peninsula,"[17] into the family of a Danish man of noble class, Otto Brahe, who was governor at Helsingborg Castle. His father intended that he should become a lawyer, but already at the age of thirteen or fourteen Tycho's former initiation into the cosmic mysteries began to assert itself; he started to take an interest in the stars and, investing in a copy of the works of Ptolemy, occupied himself with the study of mathematics and astronomy.

His first recorded observation was made on August 17, 1563, and on August 24 in the morning, he noted that Saturn and Jupiter were so close together that the interval between them was scarcely visible. The Alphonsine tables turned out to be a whole month in error.[18]

This experience in 1563, when he discovered the gross inaccuracy of contemporary astronomical tables, led Tycho to conceive of his plan for the restoration of astronomy on the basis of a program of exact observations. *Astronomia Nova* was the name he gave to his proposed reformation. On the title page of his *Tabulae Rudolphinae* the famous astronomer and colleague of Tycho, Johannes Kepler, wrote: "[The] restoration of astronomy [was] by that Phoenix of astronomers, Tycho, first conceived and determined on in the year 1564."

Through the cooperation of Kepler and Tycho Brahe, the Astronomia Nova became realized. By using the systematic collection of observations recorded by Tycho between 1576 and 1597 at his observatory, the Uraniborg, on the island of Hveen, Kepler arrived, early in the seventeenth century, at his epochal discoveries concerning the laws of heliocentric planetary motion. The destiny that led to the achievement of the Astronomia Nova appears to have been initiated by Tycho's observation "on the evening of November 11, 1572…when he happened to throw his eyes up to the sky, and was startled by perceiving an exceedingly bright star in the constellation of Cassiopeia, near the zenith, and in a place where he was well aware had not been occupied by any star."[19]

He wrote an account of his observation, *De Nova Stella*, which was published in Copenhagen the following year. It was this book that called the attention of the Danish king, Frederick II, to

---

13 Greub, *Wolfram von Eschenbach und die Wirklichkeit des Grals,* pp. 396–399.

14 Ed. Note—Again, this is a dubious claim, as Kyot died after Herzeloyde, between 812 and 814 —JMP

15 *Herzeloyde* = "heart's grief" (literal translation)

16 Steiner and Schuré, *The East in the Light of the West/Children of Lucifer,* p. 215.

17 Dreyer, *Tycho Brahe,* p. 11.

---

18 Ibid., p. 19.

19 Ibid., p. 38

Tycho. In 1576 he summoned the astronomer to his court and offered him the island of Hveen, together with money to build an observatory there. Just prior to this offer, Tycho, who had attended Basle University in 1568, and revisited the town in 1575, was considering the idea of immigrating to Switzerland and settling down there. The attraction to this part of Switzerland evidently arose from his previous incarnation (according to Werner Greub, Herzeloyde, after the death of her husband, withdrew with her son, Parzival, to live in a small place near Arlesheim, just south of Basle, where she brought him up).[20] Thus, Tycho's meeting with King Frederick II came at a decisive moment, in his thirtieth year.

Indeed, it is so that in the life of every human being, during his thirtieth year, the remembrance of his former incarnation arises from subconscious depth, and may even threaten to divert him from the true course of his destiny intended in the present incarnation. At this stage of life, a very real choice may be presented to the human soul, a choice between the old and the new. The helping hand of King Frederick II, first extended during Tycho's thirtieth year, enabled him to fulfil his destiny as an astronomer, a destiny that proved to be of world-historic significance.

The cosmic background to the individual's destiny in his thirtieth year is the return of Saturn to the same part of the Zodiac as at the time of birth, since Saturn returns to conjunction with the same fixed star after roughly 29½ years. Moreover, on the basis of the researches of cosmic science it has been found that the planetary zodiacal positions at the moment of birth correspond to a high degree with the locations of the planets in the (sidereal) zodiac at the time of the previous death. Human destiny is literally "carried over" by the stars from one incarnation to the next.[21]

[Editor's Note—I have looked carefully at 194 different comparisons, and from one perspective one could say this is true. For example, in the case of the individuality of John the Baptist, there seems to be a fairly consistent correspondence between the position of Uranus at the death in one incarnation with Uranus's position at birth in the subsequent incarnation (see Elijah, Come Again by Robert Powell). However, this "rule" or pattern cannot be made universal—i.e., it cannot be carried over to another individuality. Therefore, it would be very difficult to determine an unknown birth or death date based off of a horoscope from another incarnation.—JMP]

Just as human beings at the end of a day's work go to sleep and resume their activity when they awake the following day, likewise our unfolding destiny on earth ceases at the moment of death and resumes at the moment of the subsequent birth. Through the rhythm of falling asleep and waking, the human ego evolves from day to day during earthly life, whereas in the rhythm of birth and death, the cosmic self, or individuality, progresses. The daily (apparent) cycle of the sun around the earth betokens the activity of the human ego, which is thus related to the sun, whereas the slow motion of Saturn around the Zodiac stands more in connection with the whole life cycle undergone by the cosmic self, since in a lifetime there are only two, or at most three, cycles of Saturn. The return of Saturn in the thirtieth year of life is an event that awakes human beings to their cosmic "I," one's individuality, and calls forth the memory of the previous earthly life (or lives).

In the case of Tycho, particularly in respect of his karmic meeting with King Frederick II, much can be learned that offers significant insight into the way destiny unfolds. The memory of previous life lives in subconscious depths of the human soul; it lives *within* the human being. In contrast, the destiny belonging to the present incarnation approaches the individual from *without*. At all times there is a subtle interplay between these two streams—the impulses arising from within, belonging to the past, and what comes to meet human beings from the outside world, which leads them into the future. Our true destiny (in contrast to a possible deflection from its rightful course) arises through the harmonizing of

---

20 Op. cit., Greub, pp. 322–24.

21 It is on this basis, knowing the exact dates of Julian's death (June 26, 363) and Tycho's birth, that the dates of Herzeloyde's life have been determined.

inner and outer impulses. If an inner impulse is true, there will invariably be a sign from the outside world, although the outer sign may not come until some time has elapsed after the arising of the inner impulse. In Tycho's case, the inner impulse to emigrate to Switzerland was not in harmony with his true destiny. The outer sign he received from Frederick II was what Tycho was really seeking. Frederick approached Tycho from without, as a benefactor, leading him to his true destiny. In this instance, the way karma unfolds can be seen clearly. The purpose of looking into the destiny of Julian the Apostate in this intimate way is, on the one hand, to elucidate the course of world destiny, and on the other hand to gain insight into the working out of individual destiny.

Insight into the working of human and world destiny can give modern human beings, even amid the calamitous events of the present time, the support needed in life. Such insight is a veritable staff of Mercury! The "Astronomia Nova" of the twentieth century—inaugurated by Steiner and fellow researchers of the Mathematical-Astronomical section of the School for Spiritual Science—seeks "to approach the wisdom of the stars rightly and righteously."[22] Steiner spoke of the great difficulties to be surmounted in penetrating the facts of karma, which may be approached through the wisdom of the stars; but he said that it *can* be done:

> We see here how great the difficulties are when one wishes to approach the wisdom of the stars rightly and righteously. Indeed, the true approach to the wisdom of the stars, which we need to penetrate the facts of karma, is only possible in the light of a true insight into Michael's dominion. It is only possible at Michael's side...through the whole reality of modern times there has come forth a certain stream of spiritual life that makes it very difficult to approach with an open mind the science of the stars, and the science, too, of karma. But difficult as it is, it can be done. Despite the attacks that are possible...we can nevertheless go forward with assurance, and approach the wisdom of the stars and the real shaping of karma."[23]

An Astronomia Nova in which the connection between cosmos and earth, and between cosmos and human, in the exploration of world destiny and the formation of human destiny was made possible through the foundation of the Michael School on earth, which took place during the Holy Nights, Christmas 1923/24. On Christmas Day 1923, the spiritual Foundation Stone was laid.[24] All those who connect themselves with the Foundation Stone may begin to find the Astronomia Nova of the twentieth century (which is an inward comprehension of the human relationship to the cosmos, the world of the hierarchies), and at the same time begin to develop a new faculty, that of karmic clairvoyance, the ability to perceive the working of destiny.[25]

The Foundation Stone—whose mantric verse expresses the cosmic secrets of humanity's relationship with the Trinity and the spiritual hierarchies—came in 1923, shortly after the start of the Age of Michael (in 1879), as an answer to the tragedy of world destiny, experienced with such deep intensity by Julian the Apostate, of the closing of the Doors to the world of the hierarchies at the beginning of the Christian era. In 1923, just over one-and-a-half millennia after Julian's death, the Doors were reopened. A modern mystery school, the School for Spiritual Science, was founded on earth. With the founding of this mystery school, the principle of initiation has been reintroduced as a factor in human evolution. Although only at a beginning, the Michael initiation will work ever more strongly as a world-transforming power—not in the same way as the initiations in the ancient Mysteries, which were based on the principle of selection, but in a free way, in a Christian way.

In the language of Imagination, the symbol of ancient initiation is the Eagle, while the sign of the Christian initiation is the Dove. Julian sought to take down the Cross and reinstate the Eagle as the banner under which civilization should proceed.

---

22 Steiner, *Karmic Relationships*, vol. 4, p. 111.
23 Ibid.

24 Steiner, *The Life, Nature and Cultivation of Anthroposophy.*
25 This does not preclude that there are those who through their destiny have already begun to develop an inner relationship to the cosmos and the seeds (or the flowering) of the new clairvoyance.

conception
(Easter Full Moon)

birth
(Christmas New Moon)

33

1923

But this could not be. The era of the Cross had to take its course so that every individual could undergo at least one incarnation in which to live a life on earth as a free and unique human personality. In 1923 the spiritual foundation for the era of the Dove was laid. Under the sign of the Dove, the principle of Christian initiation is now entering modern culture. Through the Foundation Stone, the central impulse of Christianity, the Mystery of Golgotha is taken up and brought into connection with the cosmic world of the hierarchies. Thereby, the parting asunder of heaven and earth is healed. The Foundation Stone is a bridge, built through sacrifice, reuniting the cosmic realm of the hierarchies and the earthly realm, where the Christ Impulse is unfolding.

The event of the Laying of the Foundation Stone on Christmas Day 1923 stands in direct cosmic-spiritual relation to the Mystery of Golgotha. Indeed, to the spiritual gaze looking back in time, a great Imagination appears before the inner eye; it is the relationship between the new moon and the full moon. How is this to be understood?

In the course of a lunar month, the "birth" of the month occurs when the thin crescent of the new moon first appears on the western horizon at sunset. Thereafter, the month grows to maturity, signified visibly by the waxing of the moon over a period of fourteen days; after the attainment of maturity at full moon, the moon wanes and "dies" fourteen days later, disappearing on the eastern horizon into the rays of the rising sun at dawn. Gazing back in time, the Christmas Foundation Meeting, signifying the birth of Cosmic Christianity, appears to stand in the same relation to the Mystery of Golgotha as

the new moon to the full moon. Every year, during the lunar month of Aries, the Easter Festival is celebrated as the remembrance of the Mystery of Golgotha on the Sunday following the full moon.[26] The ancient festival known to the Greeks as the *neomenia*—which celebrates the birth of the lunar month of Aries and with it the start of the lunar year—gains significance in the era of the Dove as a Grail Festival. For the new moon falling nearest the vernal equinox, the *neomenia,* "new moon of the year," is the herald of the Easter full moon (see image above). Just as the inner eye, gazing back across history, beholds first (retrospectively) the birth of Cosmic Christianity in 1923 and then the founding of Christianity on earth in 33, likewise the neomenia occurs first (in time) as the herald of Easter.

Moreover, this cosmic Imagination penetrates still further to the historical connection between the Christmas Foundation Meeting and the Mystery of Golgotha. The event of AD 33 may be regarded as the "conception" of what is coming to birth in the twentieth century as Cosmic Christianity.

Mystery of Golgotha
(founding of Christianity on Earth)

33

Christmas Foundation Meeting
(birth of Cosmic Christianity

1923

26 Unfortunately, the ecclesiastical Easter computus sometimes does not coincide with the cosmic reality of the Aries full moon. Easter Sunday should fall on the Sunday closest to the Aries full moon (but not preceding it), which is the first full moon after the commencement of the solar month of Aries at the moment of the vernal equinox.

The birth of Cosmic Christianity in the twentieth century, signified by the event of the laying of a spiritual Foundation Stone on Christmas Day 1923, is the outcome of a long embryonic development that commenced with the Mystery of Golgotha in 33. This embryonic development, from conception to birth is symbolized in the cosmos by the period from the Easter full moon to the Christmas new moon, which in the far-distant past was the usual gestation period for all human beings.[27] As Zoroaster said, "Conceptions...that take place at full moon are consummated at conjunction [of sun and moon]."[28] The earliest possible occurrence of the Easter full moon is the day of the vernal equinox, when the conjunction of sun and moon may fall actually on Christmas Day. This extreme case will happen in the year 2000. Usually, the Easter full moon takes place sometime after the vernal equinox, when the conjunction of sun and moon occurs a corresponding period of time after Christmas Day.

The significant point, however, is that the full moon is the sign of conception, and the new moon signifies birth. Thus, one interpretation of the new moon—full moon Imagination is that the full moon stands for the Easter event, the Mystery of Golgotha, and the new moon (i.e., the Grail moon) represents the Christmas event, the Laying of the Foundation Stone. Under the sign of the Cross, within the womb of time, true Christianity (i.e., Grail or Cosmic Christianity) was being prepared "behind the scenes" by individuals such as Herzeloyde and Parzival. Those (and other) individuals made preparation for the coming Age of Michael and the new Christ proclamation. Now, under the sign of the Dove, Cosmic Christianity is flowing as a mighty Impulse into human civilization.

---

27 Steiner, *Christmas*, lect. 4 (London, 1922)

28 *Passages in Greek and Latin Literature relating to Zoroaster and Zoroastrianism* (tr. W. Fox and R. Pemberton); p. 105.

EDITORIAL FOREWORD, ST. JOHN'S 1977

Robert A. Powell, PhD

The increasing interest in astrology—most evident in the West—is a phenomenon that can be understood historically through the perspective offered by spiritual science. Historically, the fifth civilization (since the destruction of Atlantis) began in the fifteenth century. We are now just over a quarter of the way through this civilization, which is identified spatially with Europe. Following the fifth civilization, there will be two further civilizations—the Slavonic and American civilizations are undergoing an evolution now in preparation for the future, when each will in turn give birth to new human capacities.

Those new capacities that have been promoted through the emergence of the fifth civilization are, on the one hand, an increasingly acute power of observation, and on the other hand an enhanced faculty of intellectual analysis. Tycho Brahe and Johannes Kepler, among those who helped to inaugurate the new civilization, typify these two capacities belonging to modern humankind. The whole development of science has relied on the application of observation and analysis. Spiritual science itself is a product of this development, but it is an extension of modern science—i.e., observations that form the basis of spiritual science are not restricted to those of the physical senses but are instead acquired through the cognition of spiritual realities beyond what is accessible to physical perception.

It is generally true that most people are not in a position to conduct scientific research for themselves. Consequently, a certain degree of faith is necessary in the acceptance of the findings of modern science. Nevertheless, the faith called for by modern science is different from religious belief.

Why is this so? Religious belief is not subject to the demands of logic. The priest is not expected to substantiate his belief in God by publishing a rigorous proof. The Scholastics in the thirteenth century—during the twilight period between the final decline of the Greco-Roman civilization (the fourth) and the emergence of the fifth civilization—already confronted this problem. Thomas Aquinas demonstrates in his *Summa Theologica* that religious belief depends on faith in revelation. Scientists, however, must be able to explain their findings logically and state their assumptions. Vast numbers of scientific journals exist solely for the purpose of publishing the results of scientific findings. Those who wish to investigate a particular scientific finding can do so, in theory, by referring to the relevant journal. Thus, the faith called for by modern science is subject to the demands of logical analysis. A scientific theory found to be logically unsound is refuted.

Astrology occupies a peculiar position in modern scientific culture. "Astrology is a faith that speaks the language of science, and a science that can find a justification for its principles only in faith."[29] This was the definition of astrology held at the end of the last century by one of the great scholars who devoted much of his life to the study of the astrological tradition. Indeed Bouche-Leclerq's definition will remain correct until astrology becomes invested with an acceptable logic. Generally, the "logic" of astrology is the same now as it was during the third civilization, identified with Egypt and Mesopotamia. "If, on the 7th of Ulul, Venus appears in the west, the harvest of the land will be successful; the heart of the land will be happy."[30] These prognostications from the "Venus tablets of Ammizaduga" (ca. 1600 BC) belongs to the reign of Ammizaduga, who became King of Babylon exactly 146 years after Hammurabi. During the Egyptian-Babylonian period, civilization was guided by priest-kings who received communications from the gods embodied in the various planets.[31] Hammurabi,

for example, was a Sun worshipper although, of course, he was devoted also to Marduk (Jupiter), the leading god of the Babylonian pantheon.

The roots of astrology lie in the third civilization, but the astrological tradition that our modern civilization has inherited is essentially a product of the Greek culture. The ideas of the Babylonians were transmitted to the Greeks during the last few centuries BC and elaborated in a great corpus of doctrines. The main center for this development was Alexandria in Hellenistic Egypt. From there, astrology was transmitted far and wide, even to India. The belief in astrological doctrines persists to the present day, yet their origin is shrouded in obscurity. Nevertheless, the same "logic" in modern astrology is recognizable in the omen literature of Babylonia. It is a logic of signs. This "logic," however, is unacceptable to modern science, which follows either a logic of concepts (e.g., in mathematics) or a logic of causes (e.g., in physics).

At the beginning of the era of modern science, Kepler recognized the dilemma of astrology. He thought, however, that astrology (or at least some astrological doctrines) could be rescued by a reformation. He raised the question: "How much science is in astrology?"

The *Mercury Star Journal* raises the same question and presents the results of an experiment to investigate the influence of the zodiac (via the Moon) on plant growth.[32] This is accompanied by a spiritual-scientific explanation, based on a logic of causes, which may help to render intelligible *why* the zodiacal location of the Moon affects plant growth. It may be that, along such lines of research and spiritual-scientific analysis, astrology can be rescued, albeit reformed, as Kepler envisaged. In view of the widespread interest in astrology, this is undoubtedly one of the great challenges facing modern humanity.

Noteworthy endeavors in the direction of a reform of astrology have been made by the French statistician Michel Gauquelin. Using massive

---

29 Bouche-Leclerq, *L'Astrologie grecque.*

30 Langdon and Fotheringham, *The Venus Tablet of Ammizaduga*, p. 11.

31 There is now an abundance of evidence from cuneiform sources that these communications actually took place. Cf., e.g., Hildegard Lewy, "The Babylonian Background of the Kay Kaus Legend," *Archiv Orientalni* 17 (1949), 28-109, esp. p. 83: "...a personal contact with a planetary deity—in Moses' case Sin (Moon-god), the divine lord of Mount Sinai—conferred upon a mortal a reflex of the divine majesty which he had been

privileged enough to approach."

32 Ed. Note—This article will be published in a future volume of Star Wisdom—JMP.

---

statistical surveys over several different professional groups of planetary positions at birth he has demonstrated that there is validity in a basic astrological doctrine.[33] Another researcher, the significance of whose work is yet to be fully recognized, is John Addey. He has introduced a concept, unique in the history of astrology, which enables certain astrological doctrines to be seen in a way that can truly be called scientific. The conception of harmonics, with which John Added has been occupied for some twenty years, offers the possibility of mathematical analysis in astrology.[34] Harmonics is an important breakthrough, providing a logic of concepts for astrology. A logic of causes is yet to be developed, but through spiritual science this will surely one day come, indeed must come, if astrology is to become scientific. For it is not sufficient to demonstrate that astrology "works" and to provide a conceptual analysis for its doctrines. The "how" and "why" of astrology must be explained, and since astrology pertains to the suprasensory nature of human beings, only a spiritual science can provide such an explanation.

At least a spiritual-scientific explanation can be offered for the present resurgence of interest in astrology. Until the Mystery of Golgotha in the year 33, during the fourth civilization, humanity was following a descending line of evolution. Since the coming of Christ, however, an ascending evolution is underway. In this ascent the fifth civilization is the reflection of the third—i.e. the Mystery of Golgotha can be regarded as a pivot, and the fifth civilization as the conscious counterpart of what was lived through instinctively in the third civilization. Since the third civilization was based on the cult of the stars, this lives subconsciously in modern humanity. The instinctive belief in the stars, however, must be penetrated with consciousness and, moreover, the life, passion, and death of Jesus Christ must be acknowledged, for it is upon this pivot that the ascending evolution depends. A step in this direction is outlined in Willi Sucher's contribution, "Astronomia Nova II." It is a great challenge that is presented to humanity—to develop a new consciousness and Christ-centered awareness of the stars. Difficult as it may seem, it can and will be achieved. Humankind will speak to the stars, as they once spoke to human beings.

ASTRONOMIA NOVA II: CHRISTIANITY AND THE HOLY GRAIL IN THE LIGHT OF STAR WISDOM[35]

Willi Sucher

"Nowadays we must search among the stars in a way that is different from that of those times (in Egypt and Mesopotamia), but the writing in stars must again become for us something that speaks to us." (Rudolf Steiner, Jan. 1, 1914)

To understand the history of the Grail movement and its special connection with Christianity, we need a sense of the interrelationship of earthly history with cosmic (spiritual) processes. We can develop this sense rightly if we bring to consciousness what actually lived in the figure of Jesus Christ. For what the Christ did, at every moment of his life, was an expression of the cosmic world, of which the stars and planets are but the outer form.[36] When the representative of the heavenly, cosmic world united himself with the earth he inaugurated what Rudolf Steiner described as the "Cosmic-Spiritual Communion of Mankind."[37] Through Christ, the cosmic, heavenly world became accessible for the first time to the *conscious* experience of all humankind. In the future,

---

33 Cf. Gauquelin, *Cosmic Influences on Human Behavior: The Planetary Factors in Personality* for a summary of his findings. His principal discovery is that the position of certain planets at birth, in relation to the earth, are correlated with profession, e.g., Saturn with scientists.

34 Cf. Addey, *Harmonics in Astrology: An Introductory Textbook to the New Understanding of an Old Science* for an account of the application of the concept of harmonics in astrology.

35 From a lecture at Shalesbrook, Forest Row, UK, June 25, 1974; transcription edited with notes by Robert Powell and Richard Zienko.

36 Cf. Steiner, *The Spiritual Guidance of the Individual and Humanity*, ch. 3.

37 Steiner, *Man and the World of Stars. The Spiritual Communion of Mankind.*

people will—indeed, must—come to experience the presence of the whole cosmos in their own earthly lives. They will realize that the zodiac finds its expression in their physical organism, that the planets live in their etheric organism. Then, conscious of these connections, people will, in a sense, be able to transform the world of stars when they take hold, morally and creatively, of what is within them as the "ingredients of the cosmos." Thus it is that a careful and deep study of the life of Christ is the means whereby human beings may awake to their own cosmic nature and being.

When one speaks of the cosmic background to the life of Jesus Christ (the whole 33 years can be taken, not just the "three years" of the ministry), it is not meant in any traditional sense. Dear friends, I am still waiting for the day when a non-Christian astrologer (a kind of Klingsor, for example!) will say: *It's no wonder that the Christ went through all those terrible experiences, finally through the crucifixion! Because these events took place when the great planets Jupiter and Saturn were in detriment, according to our old astrological traditions. Look! Saturn was in the constellation of Cancer for most of the time, and Jupiter was in Gemini in the last part of his life—all of this is very dangerous! Why, then, was this time chosen for the deed of your Christ?*

This is what I would expect a non-Christian astrologer to say. The fact is that, all through the three years of Christ's ministry, we find events that coincide with what traditional astrology would describe as disastrous aspects. Now the important thing to realize is that *precisely* this time was chosen. Why? It was so that the influence of the stars and planets could be transformed. If we can understand this, we have the basis for a living feeling, a sense for what the Christ Impulse means for the earth and humanity.

Christ was the seed of a new creation in which not only the earth and man, but also the whole cosmos will receive new life, new foundations of existence. Thus, when people freely take up the cross and follow Christ, they begin to share in this great work that the Christ inaugurated. They participate in the transformation of the whole cosmos.

This thought carries with it a wonderful, inspiring power that can enable us to confront with courage and enthusiasm the seeming chaos and destruction that threaten to engulf the humanity of today.

Now it is a fact that, in the Grail movement, we have the first tentative steps on the path that Christ inaugurated. The troubadours, the poets who wrote down the story of Parzival and the Holy Grail, cautiously mention it. Although in some cases one has the impression that they do not fully understand what they are talking about, they realized, however dimly, the fact of humanity's connection with the cosmos. For example, in Wolfram's story,[38] we find that Parzival and Feirefiz rode together to Munsalvaesche (the castle of the Grail) with great joy, when "Mars or Jupiter had once again come back all angry in their orbits to the point from which they had proceeded."[39]

Through an acquaintance with Wolfram's epic, certainty grows that the Grail movement was a first attempt to take up what the Christ had inaugurated as the "Cosmic-Spiritual Communion of Mankind." It's as if in those individuals who appear in the Grail story welled up from the depths of the subconscious the realization of the cosmic nature of human beings. The Cosmic Christ, who had been lost to human consciousness with the rise of exoteric Christianity, began to make himself known in those souls connected with the Grail movement.

As mentioned, we look forward to a future time when human beings, conscious of their true nature, actively begin to participate in the transformation of the whole cosmos. Of course, this is presupposed by our own complete moral transformation when we take Christ as our inspiration and guide—the inner foundation on which the search for the Holy Grail rests. Thus, the Grail epic portrays (albeit not yet fully consciously insofar as the troubadours were concerned) our search for our self in the spirit, our cosmic being.

Wolfram mentions the positions of Mars and Jupiter in the heavens. These two are, in a sense, opposite extremes—Mars, the aggressive one,

---

38 Von Eschenbach, *Parzival,* tr. Mustard and Passage.
39 Ibid., p. 411.

enables us to take hold of life on the earth, whereas Jupiter is more the creative, expanding element in the cosmos—referred to when Parzival and his half-brother Feirefiz are riding with great joy to Munsalvaesche. In the life of Christ, we find that Jupiter and Mars were in close proximity in Gemini at the time of the Mystery of Golgotha. And earlier, according to the Gospel accounts (excluding that of St. John), Christ went into the desert immediately after the baptism by John.[40]

After forty days he encountered the adversaries. In one Gospel, Christ is tempted by the devil. In another, he meets Satan. In fact, Christ met them both, the two tempters—the devil (Lucifer) and Satan (Ahriman)—and he stood firm before them. At that time, he would have seen the paths of Jupiter and Mars crossing in the heavens, as they stood in conjunction in Aries.[41] An astrologer of old might have said, *Traditionally, that is fatal—that this conjunction should have occurred at the very time of the temptation.* Yet, as we have said, this time was chosen deliberately to bring healing and redemption into what had hitherto been considered inimical to humanity. This is the real meaning of what we call the Mystery of Golgotha.

[Editor's Note—Willi Sucher spoke on this theme some twenty years before Robert Powell completed his work of dating the life of Christ based on the visions of Anne Catherine Emmerich in his Chronicle of the Living Christ. *Whereas Willi Sucher is correct in noting the conjunction of Mars and Jupiter in Aries on January 17, AD 31, according to Robert's research this did not occur during the temptation in the wilderness, which lasted from October 21 to November 30, 29; rather, on January 17, 31, the remains of John the Baptist (who had been executed recently by Kind Herod) were rescued by the disciples from the prison in Machaerus and properly buried in Jutta. The next day, January 18 at the Pool of Bethesda, saw the third healing miracle of Christ the healing of the*

man paralyzed for thirty-eight years (see pages 212–16 in The Visions of Anne Catherine Emmerich, *vol. 2). Surely these events can also be interpreted in the light of Willi Sucher's general theme—that Christ's life took on the negative potential of the astrological events and transformed it into a life-giving force—JMP]*

In Wolfram's epic, Christianity is brought into connection with cosmic mysteries. In several places the movements of the heavenly bodies are mentioned (e.g., when Parzival and Feirefiz rode with joy to Munsalvaesche). At the same time, the return of the planets (in this case Mars and Jupiter) caused terrible pain for Anfortas, the wounded Grail King. What does this signify?

Parzival and Feirefiz, when they first met, did not recognize each other, and so they fought. But a reunion emerged from their bitter struggle, a truly humane relationship that filled them with joy. One can say that they brought about a redemption (within themselves) of "angry" Mars or Jupiter. Now, in contrast to this, Wolfram tells us of Anfortas and how he lay sick and suffering. Earlier in his life, he had made grave mistakes that brought this about. Here we have the detrimental aspect of Jupiter and Mars, but Parzival and Feirefiz had overcome this. They realized their mistake and, because of their recognition of each other, they were now spiritually united and could ride joyfully together to Munsalvaesche.

Here, then, we have an example of the connection between the essential impulse of Christianity and the search for the Holy Grail. It emerges when we begin to approach the planetary movements in an *active and imaginative way,* as a script we are called on to learn to read. We hear also from Wolfram that when Anfortas lay sick it was Saturn who was the harbinger of his suffering. When Saturn rose high in the heavens, Anfortas' wound pained him all the more. What does Saturn do? The movements of Saturn are a visible gesture of the working of the forces of karma—indeed, that of world destiny, in which every individual takes part. In ancient times (particularly during Old Testament times when history as it is understood today began), human destiny could be very hard

---

40 Cf. Steiner, *According to Matthew,* lect. 7.

41 The traditional date for the baptism is January 6th. On January 17th, AD 31, Mars and Jupiter stood in conjunction beneath Sheratan, marking the Ram's horn, in Aries.

as nations and empires fought together to achieve security and power. Thus, Saturn was experienced as severe and harsh in its activity. The traditional astrologer would confirm this, for Saturn, Chronos, Father Time, claims everyone as his own in the end! He is as old and as pitiless as the barren rocks of the mountains or the wastes of the desert. When Saturn rises highest in the heavens, the old lore says, then it works with special strength and harshness upon the people of earth. Thus, in Wolfram's *Parzival,* we find the sufferings of Anfortas connected with this position of Saturn.

As we have seen, the troubadours of the Gail were probably not fully conscious of the cosmic background to which they pointed. They were simple; Wolfram could barely read or write. The Grail story came through direct inspiration. But the very fact that Anfortas—the old king who in the past had made mistakes that denied him the true experience of the Grail—is so directly contrasted with Parzival—the young man who bears the future within him—indicates how the striving for Cosmic-Spiritual Communion was actually taking place. Anfortas, the representative of humanity, suffers at the hands of Saturn, whereas Parzival and Feirefiz are able to take up what Christ inaugurated and overcome the detrimental aspect of Jupiter and Mars. Christ employed the cosmic forces like a craftsman and put them to good healthy use. So it was that Parzival was eventually able to relieve Anfortas of his suffering. We see, therefore, how there is living in the Grail movement one of the deepest impulses that the Christ has given to the earth. One might add that the search for the Holy Grail has never been more earnestly needed than at the present time.

We may approach the cosmic background to the Grail story from another direction. We see from the story of its origin that the presence of the Grail was recognized even in pre-Christian times. One legend says that the Grail was made from a jewel that had fallen from the crown of Lucifer. It is the visible stars in the heavens that form the crown of Lucifer. From that sphere a jewel had fallen, and it was taken, and from it the vessel was made that was used at the Last Supper. Thus, precisely what had fallen under the sway of Lucifer—which, in a sense, had become decadent—became the Grail that was to bear the Holy Host that fed the whole knighthood of the Grail. Once again, we see how what was "fallen" was taken and transformed by the healing power and life of the Christ.

In its widest and most literal sense, the Holy Grail is the body of Jesus, the man of earth. It was raised, transformed, and resurrected by the power of Christ. The physical material human body has indeed "fallen" to the earth. Through Lucifer the "fall" had gone too deep into the realm of matter, and so the human physical body, the jewel of the starry world whose archetypal form can be found in the constellations of the zodiac, became subject to the earthly forces of decadence and decay, leading finally to death. This human body was chosen by the Christ as his throne during the "three years." Thus, in the image of the Holy Grail, we see the emerging victory of spiritual life over the earthly realm of decay and death. This is what the Christ inaugurated as the Cosmic-Spiritual Communion of Mankind. What had fallen to Earth from the cosmos was transformed into the seed of a whole new creation of the future.

RUDOLF STEINER AND THE CHRISTMAS CONFERENCE
ASTROLOGICAL ASPECTS OF THE LAYING OF THE FOUNDATION, PART III

Krisztina Cseri

This year we commemorate the hundred-year anniversary of the Christmas Conference held from December 25, 1923 until January 1, 1924 by Rudolf Steiner in Dornach.

In the previous two years, two articles were issued from me in *Star Wisdom* (part 1 in vol. 3, *As Above, So Below*, 2021, and part 2 in vol. 4, *Cosmic Communion*, 2022). In these studies, I approached the Laying of the Foundation Stone from two perspectives: in part 1 from a *macrocosmic* point of view, observing the actual cosmic background of the event, and in part 2 from a *microcosmic* perspective, observing the "preparation" of Steiner for this deed.

From the macrocosmic point of view, I emphasized the movement of Pluto around the perihelion of the Earth, which was (and is) also in conjunction with the meridian of Sirius. I regarded the Pluto-Sun-Earth-Sirius relationship as a quite unique and rare event. I also stated that Steiner's death was strongly related to Pluto's last return to its positions at the Christmas Conference, and, in this respect, I drew closer from the macrocosmic to the microcosmic point of view. This whole approach meant a "thinking in actual time"— i.e., I focused to the actual cosmic background of the 1923–1925 period and the actual transits that influenced Rudolf Steiner.

From the microcosmic point of view, I concentrated on the individuality of Rudolf Steiner through the correspondence of his embryonic life and actual life. I called the attention to important etheric imprints in his etheric body that might indicate points of sensitivity in his personal preparation for the Laying of the Foundation Stone. In this approach I remained with a special etheric "time stream" that is working in the individuality on the basis of the projection of embryonic occurrences into actual life.

In this third part, I will remain in the microcosmic point of view with another special etheric "time stream" that is also working in the individuality on the basis of projection, from the newborn rather than the embryonic period. Both individual etheric "time streams" work in a constant interrelation with actual time (actual transits), and altogether they make actual life a "subjective duration" for us within the space-time we sense as "objective." This third perspective of the individual life is, however, closer to the perceiving of the "word of the time," and, opening the arms toward community, of the "word of the communal need." In the very complex web of karmic relations between individual lives and between people, with the help of this etheric stream the soul is especially working on the cornerstones of his individual and communal *future*. Through this aspect of life, we may get back to the macrocosmic perspective, as we will see in Rudolf Steiner's case.

I would like to note here that my friend Natalia Haarahiltunen and I are in a common work regarding "embryonic astrology" and many related issues.[1] This study was born within the etheric milieu in which we transmitted impulses to each other. In this sense, I write this study with her and invite the reader to join us and meditate further together with us regarding Rudolf Steiner and the Laying of the Foundation Stone and the eternal questions of space and time in relation to the cosmic ether and the inner processes in its "earthly individualization," the etheric body.

---

1 See "Conversations about Time and Space" by Natalia Haarahiltunen in the present volume.

Space and Time

To begin with, I make an attempt to summarize my thoughts regarding certain aspects of space and time. I do this because both the hundred-year anniversary of the Christmas Conference and the referred special etheric "time streams" working in the individual (in this case Rudolf Steiner) refer to "algorithms of time" (or "time algorithms"). Said "algorithms of time" may bring us impulses from times, or more precisely space-times, which we usually sense as "past" or "future" with our sense perception.

When we speak about "time" we usually think about "the time as we sense it." We sometimes call it "causal time" or "linear time" as it ensures a separation and an order between cause and effect for sense-based observation, which is a necessity at the present stage of the evolution of humanity, who lives in the world of causality. We also know, from Rudolf Steiner, that—after time came into being in the Old Saturn stage of solar system evolution—"this time" was evolved around the middle of the Atlantean epoch—i.e., after the separation of the Sun in the Hyperborean epoch and the Moon in the Lemurian epoch, and is in relation with the balance in the system and orbits of the Earth between Sun and Moon. So, through its determination by the relationship of celestial bodies, "time as we sense it" is strongly bounded to space (to "space as we sense it"), and to Sun and Moon in particular.

When we speak about "time" in the sense of its direction, we usually think of a "time stream" that is flowing from the "past" toward the "future," i.e., we interpret time in relation to our causal life in the world of our sense perception. However, when we read that "time flows backward" in various occult literature, I think the usage of the *same* word—i.e., "time," may be misleading and does not help understanding.

Insofar as I can understand thus far, if we want to penetrate further into the essence of this concept, *time* means an ordering principle for us. In this sense, it entails *space-relatedness* and *algorithms.* Beyond the order that evolves in relation to the connection of the Earth with the Sun and Moon, another order is also connecting to our space-time in the etheric world. From the world beyond our usual sense perception, certain *beings* organize through certain algorithms (known or unknown for us) the fitting of "etheric substances" (or "Akashic units") to space-time units and induce their actualization. From the earthly, physical perspective we have "space-time units" (which may also be characterized by cosmic constellations), and it is in the sense of "fitting of the etheric substances to space-time units" that time is "space-related." In the etheric world we meet "etheric substances" (or "Akashic units"). Regarding their content, these "units" may also mean units that have not reached their final content (their full quality) by crystallizing out in forms on the physical plane, in a certain space-time. We may imagine them as "etheric seeds," a part of which has already been born regarding the general evolution of humanity, another part continuously coming into being and under development in an interaction with evolution in the physical world.

Returning to "the flowing backward of time": in my view, it is the inherent feature of time, i.e., the "algorithm of time," which can "point backward" (or "forward") regarding time. So, when we step out of the world of causal time, time has "another scope," and can lead us both back and forth in relation to space-time units—unlike in the world of "causal time" where time flows from past toward future. It is not that time itself "runs backward" but rather that the "algorithm of time" makes an "etheric stream" and helps to confront us with the etheric essences of space-time units of the past and future. These special "algorithmic" recollections of space-time units (often appearing in "rhythms" for us) are "embracing" our well-known causal time flow—if we allow the use of an image. And these etheric mechanisms can be imagined as curves that connect "points of recollection." Thus, time, in the usual sense of the word, cannot flow backward. Only our individual or communal evolution receives impulses and adjustments from different space-times of evolution, and evolution curves back or reverses back this way to points in causal time, or more precisely to qualities, to etheric substances that evolve out at points in causal time.

There are macrocosmic or communal algorithms and microcosmic or individual algorithms. They may be quite different in the sense that the life of humanity differs from the life of the individual, even if the individuals themselves build up humanity as a whole. Humanity "as a whole" is living *continuously* on Earth and in the spiritual world (at least at present and during a long period of time), but the individual soul has a sequence of life during which he spends his time *alternately* in the material and the spiritual world. Though humanity is built up of these individuals, human evolution is generally related to the "ready" or conscious human being, while in the individual "evolution" of the human being there are strikingly different phases (embryonic life, newborn life, actual life, death) regarding one life. According to these differences in the *constitution* of communal and individual evolution, the time algorithms may vary for humanity and for the human being himself.

It must be added, though, that there are similar characteristics. For example, a known means of the algorithms is "projection." Here a common feature is that there is a "dilution" in the algorithm.[2] For example, 1 day = 29.5 years (humanity),[3] or 1 day = 365 days or 1 day = 93.5 days (human being/humanity)[4] of causal time, when space-time-related etheric substances appear in projection from an earlier time to a later time.

Briefly speaking, the human being is living in space-time in the complex web of time-

algorithm-related etheric streams. In this article, I concentrate only on the time algorithms belonging to the *individual*.

The Elements of "Subjective Duration"

When human beings visit the Earth again and again for their earthly lives, they are born into space-time within the framework of time we sense as causal time flow. From the viewpoint of the individuality, this time flow appears as an objective time, from which we cut a part for ourselves to participate in space-time for a while, from birth to death. This part of the time flow becomes our "subjective duration" (borrowing the expression from Henri Bergson and Dane Rudhyar) through etheric processes of "individualization of time."

I differentiate three main pillars in these processes: transits, embryonic projections and newborn projections.

Throughout life, human beings sense the actual cosmic constellations around them that have a continuous relationship to their individual bodily and psychic constitution (expressed in their conception and birth charts). Astrologers all over the world examine the stellar and planetary influences on the constitution and activity of the human being, and call the influences *transits*. The descriptions of this kind of observation constitute, I think, the largest part of astrological experience and literature of predictive astrology. It is not by chance, as according to experience, these phenomena can be perceived best by the human being, mostly from "outer events"— i.e., from the manifested forms of inner traits of destiny. In this case, the real-time cosmic effects make such a direct relation with the etheric constitutions of the human being that occurrences may reach the region of the limbs.

The other two pillars have common characteristics: both are working on a mechanism of etheric projection from the first year of the individual after conception to later times in life. This phenomenon is very subtle, and can be perceived more in the life of thought and feeling of the individual in the case when the interventions of actual transits have not reached their full effect.

---

2   "Dilution" is not the best expression, as "point-like" events which are fitted usually to planetary angular encounters cannot be diluted. Still, the underlying mechanism of moving between time-frames may be described in terms of "dilution" or "condensation."

3   From the life of Jesus Christ there originated special algorithms, which can be partly applied to humanity and partly to the individual: see for example, the "Apocalypse code" (1 day = 29½ years) for humanity or the rhythm of 33⅓ years for both the life of humanity and of the individual (see the works of Robert Powell).

4   See Willi Sucher's pondering on etheric projections regarding mundane events in Sucher, *Practical Approach II*, p. 164.

Embryonic projection is based inherently on the relationship between Moon and Earth, i.e., ten lunar months of the embryonic period correspond to 10 x 7 = 70 years in actual life. It means in "solar equivalent" that the etheric weavings in one day in embryonic life are in relation with occurrences in ca. 93½ days in actual life. This etheric mechanism was discovered and elaborated by Willi Sucher, and later by Robert Powell.

Newborn projections are widely used by astrologers. Their main types are *primary directions* and *secondary directions (or progressions).* They basically rely on the cyclic relationships between Sun and Earth. Primary directions are based on the axial rotation of the Earth: the day-and-night rhythm (of the *day*). Secondary progressions are based on the orbital revolution of the Earth: the rhythm of the seasons (of the *year*).[5] I think we can say that secondary progressions are used most often among astrologers, experiencing most effectiveness in mapping the spiritual or psychic conditions of the individual that stand behind outer manifestations. I think this preference has its base in the different relation of the etheric mechanisms to the assimilative (metabolic) forces and to the organic forces. According to Rudolf Steiner, the axial rotation of the Earth is in relation with the metabolism and assimilation of the human being, while the orbital revolution of the Earth is in relation with the building-up processes of the organs:

How are they [organic forces] built up in the human body? They are built up in such a manner that as we follow the human life during the periods of this building-up process of organs, we may recognize with a fair degree of accuracy that the process is related to the course of the year as metabolism is related to the course of the day. Observe how this building process takes place in the child, commencing at conception and proceeding until he first "sees the light of the world" as it is beautifully expressed.

After this, and especially during the first months after birth, the building-up processes proceed still further; so that, in very fact, we have to do with a year's course.[6]

Practically, secondary progression is a continuation of the embryonic movements regarding its spatial principle, i.e., the spatial dimension remains the orbital revolution of the Earth. This way the embryonic and the newborn etheric weaving may constitute an organic whole regarding their spatial viewpoint. It is as if a plant would be in the human being that would need a full cycle of vegetable life to fulfil its destiny. Primary direction means a complete change not only regarding time (change from lunar to solar etheric mechanism of projection) but also regarding the spatial factor (change from orbital to axial rotation of the Earth) from the viewpoint of the ongoing etheric weaving started by conception; I cannot regard this as interpretable in this present context. Under the usage of the word "newborn projection" I will mean secondary progression.

I find it remarkable how Dane Rudhyar thought about secondary progressions:

If the Sun in astrology represents the life principle, and each month of solar motion releases a specific seasonal kind of life energy, it seems logical to me to expect that the complete formation of man —who is thought to be a microcosmic condensation of the forces active in the macrocosm, or at least in the solar system —should take a whole year. As the embryonic development in the womb takes nine months, it would be natural to assume that the extra three months needed to complete the solar cycle would refer to the *equally embryonic* unfolding of a psychic organism.[7]

Secondary progression must work on a similar basis as embryonic projections regarding the connection of our bodily member constitution and time—i.e., events within our etheric body play a main role. I assume that the operation and

---

5   The rule is the following: What takes place in the sky each day after the birth of a person gives us an archetypal or symbolic picture of the conditions that develop during one year of that person's life. In other words, the cosmic occurrences of one day in the newborn period are reflected in 365 days in actual life.

6   Steiner, *Mystery of the Universe: The Human Being, Image of Creation*, lect. 6.

7   Dane Rudhyar, *A Key to the Understanding of Personality*, p. 143.

receptivity of our etheric body in approximately the first three months are still more similar to its operation and receptivity in its embryonic condition than in later conditions. Thus, the capacity of our being for absorbing etheric seeds is still working in that period. It is another question, however, whether the birth of the human being must be a *turning point*, so the etheric mechanisms or algorithms must be totally different from each other for the periods *before* and *after* birth, within this (9 + 3 months =) one year. And indeed, this difference is apparent in the different mechanisms—i.e., in the different "principles of extension" (*extension* in a lunar or solar sense)—and meaning of the two types of etheric unfolding that I try to describe briefly in the next section.

The "Open Space"

When we look at the movement of the Sun before the stellar background during the embryonic period, we realize that there is a "missing part" of the path of the Sun between its birth and conception positions in the zodiac, which we may call the "open space."[8]

In the light of the preceding considerations the question arises: Is there any "open space" at all?[9]

I think from one viewpoint there surely is. Even if the open space is filled with a special content (secondary progressions), this special content *never closes the circle*. In the case of embryonic projection, the projection-cycle is a closed one. We can project only the actual embryonic period in the average 10 x 7 = 70 years' timeframe to actual life. And if one has a shorter embryonic period, this projection belongs to a shorter period than seventy years, even if one lives much more than seventy years. In the case of "newborn" projection, the algorithm points toward an endless direction,

where not the end of the embryonic period but the end of the actual life produces an end point. The Moon-related perspective of "the individualization of time" is more restricted than the Sun-related.

On the following images I outlined the main characteristics that I perceive regarding the two types of etheric projections—from the geocentric point of view, in "horoscopic expression," showing the path of the Sun through the first year after conception. The path of the Sun and the Moon are obviously very important in both cases (from conception to birth and from birth to approximately three months age), but still, if I would like to express the *basic tone*, I would regard the embryonic projection as a Lunar one, with its manifold implications that come to mind of the Moon as a "cosmic weaver" or "accumulator of evolution" of inherited forces and substances; and the newborn projection as a Solar one, with its manifold implications that come to mind of the Sun as a "cosmic spiritualizer of matter" or "generator of evolution" in the spiritual development of man (and humanity). In reality, we should handle and interpret a complete soli-lunar process and background into which the human being is born with his whole first year within the sphere of the Moon and Earth, in order to see how he would like to adjust himself into his closest earthly circumstances for his psychic and spiritual growth, in his relation to the two main light bodies of our earthly world.

I indicate the Lunar Nodes as well. While the *planetary* angular relationships (between two consecutive New Moons) represent a gradual transformation in intellectual perception within the contracting and expanding life of the soul during the cycle, the *spherical encounter* of the two spheres indicates remarkable points of possibility for the connection of the lower and higher "I" to make the synthesis of intellectual thinking (Moon) and wisdom (Sun) on a *higher level*, while getting a glimpse into the Astral world and the higher aims of the "I" within. The theme of the Lunar Nodes would lead out of the scope of this study. Here I would only emphasize that the Ascending Node points to future perspectives of soul development and the Descending Node points to necessities of

---

8   For example, if I was born in Aquarius and conceived in Gemini, then the Sun never passed before Pisces, Aries, or Taurus during my conception—Pisces and Aries are the "open space." (JMP)

9   That is, since the "open space" is then filled by the first three months after birth. In the above example, the Sun would move through Pisces, Aries, and Taurus after the Aquarius birth, therefore "filling" the open space left by the gestational Sun. (JMP)

soul development coming from the past, which I also sense as main characteristics of the two types of etheric projection, keeping in mind though that both *spherical crossings* have relevance in *both* periods, similar to the connection of the Earth to the *celestial bodies* (angular aspects of Sun and Moon) in *both* periods.

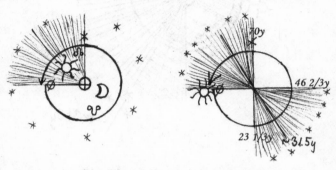

The relationship of the two etheric projections is also worth pondering on. Willi Sucher exchanges the geocentric and heliocentric viewpoint for the fourth, fifth, and sixth months of pregnancy when he speaks about the "open space," and says that "those three constellations in the 'open space' are particularly connected with planet Earth and its special significance in the universe." He also refers to the "open space" as the "Earth aspect of the nativity" and as an expression of the longing of the individual to experience the Sun spirit of the Earth, which he demonstrates with examples of historical personalities.[10]

I think what Willi Sucher recognized about the appearance of the "open space" in people's lives is a remarkable observation and interpretation, but I am skeptical that these experiences would evolve out of the embryonic period (or only out of it). Surely the two types of etheric unfolding are working in parallel in us while they interweave the pulsations of one another. But according to my own experience, the unfolding of the zodiacal forces and planetary constellations of the "open space" may be even more intense after the year of 46⅔, when the Sun leaves the opposition of the "open space" in the embryonic period and comes into opposition with its positions during the first

quarter (0–23⅓ years)—while it is still in the "open space" in the newborn period (approximately in the middle in the case of an average pregnancy). It means that if experiences after these years of age are still connected to the "open space," there must be another underlying mechanism behind the phenomenon. It is also a question why would there only be an "interplay" of heliocentric and geocentric viewpoints in the range between 23⅓ and 46⅔? Why would it not apply to the other periods of life as well?

In the embryonic period the Sun goes through the opposition of the "open space" (or the Earth goes through the "open space" from the heliocentric point of view) in relation with the period between 23⅓ and 46⅔ years of age, and in the newborn period the Sun goes through the "open space" in relation with the whole actual life. This would suggest an overlapping period at first glance. However, it must be recognized that they are not parallel periods in the projection into actual life. There is only one point in time, when the projected Suns of the two etheric mechanisms are in exact opposition—transmitting stellar substances to the Earth from the opposite directions, placing man in the focus point of this special etheric "crossfire." This occurs at approximately 31½ years of age in the case of a normal length pregnancy (273 days),[11] and comes into being with the start of life for one born after a six-month pregnancy, developing from zero to 31½ years of age according to the length of the embryonic period.

We may assume that the embryonic projections bring an impulse earlier in time, which then *later*, during the newborn projection, may shine forth as a theme in a new dress in consciousness, at that time out of a deeper and more mature conviction, and with ripe intention to create something not only for the evolution of the human being as an individual but also with a view for human evolution as a community. "Later," since the embryonic projection covers the "open space" earlier than the newborn projection. When man becomes 46⅔ years old, the embryonic "open space impulse"

10 Sucher, *Isis Sophia I* (Introducing Astrosophy), pp. 137, 142.

11 (270–180) / (270/70–1) = 31½, assuming that the Sun transits through 270° during 273 days.

disappears, but he is only at the half of the newborn "open space impulses."

The following image shows the path of the Sun from conception onward in a spiral form around the Earth, as we perceive it with our senses. At the bottom the "open space" is indicated between birth and conception, and along the spiral movement of the Sun the two etheric curves can be seen showing the projected paths of the Sun in relation to the zodiac. We can see also where the Suns on two etheric spirals get into opposition around the age of 31½ in the case of a normal length pregnancy.

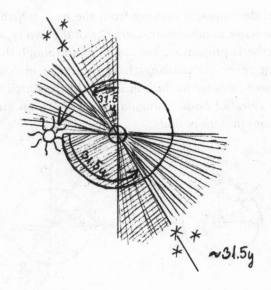

~31.5y

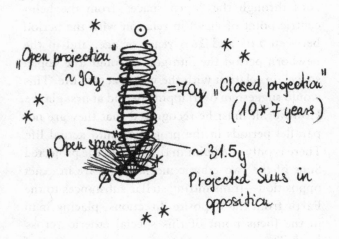

„Open projection"
~90y
=70y „Closed projection"
(10 * 7 years)
„Open space"
~31.5y
Projected Suns in opposition

As a summary of the factors of "subjective duration" (i.e., objective time made subjective through etheric projections and actual transits), the following table shows the three main etheric layers in which actual life is unfolding. "Time algorithms" are expressed in "Sun equivalents," where the "earthly" ratio is our causal time itself—i.e., it is not a time algorithm in a strict sense.

Appearance of etheric substances according to
spacetime and time-algorithms

„Algorithm of Time"		In actual life	
	In embryonic + newborn period	„In general"	„Special" (connections to thresholds)
Lunar (1: 93.5)	Actual	Projected „Actual"	
	Transits to ∅, *		Projected „Transits to ∅,*"
Solar (1: 365)	Actual	Projected „Actual"	
	Transits to ∅, *		Projected „Transits to ∅,⊛"
Earthly (1:1)	Actual		Transits to ∅,⊛ +

Projections in the Etheric

Actual effects in spacetime

Generally used in CONTEMPORARY PREDICTIVE ASTROLOGY

SUBJECTIVE DURATION

Space Became Time?

In the preceding, I focused on secondary progression amongst the etheric projections based on the birth of the individual. This does not mean that no other etheric currents would be formed in a person during his lifetime, it just means that in my experience this etheric program is the key one that represents the other pole in addition to the embryonic etheric program, and together they unfold in the "subjective duration," corresponding to the karmic background of the individual.

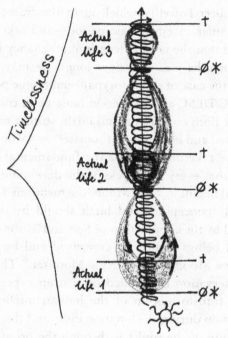

The first year counted from conception is a key point in reconciling successive lives. In my imagination, a multiple lemniscate-like etheric stream appears connecting both the durations and the threshold states (conception, birth and death) of lives, where this first year is not only the extreme point of one lemniscate, but also the center of another lemniscate.

In so far as we join into the movement between Sun and Earth with our earthly life, which is sensed by physical perception as circular or spiral, and also means our *causal time flow* here,[12]

---

12 The expression of the drawing remains in the perspective of *time (yearly time)*, and not space, where the Sun and Earth would move in a lemniscate-form.

the etheric streams belonging to space-time take a *special turn* during the first year, as if "in a point of condensation" they map down the key factors of the actual "subjective duration" of the individual incarnated on earth; key factors that are formed in the perspective of several lives. It is as if the causal space-time spiral would be split by the etheric streams, and there would be a coming into being of an *etheric vortex* characteristic only to the given individual, in the middle of which the period around birth (first year of life after conception) stands. Within the first year, in the embryonic period there is a complete silence regarding producing any karma, while simultaneously there is a beehive-like karmic weaving in the ether (into the etheric body). Our birth to earthly life as a focal point in this vortex then remains a base, which is always in relation with the "peripheral" unfolding of our life.

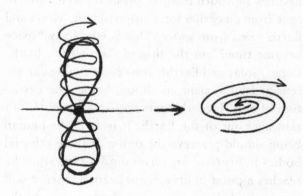

In the middle of the vortex there are two "anchorages" to the seed form of "being": the threshold experiences of conception and birth. (Death is also in the middle of the vortex in a "consolidated" perspective, that can be seen when we press the spirals together, and/or we see the image from above/below, as though looking into a tunnel). When we examine the "subjective duration" of the human being, we look for how (i.e., through what kind of cornerstones) the life of the individual unfolds. In this there are basically two principles of observation, which I marked as "in general" and "special" in the columns of the attached table. The category of "in general" contains etheric projections or actual occurrences belonging to a certain cosmic event (e.g., bound to the encounter of two planets) without comparison to threshold states, while the category of "special" means examinations bound to threshold states. Though both phenomena have their place in the unfolding of destiny, in the process of "becoming," the space-time of the threshold events gives the *seed form* for accomplishment—i.e., all of the occurrences (both projected or actual) have a basic resonance to the space-time of the threshold events, and only the repetition of the themes of the threshold conditions is under way in ever-new colors during life.[13]

This first year seems to me to carry within it in a way the spatial fragmentation that has developed for the current phase of human evolution, when man takes on a material form on Earth. The mechanism of etheric weaving and unfolding, which has its basis during the evolving of the embryo and the first few newborn months, preserves something *in time* from an earlier integration of Sun, Moon and Earth—i.e., *from space*. This is why I say "space became time?" in the title of the section. In the Lunar, Solar and Earthly *time counting* we can see reflected an ancient condition, before the extraction of Sun (Hyperborean age) and Moon (Lemurian age) out of the Earth. It is as if the human being should preserve the union of these celestial bodies in his *time organism* until a time when he reaches a point in his spiritualization when it will be not needed any more—on the way toward the absorbing of the Moon and the Sun back into the Earth. Until that time the human being may carry his longing for the experience of unity.

It is also worth pondering that the conditions of Lunar, Solar and Earthly timing (or time counting) in our life also have a relation to our individual joining into the spatial relationship of Sun, Moon and Earth at conception and birth, a joining that differs in general from a "prototypal" conception or birth. The spatial interplay of the

celestial bodies and the etheric programming based on the relationship of these same bodies constitute a quite special character for each individual. I regard this theme as important since this difference from an archetypal conception and birth has a great role in the *extraordinary difficulty* of the interpretation of the interactions in the extremely complex web of etheric layers belonging to the unfolding of our lives.

If we examine the factors of the hermetic rule (the exchange of ASC/DESC and Moon for conception and birth, see the work of both Willi Sucher and Robert Powell)—which gives the framework of the lunar or embryonic period—and take into account that the normal length of pregnancy is ten lunar months (i.e., 273 days long), we may state that in the case of a "prototypal" embryonic period the ASC/DESC and the Moon must be in conjunction for both conception and birth, so that man is conceived and born at a "Moonrise" or "Moonset."

If we take into account the fundamental experience that every new cycle of the development of the soul begins at New Moon, the mentioned "prototypal" conception and birth should be supplemented by the conjunction of Sun and Moon—i.e., human beings should be conceived and be born at "New Moonrise" or "New Moonset." This latter observation is founded on a deep experience of the transformation of the human intellectual perception during the lunation cycle and the transformation of the soul life through the progressed lunation cycles during life, which cycles have a particular starting point with the "solar impulse" released at the New Moon.

If we ponder on the different points examined by astrology when it tries to find an "average point" or index to find a "common denominator" of the relation of Sun, Moon and ASC (locality on Earth) to characterize the individual as a "personality,"[14] and we think of the "personality"

---

13 In comparing conception and birth, it is an important point of departure that the time-algorithm-frame of both etheric projections is bound to *birth* (rather than to conception), which puts before us a quite complex theme if we seek the *middle* of the vortex.

14 Speaking of the "common denominator," I think of an often-used factor, the Part of Fortune (presumably developed during the Middle Ages by the Arabs), which was observed as an indication of the type of the "personality" and loses, in a sense, its additional meaning when birth occurs at Sun-rise, when the Part of Fortune is equal with the

whose main indicator is the ASC (and not the DESC), I think that we may reduce the hypotheses to the "New Moonrise."

I think we can add that, if a New Moon occurs when both celestial bodies are in one of the Lunar Nodes (i.e., in the spherical crossing of Sun and Moon), the establishment and experience of union reach the highest level. But this cannot happen for both conception and birth, owing to the peculiar movement of the Lunar Node.

So, we may think in a prototypal or primordial, or even "paradisal" birth at a rising New Moon in the Lunar Node (meaning a rising solar eclipse), which approaches but never reaches the "ideal state," when the three celestial bodies constituted a unity. All of our *basic* differentiations, which are reflected not only in the astrological factors of our conception/birth charts *but also in our "subjective durations"*—i.e., in the lunar and solar etheric projections of the moving spatial relations of Sun, Moon and Earth, and their relations to actual transits—are basically coming from the disintegration of the union of Sun, Moon and Earth.

Rudolf Steiner and his "second birth": Additional aspects of Laying the Foundation Stone

With what I write and draw here I would like to call the attention to viewpoints for further deepening regarding the *relationship of Time and our life*, which is so important in our age when Christ has returned in the Etheric world. I am aware that the drawings express quite insufficiently the processes that reach beyond our sense perception. I also know that while in the etheric projections there are time algorithms in operation, the reconciliation of the threshold events takes into account further "cosmic algorithms" (planetary relations and house positions), which would carry this elaboration toward an even more complex view. However, for all the inadequacies, I feel that this theme, our individual relationship to Time, even in this form may induce beneficial thoughts.

_____

position of the Moon.

In the case of Rudolf Steiner, I found the most significant point in the "crossings of the three basic layers of experience of time" in the year of the Christmas Conference.

I think it is very remarkable that we can see cosmic occurrences in such a strong expression in his life. We may say in general that actual constellations and their relations to the individual's charts (i.e., transits) find their place most effectively in the material world, and the embryonic or newborn etheric projections contain a *line of development*, which is much more hidden, and takes form in the material world when the transits are well placed. In these complex processes, it is sometimes hard to characterize precisely what is going on in the individual, and all the more it is so in the case of spiritually advanced people or initiates, like Rudolf Steiner, as outer events may show other characteristics, or there are no outer events at all. And still, I regard his relation to the Christmas Conference as a very characteristic example of how these etheric streams may work, and of how they really can be adjusted to each other in an unthinkable way by the spiritual beings so that human beings can sense every impulse at the right time. I am writing in an astrological view, in a quite abstract style, but we know that the work of the beings of the etheric world and the angelic hierarchies are meant here behind any "actualization" or "taking form" of etheric substances in the material world.

In the embryonic study I think we could see a very inner landscape of Steiner's spiritual and soul development, which reached its culmination with the Sun and Mercury conjunction at the Nadir point of his birth chart. The unfolding of the given etheric impulse occurred in synch with the period just before the Laying of the Foundation Stone. I referred to Valentin Tomberg's thoughts regarding Steiner's crucifixion, which he experienced at that time with all of the possibilities and threats that may have been felt or accomplished while moving along the *vertical line* both mentally and physically. His embryonic period was adjusted completely to the *actual cosmic situation*, where Pluto reached the "vertical line" of the Sun-Earth relationship, i.e., the apsides of the Earth. The characteristics of his inner experience had already been engraved into his being during the embryonic period, taking into account the dimension of the house system (or will-pattern-framework) as well, which "provided" the Cross to which he "crucified himself" and which brought him fundamental spiritual experiences.

If we examine Steiner's secondary progressions, we can see that the progressed Sun reached his birth Pluto and then his progressed Pluto during the days of April 28 and 29, 1861, after birth, which appeared in his etheric body again in the years of 1922 and 1923.[15] Progressed Sun reached birth Pluto on April 30, 1922 at 14°57' Aries and progressed Sun reached progressed Pluto on July 22, 1923 at 16°9' Aries in etheric projection. At first glance we recognize that the theme of the relation of Pluto, Sun and Earth appears again in this perspective, as in the case of the actual cosmic situation that Steiner felt so well. It means that the *underlying mood of the time* that was created by the newborn etheric projections was completely in harmony with the *word of the actual time*. The etherically created theme could weave its way throughout the experiences that occurred during the corresponding year(s) in a way in which the actual "in general" condition, let's say here a "type of the transits," could trigger the limb region with the same cosmic forces. I think this repetition of the same forces in etheric time and in causal time made the situation—his spiritual task—even more emphasized for Rudolf Steiner.

The "type of transits" means that we speak of the relationship of transiting planets and not the relationship of a transiting planet to a birth/conception/death planet. Interestingly, the situation is the same in the case of the etheric projection, at least for the year of culmination—for 1923. Here also, we speak of the relationship of progressing planets, and not a relationship of a progressed planet to a birth planet. In these cases, where there is no "anchorage" to the purpose of life expressed by the birth chart, we face a pure

influx of cosmic circumstances (transitory actual constellation) and a boundless influx of "becoming" (progressions). According to the general rule, we usually focus on the relationship of transits and projections to the birth chart when we detect the purpose of life unfolding in the midst of the transforming life activities. The other method of examination comes to the fore in the case of individuals who experience a profound change in their life purpose, involving a metamorphosis of their being during their life, or in the case of such advanced individuals who can live according to the actual constellations. I regard Steiner as an example to show how the "subjective duration" may contain both phenomena.

In the following figure (page 65), we can see the etheric projections of Steiner for the time of the Christmas Conference. I also include an image of the transitory cosmic situation, about which I wrote in my first study.

We can see the cross of the house system, whose vertical axis was reached by the Sun and Mercury in autumn 1923 in embryonic projection. And I also indicated a little cross next to the progressed Sun and progressed Pluto—not only because the Sun-Pluto angular relationships usually mean a "second birth" for the individual, but also because the progressed Sun reached birth Pluto at 14°57' Aries and it is the zodiacal position of the Sun at the Crucifixion of Jesus Christ (14°6' Aries); and the progressed Sun reached the progressed Pluto at 16°9' Aries and it is the zodiacal position of the Sun at the Resurrection of Jesus Christ (15°40' Aries).

The embryonic image carries the *will impulse*. As the embryonic projection is *lunar* in its underlying principle, the Sun at the Nadir triggers a deep, compelling will impulse that "something must be done," and this something points toward the interior of the Earth and goes along with the potential crucifixion of the individual.

The newborn image carries the *theme* of the potential activity, but does not contain compelling will in itself. As the newborn projection is *solar* in its underlying principle, it represents a growth of consciousness and a line of development in an individual's freedom, his lifelong opportunities for

15 Data produced by www.astro.com for secondary progressions throughout the article.

creative freedom.[16] The theme is Pluto-related (regarding planets) and regarding the position of the Sun it is completely in synch with the stellar etheric imprints of the Mystery of Golgotha of Jesus Christ.

The actual (transitory) situation carries the *theme* and *external pressure* of the "duration of humanity," i.e., the necessity of the development of the greater whole around Rudolf Steiner as an individual. This theme is not only Pluto-related (regarding planets), but reaches the relationship of our solar system to star Sirius.

As Jesus Christ took on himself the karma of humanity on Golgotha, Rudolf Steiner took upon himself the karma of the earthly spiritual scientific society. The potential for this act is seen in his embryonic and newborn image. Probably we could say that in the embryonic etheric imprint there is a very individual experience expressed in the cross of the house system, and in the newborn etheric imprint there appears the *communal circumstance* both in the Plutonic situations all along the years of 1922 and 1923 (thinking of the decadent condition of the society and the burning down of the first Goetheanum), and in the zodiacal influxes embracing the period from the Crucifixion till Resurrection of Jesus Christ. Here it is interesting to see that—in addition to the orbs—we handle a *period*, as progressed Sun reached first the birth Pluto's position, and then the progressed Pluto. We could say that the former etheric imprint is in synch with the Crucifixion and with the burning

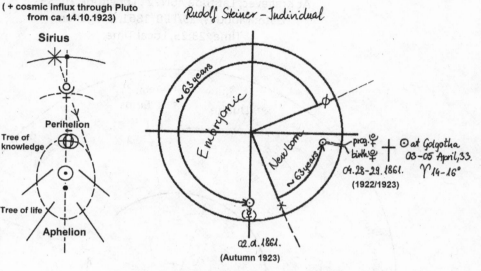

of the first Goetheanum, and the latter one with the Resurrection and the Christmas Conference—from the communal viewpoint. (We could also take into account birth Mars at 12°48' Aries to have a fuller picture of the "preparatory period.") The culmination was the Laying of the Foundation Stone, which meant at the same time the "second birth" of Steiner on a higher spiritual level.

In the cosmic image can we see the highest, planetary-cosmic factor, which represents the task for Rudolf Steiner as the next step in human and planetary evolution.

The relation between the experience of Golgotha and the Christmas Conference in embryonic and newborn images

Here, I do not want to deepen into details of Rudolf Steiner's life. I think that, if we focus on a few main focal points of his life, we can see his basic traits in order to commemorate his individuality and his contribution to human evolution.

In my study that was issued last year, I recalled that Steiner was led through his inner struggles with ahrimanic forces to a concrete encounter with Christ at the end of 1899. This encounter underlay his later esoteric lecturing activity that he started in 1900. With this encounter, a new phase began in his life, similar to the Christmas Conference. Maybe we can regard each event as a "second birth."

---

16 Human freedom is connected with the Sun forces and the lack thereof with the Moon forces. "In everything of which the poet says: 'This you must be, you cannot escape from yourself' — in all this, the past Moon existence is living on. And the Sun existence is working whenever you are conscious of freedom of choice" (Steiner, *Karmic Relationships,* vol. 6, p. 77).

Birth of Rudolf Steiner - Prenatal Geocentric Planetary Distances
At Kraljevec, Latitude 46N22', Longitude 16E39'
Date: Monday, 25/FEB/1861, Gregorian
Time: 23:25, Local Time

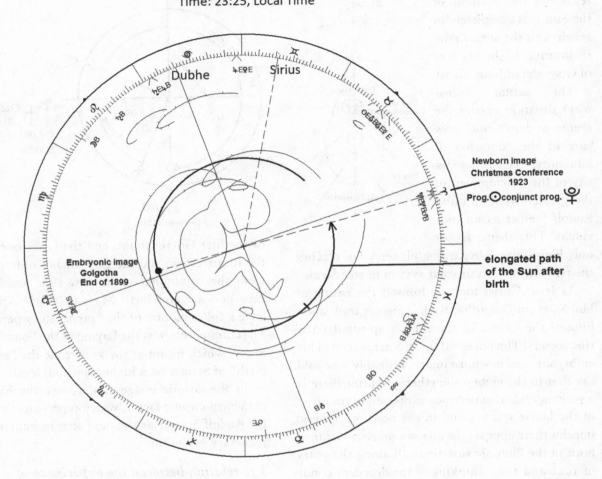

I mentioned there that during the embryonic period the Sun was in opposition to birth Pluto on October 30, 1860, which is in conformity with October 30, 1899; the Sun was in opposition to Pluto on October 31, 1860, which is in conformity with January 4, 1900. Here again, we face a *period*—though shorter due to the different etheric mechanisms—as in the case of the newborn images of the Christmas Conference, if we take into account both the unfolding of the threshold imprint (birth position) and of the actual encounters of planets. Thus, we have a period, which refers to the end of 1899, when Rudolf Steiner had his decisive experience standing in the presence of Golgotha, probably under a remarkable actual transitory constellation.

Last year I did not deal with any newborn images. I only referred to the etheric imprint of forces inherent in the Pluto-Sun opposition, that may have veiled references to the memories of Golgotha, which may have reappeared in another form, in very similar force relations at the Laying of the Foundation Stone in actual life. Here, in the third part of the study we can see that there is an interesting relationship between the two events when we take into account *both etheric mechanisms*. What appeared earlier in the embryonic period as a seed of standing in the presence of Golgotha, of an initiation into the Grail mysteries (at the age of thirty-eight), made further progress later on, in the opposite newborn seed of the Christmas Conference, where the Grail could appear also for a community (at the age of sixty-two). Here we may recall what I said earlier in general: "We may assume that the embryonic projections bring an impulse earlier in time that then later, during the newborn projection, may shine forth as a theme in a new dress in consciousness, at that time out of a deeper and more mature conviction, and with ripe intention to create something not only for the evolution of the human being as an individual but also with a view for human evolution as a community."

Of course, in the case of Rudolf Steiner this kind of general approach must be handled at an elevated level. He started his esoteric lecturing activity also for the progress of humanity, so here I think we can speak about steps between a narrower scope of human evolution and a planetary one.

I find it extraordinarily interesting that we have here a correspondence between the "standing in the presence of Golgotha" and the Christmas Conference in double aspects: Sun and Pluto encounters in opposition (embryonic) and in conjunction (newborn); and the zodiacal stellar influx for both events is the event during the Calvary of Jesus Christ through the planets' positions *at* or *in opposition* to 14°–16° Aries.

Of course, there are other cosmic, stellar and planetary forces, along which the images might be expanded, but I found the "guidance" of Sun and Pluto the most remarkable.

It is also interesting that in the case of Rudolf Steiner both etheric images are coming from the vicinity of the birth Ascendant-Descendant axis, marking the etheric seed of the Golgotha event as a more individual, or more personal event at the Ascendant, and marking the etheric seed of the Christmas Conference as a more communal event at the Descendant, which characteristics are corresponding to the general experience of the etheric imprints of the two types. It is as if *even in this respect (house system)* the etheric mechanisms were constructed for Rudolf Steiner in line with his individual and communal inner growth toward the Laying of the Foundation Stone and the consequent achievements afterward.

If we examine the actual transitory events, we may detect a correspondence to the closing of Kali Yuga in the case of the "standing in the presence of Golgotha," something that has a reference to the past. In the case of the Christmas Conference, I see something of a "promise of the future" with the Apsides and Pluto reaching the ecliptic meridian of Sirius in Gemini.

1907: An Important Cornerstone on the Path toward the Christmas Conference

In my study last year, I included a drawing on the path of Sun and Mercury during Rudolf Steiner's embryonic period, which I would like to recall here:

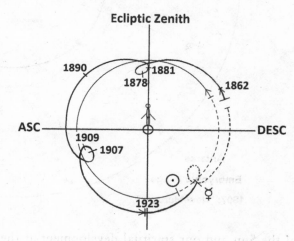

Path of Sun and Mercury during the embryonic life of Rudolf Steiner

On this image we can see the loop of Mercury under the Ascendant with the inferior conjunction of Sun and Mercury at 1907 in etheric projection. I wrote at that time: "Interpreting the effect of the inferior conjunction up to the beginning of the direct phase, these times were characterized by seeking the path and planting seeds."

In the embryonic image we can see *an inner landscape*, as in the case of the Laying of the Foundation Stone. I do not want to repeat myself, but maybe it is useful to recall a few sentences from my last study to show how important the phases of a cycle of a direct-retrograde movement of a planet may be, which colorize the path

Birth of Rudolf Steiner - Prenatal Geocentric Planetary Distances
At Kraljevec, Latitude 46N22', Longitude 16E39'
Date: Monday, 25/FEB/1861, Gregorian
Time: 23:25, Local Time

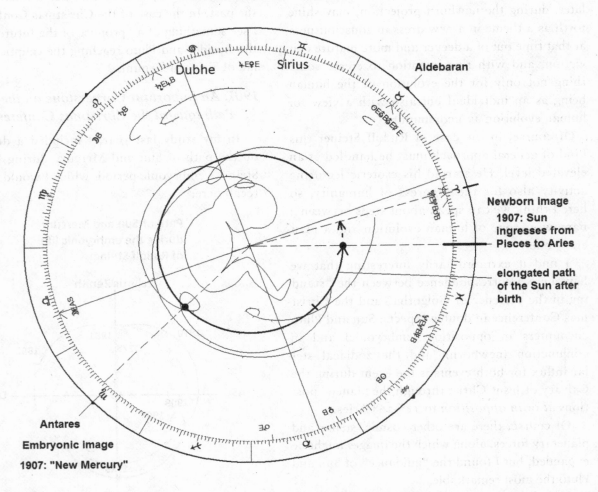

of the Sun and our spiritual development at the same time.

"In the case of the inferior conjunction of the Sun and Mercury the planet is between the Sun and the Earth: it is in the state of "New Mercury." In this dark time a new seed can be planted in consciousness. In the case of the superior conjunction, Mercury is farthest from the Earth and is behind the Sun: it is in the state of "Full Mercury." In this brightness can the fruits that evolved from the seed in the consciousness be manifested in their fullness. The result that is apparent here is a reflection of the action taken in the direct phase, based on the contemplation that was engaged in during the preceding retrograde phase. The result then remains in focus until the next 'sowing.'"

That is, I regarded the New Mercury at 1907 as a turning point, a "sowing" of a new cycle in Steiner's consciousness, while the Full Mercury at the Christmas Conference was the "manifested fruit"—though in that explanation I took into account the former loop of Mercury as well.[17] When we turn toward the newborn images, we

17 I indicated on the chart Antares and Aldebaran as well. In addition to the New Mercury condition there was a Sun-Uranus opposition at around the Antares-Aldebaran axis in projection to 1907, producing probably quite a challenging etheric pulsating, given the influences of the Uranic beings and the influence of the megastars.

find an interesting phenomenon. The Sun reached 0°1' Aries on Apr 12, 1861, in the newborn period that means January 1, 1907, in projection.

Here again, we face a turning point of a cycle, though quite another one: Aries is the first sign of the Zodiac. It stands in the cosmos as a sign of something that is a new beginning. Pisces is the last constellation and, therefore, signifies something that has come to an end, to a certain perfection.

If we take into account only the newborn images in Steiner's life, we can see that he had etheric Sun imprints for his first approximately sixteen years from Aquarius (1861–1877), then approximately thirty years from Pisces (1877–1907) and approximately eighteen years from Aries (1907–1925). We may say that Pisces and Aries were the most important constellations that etherically underlay the unfolding of his lifework—while he manifested his basic Aquarius character of his birth Sun throughout life.

Pisces is a very unique constellation as it is not only the last one of the twelve constellations, but contains all of their meaning in a way. It consists of two fishes, which represent a polarity: One is swimming backward and one is swimming forward/upward. The polarity is about past and future. "They symbolize the beginning and the end, and thus they repeat between them what otherwise is spread out in cosmic space and time. They hold the key of all evolution, of the destiny of the world. The Godhead working through them has established everlasting transformation (in earthly terms we could say death) whose external manifestation is life"—as Willi Sucher formulated it.[18]

This was the period when Rudolf Steiner indeed worked on showing to humanity the eternal countenance, image or aim of humanity, and the tremendous struggle of humanity to conform with and to manifest this divine image of the human being, through many of his lectures and books, including his main work, *The Philosophy of Freedom*, which I focus on in the next section. But when the etheric Sun entered Aries, in projection to 1907, he probably felt the urge of the "Aries

call," and as Aries is the force of the inauguration of new impulses and also of making sacrifices for the new impulses, he acted in synch with his inner etheric images, attuning himself toward sacrificial deeds and taking responsibility for the manifestation of the new. It is also interesting to consider that he finished his *Autobiography* with 1907 marking the end and the beginning of something in his life.

The lecture cycles of the year 1907 appeared as the hundredth of the Collected Works (CW) as *Menschheitsentwickelung und Christus-Erkenntnis. Theosophie und Rosenkreuzertum. Das Johannes-Evangelium.*[19] The original German version of the title expresses the Pisces and Aries side of the turning point: "human evolution" refers backward to the cosmological side of spiritual science (as theosophy), and the "knowledge of Christ" refers forward to the Christology side of spiritual science (as Anthroposophy). While the etheric Sun in Steiner entered the sign Aries, where the Father sacrificed his Son as the Lamb for humanity, he started to hold lecture cycles in Christological-evangelical and Rosicrucian themes. And while the etheric Sun entered the sign Aries where the very first steps of all creation are remembered (i.e., the divine creative world of Aries), he started to manifest new ideas and instinctive capacities: new artistic impulses in Anthroposophy.

While in the embryonic image we may perceive the more individual characteristics of Rudolf Steiner's experiences, in the newborn image there appears the theme of the later stations of the movement and society itself.

In 1907, there was an important Theosophical Congress organized in Munich for Whitsun, and in relation with his experiences Rudolf Steiner's thoughts may be found in the last chapter of his *Autobiography*: "What it would have been well to understand, but what was clearly grasped at that time by exceedingly few, was the fact that the anthroposophic current had given something of an entirely different bearing from that of the

_____

18 Sucher, *Isis Sophia II*, pp. 52–53.

_____

19 Published by Rudolf Steiner Press in 2015 as *True Knowledge of the Christ: Theosophy and Rosicrucianism—the Gospel of John.*

Theosophical Society up to that time. In this inner bearing lay the true reason why the Anthroposophical Society could no longer exist as a part of the Theosophical Society." The *next* and *last* planet that followed the Sun and crossed the border of Pisces to Aries in the newborn period was Venus. This ingress occurred in February 1913 in projection, and probably indicated impulses for the foundation of a new building—not only as the center for Anthroposophy but a home for artistic productions (first Goetheanum, 1913–1922).

There is a direct connection between the consequences of the Whitsun Conference in Munich 1907 and the design and construction of the first Goetheanum, which may have to do with the successive transits of Sun and Venus on the border of Pisces/Aries.

The Philosophy of Freedom *in the Crossfire of Embryonic and Newborn Images*

In a conversation with Rudolf Steiner in 1922 Walter Johannes Stein asked, "What will remain of your work in thousands of years?" Steiner replied: "Nothing but *The Philosophy of Freedom*," and then he added: "But everything is contained in it. If someone realizes the act of freedom described there, he finds the whole content of Anthroposophy."

I stated in last year's study that Steiner wrote his doctoral dissertation and its book version *Truth and Science* (1892) and then *The Philosophy of Freedom* (1894) in connection with the Sun-Mercury superior conjunction in his embryonic life, which etheric influence appeared in 1890 in

projection. I assumed that this culmination within the dynamics of the cycle of Sun, Mercury and Earth may have contributed to the urge for Steiner to present his thoughts to the public.

If we determine the etheric zodiacal "crossfire," about which I wrote in the introductory part of this study, we can see that it falls to April 1892 in Steiner's case.[20] That is, the embryonic and newborn projection of the path of the Sun got into alignment in 1892, when Rudolf Steiner was thirty-one years and two months old. At that time *Truth and Science* was already accomplished, and with great probability Steiner started to work on *The Philosophy of Freedom*. As he said that the *whole content of Anthroposophy* can be found in this work, these etheric influxes need closer attention.

It needs much meditation and experience to deepen into the question how the spiritual forces are streaming from the zodiacal signs toward us. May we speak about a stronger effect appearing in the center or at the periphery of the zodiacal signs? How do the peripheries of the zodiacal signs encounter each other? And how do the forces of opposite signs encounter each other?

In the alignment of the etheric Suns in the opposite zodiacal forces in the etheric projections of two types I assume a *force emphasis*, which may produce a creative tension in the human being. If we indeed may speak about such an etheric tension, then this may give a completely individual pattern—around a normal length pregnancy—to the human being regarding the so-called Christ age, which we generally interpret for the age between thirty and thirty-three years according to the incarnation of Christ.[21]

In the case of Rudolf Steiner, there is a peculiar situation, where the zodiacal etheric tension

---

20 The zodiacal positions of the two etheric Suns were in opposition on April 10, 1892 at 15°32' Virgo and at 15°32' Pisces according to my calculations based on data in Astrofire (embryonic projection) and wwww.astro.com (newborn projection - secondary progression).

21 The incarnation actually happened between 29 years and 9½ months of age and 33⅓ years of age of Jesus Christ according to the researches by Robert Powell.

Birth of Rudolf Steiner - Prenatal Geocentric Planetary Distances
At Kraljevec, Latitude 46N22', Longitude 16E39'
Date: Monday, 25/FEB/1861, Gregorian
Time: 23:25, Local Time

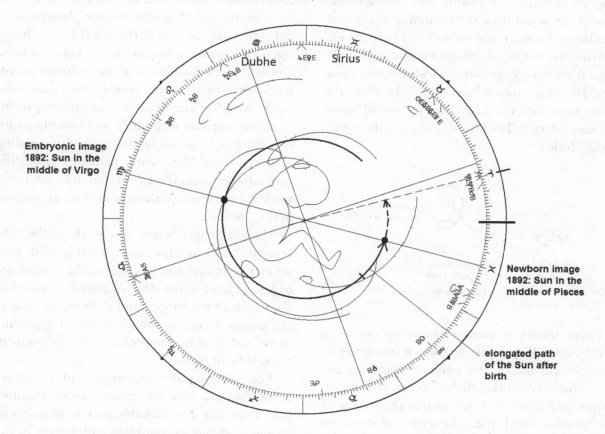

Embryonic image
1892: Sun in the
middle of Virgo

Newborn image
1892: Sun in the
middle of Pisces

elongated path
of the Sun after
birth

comes into being *in the middle* within the two opposite signs: with the embryonic Sun in the middle of Virgo and with the newborn Sun in the middle of Pisces.

In transformation or projection to actual lifetime, while in the embryonic period it took around 7.8 years for the Sun to go through the constellation of Virgo (1888–1896), in the newborn period it took around thirty years for the Sun to go through the constellation of Pisces (1877–1907). It means that the embryonic background impulse may be more localized than the newborn one, since the latter one derived from Pisces for a whole thirty years. At the same time, it is interesting to see that the opposition came into being in the middle of the signs. Thus, if we assume a heterogenous streaming of forces regarding the constellations, or at least a difference in forces at the center versus the periphery, the question arises whether the force

line in the middle bears a striking role regarding the influence on the human being.

Anyway, at least in a pictorial sense, we can see here that *The Philosophy of Freedom* was born with the force of a newborn etheric Sun in the middle of Pisces, which points toward the middle of the "human evolution" mentioned in the previous section. It points toward the middle, where the ribbons that bind the two fishes together touch each other and constitute a union. This center may represent the urge of the birth of the principle of freedom in the evolution of human consciousness, in the crossroads of the continuous streaming between past and future.

Pisces and Virgo demonstrate two perspectives of the "world vortex." In the image of Pisces the past and the future are flowing into two directions. The map of evolution is spread out. If we transpose our approach to the life of nature, we can imagine a field soaking in water, and the seeds in it like little fishes absorb their whole life program of cosmic water with this earthly water. This life program contains the cosmic laws and spiritual aims of the world from the beginning to the end: here there is a start and an end—so that the life in Aries may begin according to a precise plan. In Virgo there is no beginning or end, because these principles have already been united. In Virgo the future *turns into* the past. The "outspread" plan becomes *internal*. The future appears in the womb of the Mother.[22]

Pisces means a quality spreading out as a world-ocean. Virgo aids the coming into being of a condensed quality and point of manifestation in the material world. In her forces of transformation and creation, Virgo guards the secrets of this "coming into being," the secrets of the transformation of cosmic substances into matter, the essence of the transformation and transubstantiation between the material and the spiritual world. Fishes are like substances floating in the cosmic ocean. Though there is a beginning and an end in this floating cosmic plan, for us this ocean is still perceivable as *without order*. The forces of Virgo introduce us into the *manifested world* within the cosmic ocean, and they bring the Great Plan into an *orderliness* perceivable for us.[23]

The Philosophy of Freedom as the central principle of human evolution was born with a newborn etheric Sun image pointing to the middle of the evolution represented by Pisces: to the driving force in the middle. Rudolf Steiner placed ethical individualism, the idea of the moral human being, the human being who can choose between good and evil, at the focal point of the evolution of consciousness. This was the *fruit* coming into being in the womb of the Mother, that Steiner gave to humanity with an embryonic Sun vibrating with the forces of Virgo in the background, reminding us of the Great Plan, where humanity struggling with adverse forces is the expectation of the divine world for the accomplishing of the idea of freedom in the Cosmos.

Though Steiner wrote this work in his "philosopher" and not spiritual teacher period, here we may recognize also (and again) the appearance of Jesus Christ in the etheric images: as a fruit in the womb of the Virgin, and at the same time as the sample image of human evolution appearing in the middle of human evolution (symbolically in the middle of Pisces).[24]

Remembering the importance of transitory constellations, here we cannot avoid recalling that 1892 was a remarkable year in human evolution. And though the transit of Jupiter in the

22 This is a further pondering on Sucher's images in *Isis Sophia II*, p. 51.

23 Steiner associated the worldview "psychism" to the forces coming from Pisces, where the basic assumption is the "ensoulment of the world." And he associated the worldview "phenomenalism" to the forces of Virgo, where the observation of phenomena, of experience is in the focus. As Virgo offered the *very inner landscape* for Steiner for his work during 1888–1896, it is interesting to see how his Anthroposophy, and *The Philosophy*

of Freedom, in which the whole content of Anthroposophy can be found, have developed out of his conception of Goethe's worldview, which he described as "pure phenomenalism.... This newer age must strive toward pure phenomena, toward pure phenomenology, with regard to the observation of external natural processes. And this was Kant's antipode Goethe. He demanded that the phenomena, the appearances, express themselves purely. He sharply emphasized that what takes place in the development of the intellect must remain quite distant from what is presented as a description of the phenomena and the phenomenal process itself. And Goethe repeatedly demands this *pure phenomenalism* in the sharpest, most admirable way" (*Die befruchtende Wirkung der Anthroposophie auf die Fachwissenschaften*, April 4, 1921, CW 76).

24 It is interesting to see the resonation with the etheric image of the birth of Solomon Jesus with a Pluto/Moon-Sun opposition at Virgo 14°10'/14°48' and Pisces 15°47' on March 5, 6 BC.

middle of Pisces and the transit of Saturn entering Virgo could have been main trigger points for the coming up of etheric images to consciousness for Steiner, the approximately 494-year megacycle of Neptune and Pluto, which reached its culmination in April 1892 geocentrically at 14°27' Taurus, at the ecliptic meridian of Aldebaran—which is also the position of Uranus throughout Steiner's first year after conception—gave a perfect timing for the elaboration of Rudolf Steiner's insights, for the broadest communal need.

The newborn Sun image of Pisces has a relation here to the transitory constellation through *Neptune*. Neptune, as the Lord of the Seas, is associated as a ruler with Pisces in classical astrology, besides Jupiter, and it was standing in Pisces at Rudolf Steiner's birth, at the point of the vernal equinox. As Willi Sucher said, "he lived and worked out that 'spring' situation in his message of Anthroposophy."[25] In 1892, when Neptune reached Pluto, we can see the encounter of impulses that may have led *in a profound way to the supersensible* and to *methods of its comprehension*. All this was in the constellation of Taurus, from where humanity was given forces for learning a *new language* and practicing it in life.

And if we consider the "last transits" of Rudolf Steiner (i.e., if we examine his death constellation), we arrive at an interesting point. He died on March 30, 1925, when the Sun was at about 15° Pisces. According to my calculations, his death Sun position was within 0.5° orb of the "etheric crossfire" on the embryonic-newborn axis in the middle of Virgo and Pisces. If we take into account the death chart as a profound "summary" of his connections to the starry world, Steiner died not only in close relation with the Pluto transits related to the Christmas Conference, but also with the Sun at a point in the zodiac that was a basic point of influence for *The Philosophy of Freedom* in his etheric constitution. The substance from this great work amalgamated with the Sun back to the cosmos at his death *at the same point* where the etheric seeds were born for it.

25 Sucher, *Practical Approach I*, p. 64.

Conclusion and "Where Are We Now?"

Practically, we should prepare a comprehensive study, where we look for all of the embryonic, newborn and transitory events in order to see how the individual unfolds throughout his life the impulses that came into being in his etheric body, making his life an individualized (or subjective) duration. A very special study would be the following up of the soli-lunar cycles, taking into account the ten cycles during the embryonic and the two cycles during the newborn period.

Here we could see main points of all of the three effects in the case of the Christmas Conference. In the case of 1907 we considered the embryonic and newborn effects. Between the Grail initiation (1899) and the Christmas Conference (1923) occurring at different times we could see a relationship between the embryonic and newborn images. And in the case of the birth of *The Philosophy of Freedom* (1892) we could see an etheric "cross-influence," when the etheric projections of two types manifested opposite zodiacal forces through the etheric Suns to the same years of age.

On the following chart (page 74), we can find the transiting trans-Saturnian planets for promoting further considerations for the reader.

In the introduction part of this article, I wrote about the one-year rhythm of the development of organic forces, and I assumed that the embryonic period can be expanded regarding the evolution of the etheric body for the first three months or so of actual life. Certainly, in everyday classical astrology, where there is a large number of examples for the working of secondary progressions, it is only the first two to three months that can be taken into account for examining people not on the level of initiates. Thus, this three-month extension seems to give the general rule for observations. However, if we raise the question of how the etheric body of an initiate is working, we may get to special phenomena.

If we extend the "open projection" of the Sun according to secondary progression to further newborn months in the case of Rudolf Steiner, the Sun reached Dubhe on August 5, 1861, after his birth, which comes up to the turn of 2021/2022

Transits of trans-Saturnian planets between 1861 - 1923/24
movement of embryonic and newborn Sun is highlighted

Birth of Rudolf Steiner - Prenatal Geocentric Planetary Distances
At Kraljevec, Latitude 46N22', Longitude 16E39'
Date: Monday, 25/FEB/1861, Gregorian
Time: 23:25, Local Time

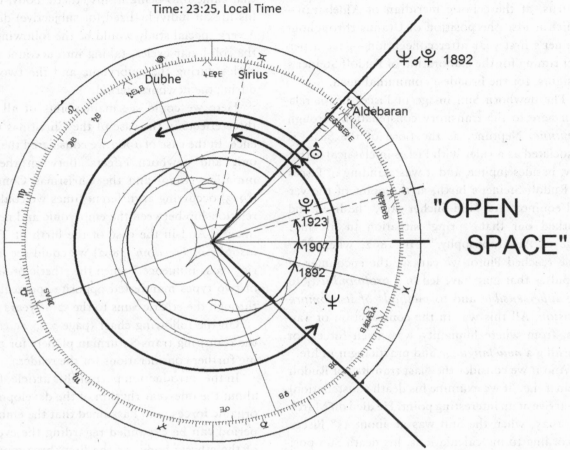

in projection (see figure on page 75). This position is in the 1° orb of his ecliptic Zenith, which was reached by the progressed Sun at the beginning of 2021 in projection. I think we may assume at least for an additional year (this way including the beginning of 2023) in the vicinity of the star's meridian if we accept a 1° orb.

If we take Rudolf Steiner's death into account as a point of departure and apply the secondary progression of the Sun to his first months after death, the Sun reached death Pluto—which was at the position where it was at the Christmas Conference (17°43' Gemini)—on July 3, 1925, which would fall to February 2021 in projection. The progressed Sun reached progressed Pluto and Sirius at 19°21' Gemini on July 5, 1925, which would fall to November 2022. Here I think we may again account for an additional year for 2023 as a scope of influence in our considerations.

Certainly, many questions arise. The etheric body is a time-force center for the human being, in constant connection with the etheric forces of the cosmos. On the basis of the researches, it is sure that there are etheric time mechanisms behind the physical and psychical manifestations in our life. However, it is still a question what happens with and within the etheric body of the *initiates*, who do not have to entirely remold their etheric

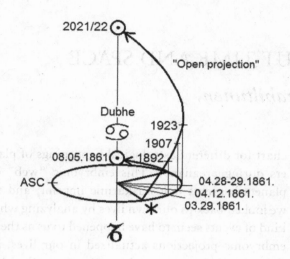

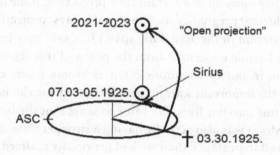

body between two incarnations, and what is the relationship of their etheric body to our causal time flow. Can there be any cosmic etheric activity extending into their special etheric body, even after their death, which makes itself felt much later in causal time—for them and for their followers—independently from the threshold events of their next incarnation?

If we attach great importance to Dubhe and Sirius in Rudolf Steiner's achievements, the question arises how we could have a connection with these achievements and with Steiner himself in these indicated special times, before and during the hundred-year anniversary of the Christmas Conference.

I would like to express my acknowledgements and gratitude to Joel Matthew Park, who allowed me to publish my thoughts here, and who helped with the correction of my English writing to make the text more understandable.

> "His image was always with me. He could always reach anyone. It is still the case now, when he has been long in the spiritual world. 'If people read only one line of my book *How to Know Higher Worlds*, I feel it is my duty to accompany them in all of their following earthly lives,' he said. I am absolutely sure that he does so, that he accompanies his disciples in his spiritual body. He was able to do it, because he was so inwardly connected with Christ."
>
> —WALTER JOHANNES STEIN

CONVERSATIONS ABOUT TIME AND SPACE

Natalia Haarahiltunen

This past year, 2022, started for me with an intense correspondence with Krisztina Cseri (see her article in the present volume) from Hungary, while my husband was translating the latest book of our Norwegian friend Are Thoresen, *Travels on the Northern Path of Initiation*. After a few months Krisztina and I had ended up in the middle of huge astrological themes with which we wanted to come to terms, and Are's book was released in print as an extended version in Finnish with the very latest teachings of Archangel Vidar. After a while we realized there was an interesting link with our astrological point of view to what Vidar was teaching. It all had to do with Time from different points of view.

How Our Friendship, Conversation, and Research Was Building Up

What we did first with Krisztina was to ponder quite a bit about the birth chart ascendant because it is such an important factor in the horoscopes; it is holding complicated metamorphoses with it when one approaches it from the conception moment throughout embryonic development as a certain goal for a person. We choose our ascendant (the moment and sign) long before our incarnation, to have it in synchronicity with our bodily form, vitality, world view, personality, etc. It has a condensed quality and it is in itself like a door to our birth chart. The degree of the sign of the ascendant (for example, 23° Leo)—or sometimes the opposite, descendant (23° Aquarius)—has a relationship to the Moon in the moment of conception.

From conception onward there occurs the cycle of the Moon ten times before birth, while the Sun moves across nine signs, if we are talking about the normal length of pregnancy. Through the Astrofire program, it is possible to produce an embryonic chart for different astrological happenings of planets during pregnancy. This embryonic "web" of planetary events holds a karmic imprint, and so we looked back to our own lives by analyzing what kind of events seem to have happened to us as these embryonic projections actualized in our lives, as they open up in a certain time projection. (One day during pregnancy is about 93½ days projection later on in the actual life span.) It is said they hold a karmic undertone from the past and this showed up in our observations often as events where certain important karmic people arrived for the first time into our lives. We came to sense that the birth Moon was also actually having a stronger influence and importance than we had previously realized. It is also very interesting to see how the ascendant degree in conception comes to be the same degree for our birth Moon. When we incarnate, we have our entry point from the cosmos from this degree of conception ascendant to be the later birth Moon. So, we can see the birth Moon and sign where it is situated as a link or "way back" to our incarnation approach. We are definitely very familiar with the qualities of our birth Moon sign. Moon holds our karmic past, and we can sense this lunar quality in the embryonic period and our own Moon, as well. The Moon is also a mediator of Solar impulses and it is always in some kind of relationship with the Sun, so we are all born at a certain point of cosmic discussion between the Moon and the Sun. After we are born there are still three months ("the newborn period") during which, especially, this Soli-Lunar relationship is very important for the coming life.

In general, we always find ourselves in the company of the Moon, Sun and Earth (especially in connection to the ascendant, as it shows which sign is on our horizon).

We are closely related to these three celestial bodies in our development both as humanity and as individualities. On this side of the threshold, in this world of illusion we live in, they are our ways of orientation and from them we "measure" our time, this causal time we are familiar with for the most part.

So, we had references to the past with embryonic projection, having many Moon-type qualities and methods of counting (e.g., the Hermetic Rule), and then there is a special moment when we incarnate here: our birth chart which holds a seed-potentiality of our spirit. We could also look to more of a "Sun" quality in the possibilities of our creative life unfoldment, known as the secondary progression. We also cannot forget the actual celestial events—the transits—as it seems we are "triggered" by the transits as they touch our birth chart or the progressive chart. It can be that we need this "transit push" to remind us of our chart possibilities. Still, it can seem sometimes to be a bit mysterious how the general time stream can have such an impact on our "individual duration of time" and potentialities in our charts. Probably, there is happening in our karmic sheaths exchanges of information between individual and general "times."

Searching for a Full Circle

As human beings we can find ourselves in many projections at the same time; in embryonic development, one can go through a period of "Sun in Pisces," for example (which can bring more Pisces quality and life challenges with it), meaning a projected period from when the Sun traversed the Pisces constellation during pregnancy, and is now projected to actual life—depending on the sign in which a person was conceived (e.g., in one's middle age if the conception moment was in autumn, Sun in Libra)—as a period of about seven to eight years. The same person has Sun in Cancer in the birth chart as a potential Spirit Sun shining and motivating that person. From the secondary progression which we call with Krisztina the "newborn period," we can still find one more Sun that is in this case in Leo. I say

"in this case" because in the " newborn period," which refers to the first three months after the birth, those three months become projected into the subsequent life span, starting from Cancer (because the person was born in Cancer), and then later on in life goes through Leo for thirty years, and then to Virgo, during which projection the person most probably will die because in the newborn period one degree is one year in the projection. Going through one zodiacal sign like Leo in our lives as a " "newborn" projection is then a projection which lasts thirty years. This secondary progression is known to be a more creative and Sun-like projection from its qualities, and it is deeply related to our "love for earth" as our wish for creative deeds.

The reader might have been able to comprehend that nine months of pregnancy plus three months after birth creates twelve, a full cycle in the zodiac. Through the astrosophical tradition of Willi Sucher and Robert Powell, we are more familiar with embryonic projection, but taking into consideration also the secondary progression we would create this full circle. Secondary progression ("newborn period") was very important, for example, for seer Edgar Cayce and astrologer/theosophist Dane Rudhyar, each in his own way. This possibility of creating a full cycle of twelve drew our attention and we started to explore more of the secondary progression which led Krisztina to research and write about it in connection to Rudolf Steiner's life. The reader can find a great deepening of many of these themes in her article.

Still as a summary we could say that we can have background tones that give hints as to where we are at the moment with certain lessons of karma and the zodiac (embryonic), and then we have the "birth seed" (birth chart) and a "future orientated" secondary progression (newborn) as our "love for earth creativity."

Now I would like to concentrate more on the general side of the questions that came up in our conversations from a meta-level concerning Time.

A lot of email exchange went on in May 2022:

Dear Krisztina!

I have been reading Steiner's lectures from 1924, 4 June. He speaks about Time and Sun and how Christ brought Time back from Sun to us. Steiner also says we can't experience time at all in space/spatial world. That we are always measuring it: from the Sun or clock. He points out that we experience time only as a soul experience and then we come out of spatial experience. Only then do we have time as a reality. On Earth, Time is not a reality at all.

So, what Steiner points out in this lecture, is that time belongs to our soul/inner life experience. Somehow, as a summary I understand that there is a real spiritual time. Christ brought something of a (real) time aspect back to us. It seems we only experience time in the soul.

This came up also in the Vidar teachings, that Time is the fourth member of Soul beside thinking, feeling and willing.

This Time aspect in us has been developing and growing more since "The Turning point of times" in Golgotha.

Love, Natalia

Dear Natalia!

Now I could read them and also RS's lecture. Quite difficult…I have the feeling that RS refers to the beings of time (to the being perspective of time) somehow when he says time is not reality here "in space." Because we definitely sense in a way time and this way it is a reality for us. Just in another consciousness, entering into the etheric world we perceive time in a different way as we get to know its other features. Probably we can see the activity of the beings of time as well. For example, the "algorithms" which the beings of time use seem to us a "reality" there.

It is quite difficult to adjust different approaches, as we spoke about it. Astrology provides the given time-projections which really happen. Somehow, we should differentiate where the activity of the time beings starts and ends with their algorithms and where starts and ends the work of the elementals (and other beings) when they "pack in" and "pack out" the etheric packages into our etheric body (coming to/from the embryonic and New Born period)

But it is also interesting how the "transits" are working. How the etheric imprints of epoch, birth, death are actualized by a spatial occurrence. Though there something spatial meets spatial influence. Time has no role there—in a strict sense.

Love, Krisztina

As a summary, we could say that there is time we are able to think as incarnated human beings—our causal time. Perhaps we can sense something of time as a member of soul? We have programs that are not exactly from this realm of time, but which have an inner link to the unifying aspects of Moon, Sun and Earth. How unconscious are those astrological projections and should we become more conscious about them: Can it help our inner orientation to accept better some challenging periods in life and have faith in creative good times, too? Could it help us to be more in harmony with our starry destiny and bring forth impulses still more in tune with divine timing? Are we really having more freedom when we are realizing our destiny?

Finally Traveling to See Friends

As was mentioned before, it is not easy to turn the calculating astrological methods into spiritual scientific questions, where we usually confront different beings that work behind everything.

Also, different spiritual beings might have their own point of view. Time understood in the basic human way might differ quite a bit from how gnomes might think about it.

This June as I travelled to Norway to visit our friends, I was able to ask directly from Archangel Vidar via Are more about the spiritual aspect of Time. Vidar is an Archangel that is well known in Edda and he has a special relationship to the Nordic countries. Are Thoresen is a veterinarian, healer and clairvoyant and he has written several books about his spiritual development that led him to work with the Christ-force and with Vidar and new etheric dimensions, where Christ dwells in his second coming.

Vidar had pointed out earlier that Time is actually the fourth member of the soul and that this aspect is growing in us. Actually, Vidar calls it Time-Christ-Karma. It seems to me that if we want to understand more about Christ's second coming we need to do our best to understand also about time and karma.

If we could grasp more about the real origin of time, could we better understand karma, too?

One can follow up a thought line of the Vidar-teachings already in Are Thoresen's book *Travels on the Northern Path of Initiation* to reach a fuller understanding of the gradual descent from the spiritual worlds and from the time dimensions that led to our very spatial experience. This happened in stages as the different etheric realms closed, one after another, before the time of Golgotha, and since then there have been gradual openings: in 1879, 1949, and 2019.

The following conversation will appear soon in a book by Thoresen, consisting of people's questions to Vidar.

A Question for an Archangel

NATALIA: "Vidar, what is time really about?"

ARE: The answer started with an imagination, and this imagination took two days. It showed clouds, masses of clouds. Not like those in the outer etheric realm,[1] but like those here in our world, cumulus clouds.

The second day the masses of white cumulus, these earthly-side clouds changed into stone, like streams of granite, like the rocks you may see in the coastline of Norway, polished by water and ice, by sea and storms.

There were three main streams of rock.

The third day the explanation came, with an overwhelming strength.

The explanation, received in intuition, was that time originated in the clouds of the outer etheric. From these clouds time then gradually materialized and hardened and became more and more materialized throughout history. It remains as three streams though. Then, at a certain point this hardening of time turned, and this point is called the "turning of times,"

in Rudolf Steiner's words "Zeiten-wende" (Zeiten is plural of Zeit, which means that several times turned at this time). This time was the year 33 after Christ, with the mystery of Golgotha, when the three streams of time turned from a downward and hardening path to an upward and spiritualizing path. This path will and must be our path back to the outer etheric where Christ can be found, and through which the three elemental realms can be transformed and Christianized.

The three streams of time also relate to the three elemental realms, one stream from the future, one from the past and one in the present.

The third realm, relating to Lucifer, comes from the future.

The second realm, relating to Ahriman, from the past, and the first realm from the present, where both Christ and the azuras may be found.

Vidar then also revealed a further aspect of our soul parts, namely the feeling, willing and thinking. These, too, originate in the outer etheric world, in the forces or parts of this world, which is the spiritual world.

The feeling is coming from the waters of this world, the thinking from the winds and the willing from the solid ground. All these parts of the outer etheric world had mirrored or reflected into the human soul, there creating soul abilities or faculties, that we with time can spiritualize and make our own, the spiritual thinking, the spiritual feeling, the spiritual willing and the spiritual "Time-Christ-Karma," for which we today have no specific name.

This knowledge also made sense of—or understandable—my earlier observation from thirty years ago, that I, by stepping into the etheric streams that stream between trees, can travel in time. As described in several of my earlier books, I can travel to the past by entering the etheric streams and move to the left, to the luciferic side of the body. By moving to the right, to the ahrimanic side of the body I can travel to the future.

These etheric streams between the trees are closely related to the clouds of the outer etheric world, where I now understand the origin of time is.

---

1   See description of the outer etheric realm in Are's book, *Travels on the Nordic Path of Initiation*.

The three time streams are thus also related to the luciferic, ahrimanic and Christ-forces (as well as the azuric forces), which thus give us the illusion of a physical existence. Time is thus part of that illusion, but in origin highly spiritual, as the clouds of the outer etheric are also the medium in which Christ will reappear in the etheric.

As such the fourth area of our soul is called "Time-Karma-Christ" by Vidar.

Many years earlier I had written about going back in time, of healing, and then connected this with the clouds. Here is a quote from my book *Pappel:*

During the following days, I had strong feelings for the Silurian age.

I read about it from different sources.

One night I dreamt about it: I saw the old clouds soaring across the sky, the sun sending its light down to the earth and the stars talking their ancient silent language. I saw it from above, 80 million years ago. However, I woke from this special feeling, and these old times disappeared. The old times when the earth conceived the sunlight with innocence. When the earth was still an altar, not a grave. When humanity itself was only a star glimmering thought.

It was difficult to come back to our time after this emotion, this dream....

Many years later, when I was sitting on the edge of a swimming pool far out in the countryside of Southern Florida, those feelings came over me again. I was there to teach American colleagues the art of pulse diagnosis. I stayed in the house of the organizer of the seminar and enjoyed her hospitality in the afternoons and evenings. The day's lesson had ended; I was at peace. A tiny chameleon crept up on the round glass table in front of me, between the can of Diet Coke and the cup of green tea. It sat motionless, for a long time. Every now and then, it blew up its bright red throat bladder; let it proudly play in the warmth, just to let it sink back into its motionless throat. Otherwise, there were no other movements. Then, slowly, it turned its head and with intensive eyes it stared at me. Unfathomably. With an

expression I had never seen before. We sat for a while like this, both equally still. I could see immemorable ages in those eyes, a depth of time with unsuspected proportions. The heat vibrated over the brown scorched pastures. The horses stood with heads hanging low in the shadow of a large oak tree that had huge amounts of Florida moss hanging from its branches. A herd of cows lay in the shadow of another oak tree. A mockingbird imitated his flying fellow creatures, whilst the lizard and I met eye-to-eye in ancient times.

Again, I felt "Silurian."

– And the old clouds still drifted on in the sky –

A few hours later a further teaching on time entered my soul, and to understand this we must recapitulate the concept of soul.

The soul has up till recently consisted of Thinking, Feeling and Willing. Thus, the spiritual understanding of different matters has consisted of Imagination, Inspiration and Intuition, the Imagination being the understanding in the thinking in the spiritual part of the etheric body, which also is described as the intellectual soul, the precursor of the Life Spirit, the Buddhi.

Further, the Inspiration being the understanding in the feeling in the spiritual part of the astral body, which also is described as the sentient soul, the precursor of the Spirit Self, the Manas.

Lastly, the Intuition being the understanding in the willing in the spiritual part of the physical body or the "I"-organization, which also is described as the consciousness soul, the precursor of the Spirit Man, the Atma.

Now, if it is so that a fourth part of the soul is under development, a part that Vidar calls or describes as "Time-Karma-Christ," then there must be a fourth level of cognition or understanding, a level of pure experience, of not "seeing," as in Imagination; of not communicating, as in Inspiration; and of not "being inside or one with" the spiritual being aspect of reality," as in Intuition; but "living or experiencing" the understanding. This level may need a new word (if it doesn't already exist in India), such as "Inexperiation."

Well, this level reached me after some hours. I experienced time and space being switched. I was almost sure that I was dying, but I did not. Later I thought that, after death, time and space become switched, so it was not strange that I thought I was going to die.

My Final Thoughts (for the Moment) about Time

Time is in its origin very spiritual, so much so that it is at times a bit hard to understand. We can read here above that as we are developing spiritually this mystery will be opening up more and more to each of us. My thoughts also go toward the resurrection body, which is developing in us. Could time as a soul member could be connected to the development of this spiritual body? That

would naturally be my next question that arises. Perhaps you, dear reader, also have a few questions arising by now. I am sure that our questions are always important for the spiritual world.

I have the feeling that adversarial powers might try "to steal our time" but we need enough time as humanity, to develop ourselves and be able to work for helping the Earth. Perhaps we can ask in our prayers for more Time for humanity, so that the future is met with enough spiritual preparation from our side and that the challenges of the sixth and the seventh cultural epochs won't meet us too soon.

> "The first chapter [of Genesis] presents the evolution of our planet through the first three earth rounds up to the fourth round, up to the moment when the human being was created. It closes then with the creation of the human being—right there, where the human being of the fourth round in the third root race first enters into incarnation. The Mosaic Genesis and Greek mythology present this in a very similar fashion. It is more clearly expressed in Greek mythology, which tells us of three streams from the three *Logoi*: Uranus, Chronos, and Zeus. At the beginning of our earth evolution, Uranus represents the first *Logos*, which altogether brings forth the first separation from the undifferentiated condition that was present in the preceding pralaya. Uranus was the being driving this forward; his opposite was Gaea. The origin of this earthly planet is rooted in them. Uranus is then, in connection with Gaea, the creative force. One could then say: 'In the beginning were Uranus and Gaea.' The second stream is the stream of soul: Chronos, who represents the purely psychic aspect of the soul. Then begins what is characterized as the pilgrimage of the soul, the union with Zeus, the god of kama-manas."
>
> —RUDOLF STEINER, *Concerning the Astral World and Devachan*, Dec. 8, 1903

THE STAFF OF MERCURY
AND THE SIGNIFICANCE OF THE PERIOD OF 39 HOURS
FROM CHRIST'S DEATH ON THE CROSS TO HIS RESURRECTION

Robert Powell, PhD

In antiquity the average embryonic period from conception to birth was considered to be ten lunar sidereal months, where one lunar sidereal month is the period of time taken by the Moon to orbit once around the zodiac and return to conjunction with the same star, which takes approximately 27.3 days. Multiplying by ten, we arrive at 273 days as the average length of the embryonic period from conception to birth. This is a period of thirty-nine weeks.

Nowadays, the period from conception to birth is generally reckoned to be thirty-eight weeks.[1] We shall return below to the theme of the shortening of the length of the embryonic period in modern times, a shortening that generally can be attributed to environmental influences.

If we take 30½ days as the average length of the solar month, twelve solar months equals 366 days, which is slightly more than 365.2422 days that is the actual length of the tropical solar year in days. The exact period of the average solar month is therefore closer to 30.437 days, rather than 30½ days, since 12 x 30.437 = 365.244 days.

Nowadays the formula used for determining the date of a child's birth is to add 266 days (thirty-eight weeks) to the last date of ovulation.[2] (Note that 266 days is one week less than the traditional 273 days of antiquity.) And according to WebMD Archives from March 23, 2006, the average length of pregnancy in the United States at the present time is approximately one week shorter than it was just over a decade earlier.[3] In general, it appears that influences of the modern world are affecting the length of pregnancy, generally shortening it.

Here we shall not go into the complexity of present-day medical research concerning the shortening length of pregnancy. Instead, we shall stay with the ancient comprehension of the embryonic period. It was that the cosmically determined period from conception to birth amounts on average to ten lunar sidereal months (273 days), and this plays a central role in star wisdom.[4] Simplifying this, since nowadays we do not think in terms of lunar months, but rather in terms of solar months, generally nine solar months is considered to be the duration of the embryonic period in modern consciousness. This would amount to 9 x 30.437 = 274 days, which is only one day different from the ten lunar months of antiquity.

Summarizing: 273 days is thirty-nine weeks, equating with ten lunar sidereal periods, a time period that was considered to be the average length of the embryonic period in the consciousness of human beings in antiquity. Interestingly, the average length of a full-term pregnancy in modern popular thinking is reckoned to be nine solar months, which equates with thirty-nine weeks plus one day, virtually identical to the time period in antiquity considered to be the length of pregnancy. However, as mentioned above, nowadays the length of the

---

1 Cf. https://calculator.net.

2 Cf. https://www.duringpregnancy.com.

3 Cf. https://www.webmd.com/baby/news/20060323
   /typical-pregnancy-now-39-weeks-not-40.

---

4 In my books *Hermetic Astrology*, vols. 1 and 2, I elaborate upon the discovery of my teacher in star wisdom, Willi Sucher (1902–1985), the founder of astrosophy ("star wisdom"), and that during each of these ten lunar sidereal months, a person's destiny for seven years of life is formed, giving rise to the "astrological biography" of each, lasting on average 10 x 7 = 70 years, the archetypal length of life indicated in Psalm 90:10. In the two *Hermetic Astrology* volumes, the connection of the embryonic period with the lunar sidereal months, which is not immediately obvious, is also made clear. It should be noted that we have to distinguish between the lunar sidereal month of approximately 27.3 days and the lunar synodic month—for example from New Moon to New Moon—of approximately 29.53 days.

embryonic period is considered to have shortened and is reckoned to be one week less than it was before, probably due to environmental influences such as electromagnetic radiation, etc.

In connection with this period of thirty-nine weeks, we come now to the main consideration of this short article. In antiquity it was not uncommon to draw parallels, by way of analogy, between a day and a year, or a day and a week, or other time-period correspondences of this kind. Thinking of thirty-nine weeks as an average gestation period, the thirty-nine hours between Christ's death on the cross and his birth as the Risen One can be seen, by way of analogy,[5] as a kind of "embryonic period." These thirty-nine hours comprise the time—following His death on the cross—of Christ's descent to the heart of the Earth, to the realm of the Earth Mother, the golden realm known as Shambhala (from the Tibetan tradition), together with the time of Christ's presence indwelling Shambhala, and His subsequent ascent from Shambhala back to the Earth's surface at the resurrection.

Following the archetype of fetal development, pregnancy is usually divided into three trimesters. Conveniently, thirty-nine weeks divides into three periods of thirteen weeks. By way of analogy, if we divide thirty-nine hours into three periods of thirteen hours, as an approximate indicator of this "embryonic period" of Christ in relation to what is referred to above in connection with His descent to the Earth Mother, we would arrive at the following outline of the unfolding of the three periods of thirteen hours:

(1) Good Friday, 3 p.m., to Holy Saturday, 4 a.m.: Christ's descent from the time of His death on the cross to His arrival in Shambhala, the realm of the Earth Mother.

(2) Holy Saturday, 4 a.m. to 5 p.m.: the time of Christ's indwelling of Shambhala, during which He received the resurrection body from the Earth Mother.

(3) Holy Saturday, 5 p.m., to Easter Sunday, 6 a.m., the time of Christ's ascent from

Shambhala back to the surface of the Earth and His encounter as the Risen One with Mary Magdalene.

Altogether, these three thirteen-hour periods, which are to be considered essentially as *approximate* time periods, comprise an *embryonic period* from the time of Christ's soul and spirit separating at His death from the physical body on the cross ("conception") to his "birth" as the Risen One at sunrise on Easter Sunday, beheld by Mary Magdalene.

The end of period (2), at about 5 p.m. on Holy Saturday, is very interesting. In connection with the Mystery of Golgotha, Rudolf Steiner often used the expression "the turning point of time." This was intended to convey the transition from the *descending* half of Earth evolution that lasted up until Christ's sacrifice, His death on the cross, whereby the descending half is associated with the planet *Mars*,[6] and the *ascending* half of Earth evolution, having to do with Christ's sacrifice leading to His resurrection and ascension, associated with the planet *Mercury*.[7]

"The turning point of time" is a temporal conception, the validity of which is indicated in footnote 6. However, in terms of Christ's descent to Shambhala

---

5 With one hour corresponding to one week in this analogy.

6 Mars is traditionally associated with the impulse of war. The crucifixion can be seen symbolically—but, in fact, *really and truly*—as a culmination of the warlike impulses of human beings of antiquity, with the nailing of the hands and feet of the Son of God to the cross in preparation for the cruel and agonizing crucifixion that lasted 2½ hours from the raising up of the cross until His death on the cross at 3 p.m. The spiritual dimension of the crucifixion is that thereby the Lamb of God sacrificed Himself for humanity and the Earth for the overcoming and transformation of the consequences of the Fall, pouring out Divine Love with the sacrifice of the blood pouring from His wounds, in order to bestow on human beings His *Christ consciousness* as the Cosmic "I AM," bearing in mind that the "I" lives in the blood. As a help in grasping the crucifixion as an archetypal healing of humanity, see the description of the *Staff of Mercury* at the end of this article, against the background of which we can understand the crucifixion as "the turning point of time" from Mars (descending half of Earth evolution) to Mercury (ascending half of Earth evolution), whereby Mercury represents the impulse of healing.

7 Ibid.

and the three "trimesters," each thirteen hours long, the deepest part of Christ's incarnatory descent was Shambhala, which He indwelled during period (2). At the end of this period (around 5 p.m. on Holy Saturday), His ascent began. As a spatial concept, this could also be thought of as "the turning point in time": from His descent to the beginning of His ascent, which, after the resurrection and His teaching the disciples for forty days, continued with His ascension.

Also highly significant, as indicated in the following quote from the visions of Estelle Isaacson, was His entry into Shambhala at the start of period (2) around 4 a.m. on Holy Saturday, which, as emerges in the following description, could also be thought of—from yet another perspective—as "the turning point in time," with the beginning of the reuniting of the Heavenly Father and the Earth Mother through the Divine Son:

> Through the anointing [by Mary Magdalene of] Christ Jesus [he] was prepared for the time immediately after his death on the cross, for the descent he would then make to the center of the Earth, where one must journey to receive the resurrection body. [Through the anointing] Magdalene was preparing him to descend to the center of the Earth, where he would lay gifts at the feet of the Mother, and where the Mother would cloak him in the resurrection body. I was taken then in vision to the center of the Earth, to the golden realm of the Mother. I saw the Holy Mother like a Sun at the center of the Earth. Her head was crowned with a headdress like a Sun. She glowed in an effulgence of warm, golden light. Countless beings, whom I can scarcely describe, lined a path leading to Her. They were thus arrayed to greet the Christ at his triumphant entry into Shambhala. They emanated golden light also. I saw Christ descend into their midst as they sang in ethereal voices that resonated throughout the Earth. This took place just after Christ Jesus died upon the cross. When he reached the realm of the Mother, these beings were present to greet him and touch him as he passed by, praising him and rejoicing in triumph. I could feel that this was the most important

moment of all time.[8] Never before had Christ penetrated into the fallen Earth to visit the Mother! I could hardly fathom that by anointing him, Magdalene—a human being—had prepared him for this moment! As he reached the Mother, She "cloaked" him in his resurrection body. The light streaming from him was astonishingly brilliant! There at the center of the Earth he became a luminous star.[9]

The Staff of Mercury

Among the healing impulses we are working with on the Shambhala path is the *Staff of Mercury,* the ancient symbol for healing used in the medical profession (see the final footnote to this article). It is interesting to consider historically when we first hear about this symbol as a healing impulse. It is with Moses. The Book of Numbers 21:4–9 says:

> Then the people of Israel returned to Mount Hor, and then continued southward along the road to the Red Sea in order to go around the land of Edom.
>
> The people were very discouraged and began to murmur against God, and to complain against Moses, "Why have you brought us out of Egypt to die here in the wilderness? There is nothing to eat here, and nothing to drink, and we hate this insipid manna. *[They are being fed from Heaven by manna!]*
>
> So, the Lord sent poisonous snakes among them to punish them, and many were bitten and died.
>
> And the people came to Moses and cried out, "We have sinned, for we have spoken against Yahweh and against you. Pray to Him to take away the snakes." Moses prayed for the people.
>
> Then Yahweh told him, "Make a bronze replica of one of these snakes and attach it to the top of a pole, and anyone who is bitten shall live if he simply looks at it."

---

8   The expression "the most important moment of all time" could be equated with Rudolf Steiner's designation "The turning point of time."

9   Estelle Isaacson, *Through the Eyes of Mary Magdalene* trilogy, vol. 2, p. 99.

So, Moses made the replica and whenever anyone who had been bitten looked at the bronze snake, he recovered.

This is not the whole of the Staff of Mercury, which shows two snakes curving up around the vertical axis, described here as a pole. It is one snake, but obviously this is the earliest reference, as far as I know, that one can find to the Staff of Mercury.

There is another very interesting reference to the Staff of Mercury in chapter three of the Gospel of St John. This is where there is the night conversation between Jesus and Nicodemus.

The indication that it is a *night* conversation points to the fact that Nicodemus is one of the seven "night" disciples of Christ. The twelve disciples referred to in the Gospels are the twelve "day" disciples. And there are seven "night" disciples such as Nicodemus, Lazarus, Joseph of Arimathea, and others. This is a much deeper level conversation than what one normally finds with the day disciples who are not necessarily spiritually orientated in the same way to the esoteric background of things as the night disciples.

In this conversation, some very profound things are spoken. The conversation begins in the Gospel of John (3:5, 9–12, 14–18), with Jesus saying:

What I am telling you is this, "Unless one is born of water and the Spirit, he cannot enter the kingdom of God."...
Nicodemus asks, "What do you mean?"
And Jesus replies, "You are a respected Jewish teacher and yet you do not understand these things? I am telling you what I know and have seen, and yet you won't believe me.... For only I, the Messiah, have come to Earth and will return to Heaven again. And as Moses in the wilderness lifted up the bronze image of a serpent on a pole, even so I must be lifted up upon a pole. So, anyone who believes in me will have eternal life. For God loved the world so much that He gave His only Son, so that anyone who believes in Him shall not perish but have eternal life. God did not send His Son into the world to condemn it, but to save it. There is no eternal doom awaiting those who trust Him to save them.

These words connect back to this first mention of the Staff of Mercury in relation to Moses and the bronze serpent. What is pointed to in the words that Christ speaks to Nicodemus? He is anticipating when He Himself will be raised up on a pole, or on a cross. Just as at the time of Moses, simply looking at the bronze serpent on a pole healed the people, so beholding inwardly (or outwardly[10]) Christ on the cross is analogous to that. Christ Himself is the Staff of Mercury. People will be healed and transformed through this experience.

This theme is taken up by Estelle Isaacson in volume 2 of her trilogy *Through the Eyes of Mary Magdalene*. First it should be mentioned that the present time is truly the time when the life and spiritual impulse of Mary Magdalene should come to awareness in human consciousness. This is told in a profound way in these three volumes by Estelle Isaacson out of her remarkable visionary capability. In receiving these visions, she was transported into the realm of spirit and she was able to speak everything that she beheld. There had to be somebody there to write it down.

Essentially, what emerges by way of her visions is what could be called "The Gospel of Christ's Second Coming." And this new Gospel is revealed through Estelle Isaacson by way of her beholding the Christ Mysteries through the eyes of Mary Magdalene, a woman who was a close disciple of Christ Jesus two thousand years ago. She was the one who anointed Him two days before His sacrifice on the cross. She was there to behold His death on the cross. She was there also for the entombment of His body. And then again, she was there in the garden of the Holy Sepulcher as (according to the Gospel account) the first person to behold Christ who had risen from the dead—risen from the realm of Shambhala, to which he had descended—Shambhala being the golden realm of the Mother in the heart of the Earth, as comes to expression in the previous quote from volume 2 of Estelle Isaacson's *Through the Eyes of Mary Magdalene*.

---

10 For those who were actually present at the crucifixion.

This extraordinary series of visions of Estelle Isaacson—which she has written down in the three volumes (or books) titled *Through the Eyes of Mary Magdalene*—tells us much that we do not find in the Bible. It gives the perspective of the eternal feminine, whereas what we find in the gospels is in general the masculine perspective of the male disciples of Jesus who are communicating what they beheld and experienced. *Through the Eyes of Mary Magdalene* is a testimony of the closest female disciple to Christ Jesus, noting that the Blessed Virgin Mary, as the mother, was more than a disciple. This trilogy was published in 2012 to 2014—again a very important time. The three volumes are hardly known to the general public, but they include deep and profound truths that are appropriate for our time if we wish to awaken and proceed further on our path of spiritual development.

Some of us were able to meet Estelle Isaacson, and I was fortunate to be able to work closely together with her for a period of ten years.[11] She had many other visions apart from what is contained in this trilogy. However, in my estimation the trilogy *Through the Eyes of Mary Magdalene* may be regarded as her main work.

What she beholds in the following vision at the tomb in the garden of the Holy Sepulcher is very significant. She beholds the Risen One:

> His body hovered over the tomb, arms extended in a cross. Rising up and intertwining like the caduceus [Latin for the staff of Mercury] along the axis of his Being were two serpents of light. The cross became the Tree of Life, the Sephiroth. His head was as the Sun, radiating dazzling beams of golden light. He stood upon a chalice Moon, and was surrounded by many angels. Behind him was a powerful winged being of light with wings outspread like those of an Eagle. All these things that I saw were *within* his resurrection body.[12]

---

11 Apart from various events and conferences that we did together in the United States and in France, we also wrote two books: *Gautama Buddha's Successor: A Force for Good in our Time* and *The Mystery of Sophia: Bearer of the New Culture: The Rose of the World*.

12 Isaacson, *Through the Eyes of Mary Magdalene*, vol. 2, p. 234.

This description implicitly links on to what was quoted above from the Old Testament regarding the healing power of the Staff of Mercury, which Moses, instructed to do so by Yahweh, raised up for the healing of those children of Israel who had been bitten by poisonous snakes. And this description also follows on from the prophetic words of Christ Jesus in the conversation with Nicodemus, where Christ indicates that He Himself would be raised up—here He is referring to His crucifixion—to be the healing remedy for all human beings beholding His sacrifice on the cross. And then, in these words of Estelle Isaacson, we see that the form of the caduceus, the *Staff of Mercury*, is intrinsic to the resurrection body of Christ.

When we put these together, we can begin to see the power of working with the *Staff of Mercury* exercise, bringing in the healing power of both the crucifixion and the resurrection into the weaving, joyous dance of life of our DNA. As modern science reveals, our DNA moves in this same form as that of the *Staff of Mercury*, whereby—as indicated in the above words of Estelle Isaacson, we can also hold in consciousness the connection between the *Staff of Mercury* and the Tree of Life, the Sephiroth Tree as it is also referred to.[13]

(To be continued...)

---

13 See the video "Introduction to the Shambhala Path" on the website of the Sophia Foundation (www.sophiafoundation.org) under Resources, for a video presentation of a way of working with the *Staff of Mercury* through movement, thereby offering a possibility (i.e., one possible way) of connecting with Christ's resurrection body. Through the Staff of Mercury, one can experience the ascending movement of Christ in His resurrection body, thus connecting consciously with the ascending half of the evolution of the Earth—the ascending half known as the *Mercury* period of Earth evolution that is generally recognized to have begun with Christ's ascension.

Asclepias

Embody Asclepius archetypes to become healthy. Diagnose, prescribe, and administer treatments to cocreate healing landscapes. Help nature by thinking like an insect. Cultivate care with compounded, segmented, and diversified actions.

Medicinal plants and parasitoid wasps cocompose hygienic farmscape immune systems. Biodynamic farmscaping restores habitats, prevents pests, and eliminates pesticides. Work with Ophiuchus rhythms to heal, defend, and beautify environments.

INTRO

Asclepius mythology offers methods for diagnosing health, prescribing treatments, and administering cures. Asclepius rhythms can be tracked with biodynamic calendars to practice auspicious habitat restoration. Biodynamic restorationists are healers who pledge to beautify landscapes and maintain healthy environments. Biodynamic farmscapes are healing temples and living pharmacies.

We have achieved successes during years spent practicing biodynamic restoration with Asclepius rhythms: Acres of habitats that restore populations of native plants and wildlife were established; Rare and vulnerable species of pollinators were hosted; Environmental quality was improved; Harvestable goods were yielded; Pesticides were eliminated.

First, we will introduce the Greek demigod Asclepius, his daughters the Asclepiades: Iaso, Panacea, Hygieia, Aceso, Aglaea, his teacher: Chiron the centaur, and his zodiac constellation: Ophiuchus. Second, we will introduce insects and link Ophiuchus to parasitoid wasps. Third, we will define farm anatomy and connect the Asclepiades to landscape features.

Fourth, we will define farmscaping, present biodynamic farmscaping, provide pest prevention practices, and profile *Asclepias*, Milkweed. Fifth, we will present astro-ecological calendrics and offer recommendations for how and when to work with Ophiuchus rhythms to beautify landscapes and defend healthy environments. Sixth, we will conclude, offer thanks, and provide references.

ASCLEPIUS

Asclepius ("to cut open") is the Greek demigod of health and medicine, son of sun god Apollo and human Coronis. One legend tells that Artemis killed Coronis because she was unfaithful to Apollo, while another tradition says she died in labor. Apollo rescued his son by cutting open (cesarean, scalpel) the womb of Coronis. Coronis was immortalized as the constellation of Corvus, the crow.

Asclepius first learned medicine from Apollo before being mentored by Chiron the centaur.

Chiron was a renowned healer and teacher who was accidentally wounded by his student Hercules during battle. Chiron could not cure himself despite his supernatural healing powers, so he was immortalized as the constellation Sagittarius.

Asclepius learned the secret arts of healing from observing or saving wounded serpents. The single snake-entwined rod of Asclepius (⚕, the *asklepian*) continues to signify the medical arts to this day. The asklepian represents healing processes: the snake symbolizes medication and regeneration, while the rod symbolizes recuperation and sanitation.

Epione ("soothing") and Asclepius had five daughters, the *Asclepiades*: Iaso ("recuperation"), Panacea ("all-curing"), Hygieia ("health"), Aceso ("inflamed"), and Aglaea ("glow"), and three sons: Machaon (medic, herbalist, surgeon), Podalirius (medic), and Telesphorus ("completion," child care). Asclepius and his lover Aristodama had one son, Aratus (poet).

Zeus killed Asclepius with a thunderbolt when the physician's supernatural ability to revive the dead threatened the balance between mortals and immortals. The body of Asclepius was immortalized as the constellation Ophiuchus ("serpent-bearer") and the spirit of Asclepius was resurrected as a god of Mount Olympus. Asclepius was worshiped in Greece as the god of healing, medicine, and doctors.

The cult of Asclepius was most popular in Greece during the sixth century BC. More than three hundred healing temples (*Asclepieia*) are known, including the largest in Epidaurus on the Argolid Peninsula. Asclepieia are often mountain temples or spas where "forest bathing" and social medicine were practiced by physicians, priests, and therapists. Both the physical and spiritual health of patients were treated.

Asclepieia healthcare practices included incubation: sleeping in sacred spaces to receive curative dreams or experience meditative consciousness; purgation of food, art, and offerings; medication; dietary nutrition; internal surgery; cleansing in baths; physical fitness in gymnasia. Asclepieia mascots were often Aesculapian

Snakes [*Zamenis longissimus* (Laurenti, 1768)], dogs, and roosters.

Asclepiad was an honorary title bestowed on generations of Greek physicians who followed the healing arts of Asclepius. One notable Asclepiad was Hippocrates of Kos, the "father of modern medicine." The Hippocratic Oath was sworn to uphold medical ethics. The oath begins:

I swear by Apollo Healer, by Asclepius, by Hygieia, by Panacea, and by all the gods and goddesses, making them my witnesses, that I will carry out, according to my ability and judgment, this oath and this indenture.

The Asclepiades each represent components of health and healing, here linked with sacred elements:

1. Iaso = Recuperation = Earth
2. Panacea = Medication = Water
3. Hygieia = Sanitation = Air
4. Aceso = Regeneration = Fire
5. Aglaea = Beautification = Spirit

Health occurs when the five Asclepiades are balanced and unified as one polyrhythmic system.

The Asclepiades can inspire observations that indicate health diagnoses and treatments. When diagnosing health ask: Which of five Asclepiades processes are present? What features show such health processes? Which of the five processes are balanced? What degree of balance is present in a health system? How can systems become unhealthily imbalanced? Which of five health processes are absent? How can absent processes become present through treatments?

The principles of healing represented by Asclepius and the Asclepiades are not restricted to the health of human beings alone. Asclepius is a demigod who is connected to the nonhuman world through his teachers: the god Apollo, the centaur Chiron, and the wounded serpents. The mythology of Asclepius can inspire us to diagnose and treat not only human bodies, but the bodies of societies and environments.

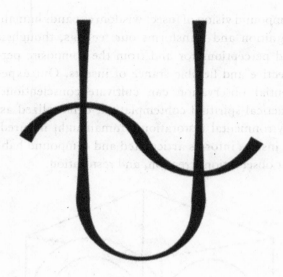

OPHIUCHUS

Ophiuchus or Serpentarius ("The Serpent Bearer") is a constellation that represented Asclepius and his snake-entwined rod to the Romans. Ophiuchus represents the paradoxical concept of pharmakon (remedy/poison, healer/destroyer), a unified duality that forms the basis for contemporary pharmacology: lightness and darkness; composition and decomposition; fertilization and putrefaction.

Ophiuchus is aligned with the Galactic Center, the dark heart of the Milky Way, and rests between 5° Scorpio and 11° Sagittarius (Nov. 29 to Dec. 21). Ophiuchus is excluded from dominant twelve-sign zodiacs due to odd indivisibility or superstitious fear of the "unlucky" number 13. Ophiuchus has similar yet distinct attributes of both stinging Scorpio and six-limbed Sagittarius.

Scorpio is a fixed water sign represented by the scorpion. Scorpio was traditionally ruled by the planet Mars and is now also ruled by Pluto. Greek myth recounts how Orion the hunter bragged that he could kill any animal. When Orion then threatened to kill every animal, Earth goddess Gaia sent the scorpion to challenge Orion. Scorpio cautions against human arrogance toward the nonhuman world.

Sagittarius is mutable fire, associated with the transformational power of the ember. Sagittarius recalls the earthly and cosmic wisdom of Chiron through its rulership by the benefic planet Jupiter. The Centaur is a sign of duality and the fusion of opposites. Sagittarius appears at the darkest time of the year in the northern hemisphere, signifying the warmth generated by inspired creativity.

Ophiuchus is ruled by both heavenly Jupiter and underworldly Pluto and is no more fixed-water (ice) than mutable-fire (ember). The constellation contradictorily represents the dark-light occurring at the death-birth time of Solstice. Ophiuchus no more rests than changes between archetypes of stinging Scorpion and six-limbed and arrow-shooting Centaur.

Ophiuchus is both shrewd terrestrial hunter and rebellious cosmic predator, an autonomous and dangerous regulator of nonconformity and self-authority. The constellation becomes archetypally element-fluid by simultaneously phasing from water to fire and fire to water through air and earth. Ophiuchus expands and contracts, from both outside to inside and inside to outside.

Ophiuchus represents the outsiders and outcasts of society: heretics, pirates, or witches. Ophiuchus challenges the harmonious structure of the twelvefold zodiac, reminding astrologers to remain fluid, non-dogmatic, and open to new elements in their practice. Scorpio shows the antagonism between human and insect, while Sagittarius represents the possibility for human and non-human collaborations. Ophiuchus shows ways for humans to heal environments.

ORGANICS

Organics is a living science of metamorphosis, here defined as the synergy of two disciplines: *anthoposophy* and *arthroposophy*. Anthoposophy (*ánthos* = flower) is a method of cognitive transformation wherein *human becomes plant*. Such *plant wisdom* is learned through feeling, thinking, and willing the stages of plant metamorphosis. Arthroposophy (*árthron* = joint) is a method of cognitive transformation wherein *human becomes insect*. *Insect wisdom* is synchronized and syncopated with plant wisdom.

Organics observes from compound perspectives and articulated stances, interlinking humans and plants through insects. Plants and insects form one unity, the *plant-insect*, here defined according to organics as *antho-arthroposophy: wisdom from plant-insects*. Plants mutually share life with insects, which reciprocally distribute spirit for plants. The following sections describe insects, plant-insects, and insect-humans from the polyrhythmic stance of organics.

Insects

Arthropods (Phylum: *Arthropoda*) are invertebrate animals (multicellular *eukaryotes* that are motile, consume organic matter, and reproduce sexually) with *exoskeletons, segmented bodies,* and *jointed appendages*. Insect wisdom is practiced from the becoming-process *"arthro-pod."* "Arthro" are articulated, jointed, or limbed bodies connected to turn and flex as fulcrums. "Pods" are bodies that expand-contract between inside and outside, beings grounded with bases that provide movement.

Arthropods with six legs belong to subphylum: *Hexapoda*. *Hexapods* constitute the largest number of species of arthropods. Hexapod *heads* [roots] are composed of six fused segments, affixing *antennae* and *mouthparts: mandibles, maxillae, labium, and labrum; thoraxes* [leaves] are composed of three fixed segments, affixing *three pairs of legs* and variably *two pairs of wings;* abdomens [flowers] are variably composed of four to eleven segments bearing *reproductive and sensory appendages*.

Hexapods with *chitinous exoskeletons,* threefold physical body of *head-thorax-abdomen, six legs, compound eyes,* and *two antennae* belong to class: *Insecta* (*éntomos,* "cut into pieces"). Insects are the most speciose class of life on Earth. Insect exoskeletons are sclerotized polysaccharide crystals composed of *chitin* (plant cellulose [earth-carbon + water-oxygen + fire-hydrogen] + [air] nitrogen). Plants and insects exist in synchrony, syncopation, and supplementation through coevolution.

Insect eyes are composed of multifaceted and tessellated *ommatidia,* independent photoreceptors that are sensitive to light and movement. The

compound vision of insect wisdom expands human cognition and transforms our feelings, thoughts, and perceptions for and from the composite perspective and flexible stance of insects. Our experiential observation can cultivate conscientious practical-spiritual contemplation, externalized as environmental restoration. Human sight inspired by insects informs articulated and compound habitat observation, creation, and restoration.

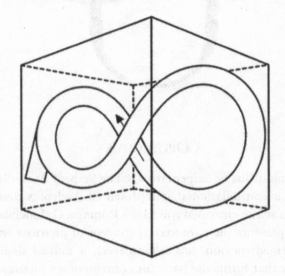

Plant-Insects

Plant and insect morphology is comparative yet nonlinear. Insects exhibit complete or incomplete metamorphosis, which synchronizes and syncopates with plant metamorphosis. While plants sustain polyphonic chords, insects arpeggiate monophonic melodies. Plant stages can be seen at once; insect stages are hidden through time. Plants drone while insects melodize.

Organics proceeds with fully conscious, intentional imaginations of metamorphological stages. Transpositions from Earth-Water-Air-Fire; Mineral-Plant-Animal-Human; Root-Leaf-Flower-Fruit; and Egg-Larva-Pupa-Imago tetrads are thought in chorus:

1	Earth	Mineral	Root	Egg
2	Water	Plant	Leaf	Larva
3	Air	Animal	Flower	Pupa
4	Fire	Human	Fruit	Imago

Involution coils from earth to water, air, fire, and back to earth; *Evolution* spirals from fire to air, water, earth, and back to fire. Involution is becoming self, while evolution is becoming other. Thereby, organics is an evolutionary theory of humans becoming animals and plants through cognitive metamorphosis. Human minds blend patterns and processes obscured to our senses. One imagines juvenile and senile rhythms at once, life flowing no more backward than forward. Continuous and discontinuous sequences cycle together and are observable in both patterns and processes.

The pattern of *spherical* Earth-Root-Egg becoming *radial* Air-Flower-Pupa is one unified process mediated by polyrhythmic Water-Leaf-Larva and Fire-Fruit-Imago. Spherical centers expand and distort as amplified roots or eggs. Radial peripheries contract and compress as condensed flowers or pupae. Water-Leaf-Larva and Fire-Fruit-Imago flow together to form midpoints of lemniscates. Metamorphosis is a *panarchy* of complex adaptive cycles among linked systems.

Insect-Humans

Internal duplets of *imaginal discs* grow within larvae and transform during pupation to form external duplets of "pods," such as antennae, legs, or wings. Thus, imaginal discs are inner larval ghosts masking outer imago selves. Below ground, the larvae dream of above ground eclosions. From the maggoty solum through the wormy subsoil, agents of putrefaction grow intestinal and parasitical, sacrificing sunlight and resigning mutation, but retaining formative forces. The suppression of larva-force secretes invaluable soil health and a corresponding larva-imago hybrid: *the human brain*.

Humankind is a puzzle of all taxa, one *subscendent* organism less than the sum of organs, each unique being-in-becoming. Vertebrae contract to skulls, which expand to brains. Without contraction, the torso would interminably radiate. Instead, rhythmic forces condense the swelling brain, fluids folded over-in-around themselves, compressing tessellated hemispheres

as unfurled wings. The brain swells in a well of damp darkness, bound within bone, excluded from eclosion. Our brain-larva compresses forces of imagination that *eclose* and *echo* as imagos: living thought butterflies.

Solum is soil ensouled by sun. Inner-solum rests within the terrestrial; outer-solum cycles within the celestial. The soil-larva hatches with inner-solum nutrition assimilated from respiration and digestion; the brain-larva hatches with outer-solum perception digested from thinking and feeling. Imagine our brain-roots within mobile skull-containers, inverted toward astral terroir. Humans and insects are plants inverted in form and function:

- Air–Flower–Pupa–Abdomen–Reproduction
- Water/Fire–Leaf/Fruit–Larva/Imago–Thorax–Motion
- Earth–Root–Egg–Head–Perception

Imagine a threefold plant-insect-human-system *lemniscate*: Amplifications and compressions phase-synchronize-syncopate at once among two morphological fields. Perception amplifies from root-egg-head, reproduction compresses from flower-pupa-abdomen, and locomotion filters and echoes from leaf-larva/imago-thorax at the crossing point. Locomotion is the rhythmic element that phases perception with reproduction in synchrony and syncopation. Humans can imagine transformation from one organism into another through cognitive metamorphosis as one locomotive plant-insect self.

Imagine insect metamorphosis in *reverse*: larval involution flowing to evolution, inverted during pupation. Such motion is an inversion of the involutionary enactment of imaginal reproduction. Pupal countermovement puppets larval and eggy ingress. Inward folding flows from pupae to gastrulae: concave buds forming larval mouths. Evolutionary drive from pupae effects imaginal egress. Outward folding flows from the pupae to *blastulae*: convex buds forming potentiated embryos. The first insect embryonic fold becomes input, while the first human fold becomes output, defining body cavities.

Pupal inversions illuminate how embryonic germ layers contract *ambience*: endoderms and ectoderms with intermediate mesoderms sequester outer worlds and reproduce interior environments through invagination. The ambient embryonic fold is illuminated with inner light, an internalized projection of nature as consciousness. *Protostomes* fold spirit inside-out, while *deuterostomes* fold spirit outside-in. Thus, arthropod, mollusk, and nematode consciousness are externalized as an *environmental soul*, while chordate and echinoderm consciousness are internalized as an *organismal soul*.

Environmental soul is continuously transforming, encompassing all species and individuals. Insect souls are from outside at one with inside; human souls are from inside at one with outside. The outer souls of insects include our inner human souls, while our inner human souls are nested in the outer souls of insects. Humans are the habitats and souls of insects. Thus, naive *entomophobia* not only threatens, but kills our environmental consciousness. Why are we afraid of our environmental souls?

We are afraid to sacrifice our egos for our environments. Our entomophobia disables our physical and spiritual growth. We worsen our abilities to establish healthy soul habits and habitats with our persistent, irrational fears of insects. Our unreasonable and uncontrollable anxieties negatively affect Earth. We estrange ourselves from nature and exacerbate extinctions by avoiding insects. We must systematically desensitize ourselves through collaboration with insects to help restore our planet.

Parasitoid Wasps

Parasitoid wasps are the most speciose animals on Earth. Mated female parasitoid wasps hunt and sting prey with syringe-like *ovipositors* to lay eggs either inside or outside hosts. Internal parasitoid wasp eggs are often injected with secretions including venoms and viruses, which help protect wasp larvae and avoid detection by hosts. Hatched wasp larvae feed inside or outside of hosts who are either immediately immobilized or gradually

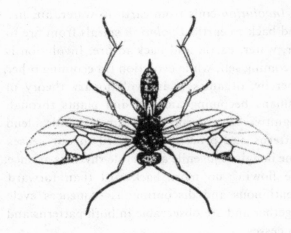

killed. Hosts include eggs, larvae, pupae, or adults of various arthropods, including crop pest beetles, bugs, flies, and moths, and other parasitoids (*hyperparasitoids*).

Wasp larvae selectively feed on inessential host organs during growth until spinning cocoons and pupating either inside or outside of dying hosts. Eclosed adult wasps feed mostly on nectar and mate. Sexes of wasp offspring are actively determined by mothers in a process known as *haplodiploidy*: daughters hatch from fertilized eggs (mother + father chromosomes = *diploid* sisters); sons hatch from unfertilized eggs (mother chromosomes = *haploid* brothers). Sisters are often more genetically similar to each other than to their mothers; sons are fatherless clones of their mothers.

We posit that parasitoid wasps symbolize Asclepius: Six-limbed hunters who kill with venomous yet life-giving stings; queer reproducers and strange selves who grow inside/outside others; odd carnivores/vegetarians who are no more guests than hosts; and wounded healers who are vilified by entomophobes. We can feed, shelter, and sustain populations of parasitoid wasps with annual and perennial insectaries, sources or alternate prey, and diverse and pesticide-free landscapes. Overall, abundance, richness, and diversity of parasitoid wasps indicate healthy landscapes.

ASCLEPIADES

The fivefold path of healing represented by Asclepius and the Asclepiades can be applied to landscapes through an understanding of occult anatomy and physiology. Occult physiology posits: organ systems are internalized for organisms and externalized for environments; internal organ systems correspond with external environments. Farms are living multicellular organisms composed of complex relations of specialized tissues and organs. Farm tissues are assemblages of similar biological, structural, or functional units; farm organs are composed of tissues that collaborate to perform similar functions.

If farm anatomy is classified and described according to occult physiology, then farm organs can be identified, conserved, and enhanced to address and prevent farm disorders. Our model environments-organisms will be habitat features that host insects, the most abundant and diverse class of life on earth. Articulated and compound observations from insect wisdom can inform therapeutic practices for farm restoration via *conservation biocontrol* and *biodynamic farmscaping*.

Farm anatomy will be classified and described according to the physiology of ten insect organ systems. First, each insect organ system will be briefly explained. Second, insect organ systems will be related with insect habitat features to identify farm organ systems. Third, farm organ systems will be described in form and function. The resulting ten farm organ systems combined constitute a biodynamic farm organism or farmscape. Farmscapes are enhanced for the benefit of basic life processes: breathing, warming, nourishing, secreting, maintaining, growing, and generating.

Farm Anatomy

The Asclepiades and associated health processes are linked to insect organ systems as follows:

1. *Iaso* = Recuperation = Exoskeletons + Muscular Systems + Respiratory Systems: *Exoskeletons* are external shells that protect and support arthropods as living vessels. The internal body cavity (*haemocoel*) sequesters life and secretes spirit. Thereby, arthropods are living vivariums, microcosmic presentations of macrocosmic nature that transport habitats across and within environments. *Farm skeletal systems* are both invisible *boundaries* and visible *parent materials*. Farmscape exoskeletons welcome wildlife from exterior to interior, balancing temporary-permanent exclusion-inclusion for privacy-publicity, while supporting organisms with physical structure-texture. *Muscular systems* provide flexibility and strength for digestion and locomotion, allowing for dispersion and colonization. Appendages such as legs and wings are powered by striated muscles that run through the exoskeleton and control motion. *Farm muscular systems* are *beetle banks* and *hedgerows*. Beetle banks (*apodemes*) and hedgerows are linear structures composed of earthen mounds and native grasses or dense woody vegetation that provide foods, nests, and shelters for wildlife. Farmscape muscles work with exoskeletons to delineate field boundaries, while improving soil, water, and air quality. *Respiratory systems* actively or passively transport oxygen and carbon dioxide to and from tissues. Air is inhaled and exhaled through *spiracles*, pairs of apertures on the thorax and abdomen, which open to *tracheae* and *tracheoles* that aerate internal organs via diffusion. *Farm respiratory systems* are *windbreaks*. Windbreaks are composed of permanent dense yet porous vegetation that filters airborne sediments. Farmscape respiratory systems protect crops and wildlife, while improving soil, water, and air quality by reducing erosion, trapping sediment, and screening pollutants.

2. *Panacea* = Medication = Digestive Systems + Endocrine Systems + Circulatory Systems: *Digestive systems* extract nutrients from foods, which are ingested, metabolized, and assimilated for energy, growth, and reproduction. One-way closed systems or *alimentary canals* process food from the head and *salivary glands* to the storing-grinding *foregut*, secreting-absorbing *midgut*, storing-excreting *fat body*, and absorbing-excreting *hindgut*. *Farm digestive systems* are *cover crops*. Farmscape digestive systems composed of grasses and forbs

planted for seasonal vegetative cover identically improve soil and water health, while regulating crop pests and enhancing wildlife. *Circulatory systems* cycle *hemolymph* (blood) openly and freely within exoskeletons, bathing substances among tissues and organs, while protecting against disease or predation, and facilitating motion and reproduction. *Farm circulatory systems* are *rivers, streams, and water bodies.* Farm circulatory systems can be conserved by enhancing areas adjacent to watercourses or water bodies with native trees and shrubs that create shade and habitat, while reducing pollution. Farmscape wetlands can be created, restored, and maintained for improved circulation of nutrients and wildlife. *Endocrine systems* transport *hormones* within the haemocoel and throughout the hemolymph. Hormones carry messages secreted from specialized glands to direct processes of growth, molting, metamorphosis, and reproduction. *Farm endocrine systems* are *field borders* and *paths.* Field borders interconnect farm organ systems with trails of permanent herbaceous buffer strips, filter strips, wind barriers, or other strips of vegetation established at edges or around perimeters of fields. Farmscape endocrine systems can protect crops and wildlife, while improving soil, water, and air health.

3. *Hygieia* = Sanitation = Immune Systems: *Immune systems* innately fight infections with physical barriers and immune responses. Physical barriers include the outer *cuticle* of the *integument* and inner *peritrophic membrane* of the midgut. Immune responses against haemocoel infections include *humoral production of antimicrobials* and *cellular encapsulation, nodulation, and phagocytosis by hemocytes.* *Farm immune systems* are *insectaries and meadows.* Annual or perennial insectaries are composed of abundant and diverse communities of companion plants and wild beneficial insects that prevent or regulate crop pests. Farmscape immune systems link farm organs, from outer exoskeleton to inner circulatory, digestive, and endocrine systems. Thus, conservation or restoration of annual-perennial insectaries is of fundamental importance for healthy farm anatomy and physiology. The

foundation of harmonized disease regulation must be grounded from prevention rather than medication. Therefore, preventive enhancement of annual or perennial insectaries should be of primary concern when planning balanced farmscapes.

4. *Aceso* = Regeneration = Reproductive Systems + Excretory Systems: *Reproductive systems* sexually produce offspring via eggs from females that are fertilized by males and oviposited by females or asexually produce offspring without males via *parthenogenesis.* Eggs are oviposited near, on, or within foods for *neonate* larvae or nymphs. High reproductive rates and short generation times afford rapid adjustment to environmental changes. *Farm reproductive systems* are *croplands* or *greenhouses.* Farmscape reproductive systems can be enhanced with crop rotations that improve soil health, regulate weed pressure, provide forage for wildlife, and improve crop vigor. *Excretory systems* expel toxic metabolic waste products while conserving water. *Malphighian tubules,* a system of branching ducts, extract waste products from the hemolymph to the hindgut, where excrement is voided primarily as solid nitrogenous compounds. *Farm excretory systems* are *pastures and compost.* Pastures established to process and eliminate wastes for fertility can improve both livestock and wildlife nutrition and health, while protecting soil and water. *Silvopasture systems* of integrated trees, shrubs, wildflowers, and grasses provide diverse forage for enhanced farmscape excretion and fertility.

5. *Aglaea* = Beautification = Nervous Systems: *Nervous systems* embody internal and external sensory information. *Central nervous systems* coordinate body functions, while *peripheral nervous systems* sense stimuli from environments. External senses of taste, smell, sight, warmth, and hearing are detected by sensory organs including antennae, compound and simple eyes, hairs (*setae*), and *tympana.* *Farm nervous systems* are *farmers.* Farmers remain attentive with internal senses of life, self-movement, and balance that are deepened with external senses of speech-tone and concept.

Farm nervous system health can be enhanced through mindful practices and studies that assess, inventory, and monitor internal and external farmscape features. Farms become beautified when farmers themselves embody Aglaea by farmscaping with Iaso, Panacea, Hygieia, and Aceso features.

The five Asclepiades with equivalent health processes and features are summarized as follows:

1. *Iaso* = Recuperation = Beetle Banks + Boundaries + Parent Materials + Windbreaks

2. *Panacea* = Medication = Cover Crops + Field Borders + Rivers + Streams + Water Bodies

3. *Hygieia* = Sanitation = Hedgerows + Insectaries + Meadows

4. *Aceso* = Regeneration = Croplands + Greenhouses + Pastures

5. *Aglaea* = Beautification = Farmers

Habitat-Humans

Humankind can enrich habitats from expanded cognition when we collaborate with nature, *antho-arthropomorphized*. Insect-humans sense with compound perspective, move with segmented articulation, breathe rhythmically with environments, and reproduce with abundance, richness, and diversity. Thereby, insect-human observation becomes one with observable habitats through living polyrhythmic collaborations: planned, prepared, installed, and maintained together.

The process of insect habitat restoration or enhancement is mutually dynamic: The human is *becoming a habitat* and the habitat is *becoming a human* through interconnected actions. *Becoming habitat* helps humans integrate patterns and processes from nature. Integration pauses anthropocentrism, cycles empathy, and flows from observation toward health. We imagine habitat with plants, we inspire habitat through insects, and we intend habitat as humans.

Insects show humankind that habitats *subscend* (are less than the sum of their parts), metamorphose, and are one. A plurality of perspectives plus free mobility of thought afford humans the expanded capacity to help nature heal. Practices modeled after such polyrhythms include habitat observations, creations, and restorations, together transforming the practice and spirit of habitat restoration. Humankind manages and supervises habitats from within as the nervous systems of our eco-selves.

Humans must learn to reciprocate the inescapable soul embrace from insects to decelerate anthropogenic extinctions. Conscious reciprocation proceeds through restoration. The process includes internal integration of our external soul as intelligible by mind. Once integrated, our external souls eclose as insect-humans, with the plant and mineral worlds as grounds for presentation. Thus, willful inhabitation of our environment-soul can inspire imaginative habitat-human performances via *rhythmics*.

Habitat-humans become one through rhythmics. Farmscaping performed in time, self-metamorphosing from humans to animals, plants, and soils. Equalizing the heard and ~~heard~~, human and non-human, celestial and terrestrial—cycling between soils and stars. Ourselves becoming-gardened through seasonal festivities: ritual practices perennially performed according to prescriptions of nature. Sharing aesthetics flowing between Earth and Cosmos, human-habitats live in concert: one audience-stage-venue, producer-consumer-decomposer, composer-performer-listener.

BIODYNAMICS

Farmscaping

Farmscaping is an ecological pest management strategy that enhances habitats for wild beneficial organisms who prey on crop pests, thus eliminating any need for pesticides. Farmscaping aka *conservation biocontrol* is the sum of *conservation biology* and *integrated pest management (IPM)*. Conservation biology is the study of nature for the protection of biodiversity. IPM monitors and suppresses pests with coordinated methods for environmental, social, and economic sustainability.

Quantitative farmscaping prevents pests with *predator-specific habitats* that host *pest-specific predators* who prey on *crop-specific pests*. In North America there are > 200 species of parasitoids, predators, and pathogens who prey on ~70 species of injurious pests. Natural enemies of crop pests are most often *parasitoid wasps, predatory beetles, and predatory bugs. Parasitoid flies, entomopathogens, lacewings, lady beetles, ground beetles, and spiders* also contribute crucial pest regulation services.

Farmscape features offer natural enemies foods, such as *nectar, pollen, and alternate prey*, while providing places to build nests, take rest, or be sheltered from disturbances. *Rock piles, stone walls, brush piles, dead wood, and snags, living groundcovers, bark mulches, leaf litters, or windbreaks* provide shelters. *Sandy soils with sparse vegetation* offer nesting opportunities. *Field borders, hedgerows, beetle banks, cover crops, or pastures* conserve, support, and sustain natural enemies.

Insectaries of native flowering plants with *yearlong blooms* feed parasitoid wasps and other natural enemies. *Sources of alternate prey* can sustain predators when crop pests are absent. *Increased crop diversity, reduced tillage, and organic soil amendments and mulches* reduce pest outbreaks and preserve natural enemy populations. *Pesticide-free crop fields* are crucial for the conservation of all beneficial farm organisms. Farmers must *divest from pesticides* to perform farmscaping.

Biodynamic Farmscaping

Qualitative biodynamic farmscaping heals farms according to therapeutic spiritual ecology. Such curative practice intuitively diagnoses from occult physiology to harmonize mixtures of elemental substances for the restoration of vitality. Illnesses meaningfully indicate imbalances, which are themselves opportunities for physical-spiritual growth. Practitioners assess farm organism *biography*, including: farm history or age, ecoregion or stature, soils/flora/fauna or build; mission or *behavior*; farming practices or *personality*; crops or farm *preferences*; and disturbances, imbalances, or *symptoms*.

Farm biographies help diagnose chronic illnesses, while ephemeral conditions assist in the diagnosis of acute illnesses. The resulting consultations inform curative treatments, which must remain living to help nature heal. Farmscape cures heal *in situ* and *in vivo*: site-specific dynamic potencies remain embodied within and flow from living medicinal plants. Balanced mixtures of *aboveground* celestial-air, *surface* biological-water/fire, and *belowground* terrestrial-earth forces-substances are prescribed to regulate farm organisms and support present and future conditions for farmscape health.

Aboveground, surface, and belowground cures balance farmscape instabilities. *Aboveground cures*, such as leaves, flowers, or fruits can create light and exposed habitat conditions for organisms to *feed*. *Surface cures* such as leaves or stems can create a continuum of moist-dry habitat conditions for organisms to *rest*. *Belowground cures* such as bulbs, rhizomes, or roots can create dark and sheltered habitat conditions for organisms to *nest*. Such threefold rhythmic treatments produce qualities of lightness, wetness, dryness, or darkness from the living bodies of aromatic and flavorful herbs.

Aromatic herbs treat *internal* farmscape disparities, while flavorful herbs treat *external* farmscape imbalances. For example, aromatic Apiaceae (Carrots), Asteraceae (Asters), and Lamiaceae (Mints) cure farm interiors, while flavorful Ericaceae (Heaths), Rosaceae (Roses), and Salicaceae (Willows) cure farm exteriors. Both internal and external farmscape symptoms are treated with mixtures of aromatic and flavorful herbs, including Brassicaceae (Mustards) and Fabaceae (Peas). Medicinal plant families are multisensory and multifunctional, thereby combinations of aromatic and flavorful herbs work together to balance overall farm organism health.

Medicinal herbs heal among environments and organisms through formative, rhythmic life forces. Life forces similarly flow throughout mineral, plant, animal, and human worlds. A dearth or surplus of life forces is expressed as either compressions or distortions in physical-spiritual bodies. Phasing qualities, similar throughout life worlds, constitute curative substances when synchronized or syncopated in concert. External and internal formative forces can be willed as therapies, which phase, synchronize, and syncopate together to heal symptoms of farm imbalances with medicinal herbs.

Farm organism imbalances are mainly *depression, stagnation, excitation, or desiccation*. Such tissue states are respectively synchronized with surplus forces of earth-Iaso, water-Panacea, air-Hygieia, and fire-Aceso. These four complexes are respectively synchronized with qualities of aromatic and flavorful herbs: *decayed-minty-pungent essential oils, chemical-bitter-tannic tonics, citrus-floral-sour flavonoids, and fruity-nutty-sweet polysaccharides*. Such qualities of aromatic-flavorful herbs respectively provide therapeutic properties of *sedation, digestion, stimulation, and circulation*.

1. *Earth* = Iaso = Recuperation = Depression / Sedation = Decayed-Minty-Pungent Essential Oils

2. *Water* = Panacea = Medication = Stagnation / Digestion = Chemical-Tannic-Bitter Tonics

3. *Air* = Hygieia = Sanitation = Excitation / Stimulation = Citrus-Floral-Sour Flavonoids

4. *Fire* = Aceso = Regeneration = Desiccation / Circulation = Fruity-Nutty-Sweet Polysaccharides

Farmscape *depression is balanced with stimulation* from citrus-floral-sour herbs, while *stagnation is balanced with circulation* from fruity-nutty-sweet herbs, *excitation is balanced with sedation* from decayed-minty-pungent herbs, and *desiccation is balanced with digestion* from chemical-tannic-bitter herbs. Such herbal remedies can be administered alone or in combination with each other in farm organisms through the creation and conservation of abundant and rich farmscape features. Biodiverse farm organ

systems are *living pharmacies* that treat a wide range of afflictions.

Beetle banks of decayed-minty-pungent Apiaceae, Lamiaceae, and Poaceae (Grasses) cultivate sedation for healthy farm exoskeletons-muscular systems. Cover crops of chemical-bitter-tannic Asteraceae and Brassicaceae encourage metabolization for healthy farm digestive systems. Hedgerows or insectaries of citrus-floral-sour Apiaceae, Asteraceae, Ericaceae, Rosaceae, and Salicaceae foster excitation for healthy farm immune-muscular systems. Cover crops composed of fruity-nutty-sweet Asteraceae, Fabaceae, Poaceae, and Polygonaceae (Buckwheats) nurture circulation for healthy farm digestive-excretory systems.

Pests

Pests are *symptoms* of farm imbalances, which are remediated with medicinal herbs administered as farmscape features. Insect metamorphosis is synchronized with plant metamorphosis and elemental forces. *Holometabolous* insects experience *complete metamorphosis* from egg to larva, pupa, and imago, while *hemimetabolous* insects experience *incomplete metamorphosis* from egg to nymph and imago. Egg is to earth-mineral-root as larva/nymph is to water-plant-leaf, pupa is to air-animal-flower, and imago is to fire-human-fruit. Such compound polyrhythmics inform three phases of treatments:

1. *Eggs are regulated with aboveground cures that create lightness, larvae/nymphs and imagos are managed with surface cures that create wetness or dryness, and pupae are balanced with belowground cures that create darkness.*

2. *Eggs are regulated with insectaries, meadows, and hedgerows of citrus-floral-sour* herbs, while *larvae/nymphs are managed with cover crops of fruity-nutty-sweet* herbs, *pupae are balanced with beetle banks of decayed-minty-pungent* herbs, and *imagos are regulated with cover crops of chemical-tannic-bitter* herbs.

3. *Insect orders* are associated with elements and sages. Regulate pests with targeted cures and features:

- *Diptera* (Flies) = Earth-Root-Egg = Aboveground = Insectaries, Meadows, *Hedgerows* = Citrus-Floral-Sour

- Hemiptera (Bugs) and Lepidoptera (Butterflies and Moths) = Water-Leaf-Nymph/Larva = Surface = Cover Crops = Fruity-Nutty-Sweet

- *Hymenoptera* (Ants, Bees, Wasps) = Air-Flower-Pupa = Belowground = Beetle Banks = Decayed-Minty-Pungent

- *Coleoptera* (Beetles) = Fire-fruit-Imago = Surface = Cover Crops = Chemical-Tannic-Bitter

Prevention of pests is basic for balanced farmscapes. The eight most recurrent pests of North American farms are mostly Lepidoptera, Coleoptera, and Hemiptera:

1. True Armyworm, *Mythimna unipuncta* (Haworth, 1809) [Lepidoptera: Noctuidae]

2. Wireworm, *Melanotus spp.* or *Limonius spp.* (Eschscholtz, 1829) [Coleoptera: Elateridae]

3. Saltmarsh Caterpillar, *Estigmene acrea* (Drury, 1773) [Lepidoptera: Erebidae]

4. Corn Earworm or Tomato fruitworm, *Helicoverpa zea* (Boddie, 1850) [Lepidoptera: Noctuidae]

5. Tarnished Plant Bug, *Lygus lineolaris* (Palisot de Beauvois, 1818) [Hemiptera: Miridae]

6. Aster Leafhopper, *Macrosteles quadrilineatus* (Forbes, 1885) [Hemiptera: Cicadellidae]

7. Harlequin Bug, *Murgantia histrionica* (Hahn, 1834) [Hemiptera: Pentatomidae]

8. Variegated Cutworm, *Peridroma saucia* (Hübner, 1808) [Lepidoptera: Noctuidae]

Lepidoptera and Hemiptera pests indicate imbalanced wet or stagnated farmscapes, which can be balanced with dryness from cover crops of fruity-nutty-sweet buckwheat, clover, pea, safflower, and sunflower. Coleoptera pests indicate imbalanced dry and dessicated farmscapes, which can be balanced with wetness from cover crops of chemical-bitter-tannic chicory, mustard, and radish. Therefore, you can prevent the most recurrent pests with cover crops that feed parasitoid wasps and other predators.

Quantitative conservation biocontrol and qualitative biodynamic farmscaping can mutually reciprocate in theory and practice to help nature heal. Therapeutic physical-spiritual ecology diagnoses and administers living herbal treatments that cure illnesses for the restoration of vitality. Illnesses meaningfully indicate imbalances, which are themselves opportunities for physical-spiritual growth. Thus, qualitative-quantitative studies of nature can help humans protect biodiversity with coordinated methods that enhance habitats for wild beneficial organisms that prey on crop pests.

ASCLEPIAS

Medicative herbs are panaceas that produce poisons for the protection of self and others. Specialized herbal curing-poisoning compounds both attract and repel herbivores. *The dose makes the poison*: Palatable herbs can nourish and protect herbivores after consumption; unpalatable herbs protect plants and can harm herbivores once eaten. Protective poisons often regulate plant-insect specializations.

Milkweed, genus *Asclepias* L. (*Apocynaceae*), was named after Asclepius. North America hosts seventy-two native species of Milkweed, each perennial, mostly deciduous. Milkweed roots are rhizomes or taproots, stems are upright or branching and often contain milky latex sap, flowers are often pink-purple, green, or orange umbels that bloom during summer, pollen grains are enclosed in ochre-umber *pollinaria*, and fruits are spindle-shaped follicles with tufted seeds.

Asclepias bodies contain protective medicinal/toxic metabolites called cardenolides (steroid cardiac glycosides). Cardenolides are unpalatable and potentially toxic to livestock. Cardenolides drive specialization by some herbivores such as Monarchs, *Danaus plexippus* (Linnaeus, 1758) and Queens, *Danaus gilippus* (Cramer, 1775). Milkweed butterflies sequester cardenolides from foliage as caterpillars and maintain the medicines through metamorphosis to adulthood for self-defense.

Butterfly Milkweed, *Asclepias tuberosa* L., is an upright and branching perennial that grows from taproots and has hairy stems with alternate, light to dark green, lance-shaped, and fuzzy leaves, orange umbels of eight to twenty-five flowers with five petals, hoods, and horns, and spindle-shaped follicles with tufted seeds. Butterfly Milkweed grows in full sun, dry–moist, and well-drained, acid, sand, or gravel soils, in glades, canyons, fields, grasslands, prairies, roadsides, and savannas across North America. *Asclepias tuberosa* has benefits including: biocontrol, butterflies, ceremony, clothing, compaction, and medicine.

Butterfly Milkweed has the following medical indications:

- Tastes slightly sweet, bitter, and salty or earthy
- Treats tissue states of atrophy, constriction, and excitation
- Decreases inflammation and pain

- Increases circulation, detoxification, digestion, relaxation, and respiration
- Causes illness if consumed in large quantities

Asclepias is a living remedy that helps restore, recover, soothe, and clean landscapes with nectar. Milkweed depends on insects for reproduction and produces surplus nectar that is highly attractive to parasitoid wasps and other pollinators. *Asclepias* hosts specialist herbivores that often feed generalist predators and parasitoids as sources of alternate prey. Milkweed eases landscape inflammation and pain caused by herbivores through increasing the circulation of predators that detoxify and digest pests.

Plant native Milkweeds in sun–part shade conditions in dry–moist or wet soils within field borders, hedgerows, insectaries, and meadows to enhance both Panacea and Hygieia rhythms. Grow *Asclepias* to help reduce compaction and erosion while yielding harvestable medicines, fibers, foods, and seeds.

Propagate local, sustainably collected Milkweeds by dividing or sowing. Expose seeds to cold and moist stratification and/or sow milkweed at ¼ inch in soil or containers during fall. *Asclepias* seeds germinate following winter dormancy. Protect young Milkweeds from competition, herbivory, and pollution. Asclepius and *Asclepias* together help humans restore health.

RHYTHMICS

Calendrics

Yearly, monthly, and daily celestial rhythms interact to influence the lives of all Earthlings. Sun, moon, planets, and stars radiate or reflect descending intensities of light energy. Seasonal sunlight cycles interact with monthly moonlight phases and daily planetlight and starlight patterns. Light intensities are variable and have both lurid and subtle effects on plant and animal growth and metamorphosis.

Lunar cycles can be followed to schedule gardening activities. Biodynamic gardeners and farmers enhance crop growth with geocentric calendars composed of Sun, Moon, planet, and star rhythms. Gardening habituated from biodynamic calendars connects gardens with environments, humans with (non-)humans, and earthlings with cosmos.

Biodynamic calendars track rhythms of the sun, moon, and planets cycling through twelve constellations of the zodiac. Zodiac signs activate archetypal images or symbols rooted in our collective unconscious that inspire collective conscious gardening impulses. Astronomy and astrology become applied astro-ecology through the spiritual consciousness and active mediation of biodynamic practitioners.

Biodynamic farmers and gardeners grow plants according to place/space-based and plant stage-specific astrological conditions. Cosmic rhythms can also guide the restoration of healthy habitats for beneficial insects that pollinate crops, regulate pests, and recycle wastes. Standard twelve-sign biodynamic calendars can be supplemented with a thirteenth sign that symbolizes "health" and "medicine": *Ophiuchus*.

Local apparent astrology affects auspicious or inauspicious conditions for farmscaping. Transits, phases, and cycles focus, magnify, push, pull, shine, or symbolize with different degrees of force, luminance, or meaning. Lunar cycles and courses interact with patterns of planetary events, including nodes, eclipses, and trines. Moon phases transit new constellations every two to three days and return to constellations every ~27 days.

Gardening according to lunar cycles and courses during plant-specific times can enhance establishment, growth, and yield. Moon in constellations is linked with elements, stages of plant-insect metamorphosis, and the healing actions of the Asclepiades as follows:

- Moon in Taurus, Virgo, or Capricorn = Earth-Root-Egg = "Recuperation Time"
- Moon in Cancer, Scorpio, or Pisces = Water-Leaf-Larva = "Medication Time"
- Moon in Gemini, Libra, or Aquarius = Air-Flower-Pupa = "Sanitation Time"
- Moon in Aries, Leo, or Sagittarius = Fire-Imago-Fruit = "Regeneration Time"
- Moon in Ophiuchus = Spirit-Stage = "Beautification Time"

Consult existing calendars including Maria Thun, Stella Natura, or various apps to track daily, monthly, and yearly celestial rhythms. Mark the Rod of Asclepius symbol (⚕) on biodynamic calendars between Scorpio and Sagittarius.

Adapt *monthly* lunar Ophiuchus actions according to *annual* solar cycles. Yearly (±1–4 days) times with thirteen signs, modes, elements-stages, and actions are presented below. Three modalities are associated with each zodiac sign: cardinal signs begin, fixed signs continue, and mutable signs change:

1. *Aries*
   - April 19–May 13
   - Cardinal Fire-Fruit-Imago
   - Cultivate soils and begin maintaining croplands, greenhouses, and pastures.

2. *Taurus*
   - May 14–June 19
   - Fixed Earth-Root-Egg
   - Transplant annuals, perennials, and woody plants and avoid preparing and maintaining beetle banks, boundaries, and windbreaks.

3. *Gemini*
   - June 20–July 20
   - Mutable Air-Flower-Pupa
   - Prepare hedgerows, insectaries, and meadows.

4. *Cancer*
   - July 21–August 9
   - Cardinal Water-Leaf-Larva
   - Begin preparing, propagating, installing, maintaining, and monitoring cover crops, field borders, rivers, streams, and water bodies.

5. *Leo*
   - August 10–September 15
   - Fixed Fire-Fruit-Imago
   - Continue preparing, propagating, installing, maintaining, and monitoring croplands, greenhouses, and pastures.

6. *Virgo*
   - September 16–October 30
   - Mutable Earth-Root-Egg

- Transplant annuals, perennials, and woody plants and avoid maintaining beetle banks, boundaries, and windbreaks.

7. *Libra*
- October 31–November 22
- Cardinal Air-Flower-Pupa
- Begin preparing, propagating, installing, maintaining, and monitoring hedgerows, insectaries, and meadows.

8. *Scorpio*
- November 23–November 29
- Fixed Water-Leaf-Larva
- Continue preparing, propagating, installing, maintaining, and monitoring cover crops, field borders, rivers, streams, and water bodies.

9. *Ophiuchus*
- November 30–December 17
- ~~Mode-Spirit-Stage~~
- Reflect on and adapt assessing, designing, and evaluating; begin preparing, propagating, installing, maintaining, and monitoring; continue preparing, propagating, installing, maintaining, and monitoring all habitats.

10. *Sagittarius*
- December 18–January 18
- Mutable Fire-Fruit-Imago
- Cultivate and avoid installing croplands, greenhouses, and pastures.

11. *Capricorn*
- January 19–February 15
- Cardinal Earth-Root-Egg
- Transplant and avoid maintaining beetle banks, boundaries, and windbreaks.

12. *Aquarius*
- February 16–March 11
- Fixed Air-Flower-Pupa
- Sow and prune perennial hedgerows, insectaries, and meadows.

13. *Pisces*
- March 12–April 18
- Mutable Water-Leaf-Larva
- Reflect on and adapt assessing, designing, and evaluating or sowing annual cover

crops, field borders, rivers, streams, and water bodies.

Gardening during adverse conditions can diminish results. Constellations have unequal sizes and shapes that often overlap: Avoid farmscaping four hours around moon transits between constellations. *Eclipses* cause chaos: Avoid farmscaping twenty-four hours around lunar and solar eclipses. *Nodes* cause stress for seeds: Avoid sowing four hours around moon nodes and twenty-four hours around Mercury and Venus nodes. *Apogee* (moon farthest from Earth) causes bolting: *Root-Recuperation Time* and *Leaf-Medication Time* become *Flower-Sanitation Time*. *Perigee* (moon nearest to Earth) causes stunting: Avoid sowing seeds 24 hours around perigee.

Recommendations

Schedule and perform farmscaping during *Auspicious* lunar and solar times:

Practicing
- Reflect on and adapt assessing, designing, and evaluating during *Ophiuchus* and *Pisces*.
- Begin preparing, propagating, installing, maintaining, and monitoring during *Ophiuchus*, *Cancer*, and *Libra*.
- Continue preparing, propagating, installing, maintaining, and monitoring during *Ophiuchus*, *Leo*, and *Scorpio*.

Preparing
- Burn, graze, or mow during Aries, Gemini, Libra or Aquarius during 4th quarter waning crescent moons.
- Sheet mulch during *Ophiuchus* or *Cancer*.
- Cultivate dry-soils on afternoons *Aries*, *Leo*, Sagittarius, or Gemini during waning crescent moons.
- Cultivate wet-soils on mornings during *Aries*, *Leo*, Sagittarius, or Gemini during waning crescent moons.

- Sow annual smother crops on afternoons during *Pisces*, *Cancer*, or Scorpio within three days before full moons.
- Sow perennial cover crops on afternoons during *Libra*, *Scorpio*, Aquarius, or Gemini during waning moons.
- Avoid preparing habitats during Taurus.

Installing

- Begin installing during *Libra* and maintain installations during *Scorpio* or *Ophiuchus*.
- Sow annuals on afternoons during *Pisces*, *Cancer*, or *Scorpio* three days before full moons.
- Sow perennials on afternoons during *Libra*, *Scorpio*, or Aquarius during waning moons.
- Transplant annuals, perennials, and woody plants on afternoons during *Taurus*, *Virgo*, *Libra*, and Capricorn within three days before full moons and during descending or 3rd quarter waning gibbous moons.
- Avoid installing during Aries, Gemini, and Sagittarius.

Maintaining

- Begin maintaining during *Aries* and continue maintenance during *Leo*, *Scorpio*, or *Ophiuchus*.
- Prune herbaceous perennials on mornings during *Scorpio*, Cancer, or Pisces, Cancer during 1st–2nd quarter waxing crescent or gibbous moons.
- Prune woody perennials on mornings during *Aquarius* or Pisces during 1st–2nd quarter waxing crescent or gibbous moons.
- Avoid maintaining during Taurus, Virgo, and Capricorn.

Celebrate by performing rituals that honor nature during both new and full moons: Burn incense; honor nature spirits; chant, drum, or sing to ground and release intentions; offer acknowledgements and express gratitude.

OUTRO

You can work with Ophiuchus rhythms to heal, defend, and beautify landscapes. Biodynamic farmscaping restores habitats, prevents pests, and eliminates pesticides. Medicinal plants and parasitoid wasps co-compose hygienic farmscape immune systems.

You can help nature heal by thinking like an insect. Cultivate care with compounded, segmented, and diversified actions. Diagnose, prescribe, and administer treatments to co-create healing landscapes. Embody Asclepius archetypes to become healthy.

ADDENDUM I: HOUSE SYSTEMS

Ophiuchus is aligned with the Galactic Center (2° Sagittarius), the heart of the Milky Way Galaxy. Across the zodiac from Ophiuchus is Orion, honored by the ancient Egyptians as the cosmic form of Osiris. The Great Pyramids at Giza were built in such a way as to align specifically with Orion at a certain time of year. Ophiuchus is the complement and counterpart to Orion/Osiris. The gigantic black hole at the center of the Milky Way is simultaneously a central Sun, a "Sun of Suns," a darkness-lightness of high degree. The original Pentecost (Whitsun) took place while the Sun was opposite the Galactic Center.

Further Recommendations

1) Current practice in most biodynamic circles is to use the uneven division of the zodiac into the twelve constellations delineated by modern astronomy. In contradistinction to the astronomical division of the visible starry heavens, there has arisen since the time of Ptolemy an astrology based on an evenly divided zodiac of tropical *signs*. Although these signs, at the time of Ptolemy, corresponded with the actual positions of the visible constellations, Ptolemaic astrology failed to take into account the reality of precession; increasingly over the last 2,000 years, therefore, tropical astrology has deviated from sidereal (observational)

astrology and/or astronomy. The Sun's positions in the various tropical signs are based on a calendar of fixed dates, rather than an actual tracking and observation of celestial maps.

Originally, astronomy and astrology were one. This original astrology was developed in several ancient cultures, and eventually codified in ancient Babylon, around the time of Zaratas and Pythagoras. Babylonian sidereal astrology was based on both a direct observation of the movements of the planets through the zodiac, as well as the last vestiges of the picture-clairvoyance of the ancients. Out of this combination of clairvoyance and observation, the Babylonians divided the zodiac into twelve equal-length signs of 30°. The axis upon which this division was based was between the star *Aldebaran*, the Eye of the Bull, designated by the Babylonians as 15° Taurus, and *Antares,* the heart of the Scorpion, designated by the Babylonians as 15° Scorpio. In this original, ancient practice, "sign" was the same as "constellation." The phenomenon of precession was taken into account, and so this connection between sign and constellation was never severed. Indeed, until close to the modern era, there was never seen to be any difference between the two.

The original sidereal astrology was maintained more-or-less intact only in Hindu Vedic astrology. However, in the past century a number of modern astrologers in the West have, in seeking the authentic origins of astrology, also made the choice to approach astrology through the lens of an equally divided, sidereal zodiac. The authors contributing to *Star Wisdom* and its predecessors, *The Journal for Star Wisdom* and the *Christian Star Calendar,* by and large include themselves in this group of researchers rediscovering the ancient astrology. It would be valuable research to experiment biodynamically with the equally divided, sidereal-astrological zodiac vs. the unequally divided astronomical zodiac in order to see which is more effective and harmonious for the farm organism. This would be a phenomenological approach to discovering the actual and active boundaries from one sign to the next. The dates for the solar and lunar ingresses, from the equally divided sidereal perspective, will be somewhat different from the dates listed above. The ingress of Sun, Moon and all the other planets is listed in the monthly ephemerides included in every edition of *Star Wisdom*.

2) A careful study of Rudolf Steiner's work seems to indicate that he utilized a clockwise house system.[1] Certainly, many of his indications make little to no sense in astrological terms without taking this perspective, as he often indicates the Sun being in Aries when it rises, Libra when it sets, in Capricorn at midnight, and in Cancer at midday.[2]

One could begin to utilize the positions of the planets in the various houses in biodynamic practice in order to find not just the right season, month, and/or day for a certain activity, but even the right *hour* in the day. In terms of the clockwise house system in development by Joel Matthew Park, the First House is analogous to Aries. The eastern horizon is the center (15°) of this house, with half of it above and half of it below the horizon. The Second House (Taurus) is the next 30° portion above and to the south; then the Third House (Gemini), the next 30° portion above and to the south. Then the Fourth House (Cancer) in the midheaven, the house directly south and highest overhead. And so on and so forth.

Ophiuchus straddles both Scorpio and Sagittarius. In terms of her equivalent in terms of the earthly houses, we would look to the portion of the sky midway between the western horizon (Seventh House, Libra) and the nadir, directly below and to the north (Tenth House, Capricorn). While the Sun's ingress into the "Ophiuchus house" varies somewhat from day to day, generally speaking it is around 10 p.m. that the Sun is in this region. Considering, however,

---

1 See, for example, *Calendar of the Soul* (CW 40); *Human and Cosmic Thought* (CW 151); *Toward Imagination: Culture and the Individual* (CW 169), and *Secret Brotherhoods and the Mystery of the Double* (CW 178).

2 See Joel Matthew Park's articles "Saturn in Cancer" in *Saturn-Mary-Sophia: Star Wisdom,* vol. 2, and "The Tree of Life" in *As Above, So Below: Star Wisdom,* vol. 3, for a fuller investigation of this hypothesis.

Ophiuchus's relationship to both Jupiter (ruler of Sagittarius) and Pluto/Mars (modern/traditional rulers of Scorpio respectively), one might also want to track when those planets are between setting and nadir. While the Sun will be consistent in its Ophiuchus position from one cultivation season to the next, Jupiter, Mars and Pluto will vary. This is because there is a very close alignment between the Sun's seasonal cycle and zodiacal year, whereas the zodiacal years of Jupiter, Mars, and Pluto bear no resemblance to the Earth's seasonal cycle.

There are not ephemerides for the clockwise house system. This system is *place-based*—e.g., the Sun is in the center of the Fourth House on the east coast of the United States, while simultaneously still in the Second House in California; therefore, there cannot be a globally consistent ephemeris. It is something the farmer would have to dutifully work out and keep track of, day by day, in order to integrate the diurnal positions of the planets (in terms of *north-south-east-west-above-below*) into her gardening.

In astrological tradition, there is a Hermetic correspondence between the cosmic signs above and the earthly houses below. Rudolf Steiner always referred to the houses by their sign, their astrological equivalent, which is part of what makes his indications confusing. Note that each astrological sign, as it revolves around the earth from the geocentric perspective, spends about two hours of the day in each earthly house. Therefore, we can have the confusing situation of, for example, Taurus (astrological sign) in Aries (first house)!

ADDENDUM II: ECOSYSTEMS

Astrology divides the ecliptic plane into twelve houses, each associated with a zodiac sign. Houses are traditionally numbered *counterclockwise* from the cusp of the First House (Aries), with the first six houses below and the second six above the horizon. The Greek word for house is *oikos*, ancestor of the prefix *eco-*. Research indicates that Rudolf Steiner used an earthly *clockwise* astrological house system. Thus, an earthly

astrological ecosystem grounds biodynamic theories and practices.

The positions of planets in the earthly houses can be observed to determine the most favorable *hours* for biodynamic practices. According to the clockwise house system, the eastern horizon is the center (15°) of the First House (Aries), which is divided by the horizon. The Second House (Taurus) is the next 30° portion above and to the south and the Third House (Gemini) is the next 30° portion above and to the south. The Fourth House (Cancer) is in the midheaven, directly south and overhead at 12:00 hours.

The Seventh House (Libra) is located at the center (15°) of the western horizon, while the Tenth House (Capricorn) is in the nadir, directly north and underfoot at midnight. Ophiuchus rests between the Eighth House (Scorpio) and Ninth House (Sagittarius). Thus, the sun transits the Ophiuchus House daily from 19:00 to 22:00 hours. Many predators of crop pests are active in the evening or at night. Is farmscaping most embodied or successful when performed around sunset, but before midnight?

The Sun transits the Ophiuchus House every day from 19:00 to 22:00 hours, but other planets transit the Eighth–Ninth House at different hours, which shift daily, monthly, or seasonally. Such time shifts are due to unique durations of planetary orbits according to our geocentric model. For example, each day the Moon appears to enter the Ophiuchus House around forty-five minutes later than the previous day. What appearances of other planets in the Ophiuchus House might be particularly significant for farmscaping?

Ophiuchus is ruled by Jupiter and Pluto; therefore, the appearance of these planets in the Eighth and Ninth houses marks an auspicious duration. Such transits affect spiritual peace, expansive action, supernatural depth, and transformative vision. Both Jupiter and Pluto are slow-moving planets with variable orbits that appear in the Ophiuchus House between one minute or four seconds later respectively than the previous day. Are long-lasting Jupiter-Pluto rhythms lucky for predators and unlucky for pests?

The earthly clockwise house system is *place-based*. For example, the Sun is in the center (15°) of the Fourth House (12:00) on the East Coast of the United States, while simultaneously still in the Second House (09:00) on the West Coast. Therefore, there are no global ephemerides for the earthly house system. Biodynamic farmscapers must track site-specific planetary rhythms to create unique place-based calendars that help schedule timely habitat preparation, installation, and conservation practices.[3]

---

3 Bibliographic references for this article are available online at https://zizia.xyz/sclps.html.

THANKS—

Natalie Adams, Donat Bay and Plowshare Farm, Eric Buteyn, Alice Groh and Temple-Wilton Community Farm, Craig Holdrege and The Nature Institute, Robert Karbelnikoff, Don Keirstead, Eric Lee-Mäder, Ian McSweeny and Agrarian Trust, Mac Mead and The Pfeiffer Center, Brad Miller, Joel Park and Star Wisdom, Dan Pratt and Astarte Farm, Erika Rosenfeld, Nicole and Jeremiah Vernon and Vernon Family Farm, Claudia and Conrad Vispo and The Hawthorne Valley Farmscape Ecology Program, Severine von Tscharner Fleming and Greenhorns, Sherry Wildfeuer and Stella Natura.

At the turn of time,
cosmic spirit light descended
into the Earth's stream of being.
Night's darkness
had run its course.
Day-bright light
streamed into human souls—
light that warms
poor shepherds' hearts,
light that illumines
the wise heads of kings.
Divine light,
Christ Sun,
warm through our hearts;
illumine our heads,
so that what
we would create
from our hearts
and guide from our heads,
in sure willing,
may be good.

—RUDOLF STEINER
(*Start Now!* pp. 241–42)

THE SACRIFICES OF JESUS AND CHRIST, PART II

Joel Matthew Park

Over the course of the first part of this article series, the attempt was made to paint a picture of the gradual precipitation of the various levels of the human being (physical body, etheric body, etc.) out of a general homogeneity over the course of human evolution since the Fall in Ancient Lemuria. We are working with the hypothesis that the ancient Hebrew sacrificial rite began at the time of the first sacrifice of Jesus and Christ in Ancient Lemuria in order to organize the physical body and plant the seed for the developing ego organization. This rite lasted from that earliest time of our material existence up through the time of the fourth sacrifice, the Mystery of Golgotha, the turning point of time. We saw Abel's animal sacrifice as the first enactment of this Hebrew rite, whereas Cain's plant sacrifice was a precursor of a different rite—what held sway more or less for the entirety of Ancient Atlantis. This rite was bound up with the second sacrifice of Jesus and Christ at the beginning of Atlantis, one that organized the etheric body of the human being and simultaneously planted the seed for the birth of the astral body in the latter portion of Atlantis, during the third sacrifice of Jesus and Christ. After that point, the "Cain rite" overstayed its welcome, and its decadence led to the destruction of Atlantis. And so, the image we have is the "Cain rite" as a smaller era embedded in the overarching era of the "Abel rite" of the Hebrew.

We then saw that the first three sacrifices of Christ were in a certain sense recapitulated in the first three post-Atlantean zodiacal ages: the first sacrifice in the Age of Cancer (bridging Atlantis and India), the second in the Age of Gemini (bridging India and Persia), and the third in the Age of Taurus (bridging Persia and Egypt). This recapitulation led to the perfecting of the astral body born at the end of the Age of Atlantis.

By the time we come to the Age of Aries, which began in 1946 BC, a special event occurs: the birth of Philosophia, she who is the expression of Old Sun evolution within our Earth evolution. This birth of Philosophia coincided with the life of Abraham, the one who was the first brain-bound conceptual thinker, the one who led humanity away from picture-consciousness. With Philosophia's birth comes the gradual dying away of the ancient clairvoyance, expressed through her biographical periods—which, rather than seven-year cycles, are 720-year cycles, each cycle one third of a zodiacal age of 2,160 years. The years of the development of her "physical body" coincided with 1946 to 1226 BC, from the time of Abraham to Moses. The years of development of her "etheric body" coincided with 1226 to 506 BC, the time of Moses up through the so-called Axial Age, of Gautama Buddha and the ancient Greek philosophers. It is during the time period of her astral body in particular—from 506 BC to AD 215—that we see the complete loss of pictorial consciousness and the birth of "thought perception." Since, at the start of this period, the human "I" had not yet been born, thoughts were not experienced as being created through the activity of the personality; rather, they were perceived as objective entities in a similar way to external sensations.

These thought-perceptions came to full expression first in the Platonic school (which sought the highest origin in the One through a kind of "vertical memory"), and then in the Aristotelian school (which sought the expression of this One in the multiplicity through precise horizontal perception).

However, the thought streams of these two schools stagnated and then died out in their homeland, being preserved primarily in the Alexandrian schools and in the Middle East through the travels of Alexander the Great. At that point, they had no possibility for further development; a developmental shift on the part of the human being was necessary before this could happen, one that necessitated the presence of the ego as "thought-creator" rather than the astral body as "thought-perceiver." Therefore, they had to wait for a future age to truly integrate themselves into human culture.

Theirs had been the time period of Michael, the Solar Archangel, which lasted from 602 to 248 BC. This culturally prolific age was followed by the time of Oriphiel, the Saturn Archangel, from 248 BC to AD 107, a time of incredible darkness and divine wrath.[1] In the Greco-Roman lands, philosophical perception gave way to absolute sensual decadence on the one hand, and the rigid strictness of Roman law on the other. In the midst of this downfall (one could say in darkest winter, at midnight, in a cave for animals) of the idyllic Greek civilization came the event of the fourth sacrifice of Christ and Jesus—the Mystery of Golgotha. This sacrifice precipitated out the human personality (the concrete ego) from the admixture of atman, buddhi, manas, and ego that had prevailed as the "higher self" prior to this event. It was this ego that was the necessary implement for working with the Platonic and Aristotelian worldviews in a truly practical, widespread way.

As we pointed out earlier, the ego had been gestating and developing ever since its germination at the time of the *first* sacrifice of Jesus and Christ, around the time of Cain and Abel. The sacrifice of the "I" of Archangel Jesus allowed for the organization and precipitation of the material, physical body, yet simultaneously planted the seed for the eventual birth of the ego in each human being. The ancient Hebrew sacrifice was the rite that accompanied this development, from Abel's sacrifice through to the Last Supper.

The fourth sacrifice is in a sense a reversal of the first: it gives birth to the ego of the human being, and simultaneously plants the seed for the gradual development of the transformed physical body, the highest member of the human being: *atman*. The establishment of the Eucharist at the time of the Last Supper is a rite that accompanies the development of the highest in the human being, a rite that will accompany humanity through to the end of its earthly incarnations at the dawn of the Anglo-American epoch; just as the Hebrew rite held sway in an overarching way from the first through the fourth sacrifice, so the Eucharist holds sway from the fourth to the seventh and last sacrifice.

And so, since the end of the Age of Aries (and the Mystery of Golgotha in particular), we have had a two-fold development of human culture. On the one hand, with the coming-to-birth of the personal ego, humanity became ever more equipped to grapple with the Greco-Roman world views *in an experiential way*, recreating the thoughts out of their own inner activity, rather than perceiving the thoughts as a finished objective reality approaching from "without", so to speak. As humanity felt the presence, the loneliness, of the individual ego more and more strongly over the course of the Age of Pisces (right up to the present), the more this could occur. Thus, the seeds planted at the end of the Age of Aries could unfold to their fullness over much longer periods of time: the first third of the Age of Pisces, the birth of the sentient soul of Philosophia (AD 215–935), saw the full integration of Platonism into Christian, European culture. Subsequently, during the second third of the Age of Pisces, the birth of her mind soul (AD 935–1655) saw the full integration of Aristotelianism into Christian, European culture. The "Christ years", i.e., ages 30-33 of Philosophia fell precisely at the crossing point of the Platonists and Aristotelians, from about 1140 to 1450, when the School of Chartres (Platonism) gave way to Scholasticism (Aristotelianism).[2] We could say that the Platonist years saw the human being primarily concerned with the realm of spirit and religion, while the Aristotelian age was primarily concerned with the realm of the human being and the arts. It then transitioned into the

---

1 See Steiner, *Concerning the History and Content of the Higher Degrees of the Esoteric School, 1904–1914,* in particular the lessons of Nov. 1, 1906; Oct. 18, 1907; Dec. 5, 1907; Aug. 9, 1908; and Feb. 12, 1911.

2 The most comprehensive and scholarly description of this process can be found in Steiner's *Riddles of Philosophy.*

final third of the age of Pisces (the consciousness soul of Philosophia, in the midst of the Age of the Consciousness Soul!), in which we have lived since the Cartesian revolution, a time concerned primarily with nature and science.

So, the years AD 215 to 1655—the fourth and fifth life cycles of the being Philosophia, her sentient soul and mind soul years—set the stage for a flourishing of the ego in the last third of the Age of Pisces (AD 1655–2375), analogous to the flourishing of the astral body at the time of Plato and Aristotle. This flourishing came in the form of Goetheanism and German Idealism in the late eighteenth and early nineteenth centuries (the equivalent of Platonism) and Anthroposophy in the late nineteenth and early twentieth centuries (the equivalent of Aristotelianism).[3] Similar to Platonism and Aristotelianism, thousands of years

earlier, these cultural pinnacles of the experience of the individual ego are in the process of stagnation and being cast to the four winds, forgotten in the decadent materialism, rigid legalism, and suicidal technophilia, which began to take hold after the fall of the spirits of darkness in 1917.[4] To be fully realized, they will require a concrete capacity that the human being has yet to fully integrate: manas consciousness, the gift of the Etheric Christ. It will take over a thousand years for them to fully develop.

At the end of the Age of Aries, we have the progression: Platonism—Aristotelianism—Christianity, as the key elements that went on to create the culture of the Age of Pisces. We can see clearly the modern equivalents of Platonism and Aristotelianism—what of the Mystery of Golgotha, the whole context of the fourth sacrifice of Jesus and Christ? Let's take a step back, and look at the difference between cultural ages and zodiacal ages. The cultural ages, according to Rudolf Steiner, progress from: Indian epoch (7227–5067 BC) to Persian epoch (5067–2907 BC), to Egyptian epoch (2907–747 BC), to Greco-Roman epoch (747 BC–AD 1414), to Central European epoch (1414–3574, the one in which we now live). On the other hand, the zodiacal ages run from the Age of Cancer (8426–6266 BC) to the Age of Gemini (6266–4106 BC), to the Age of Taurus (4106–1946 BC), to the Age of Aries (1946 BC–AD 215), to the Age of Pisces (215–2375, the one in which we now live). For more information as to *why* there is a lag between zodiacal age and cultural age, consult the work of Robert Powell, e.g., *Hermetic Astrology*, vol. I.

Plato and Aristotle arose out of ancient Greek culture. They are *the* representative products and producers of "Greco-Roman" culture. However, Jesus Christ and Christianity, the third in the progression "Platonism—Aristotelianism—Christianity", do *not* emerge from or fit into Greco-Roman culture. They are the end result of the ancient Hebrew culture. This culture was more or less at odds with the Greco-Roman culture at the time of Christ; at best, they tolerated each other.

---

3   There are any number of statements from Rudolf Steiner that could justify this point of view, but of course from another point of view this is an oversimplification. One could, for example, look at the progression from Goethe to Kaspar Hauser to Rudolf Steiner as somehow akin to the progression from Socrates to Plato to Aristotle. However, in this case, it is Goethe who is the equivalent of Plato, Steiner the equivalent of Aristotle, and Kaspar Hauser, who plays the role of Socrates. Note that Socrates is the common root of the seemingly opposite Plato and Aristotle; Hauser plays the same role for Goethe and Steiner on a spiritual level. And just as Socrates was seen as a threat worth killing by the authorities of his day, Kaspar Hauser suffered a similar fate. On the other hand, one could look directly at the progression of the literally reincarnated Socrates, Plato, and Aristotle: Tobias Gottfried Schröer (a.k.a. Christian Oeser), Karl-Julius Schröer, and Rudolf Steiner (see for example the chapter "Pictures from the Thought-life of Austria" in CW 20, *Riddle of Man*). Finally, one could also perceive the progression Bach—Mozart—Beethoven as the modern "Pisces" equivalent of the "Aries" Socrates—Plato—Aristotle, inasmuch as 1) the analogy holds remarkably well, and 2) these individuals incarnated almost exactly 2,160 years after the Greek philosophers in question. This raises the perspective that while the Age of Pisces was concerned primarily with imbuing the world views of Plato and Aristotle (both born of Socrates) with Christian "I"-consciousness, the Age of Aquarius may be more concerned with imbuing the musical impulses of Mozart and Beethoven (both born of Bach) with Christian manas consciousness.

---

4   See Steiner, *The Fall of the Spirits of Darkness*, particularly the lecture from Oct. 14, 1917.

And yet the Hebrews do not fit properly into the ancient Egyptian cultural epoch either. They were for the most part at odds with and strangers to this culture as well. Where do they find their place?

The Hebrews were the bridge from the ancient Egyptian to the Greco-Roman cultures. They were the primary people of the *Age of Aries*, which bridges that gap. And the advent of Jesus Christ, the God-Man, was the fulfilment of the mission of this people and that Age.

If, in the modern time, Goetheanism and Anthroposophy (both strongly Central European impulses) are the equivalent of Platonism and Aristotelianism, where might we look for the "third term," the culture that has brought to birth the advent of the Second Coming, the fifth sacrifice of Jesus and Christ? Both Goetheanism and Anthroposophy are representative of the fifth cultural age, the Central European epoch. But what movement or stream has been the modern equivalent of the ancient Hebrews, a kind of bridge from the Greco-Roman epoch to the Central European?

We can discover this quite clearly and distinctly by looking to the story of the immediate aftermath of Christ's resurrection for his followers, particularly Lazarus and Mary Magdalene.[5] They are sent adrift on the Mediterranean Sea and miraculously land in *Marseilles*, in France. The modern equivalent of the ancient Hebrews can be found in this region of France. It is the stream running from Lazarus and Magdelene, to the events of the Grail in the Carolingian era, to the School of Chartres and the Knights Templar, to the Tarot of Marseilles, Rosicrucianism, Freemasonry, Martinism—in a word, the French Hermetic tradition. This French spiritual stream is the main shoot of cultural development in the Age of Pisces (AD 215–2375) versus the main shoot of the Central European epoch (1414–3574)—the Germanic cultures.

And so, if we want to seek out the third term, the equivalent of the incarnation of Christ in the ancient Hebrew culture 2,000 years ago, we can

look to the French Hermetic stream of the modern time—specifically in the work *Meditations on the Tarot,* composed anonymously by Valentin Tomberg from 1958 to 1967. We can consider this work a kind of Gospel or Testament of the Etheric Christ—or perhaps better said, Epistles or Letters concerning the Etheric Christ.

It is in working rigorously and intensively with the Tarot of Marseilles (both Major and Minor Arcana) that we can begin to develop our manas cognition. Why is this? At the time of Christ, the Ego that had been planted by Archangel Jesus eons before came to fruition; at the same time, the seed for *atman* was planted, only to come to fruition at the time of the *seventh* sacrifice of Jesus and Christ at the dawn of the Anglo-American Age. However, now at the time of Christ's fifth sacrifice, it is *manas* cognition that comes to birth in each human soul, while the seed is now being planted for *buddhi*, a seed that will not fully develop until the *sixth* sacrifice of Jesus and Christ in the Slavic-Russian epoch.

Now, Christ's *buddhi,* his transformed etheric body (also known as "life spirit") was given over to Lazarus (Christian Rosenkreutz) at the raising of Lazarus from the dead. Christ's *buddhi* is manifested through the Sephiroth Tree, the Tree of Life—a Tree that bears within it twenty-two paths of Wisdom through ten Sephiroth operating on four planes of existence. This Tree is a multivalent being: it is simultaneously the archetypal foundation for the Hebrew language, the Ten Commandments, the Lord's Prayer, and the Tarot of Marseilles. The development of the Tarot of Marseilles has been under the spiritual guidance of Christian Rosenkreutz from their origins. We might say that, in particular, the Tarot of Marseilles is a *living symbol* of Christ's transformed etheric body. A living symbol represents a spiritual being or reality, yet simultaneously *is* what it represents. When we work with the Tarot of Marseilles, *we are working with Christ's etheric body to activate our manas consciousness.* This is what Valentin Tomberg has offered to us through composing *Meditations on the Tarot*—an example of *how* to work with Christ's etheric body. And this work to activate our manas

---

5   See Isaacson, *Through the Eyes of Mary Magdalene,* vol. 3, as well as my article "Eternal Israel": www.treehouse.live/2016/11/01/eternal -israel/.

consciousness will remain crucial for our cultural development for approximately 1,900 years.

And so, we have come to the following picture of the time of the fourth sacrifice of Jesus and Christ, the Mystery of Golgotha: it took place during the last third of the third life phase of Philosophia, in the Age of Aries; it was preceded by and was the natural culmination of the ancient Hebrew culture; it was also preceded by two critical schools of wisdom: Platonism and Aristotelianism. Initially Christianity had nothing to do with the two schools of Platonism and Aristotelianism; eventually, it integrated and brought to perfection first Platonism (in the Neoplatonic movement, in about the fourth century), and then Aristotelianism (during the Scholastic movement, around the thirteenth century).

And now we find ourselves in the time of the fifth sacrifice—the so-called Second Coming (although this title is confusing in the fuller context of the seven sacrifices), Christ's appearance in the etheric realm. Analogous to Christ's physical incarnation, this appearance in the etheric takes place in the last third of the sixth life-phase of Philosophia, in the Age of Pisces; it has been preceded by and is the natural culmination of French Hermeticism (Rosicrucianism); and it has also been preceded by two critical cultural movements: Goetheanism (German Idealism and Romanticism) and Anthroposophy. In fact, we might say that the deed of Christ's death and resurrection in the etheric sphere has been occurring over a much longer time period than the physical sacrifice 2,000 years ago. The crucifixion of Christ on the etheric plane—actually better described as a suffocation—took place in the nineteenth century, according to statements made by Rudolf Steiner on May 2, 1913.[6] He refers there to the swooning of the angel with whom Christ had united in order to appear in the etheric. This "swooning" is both the perfecting and sacrifice of ego-consciousness that had been developing since the time of the Mystery of Golgotha. Just as Platonism and Aristotelianism

represented the perfection of the astral body in preparation to receive the ego from Christ's deed, Goetheanism and Anthroposophy represent for our time the perfection of ego-activity in preparation to receive *manas* consciousness—the re-enlivened picture consciousness, now able to be a totally conscious and participatory experience, rather than strictly revelatory and dream-like.

The full sacrifice of Christ—Crucifixion, Descent, Resurrection—now takes place over the course of hundreds of years rather than three days—approximately 300 years. For the etheric crucifixion, the suffocation of Christ, which took place in the nineteenth century, coincided with and was reflected in the untimely death of Kaspar Hauser, the Child of Europe, in 1833, at the age of twenty-one—the age of the birth of the "I" in human development. A century later, around the year 1933, marked the start of the second phase—the Descent into Hell—with World War II marking Christ's descent through the nine sub-earthly spheres in order to reawaken humanity's awareness of the Mother in the Depths, to reopen the Path to Shambhala (Paradise) in the heart of the Earth.

This second phase is reaching its culmination, as in our time—around 2033[7]—Christ will have penetrated all the way to the Heart of the Mother, after a century-long journey to find Her (more on this, from various perspectives, can be found in the work of Robert Powell, for example *The Christ Mystery*). The third phase of resurrection will begin at that point, culminating in 2133. And so, the Christ event of the modern age is happening—due to it taking place over centuries rather than days—more or less *simultaneously* with the modern Aristotelianism of Anthroposophy. They are therefore not nearly so foreign to each other as the Mystery of Golgotha was to Aristotelianism.

One final thread for us to survey is the development of the Eucharist since the time of Christ. This rite splintered into several streams of Orthodoxy. Between 431 and 451, the Oriental Orthodox Churches and the Church of the East split off, both from each other and from the main trunk of

---

6 Steiner, *Christ at the Time of the Mystery of Golgotha and Christ in the Twentieth Century*, pp. 34–35.

7 Between 2028 and 2040, according to Robert Powell.

Orthodoxy, the Roman Catholic Church. About 600 years later, the Eastern Orthodox Churches split off from this main trunk during the East-West Schism of 1054. Another 500 years later, at the passing of the Act of Supremacy in 1534, establishing the King of England as head of the Church of England rather than the Pope, the third split from the main trunk occurred (simultaneous with the enormous fracturing of the Protestant Revolution).

So, over the first two thirds of the Age of Pisces, more or less four separate Orthodoxies developed: Roman Catholicism in Europe (and eventually South America); Oriental Orthodoxy in Africa, the Middle East, and the Far East; Eastern Orthodoxy in the Slavic and Russian nations; and Anglicanism in the English-speaking nations. The rite, which is meant to last through to the dawn of the Anglo-American age, has splintered completely.

In the sixteenth century, the world saw the widespread publication of the earliest decks of the Tarot of Marseilles—the earliest exoteric expression of the Tree of Life in our time. On the other hand, we also saw the final split in Orthodoxy occurring in the sixteenth century, with the rise of Protestantism, and the last "branch" of Orthodoxy, the Anglican Church. However, a healing also begins during this time. It is from the sixteenth century up through the modern age that certain of the Eastern and Oriental Orthodoxies begin to rejoin the Catholic Church, making up what are known as the Eastern Catholic churches. These are special churches which are under the auspices of the Catholic Church and the authority of the Pope, and yet have maintained their own particular rites (represented among the twenty-three Eastern Catholic Churches are five liturgical rites: Alexandrian, Armenian, Byzantine, East Syriac, and West Syriac). Therefore, they represent a kind of bridge between Catholicism and the other Orthodox faiths.[8] Perhaps along with the sacrifices of Jesus and Christ—now and into the future—there will also be a gradual reunion of the various splinters of Orthodoxy into a truly Catholic Church—an *Ecclesia Universalis*.

Therefore, we have several strands to weave together in the coming years. Just as the Eucharist established at the Last Supper facilitates the long-term goal of birthing the Resurrection Body (atman) of Christ in each individual human being at the dawn of the Anglo-American epoch, we ought to have a rite, some ritual, which is appropriate to the appearance of Christ in our time. This rite should exist with the goal of facilitating the germination and gestation of buddhi consciousness in humanity, a level of consciousness that will be able to come to birth at Christ's appearance on the astral level around 3800 to 3900.

Second, we have the need for the eventual full integration of Goetheanism and Anthroposophy into all of cultural life through the agency of the Hermetically-awakened manas consciousness over the course of the next 2,000 or so years. If the new rite is the equivalent of the Eucharist, a Hermetic Goetheanism and Hermetic Anthroposophy would be the equivalent of the Neo-Platonic and Scholastic movements.

And finally, we have a need for the continuing reformation and reunion of the Orthodox faiths. Perhaps, by the time of the sixth sacrifice of Jesus and Christ during the Slavic-Russian epoch, we can see the complete reunion of Eastern and Oriental Orthodoxies with Catholicism, and the beginnings of the reintegration of the Anglican and Protestant faiths.

The modern equivalent of Judaism is French Hermeticism; of Platonism, Goetheanism; and of Aristotelianism, Anthroposophy. But the fourth element at the time of the Mystery of Golgotha was the actual *rite* itself, the Eucharist, which abolished the old sacrifice—and is valid until the end of time, i.e., until the end of the cycle of birth, death, and reincarnation as we currently experience it, around the year 5733.

When we look at the development of the Eucharistic rite two thousand years ago, we can see that it took hundreds of years to take on its final form. Even to this day, with the reintegration of some of the churches of the Oriental Orthodox (the twenty-three Eastern Catholic Churches) there is some variety in the way that the Mass is celebrated

---

8 Cf. https://en.wikipedia.org/wiki/Eastern_Catholic _Churches.

within just Roman Catholicism alone. But perhaps if we can find the "guiding motif" for the Eucharist, we can try to discover what the "guiding motif" for the modern rite might be.

The core of the Eucharist is the communion of bread and wine. It is based on the events of the Last Supper as recorded in the synoptic Gospels of Luke, Mark, and Matthew, in which Christ inaugurates the very first Mass and instructs the apostles to "do this in remembrance of me." According to the visions of Anne Catherine Emmerich, the development of the elaborate ritual of the Eucharist out of this seemingly simple phrase from the Gospels was not a matter of the apostles taking things a bit too far, perhaps out of enthusiasm. In her visions, much more was said to the apostles, and many specific instructions were given, for the establishment of the Mass.[9]

One of the early customs of the church was to administer milk and honey at the first communion, prior to or along with the bread and wine.[10] This died out, however, around the time that the Church of the East and the Oriental Orthodox Churches separated from the main body (in the fifth to sixth centuries). The realization that the Church had at that time was that many different celebratory elements were being added to the service—whether it was milk and honey, or special water, or special herbs and oils, or other elements. It was felt that all of these elements, while arising from true enthusiasm, were occluding the two elements of most crucial importance: the bread and the wine. Thus, the Mass was eventually stripped down to its essence, with the focus entirely on Transubstantiation and the union of the human being with substance transformed into Christ's body and blood.

The purpose of this rite is to build, Mass by Mass and century by century, over many incarnations, the Resurrection Body within humanity. The purpose of it is to reunite the human being with the realm of the Father—with the nine spiritual hierarchies leading up to Him, as exemplified after the Resurrection by Christ's Ascension into Heaven. The gaze of the Church since the time of Christ is *upward*, longing for our reintegration into the heart of the Father as it was in the beginning—but now as sons and daughters, not slaves (i.e., with full conscientious participation, not in a dreamlike state).

What is of note is that there was at least one instance of a Mass that took place much too early—Abraham enjoyed the bread and wine with Melchizedek some 2,000 years prior to the Mystery of Golgotha. This might remind us as well of Cain's sacrifice of plant-life, creating horizontal smoke, *too early*, during the Lemurian age at the first sacrifice of Jesus and Christ. This form of sacrifice would only become proper during the Atlantean time period, at the second sacrifice of Jesus and Christ—and would only *remain* proper for the duration of the Atlantean Age, after which it would become decadent. Indeed, it was the extension of this "Cain Rite" beyond its proper time that brought about the great Flood that destroyed ancient Atlantis.

Therefore, it seems that both rites—the Atlantean rite *and* the Eucharist—were foreshadowed before their proper time, one by Cain and the other by Abraham. Indeed, there is a very close relationship between these two beings.[11] And perhaps this is where we might find a clue as to the nature and basic form of a modern rite, one we might call the Johannine rite, as will become clearer as we proceed.

The clue lies in the individuality of Cain—for this individuality reincarnated as Lazarus (also known as Lazarus-John after his resurrection, John, or Iohanan, being an initiatory title). There is only *one* Gospel that contains the story of the Raising of Lazarus—and this is the Gospel of St. John. Now, what is very interesting about this Gospel is that it is very different in content and tone from the other three. It contains many events within it that do not appear in the synoptic Gospels;

9 See *The Visions of Anne Catherine Emmerich*, vol. 3, pp. 78–82.

10 See for example here: https://christianity .stackexchange.com/questions/8278/who-in-the -fourth-century-had-milk-instead-of-wine-at -communion.

11 See for example Steiner's *Inner Experiences of Evolution*, in which the rejected sacrifice of Cain is connected with the rejection of Abraham's sacrifice of Isaac.

and it lacks certain content that *is* contained in the synoptics. It stands apart almost completely. Whereas Lazarus and John Zebedee were the same individuality according to Rudolf Steiner, according to the research of Robert Powell and Estelle Isaacson—which builds on and elucidates the visions of Anne Catherine Emmerich—John Zebedee (the disciple that Jesus loved) was able to bear the soul of Lazarus at certain crucial times.[12] The Apocalypse of John is entirely the work of Lazarus, and the three Epistles of John are entirely the work of John Zebedee, but the Gospel of St. John is a collaborative document, produced by two eyewitnesses to the ministry of Christ Jesus (we might see the hand of Lazarus more in the first half, and the hand of John Zebedee more in the second).

Perhaps, just as Cain was the forerunner of the Atlantean rite, and Abraham was a forerunner of the Eucharist, we might find the indications for a future rite in the Gospel of John. Certainly, the final scene in the Gospel of John indicates this: seven apostles are fishing all through the night, coming up empty. A figure on the shore tells them to cast their nets on the other side, and they haul in 153 fish. This figure turns out to be the Risen One, who prepares for them a breakfast of grilled fish and honey cakes. After this breakfast, he has a mysterious conversation in which he asks Peter three times if he loves Him—counterbalancing Peter's denial of Christ three times on Good Friday—and mandates him to "feed the sheep." We could think of this as an indication to Peter, as first Pope and representative of the Church, to vigilantly administer the sacrament, from that moment onward.

Christ then turns to John, and Peter asks, "What about him?" And Christ tells Peter, "If he is to wait until I come again, what of it?" Perhaps this exchange indicates that John, too, must inaugurate a rite, but cannot do so until Christ comes again—that is, the present time. But what should this rite look like? If the transubstantiation of bread and wine makes up the core of the Eucharist, what would be the core of a Johannine rite?

First, let's look at a portion of Valentin Tomberg's *Lord's Prayer Course*.[13] Within it he indicates that there are seven levels of communion, related to the various lotuses of the human being:

Crown	— Incense
Brow	— Oil
Larynx	— Fish
Heart	— Bread
Solar Plexus	— Milk
Sacral	— Honey
Root	— Wine

Notice that it became important for the early Church Fathers that the focus of the Eucharist remain on *only* the bread and the wine, to the exclusion of the five other elements, in order to avoid the dilution of the Rite. Valentin Tomberg teaches in the Lord's Prayer Course that it will be important for the levels of communion to become reestablished in the time of the Etheric Christ.

In the fourth healing miracle of Christ, the Feeding of the Five Thousand, a boy gives five loaves of bread and two fishes, from which the entire crowd of five thousand is satisfied, leaving twelve baskets of left-overs. Perhaps we could think of the two levels of communion administered in the Eucharist as the "two fishes." This would leave the other five—incense, oil, fish, milk, and honey—as the levels of communion of concern to the Johannine rite.

We can see the first beginnings of a Johannine rite in both The Christian Community, which sprang from Anthroposophy in 1922, as well as in the Grail Priesthood of the Sophia Foundation, which began to be an official training in 2006.[14] We could think of both of these as akin to the situation in the

---

12 See also Tidball, *Jesus, Lazarus, and the Messiah: Unveiling Three Christian Mysteries.*

13 Soon to be published as a single volume with a revised English translation by James Wetmore. The references to seven levels of communion are to be found in the section which focuses on the 4th petition of the Lord's Prayer, "Give us this day our daily bread."

14 It would take me much too far afield to describe the Mass of the Lamb and His Bride adequately. I will point the reader in the direction of Powell's article "The Eucharist and the Mass of the Lamb and His Bride," pp. 59–70 of the Easter 2020 edition of *Starlight*, available at https://sophiafoundation .org/wp-content/uploads/2020/04/Starlight-Easter -2020-issue-99p.pdf.

early church, when varieties of rites were springing up in different places, gradually approaching a universal (i.e., Catholic) underlying form. The Christian Community—as is quite clear in the lectures to the Priests on the Apocalypse from 1924—certainly sprang from the right essence, but is more or less an "updated" version of the Catholic rite. On the other hand, the Sophia Priesthood offers access to an authentic *milk and honey* communion—a communion devoted to Sophia, the Divine Feminine—but also offers a dozen or so other celebrations, none of which are yet attached to a liturgical cycle of the Christian year.

Again, it is the Gospel of John that ought to offer us the right guide here. What is *missing* from this Gospel? Read closely the events of the Last Supper in John's Gospel in Chapter 13. There is no Eucharist! There is no bread and wine! Instead, there is the *Washing of the Feet*—which is *only* present in John's Gospel. And when we remember that the feet are the "fish" of the human body—related to the sign of Pisces—we can see how the Washing of the Feet fulfils the role of the "fish" level of communion. When we consider the way in which Mary Magdalene washes the feet of Christ on the day before the Last Supper (see John's Gospel, chapter 12) with spikenard oil (*incense oil*) we can see that the upper levels of communion—incense, oil and fish—are fulfilled in the act of foot washing.

We could think of foot washing as the equivalent of the sacrament of baptism in a way—whereas baptism emerged from the Age of Aries (related to the head), foot washing must emerge from the Age of Pisces (related to the feet). And it is these two activities—foot washing and the communion of milk and honey—that must be the central acts of a modern Johannine rite, inasmuch as together they contain the five levels of communion other than bread and wine, the levels of communion belonging to the Eucharist.

What might be the other features of this rite—a rite devoted primarily to the *Earth Mother* rather than the *Heavenly Father*, and one that will be necessary and appropriate for humanity for only a short time—until Christ comes again, around the year 3833, in an *astral form?*

This Rite ought to be as *authentic* as possible, stripped of arbitrary elements as much as possible; it also must be *complementary* to existing Tradition as much as possible—remembering that it is a temporal rite, developing a completely different spiritual body (buddhi or life spirit—the "Tree of Life") than the Eucharist (which is developing atman or spirit-human, the Resurrection Body).

The Orthodox Churches are concerned with reestablishing the connection between human beings and the Father God in the heights, via the nine spiritual hierarchies. In doing so, they transform the human kingdom into the tenth hierarchy—that of Love and Freedom. The center of gravity of the Church is the Eucharist, the communion of bread and wine. And the primary time of year during which the Church focuses on the birth, life, death and resurrection of Christ is from Advent through Whitsun—the rest of the liturgical year (between Whitsun and Advent) is referred to as "Ordinary Time."

Nowadays Advent begins somewhat less than four weeks prior to Christmas Day, at the end of November/beginning of December. This was not always the case. Originally, the season of Advent began on the Sunday after Martinmas (Nov. 11), and was referred to as the Fast of St. Martin. It was an approximately forty-day fast leading up to Christmas, akin to Lent leading up to Easter. This is still the custom in both the Ambrosian and Mozarabic Rites, in which the Advent season begins six Sundays before Christmas, rather than four.[15]

Martinmas, in many northwestern cultures, marks the end of the farming season. If Michaelmas is the harvest festival, Martinmas is the butchering festival. It is often celebrated with a harvest feast and bonfire. It marks the "turning within" of the Christian year, when the focus is no longer meant to be on outer affairs, but on the life of Christ.

On the other hand, Whitsun is a moveable festival that can occur anywhere from May 10 to June 13. One could say this festival marks the

---

15 See "The Feast of St. Martin" by Gregory Dipippo: https://www.newliturgicalmovement.org/2015/11/the-feast-of-st-martin.html#.YvFbjS9QimA.

proper beginning of the agricultural year (again, from a culturally Northwestern perspective)—it is usually at this time of year that animals go back out to pasture, the final frosts have occurred, and biodynamic preparations are sprayed on the fields and gardens. The "turning within" to the life of Christ ceases; we once again become concerned with outer affairs.

And now let's take into consideration the aims of the presence of Christ in the elemental realm in our time. It is his task—and ours—in this age to turn our gaze *below,* to the Mother, rather than above. We must find the Mother in the depths; and we can only find her through the redemption of elemental beings of natural and subnatural realms. If our task in the Eucharist is to return to the Father via the angels, it is our task in the Johannine rite to return to the Mother via the elementals. This time of year, during which we turn to Mother Nature—so-called Ordinary Time—is the time of year during which the Johannine Rite ought to be performed.[16]

We can find a clue to this in the mystery of the number 153, the quantity of fish that were caught by the disciples through the guidance of the Risen One.[17] One hundred fifty-three days is just one day shy of twenty-two weeks (22 × 7 = 154); the Tree of Life, the transformed etheric body of Christ, is made up of twenty-two Paths, twenty-two Arcana, represented in the Tarot of Marseilles. The "Christian year" of the Mother Service would ideally consist of 153 days (or twenty-two weeks) between Whitsun and Martinmas.

In the year 2023, this would be from Sunday, June 11 through Saturday, November 10. Generally

speaking, this is about the time of year that the Johannine season would take place—from mid-June to mid-November. The start of this liturgical season would begin after the descent of the tongues of flame on Whitsun—usually around the Feast of the Holy Trinity, the Sunday after Whitsun. In fact, this day is of some significance. It was on the Feast of the Holy Trinity (May 21, 1967) that the anonymous author finished penning his twenty-two Letter-Meditations on the Tarot. It was also on the Feast of the Holy Trinity (May 26, 810) that Parzival came for the second time to the Grail Castle and healed King Anfortas (see my article in *Cosmology Reborn: Star Wisdom,* vol 1, "First Steps Toward a Grail Timeline"). Perhaps there is an indication here that the "Grail Church service," one deeply related to the Tarot, ought to begin each year on the Festival of the Holy Trinity, one week after Whitsun. In 2023, this will fall on June 4, which would have the 153-day period last until November 3.

Shortly after the start of the cycle each year comes the celebration of St. John's Tide on June 24, when the flames of Whitsun become full bonfires. The death and resurrection of Lazarus, historically speaking, took place in the second half of July. The Assumption of the Virgin Mary is celebrated (and occurred historically) in mid-August; and the Feast of the Beheading of John the Baptist is celebrated on August 29. Along with Michaelmas (the theme of which is the rescuing of the Divine Feminine from the attack of the Dragon), comes the Feast of St. Francis—the reincarnated John Zebedee—who had a very special relationship to Nature. And the season ends with St. Martin of Tours, who could be seen as a similar figure to St. Francis—a soldier who turns to a life of piety and service.

Just as the Father Church enters beautiful stone cathedrals, from the cold of winter to the rebirth of spring, ideally the Mother Service would take place outdoors in the beauty of Nature. For this church does not exist primarily for human beings. The key gesture of this service would be to *redeem Nature,* just as humanity has been redeemed by the spiritual world—in other words, to *wash the feet* of Nature. The gesture of foot washing is

---

16 In terms of Steiner's *Four Seasons and the Archangels,* it seems that to the Father belong the Gabrielic and Raphaelic seasons, whereas the seasons of the Mother are Urielic and Michaelic.

17 In fact, this is one of the "open secrets" of the Gospel of John; whereas it is immediately revealed that there are miraculously twelve baskets of leftover bread after the Feeding of the Five Thousand, it is not obvious whether there were any leftover fish. It is clear enough for me, however, that the 153 fish are the miraculous leftovers from the 4th Miracle, undiscovered (and undiscoverable?) until after the Resurrection.

the higher bending over to honor the lower—the lower that has sacrificed itself for the sake of the development of the higher. This was the gesture of Christ toward his disciples on the night of the Last Supper.

In both Valentin Tomberg's *Lord's Prayer Course,* as well as in his meditations on the Foundation Stone Meditation, he elaborates on the foot washing that could occur for the kingdoms of nature and our fellow human beings in our time. In *The Lord's Prayer Course,* his indications are included in the meditations on the sixth beatitude in the section on the first petition of the Lord's Prayer:

"Hallowed be thy name," with special reference to the sixth Beatitude, "Blessed are the pure in heart, for they shall see God."

To be pure in heart means: to extend one's mercy (compassion) to all realms, to all beings: to those of the kingdoms of Nature and to the spiritual hierarchies, belonging to the spiritual kingdoms. This is objectivity *with* interest, where the question is not what is there but *what is lacking.* This is the *healing* gaze. The heart is radiant when it has selfless interest: the therapeutic look. If one looks at Nature this way, what does one see?

What does one find if one directs a pure look toward Nature?

There the Fall is also to be found, which comes to expression in that the kingdoms of Nature became heavier than they should be, and the spiritual kingdoms lighter. Just as light and smoke arise from a flame, so also here: the smoke came as heaviness into the kingdoms of Nature, the light as lightness into the spiritual kingdoms. Thus, a cleft formed that should not be there: a cleft between the material world and the non-incarnated world. The search of the alchemists went in the direction of bridging over this cleft, in order to attain to the regenerated condition of the old Earth, prior to the Fall. They attempted to make matter lighter through the Fifth Element, or spiritual substance heavier—so as to bring about a connection again. This attempt was successful and remains preserved in the true Rosicrucian tradition. If one asks what the mineral, plant and animal kingdoms are lacking: the three kingdoms of Nature lack tone, light and warmth.

The *stones* lack *warmth*: the *force of the Father.* If this was there, there would be a melting of rigidity of the mineral kingdom.

The *plants* lack *light*: the <u>Son</u>. Through him the plants would have their light again.

The *animals* lack <u>tone</u>: the *Holy Spirit* through whom it is bestowed to be consciously present in one's own body. The group soul bears the Holy Spirit but not the individual animal.

Thus, the Trinity is what is missing from the world of the kingdoms of Nature. In this way one attains to a perception of the Divine by asking through loving interest what is lacking.

What is the mineral world lacking?

If one asks what the mineral kingdom is lacking, one finds that it has become the sacrifice or victim of cold. In the same way that ice comes into being, so also has the mineral world arisen, through the paralyzing of movement through cold. On Ancient Saturn everything was still warm, the will of the Thrones, and everything was in movement. The mineral world is ash from burnt-out flame. The mineral world lacks *warmth.* Such a will must come, which brings warmth again, whereby the paralyzing of the will through cold ceases. Warmth of will must be conveyed: the Father force. The mineral kingdom has lost the *warmth ether.* Meditate on the mineral aspect of Nature. Meditation upon stone, which has lost its warmth, which is warmth of will rigidified by Ahriman. Liberation therefrom can be carried out through a will that is as living as that of the Father and has as much love as the Father. Experience the cold of the world and ask concerning the original form of warmth.

What is the plant world lacking?

If one asks oneself what the plant kingdom is lacking, one finds that it is *light.* It longs for light because it needs it and does not have it itself. It possesses no astral light of its own. Thus, it is dependent upon light from without. When did the plant have light? On the Ancient Sun. Then it was within the Sun. What the Sun now brings to it was at that time its root. It consisted of Sun light. Now, however, it has lost its relationship to the *light ether*. Ask what the plant world is lacking: it is the light of the Sun. The plant longs for light. At one time the plant was light, was Sun. Read Paul's Letter to the Romans: "For the creation waits with eager longing for the revealing of the Sons of God." (Rom. 8:19–22)

What is the animal world lacking?

What does the animal lack? The *word*, the voice. On the Ancient Moon the kingdom that now corresponds to the animal kingdom was gifted with the word. They sung and understood one another. (In old myths and legends there is still a reminiscence of this: the singing fish, the singing unicorn.) For the animal there now remains only a remnant of this singing: roaring, barking, etc. The animal world has lost the capacity to set the *tone ether* in motion. Ask what the animal world is lacking: it is the voice of the soul, the inner word. If the Holy Spirit were to penetrate the animal, the animal kingdom would be raised up.

What do human beings lack?

What does the *human being* lack? Everything that the kingdoms of Nature also lack, for the human being bears all three kingdoms of Nature within. Beyond this, however, the human being also lacks something else quite specific on account of being human. In the Christian tradition that is ever growing, deepening and progressing, something is spoken of that human beings have lost: this is the *seed of Eden*. Earlier, human beings lived from the forces of seeds until, after the Fall, they incarnated ever more deeply. They then ate fruit, then vegetables, and, lastly, meat. This was because the Cherubim closed off access to the Tree of Life. What was the significance of this loss of the Tree of Life for human beings? It meant that human beings were no longer able to create physical bodies for themselves, but that they had to be received by way of heredity, whereby the body is usually not suited to the individual. This is the tragic consequence of the loss of the Tree of Life.

The resurrection body of Christ is the Tree of Life *in the present*. This is the *seed of Eden*. In it death is overcome such that everything

that Nature is lacking is there. Warmth of will is there: the Resurrected One is able to accomplish deeds in the physical world with his mobile and flexible physical body. Light is there: this resurrection body is so radiant that it has what plants lack. A radiant body: the Sun is in it. It is a piece of Sun upon the Earth. Also, tone is there: the tones that the animal world lacks are in it. This resurrection body of Christ is such a fine instrument that it brings forth in tone and sound everything of the thought, feeling and will that this body experiences: this all comes to expression in it. In addition, this body contains the seed of Eden—immortality—as the fourth. It is not so terrible when an animal dies; it only sleeps somewhat longer. However, when a human being dies, this is actually a disgrace. Thus, human beings should not die, but should become transformed. It is a disgrace that a spirit is so dependent upon the body. Dying is a humiliating experience for the human being. However, the seed of Eden is immune to death. Christ died to a far greater extent and yet returned again to life.

The human being lacks the synthesis of Father, Son and Holy Spirit—the *Persona*. This is the seed of Eden, and it is this that the human being is lacking. Death is an affront to the human being, who lacks immortality in the body, the resurrection body. This is the Persona, the Divine Person of Jesus Christ.

Ask what the human being is lacking. It is the seed of Eden, the synthesis of Father, Son and Holy Spirit: the Persona, the Tree of Life.

Concerning the Tree of Life, read Genesis, chapters 1 to 3, and Revelation, chapters 2 and 22.[18]

As to the basic content and structure of the celebration, the Sophia Mass of milk and honey, introduced by Robert Powell some thirty years ago, and celebrated by many involved with the Sophia Foundation (mainly, up until now, in the United States) is a huge step in the right direction.[19] In

---

18 This is a provisional rendering from Robert Powell, available through the Sophia Foundation. A fully revised translation is soon to be available from James Wetmore.

19 Up until now the text of this liturgy/celebration has been available only to those willing and able

particular, the focus of this service is on the *Our Mother* prayer, given through Valentin Tomberg at the height of World War II in Amsterdam. This prayer ought to be as central to the Mother service as the Lord's Prayer is to the Father service in the Eucharist:

Our Mother,
    Thou who art in the darkness of the underworld,
    May the holiness of Thy name shine anew in our remembering,
    May the breath of Thy awakening kingdom warm the hearts of all who wander homeless,
    May the resurrection of Thy will renew eternal faith, even unto the depths of physical substance.
    Receive this day the living memory of Thee from human hearts,
    Who implore thee to forgive the sin of forgetting Thee,
    And are ready to fight against temptation that has led thee to existence in darkness,
    That through the deed of the Son, the immeasurable pain of the Father be stilled, by the liberation of all beings from the tragedy of Thy withdrawal.
    For thine is the homeland and the boundless wisdom and the all-merciful grace, for all and everything in the Circle of All.
    Amen.

However, the orientation of the Sophia Mass as performed currently by the Sophia Priesthood would need to be somewhat altered. As it stands currently, the service culminates in the eating of milk and honey. A separate service replicates the bread and wine communion of the Orthodox Church (the union of these two is referred to as the "Mass of the Lamb and His Bride"); and a third, only partially developed service includes a communion of fish.

First, the bread-and-wine communion belongs to the Church and to the liturgical year running from Advent through Whitsun. It does not belong in a Mother service (i.e., the Johannine rite), as

it is not a part of the Gospel of John. Remember that this new rite needs to complement and complete—not replace—the pre-existing rite of the Church.

Second, the *eating* of milk and honey should not necessarily stand at the center or culmination of the Mother service. You see, in Orthodoxy, what is of primary importance is the taking of the Eucharist in the Mass—the sacrament that is *ingested* is of primary importance. On the other hand, the sacrament of baptism—a *tactile* sacrament—is of secondary significance. With the Johannine Rite, it is the reverse. What is of primary importance is the Washing of the Feet. Foot washing is mentioned not once, but twice in the Gospel of St. John. On Holy Wednesday, Mary Magdalene anoints Christ's feet with precious spikenard oil and her tears, drying his feet with her hair. Then, on Maundy Thursday, Christ anoints the disciples' feet with water. The *tactile* sacrament is of primary importance here—the Sophia or Mother service ought to culminate in the Washing of the Feet, rather than the tasting of milk and honey. Certainly, in the early tradition of the Church, milk and honey were taken only once, with one's first communion—just as one is only baptized once, usually as a newborn in the Orthodox churches. The Johannine rite could adopt this historical tradition, giving milk and honey only at the "first communion"—or rather, first foot washing.

At the time of Christ, the actual baptism administered by John was an initiatory event performed on full-grown adults, during which they were submerged in the water until they had a near-death experience. This was adapted to a sprinkling of water on the heads of newborn infants in the tradition of the Church. The immersive and thorough foot washing performed by Christ and Mary Magdalene could be similarly adapted—one's feet would be sprinkled with the water at the culmination of the service. One would then take the water and douse the surrounding Nature, as in the application of a biodynamic preparation. In fact, a "Milk and Honey Prep" is already used in biodynamic agriculture (see chart). Here we have

to take on the Grail Facilitator's training, which happens annually through the Sophia Foundation. See www.sophiafoundation.org for more details.

THE MILK SPRAY / THE MILK & HONEY SPRAY

When certain plants in the garden experience a sudden attack by detrimental insects or when plants seem to be experiencing great stress which is not overcome by the Barrel Compost (Thun recipe) or other BD preparation spray treatment, a spray of milk, or sometimes, a spray of milk and honey, can often bring benefits. While attempts to explain what is actually happening are difficult, the most evident result is a tremendous increase in the population of so-called beneficial insects, often in such numbers as to quickly eliminate as a problem the previous onslaught by the detrimental insects.

The basic formula used is one (1) part milk to nine (9) parts water, (i.e. 1:10 ratio). The honey is sometimes added in a ratio of 1:100 to the entire volume. Particularly when using the honey, the water should be warmed to aid in dissolving the honey. Each mixture is stirred in the customary Biodynamic fashion for 20 minutes and then sprayed in a medium to fine mist, somewhere between the large drops recommended for BD #500 and the fine mist recommended for BD #501. We generally stir and spray either 5 or 10 gallon batches with the following ratios:

	FIVE GALLONS	TEN GALLONS
MILK	½ gallon	1 gallon
WATER	4½ gallons	9 gallons
when used with HONEY	6.4 oz. by volume	12.8 oz. by volume

Josephine Porter Institute, www.jpibiodynamics.org

---

an excellent beginning to the holy substance that would be regularly sprayed on the feet of the celebrants, as well as the "feet" of Mother Earth. One might only need to add to this a small amount of spikenard oil (and/or frankincense oil) in order to have the fullness of the five communions:

> (1) Incense and (2) Oil = Spikenard Oil
> (3) Fish = Feet
> (4) Milk and (5) Honey

I originally began developing the form of this service in the summer of 2020. My friend and colleague Natalia Haarahiltunen expressed a great deal of interest in attempting this new ritual, which she did for the first time in the summer of 2020 in Italy. We then had quite a bit of back and forth, developing the ritual further between us. It has very much been a collaborative experience—and not only between us, but also in our dream life, influences have come. Each of us has performed it a few times since then, and gradually something concrete and central has begun to take shape.

One of the first aspects we noticed is that the administration of the incense and oil has a very different gesture to it than the administration of the milk and honey. We felt the incense and oil to have more of an "embalming" feeling to them, related more to the stones, versus the milk and honey, which reach out to the plants and animals in an enlivening/awakening way. Eventually we saw the following:

We bring warmth to the stones through the
    incense and oil.

We bring moral ether to the human being
    through the foot washing.

We bring light to the plants through the
    dousing with milk and honey preparation.

We bring tone to the animals through song and
    dance.

These became the four parts of the service.

Prior to beginning the service, one would need to potentize the milk and honey prep for twenty minutes. All would gather in a semi-circle around this preparation.

And so, this is how the service begins: after reading from John 12:1–8, the officiant speaks out the words, "The Spirits of the Elements hear it in East, West, North, South" while the participants respond, "May Human Beings hear it!" Drops of incense (spikenard and frankincense) are put onto the tip of a sword[20] by the officiant, and it is plunged into the earth. The participants kneel and recite the Our Mother Prayer.[21] All of this is done in honor of the kingdom of stones, bringing them warmth. Our consciousness is directed down

---

20 In a dream, I was guided to the image of plunging a sword into the earth and kneeling before it, as the Knights Templar once did. I was reminded of the Dagger of Djemshid, the father of agriculture. I was reminded of "burying the hatchet," of swords becoming plowshares.

21 Alternatively, this would be spoken accompanied with the eurythmy gestures from the Prayer Sequence, available here: https://sophiafoundation.org/product/prayer-sequence-in-sacred-dance/. It would also be wonderful if it was spoken in Russian, for those who know it. However, speaking it in one's own language while kneeling is the simplest and most easily accessible.

to the center of the earth, to the Mother. It is a solemn mood.

Next, an offering of the *moral ether* is brought to the human being, administered through the sacrament of *fish* (i.e., the human feet, the "fish" of the zodiacal human being).

The officiant reads John 13:1–17, 34–35.

The officiant then proclaims, "The Spirits of the Elements hear it in East, West, North, South."

The participants respond, "May Human Beings hear it!"

(At this point, an explicit invitation to those across the threshold to join in the service could be made. This could be done in the context of the Tarot of Marseilles and the ritualistic mantra and gestures of the Grail Knights Practice—a different Tarot and portion of the Practice could be focused on for each of the twenty-two weeks of the liturgical season of the Mother. See the appendix at the end of this article.)

The officiant then adds a few drops of the oils to the preparation, takes a vessel of it, and then approaches and kneels before each participant and douses their feet with the prep and drops of the essential oil. While doing this, the officiant speaks to them: "If your feet are clean, then all of you is clean. Go and wash the feet of others as I have washed yours."

The last participant whose feet is washed then washes the feet of the officiant. Alternatively, if there is more than one officiant, they can wash the feet of each other.

In the third part, we bestow *light* on the plant kingdom primarily through the sacrament of *honey* via the biodynamic preparation.

The officiant reads John 6:1–21.

The officiant then proclaims, "The Spirits of the Elements hear it, in East, West, North, South."

And the participants respond, "May Human Beings hear it!"

Each participant then gathers up their own vessel for dousing the surrounding landscape with the preparation; the dousing continues until the prep is gone.[22] Keep in mind that one's feet are

spreading this preparation as one is taking each step, returning the Earth to her original hallowed state.

Finally, we bestow *word or tone* on the animal kingdom, represented by the sacrament of milk that we have just sprayed on the surrounding landscape.[23]

We return to the circle, and together we joyfully sing for the sake of the animal kingdom. It could be a spiritual song that is somehow deeply tied to the surrounding nature, land, or folk. For example, a section from the Kalevala might be very appropriate in a Finnish landscape.[24]

The service ought to be quite grave and solemn in the first two parts, but this gravity should transform into joyful levity and playfulness in the third and fourth parts. Therefore, if only in terms of *aesthetic* and *core orientation*, the outdoor paneurhythmy celebrations of the Universal White Brotherhood developed by Beinsa Douno (Peter Deunov) in the early part of the twentieth century would be ideal for this portion of the service.[25] Additionally,

---

incorporate the threefold walking exercises from the Shambhala Path (https://sophiafoundation.org/product/the-shambhala-path), as it is not only our hands but also our feet which are spreading this preparation through the surrounding landscape as we take each step.

23 Keep in mind that the milk and honey preparation is meant to benefit pollinating plants as well as pollinating birds, insects, and bats—it is of benefit to both the plant and animal kingdoms.

24 Clearly, for those who are familiar with Choreocosmos, the cosmic dance for Sun in the appropriate constellation would be ideal; the trick would be to find musical accompaniment to this that doesn't require a piano or a recording; something that can be sung outside—i.e., an earthier, "folk-oriented" spiritual song in the appropriate key. However, one could also sing "Silent Stones", a musical rendition of Christian Morgenstern's poem "The Washing of the Feet" by Colin Tanser (https://www.uppereskmusic.com/store/p112/Colin_Tanser%3A_Star_Wished_Night.html; click on the last thumbnail image). In fact, this song could be sung consistently each time the service is performed, especially by those who are unfamiliar with paneurhythmy.

25 Beinsa Douno's book *Paneurhythmy: Supreme Cosmic Rhythm; Music Ideas, Movements* is especially helpful in this regard. See also the online instructional videos by Svetla Baltova on YouTube.

---

22 I would be more inclined to allow this to be a bit of a joyous free-for-all; however, others might wish to

paneurhythmy was developed specifically with the elemental beings and the world of Nature in mind. The songs and movements of Beinsa Douno could become an integral part of a modern Mother service. There are twenty-eight paneurhythmy exercises, as well as the culmination of these exercises in the "Sun's Rays" and "Pentagram" dances. The first ten of the twenty-eight exercises form a unity; therefore, this gives us 1 + 18 = 19 exercises and two culminating dances—twenty-one celebratory songs and movements that align very closely with the 153-day/twenty-two-week liturgical season of the Mother.

To close, the officiant then reads the entirety of chapter 21 of the Gospel of John. We then proclaim, all together:

> The Spirits of the Elements hear it
> In East, West, North, South;
> May Human Beings hear it!"

So, in many ways we have the basic elements required for a proper service. We have the *Our Mother* rather than the *Our Father*. We have Foot washing rather than the Eucharist. For liturgical music and movement, we have paneurhythmy. For a chapel we have the natural world—in fact, fields and forests are best. The biodynamic milk and honey preparation was made in order to encourage the presence of pollinators. Inasmuch as the stars above could be seen as the outer garment of the angelic hierarchies, we might consider insects (particularly pollinators) to be the outer garment of the elemental beings: a direct expression of their health and well-being.[26] And so a milk and honey foot washing is directly beneficial to the elemental beings of our fields and forests.

Therefore, an ideal celebration of the Mother would be an outdoor biodynamic foot washing using a special mixture of several sacramental elements; weaving together the work of Valentin Tomberg, Robert Powell, and Peter Deunov; focusing on the revivification of Mother Nature and the elementals. It would be celebrated during "Ordinary Time," the height of the agricultural season, the time from Whitsun until Martinmas.

It is still a question what one would call the officiants of such a service. They would not be priests or ministers. The word *priest* comes from *presbyter,* which means "elder." Those who are leading this service are not elders or masters, they are servants and children at heart. And certainly, no training or ordination would be necessary to host the above celebration—simply a willing heart.

On a personal note—what is wonderful about this service is its accessibility, not only in terms of who is able to host it, but also in terms of who can attend. For my part, when I hosted it in August 2021, it was attended by a devout Catholic. Since there is no taking in of substances, it is not a moral quandary for an orthodox individual to participate in this service. This is not the case when it comes to The Christian Community service or the Mass of the Lamb and His Bride. On the other hand, my friend Natalia was able to host this in Finland at the same time, with friends who would otherwise want nothing to do with a church service. The Finnish soul is drawn in a powerful way to Mother Nature and the elemental beings; the focus of this service was experienced to some degree as the church service for which the Nordic peoples have been waiting (more on this in part three of this series). Again, this is not so much the case when it comes to either The Christian Community service nor the Mass of the Lamb and His Bride. This is in no way meant to disparage these two services, both of which I have attended on a regular basis! It is simply to emphasize the open quality of the Mother ritual. This was even clearer in light of the social effects of Covid restrictions at the time—since it is an outdoor festival, with no taking in of substances, it was open and welcome to all—masked or unmasked, it made no difference. In fact, I felt on an intuitive level that what Natalia and I had been given in terms of this ritual was something that could be deeply healing for humanity in terms of the longer-term health effects of both Covid itself, as well as the mRNA injections—an answer to prayer!

As a reminder of the spiritual significance of this "washing the feet" of Mother Earth, let's

---

26 See the article " ♃ " by Asclepias in this volume.

recall Valentin Tomberg's indications about the second coming of Christ:

The reappearance in the etheric has significance not just for humanity, but also for nature. The purpose is to bring something new into being. After death, the human ether body "dissolves"; nevertheless, at the same time an extract survives death and goes with the individuality from one incarnation to the next. Likewise, nature will also acquire a realm related to ordinary nature, just as the extract of the human ether body relates to the ether body itself. The extract of the human ether body is, in fact, buddhi, or life spirit. Similarly, a realm of life spirit will also arise in nature as a result of the etheric second coming of Christ.[27]

We mentioned that the etheric return of Christ will also have significance for the world of nature. When Christ appeared nineteen centuries ago, he came for the benefit of humanity. His descent took place vertically in the sphere of human existence. The consciousness of nature, however, is on a horizontal plane. Consequently, the effects of the Mystery of Golgotha are accessible to nature only through human beings. The world of nature does not experience the being of Christ directly, and because of this, a certain sense of hopelessness is becoming stronger for nature. We can say that humankind is the destiny of nature; we must bring salvation to the world of nature, because we have the moral connection with the spiritual world. But nature has a dynamic connection with the spiritual world; it must obey the world of spirit. Nature can experience the warmth that comes from the Sun, but not moral warmth, which can come from human beings. Unfortunately, this does not happen. Because of this, misfortune occurs again and again only in the elemental world.

The Bible mentions the primordial chaos (tohu wa bohu). The Genesis of Moses portrays the earth's becoming, particularly from the view of the elemental world. At that time, the beings of nature, the animals, were brought before human beings, who gave them names. Through this act, a certain influence proceeded from humankind toward the beings of nature, and this determined their karma; human beings determined nature's karma. This occurred during the Lemurian epoch, and the post-Atlantean epoch is a reversed reflection of that Lemurian epoch. Chaos is again arising in the elemental world. It is the duty of humankind to return order into that chaos by using moral powers. All of this chaos makes possible certain influences upon humanity. For example, when Rudolf Steiner spoke of Bolshevism, he said that there are cruel elemental beings behind men—elemental beings who goad human beings to commit acts of cruelty. It is our human task to cure the world of those illnesses. Still, human beings do almost nothing in this way for nature, and thus much of nature has less and less hope for redemption. The etheric return of Christ will signal a restoration of hope for nature; it will be a sign of resurrection for nature. Christ will be active throughout the horizontal spatial realm. He will visit all the regions of the Earth, and this will lead to a meeting with the beings of nature and an active moral force in the world of nature. In the past, this happened through the vertical plane for humankind; today it happens on the horizontal plane for nature.[28]

The Age of Aries was focused on the perfection of the astral body in order to facilitate the birth of the ego within humanity, culminating with Aristotle, Plato and the Mystery of Golgotha in the final third of the Age of Aries. The Age of Pisces involved the perfecting of the ego in order to facilitate the birth of manas (imaginative) cognition, culminating in Weimar Classicism, Anthroposophy, and Christian Hermeticism in our time, the final third of the Age of Pisces.

The goal of the new rite that is to be established at this time of the etheric Christ is meant to help bring to birth the next higher level after manas—buddhi, which as the above quote indicates, is a concern for both humanity and nature together. It is the "extract" of the memory of Earth that we must take into the next planetary embodiment (Future Jupiter).

Notice that, for early humanity, the physical body and the etheric body were free gifts from

---

27 Tomberg, *Christ and Sophia*, pp. 363–64.

28 Ibid., p. 399.

above. Humanity had to *work*, in response to sacrifices from above, for the attainment of an astral body and—for an even longer period of time—the attainment of an ego. The Hebrew rite that existed from the time of Cain and Abel (ancient Lemuria) up through the Mystery of Golgotha was the primary rite that built up the capacity for acquiring the individual ego over long ages of time. The secondary rite lasted only throughout the Atlantean Era, and built up the capacity for acquiring a fully precipitated, individualized astral body (i.e., rather than an astral body united with the wider cosmos).

And now it is reversed. *Manas* (the transformed astral body) comes as a "free gift," building on the work done to acquire and perfect the astral body prior to the time of Christ, combined with the exercising of the free ego since the time of Christ. The highest body of the human being, Atman (the transformed physical body), requires the exercising of the Eucharistic Rite until the end of time—that is, until the end of material incarnation in the 6th millennium. We must *work* for this transformed physical body, whereas the untransformed physical body was a free gift. And similarly, we must *work* for buddhi, for the transformed etheric body, whereas the original etheric body was a free gift—and this work involves the Mother ritual, a work that must last through to the sixth sacrifice of Jesus and Christ—Christ's appearance in an *astral* form rather than an *etheric* or *physical* form, in approximately 1,900 years.

And so, our time to establish and practice this Johannine Mother ritual is relatively brief. It extends from our current time period, the end of the Age of Pisces, until the last third of the Age of Aquarius, around 3900 (the Age of Aquarius ends in 4535), as a kind of miniature reflection of the Atlantean Era. Pisces: this points us to the honoring of the feet in the Mother ritual; Aquarius: each person participating in the ritual becomes a Water Bearer.

But the cultivation of this Mother ritual must go hand in hand with the full development of the independent manas consciousness:

For the first time, the Mystery of Golgotha will be repeated, but now with an added new

element...a new "karmic clairvoyance" will be evoked through the activity of the Christ being. This etheric clairvoyance will be entirely new and not a repetition; it will be the result of the fifth sacrifice of Christ.

Try to understand this new, fifth sacrifice... The earlier sacrifices involved harmonizing the physical, etheric, and astral bodies and the "I." The fifth sacrifice, however, harmonizes the human manas organization, or spirit self. Harmonization of the form always comes before the harmonization of the essence, which can take effect later and develop on the foundation thus created. This is precisely a matter of harmonizing the manas, the relationship between the "I" that ascends and the ego that descends. It is the harmonizing of the two "eyes"; the upper eye sees the mysteries of goodness, the future, and the world of spirit, while the lower eye perceives the mysteries of evil. The manas organization is harmonized by uniting these "eyes" in the I AM of the Christ impulse. This is their axis of vision, which includes potential communication with the spirit world while conscious and awake...

This union will become permanent in harmony with the human spiritual organization, and not something that existed only at certain times during special states of meditation. The harmonization of the manas organization gave rise to permanent connection between the upper "I" and the lower ego. This axis of vision of both "eyes," or axis of vision in the manas organization (with the upper seeing into the upper world and the lower seeing into the lower world), unites both as a continuing, ever-present faculty.

With Christ's etheric return, therefore, we are dealing not only with a memory of the past, but also a new "memory" of the future. In other words, the awake human daytime consciousness would perceive both what the upper "eye" is able to perceive in the future of the spiritual world (the spiritual world is always in the future), and what the lower "eye" would remember from the past by "reading" the etheric body, thus gathering knowledge from earlier incarnations. This attainment of knowledge from the past and knowledge of the future through the activity of two "eyes" is linked by a unifying memory stream. Rudolf Steiner once wrote a mantra that begins, "In the beginning was the power of memory." For the human organization, the significance of the etheric return is expressed in these words; it will permanently link the upper and lower worlds within human consciousness, a link that makes possible the intended power of memory. By awaking memory, the possibility of recognizing karma arises.[29]

How exactly will this take shape? It will not be immediately apparent that human beings have been endowed with an independent manas formation, now independent from the spiritual world (the Guardian Angel). It will take time to show itself, just as the independent ego (the individual personality) took its time to reveal itself completely after the Mystery of Golgotha.

In the first third of the Age of Pisces, the independent ego displayed itself primarily in the Neoplatonist stream. The world-conception of Plato became *experiential* and *widespread* during this time (AD 215–935), primarily in the form of religious experience, expression, and expansion. Subsequently, the ego displayed itself even more strongly—that is, even more independently from religious experience—in the Scholastic trend of the second third of the Age of Pisces (935–1655), which took the world-conception of Aristotle and made it too *experiential* and *widespread*. This culminated in the first Scientific Revolution, the Age of Discovery, and eventually the French Enlightenment. The last third of the Age of Pisces has seen the full flowering of the independent personality, culminating in the development of Goetheanism/Weimar Classicism and Anthroposophy.

And now, the exercising of the new capacity of manas cognition will follow an analogous path. During the first third of the Age of Aquarius (2375–3095), a kind of "Neo-Goetheanism" or "Neo-Classicism" will arise in humanity—this time not localized to certain individuals such as Goethe, Schiller, and Novalis, but spread to a much wider swath of humanity. What Goethe strove for in the perception of his archetypal plant (a living imagination of a plant in metamorphosis) will become a much more common experience for humanity in general.

We might imagine this to be the fulfilment of Steiner's words concerning the mission of Kaspar Hauser:

South Germany should have become the new Grail-Castle of the new Knights of the Grail and the cradle of future events. The spiritual ground had been well prepared by all those personalities whom we know of as Goethe, Schiller, Holderlin, Herder and others. Kaspar Hauser was to have gathered around him, as it were, all that existed in this spiritual ground thus prepared. (communicated to Count Ludwig Polzer-Hoditz, Nov. 1916)

Subsequently, in the second third of the Age of Aquarius (3095–3815), we will see the full flowering of Anthroposophy—what Scholasticism and the Scientific Revolution were for Aristotelianism, the equivalent for Anthroposophy will arise in the fourth millennium. Only this time, what was experienced by and spoken about by Steiner will be the common property of humanity, particularly in the realm of the "karmic clairvoyance" previously mentioned.

Finally, during the last third of the Age of Aquarius (3815–4535), manas cognition will express itself completely; the new body of buddhi, of life-spirit, will be bestowed on humanity through Christ's astral appearance; and the task of both the Church of John and the Maitreya Bodhisatva will come to their conclusion.

And so, the biography of Philosophia will be complete: extending from the time of Abraham, through the Age of Aries (the equivalent of 0–21), the Age of Pisces (21–42) and finally the Age of Aquarius (42–63), culminating with the final incarnation of the Abraham individuality as Maitreya Buddha, around the year 4443 (see Powell, *Hermetic Astrology*, vol. I). He will have accomplished the mission of drawing humanity down out of picture-consciousness and into brain-bound thinking for the sake of the birth of the ego (as Abraham) and eventually rescuing humanity from this brain-bound thinking, elevating them to restore true contact with the spiritual world (as Maitreya).

---

29 Ibid., pp. 397–98.

APPENDIX: GRAIL KNIGHT'S PRACTICE

Over the course of the years 1940–1943, Valentin Tomberg led a group of individuals in Amsterdam through an in-depth study of the Lord's Prayer, what is now known as the *Lord's Prayer Course*. In the years after World War II, he distilled the essence of this study into a powerful mantra—akin to the mantra of the First Class of the School of Michael. Originally there were twenty-two of these mantras; Tomberg's handwritten notes (in German) for fourteen of these mantras are still in existence. Since 2012, they have gradually been translated into English and paired with eurythmy gestures by Robert Powell as the *Grail Knight's Practice*. Each of these mantras aligns with a certain section of both the Lord's Prayer and the Our Mother Prayer; each aligns with one of the twenty-two Major Arcana; and each is a distillation of a portion of the Christian-Rosicrucian Path developed in the Lord's Prayer Course.

For example: the first mantra is a distillation of the Nine Beatitudes, and relates to The World as First Petition of the Our Mother (or The Magician as First Petition of the Our Father). The second mantra is a distillation of the Stages of the Passion, and relates to The Fool as Second Petition of the Our Mother (or High Priestess as Second Petition of the Our Father). These readings are like the fruit of the Tree of Life, as this Tree is the underlying archetype of both the Our Father and Our Mother Prayers, as well as the Major Arcana of the Tarot.

Unfortunately, only fourteen of the twenty-two original mantras are still extant, at least from what material is currently known of and available. They are related to:

> The Nine Beatitudes
> The Stages of the Passion
> The Apocalyptic Levels of Judgement
> Nourishment from the Force of Seeds
> The Healing of the Breath
> Four Levels of Communion
> First Healing Miracle
> Second Healing Miracle
> Third Healing Miracle
> Fourth Healing Miracle
> Fifth Healing Miracle
> Sixth Healing Miracle
> Seventh Healing Miracle
> Transfiguration

And this is as far as the notes go. The remaining eight parts would have related to the seven Words from the Cross, with a final part as a closing. In a way it is fortunate that we are not given this content in its completeness: an opening has been left in the spiral to complete these twenty-two mantras—the "readings for the dead" of the twenty-two weeks of the Johannine Rite.

> **"C**hrist Himself brings the message that, when space is overcome and one has learned to recognize the Sun as the creator of space—when one feels oneself placed through Christ into the Sun, lifted into the living Sun—then the earthly and the physical vanishes, and only the etheric and the astral are present.... The stars no longer twinkle down upon us but gently touch us with their loving influence."
>
> —RUDOLF STEINER (*The Festivals and Their Meaning*, p. 311)

ON CHRISTIANIZING THE CHAKRAS

Norm D. Feather

The development of the flowers on the Tree of Knowledge, the spiritual organs, is essential for the esoteric student. While this is possible through chanting the various sounds associated with each chakra, or imagining the color, metal, plant or planet, this development can also be quickened by the use of various Christian prayers, texts and events. To memorize and recite, in other words pray these while focusing each phrase on the related location on the body can produce results that we can reflect on with thinking.

Three prayers (the Our Father, Our Mother and the Mystery Prayer), the Prologue to the Gospel of St. John, and four deeds of Jesus Christ (the healing miracles, the I AM sayings, the Stages of the Passion, and the Words from the Cross) constitute the basic eight phrases. Added to this, and perhaps less familiar, are the "words" of the Father for each Day of Creation—a kind of condensation of Genesis—and the art form:

Crown	Let there be light	Architecture
Brow	Division of the two waters	Painting
Throat	Seed principle	Sculpture
Heart	Hierarchy	Music
Solar Plexus	Ensouled movement	Dance
Sacral	Horizontal heredity	Poetry
Root	Freedom	Prose

In an effort to follow the example of a great teacher and to make these ten into twelve, I wondered if two Catholic sequences of seven could be included: The Sacraments[1] and the Cardinal Sins.

Crown	Divine Unction	Sloth
Brow	Ordination	Envy
Throat	Marriage	Wrath
Heart	Communion	Pride
Solar Plexus	Confession	Greed
Sacral	Confirmation	Lust
Root	Baptism	Gluttony

This required a change of direction in thinking from the vertical, in the saying of each, to the horizontal. Contemplating all the phrases related to the Saturn chakra, for example, to see how each one illuminates each other, resulted in this brief article. All twelve support, explain, and sustain each other logically while generating great warmth, because they reflect the same "light" from their respective chakras. The author is aware that any single line from any of the twelve could support a whole book of insights, but the intent here is to work within the phrases themselves, minimizing attenuating thoughts. Readers are encouraged to explore their own questions and find their own correspondences.

Norm D. Feather, July 2022

SATURN: Saturday, Crown Chakra:

Our Father, who art in Heaven,
  hallowed be Thy Name
Our Mother, thou who art in the darkness of
  the underworld, may the holiness of Thy
  Name shine anew in our remembering

---

1 EDITOR'S NOTE: Some readers may notice that Feather is using a somewhat different ordering of the Sacraments from what Valentin Tomberg uses in *Lazarus: The Miracle of Resurrection in World History*. Additionally, he uses a unique association of the stages of the Passion with the chakras, ascending from root to crown rather than descending from crown to root. As far as I know, the association of the Cardinal Sins with chakras is original to him. Otherwise, the associations are the same as those that can be found in the work of Tomberg (e.g., his *Lord's Prayer Course*) and Powell (e.g., *Cultivating Inner Radiance* and *The Prayer Sequence in Eurythmy*).

...and forgot your Names, you Fathers
   in the Heavens.
In the beginning was the Word, and the Word
   was with God, and the Word was God.
Raising of Lazarus
I AM the Resurrection and the Life
Resurrection
Father, into Thy hands I commend my Spirit
Let there be light
Architecture
Divine Unction
Sloth

Let us begin with two of the more Catholic correspondences associated with the crown chakra: the Cardinal Sin of Sloth, and the Sacrament of Divine Unction. This chakra contains all of our karma. It is a permanent, though unconscious link with heaven, and when we die it is our point of exit. Now the art form here is architecture, creative work extending toward the vertical, and if we are too lazy to erect some kind of link with that which is above the two waters, we are indeed spiritually slothful. Therefore, through ceremony and blessed oil, the Church provides the reconnection to heaven required at our passing.

The priest intercedes on behalf of the Son of Man who says: "I AM the resurrection and the life," because any distance from the Father is too far, and will ultimately lead to death. On the first day the Father allows an emanation from his divine embrace. Unmanifested, perfect and spiritually alive unity sacrifices a part of its very essence, the "stuff" which the hierarchies will shape into the creation: "Let there be light." When all humanity is in the divine embrace of the Son (manifested, perfect and spiritually alive unity), this now evolved light will be returned to its source. "Father into thy hands I commend my spirit," the words from the cross anticipate the Resurrection, the stage of the Passion for this chakra, as does the miracle of raising Lazarus from the dead.

"Hallowed be thy name" says the Lord's prayer, and in our heart of hearts, we venerate what is the root of creation and yet sublimely transcendent to it. Saturn is the planet of memory, and Genesis would have us recall that we were once

on speaking terms with the Father in paradise, despite the distance between us now. "The Word was in the beginning with God," agrees St. John and, as Jesus is our brother, we were, too. Name, in a spiritual sense, is what a being is comprised of, what it can do and who it represents, so in the case of the Father, everything. Yet this Name, this All is to be identified as the very center of our One, and kept Holy. In this center (and the planet's), we petition in the Our Mother prayer that the "Holiness of her name shine anew in our remembering." The hallowing of the Creator is shared with the Creation. This living being, living wisdom, the nurture from nature that has sustained our entire existence is to be discovered again, but this time also within ourselves.

The Mystery Prayer, culminating at the crown, says we have "Forgotten their (the Fathers') names," having already separated ourselves from their Kingdom. Thus, the lack of "architecture" in a spiritual sense, and instead the towering skyscrapers of today, echoes of their biblical archetype Babel. If we don't know toward what or whom we are building, it will be in our "own name," and so a product of arrogance. If our ancestors thought of the sky, especially at night, as the "face of God," who would want to scrape it?

SUN: Sunday, Heart chakra:

Give us this day our daily bread
Receive this day the living memory of
Thee from human hearts, who implore
Thee to forgive the sin of having
   forgotten Thee....
Experienced in the daily bread
In the Word was life
Feeding of the Five Thousand
I AM the Bread of Life
Bearing of the Cross
Today, you shall be with Me in Paradise
Let there be hierarchy
Music
Communion
Pride

If we take the Edict of the Father "Let there be hierarchy" and add the Son's response "I AM the bread of life," we can learn about the nature of power according to the spiritual world. The "I AM," the true human ego, is compared in this aspect of its function to "Bread," created by human effort and the effects of the Sun, and this can sustain the "Life" of the Hierarchy. The state of "sonliness" will provide nurture to all beings. Ideally, a son's wishes are to fully love, understand, and support his Father's mission so as to sustain the family. A Father wants with all his heart for his Son to succeed in this and eventually inherit all that is his. Power is not force or competition, though it is real (the father is stronger than the son), but it is always subservient to Love.

The miracle associated with the heart chakra is the feeding of the five thousand, where the self-identified "bread'" apportions "Himself'" to the surrounding crowd, and all are filled. Hierarchy is demonstrated, as the Lord distributes to his disciples, and they to the others. By uniting with this true bread, the Son, the presence of the vertical world is manifested to the crowd, and this heavenly nourishment is also *so* effective in the horizontal realm that they seek to make him a king.

The petition from the Our Father here is "give us this day our daily bread," and we can see that this doesn't mean bread from the horizontal world alone: that we should not go hungry, but receive heavenly bread each day. The Mystery Prayer shows that selfish isolation is to be "experienced in the daily bread." Earthly bread alone, without Christ's presence, will only nourish and sustain this unfortunate state. We say grace before the meal to blend the two breads, and Communion is the Sacrament. Uniting Christ to our nourishment (the transubstantiation of the Mass), we echo the miracle and become one of the "five thousand."

Music is the art form, and harmonies are a wondrous expression of hierarchy in action. Tradition describes the ranks of angels as choirs, and even in earthly choirs, individuality is happily subordinate to the whole. Also in our evolution, each voice has a precious part to contribute according to the distribution of the bread, and to "sing" too loudly (or too soon or too late) is more than that required by the harmony/hierarchy. To "stick out"

is the sin of Pride. Too much regard for one's self is simultaneously too little regard for the whole: unbalanced (un-harmonious) love.

Hierarchy manifests in three ways, as every being needs something above to learn from (angels), something on their level to work with (other humans), and something below to bring along (nature). The stage of the Passion for this heart chakra is the Bearing of the Cross. In the light of conscience from above, we see what is dying in ourselves—at first our own shadow—and pick it up. Carrying this awareness into our relations with others, we see their suffering is like our own and so in redeemed brotherhood (Cain and Abel), we must also carry each other, which provides a harmonious example for the kingdom of nature.

From the Prologue to St. John's Gospel: "In it (the Word) was Life," and so all else is death. Anyone realizing this is immediately reconnected through the Word to the Hierarchies, "Today thou shall be with Me in Paradise," even a thief. Our admission is our admission. Transformed by His mercy, we become sons and daughters working to sustain the hierarchy, and by rejoining this choir we sing, "Receive this day the living memory of Thee from human hearts, who implore Thee to forgive the sin of having forgotten Thee," from the Our Mother.

MOON: Monday, Root chakra:

Deliver us from evil
By the deed of the Son, the immeasurable
    pain of the Father be stilled, by the
    liberation of all beings from the tragedy
    of Thy withdrawal
The evil holds sway
And the darkness overcomes it not
Changing of Water into Wine
I AM the True Vine
Washing of the Feet
It is finished
Let there be freedom
Prose
Baptism
Gluttony

Gluttony is the Cardinal Sin relating to the chakra at the base of the spine. Here, the Our Father Prayer petitions that we be "delivered from evil," so what kind of evil is gluttony? Does the obvious manifestation of overconsumption on the physical plane have a spiritual aspect, fueling this deep need for more, far more, well past the point of fullness?

"I AM the true vine," says the Son, and our independent consciousness delivers the human reply, "I am a branch cut-off"—separated from all the hierarchies, the Father, even a pure relationship with the Earth Mother. Altogether too cut-off, this branch of individual consciousness will try to set its roots into anything to abate its isolation. We fear existential starvation, a hunger that cannot be filled with anything other than reconnection to the very Godhead (fullness) from which our journey to consciousness has left us apart. At a deeply moral-intuitive level our actual state—that we can never be filled without this connection—drives us to be gluttons. Separated from our spiritual parents, we have achieved an individual perspective, a private history of sorts, and the art form is prose.

The Father has called for freedom, on this the seventh day of creation. His faith in humanity is so strong, now that the work of creation is complete and we have become independent, we will freely choose to reconnect with Him through His Son through love. Freedom is the essential precondition for love, and so a true vine will be one that abides by this law, providing all the nourishment the branch needs, but only when asked. The Son asks for this "asking" at various points in the Gospels ("Come to me all ye who are . . ."), and will heal only those who wish for it and can cooperate with Him in the healing.

So how free, how "cut-off" are we? The Mystery prayer begins with this chakra, "The evil holds sway." The feeling of complete separation that comes with our fledgling ego-hood is happening in a place so far removed from heaven that from their perspective, only evil can thrive here. But the gospel of St. John tells us that through the light of the Word, this "darkness overcomes us not." Our sincere effort to send and maintain

a connection to the true vine will bring light into this darkness and this light is represented by the blessed water the priest provides at our birth. Baptism, the Catholic Sacrament for the root chakra is the reminder to the newly incarnated soul of what is needed for true nurturing here below, precisely that effort.

The true vine demonstrates awareness of our situation and His ability to overcome it at the wedding at Cana. Water—essential, neutral liquid—becomes wine, a spirit-filled liquid. Earthly water is needed for growth, but it is cooperation with the sun that brings about fruit. The custom at the time was that water was served at weddings within the family (by far the more frequent type), and wine was served where two families were coming together. By changing water into wine at a family wedding, Christ shows the vertical nature of this healing is for all humans. The love that holds families together will be expanded to include all His children, the family of humanity, so the blessing of the baptismal water provides the spirit and "repeats" this healing miracle.

If this is how "the darkness will overcome us not," the why is provided by the Our Mother: "By the deed of the Son, the immeasurable pain of the Father will be stilled by the liberation of all beings from the tragedy of Thy (Her) withdrawal." The Son's deed relating to this chakra is the washing of the feet. Not just as a master of Pisces, not simply removing too much earth (gluttony) from the part of us that touches it the most, but by completely reversing the power structure here below so that, as in heaven, the higher serves the lower. She has withdrawn because the principle of power, that might is right (Cain and Abel), is the way of things on earth: the lower serves the higher. The Father, the God of Love, has already "set us free" in faith, though unfathomably pained that our orphanage cannot intervene. Since it took some time (from the original family through countless generations) to establish the power principle, it will take a while to reverse this, but the first half of the creation is now over: "It is finished," the words from the cross. The time of the war god Mars, and our fight toward individuation, is to be transformed into Mercury, the messenger of the gods, and the Mother will be able to rise from Her existence in darkness to be present with Her children.

MARS: Tuesday (Mardi), Throat chakra:

> Thy will be done, on Earth as it is in Heaven
> May the resurrection of Thy will renew eternal faith to the depths of physical substance
> In which the will of the Heavens no longer rules
> All things were made through the Word, and nothing that was made was made without the Word
> Walking on Water
> I AM the Good Shepherd
> Crucifixion
> I Thirst
> Let there be the seed principle
> Sculpture
> Marriage
> Wrath

It is the third day of creation. "Let there be the seed principle," intones the Father, and we see reflected in the plant kingdom how propagation occurs in the spiritual world. This is how His Will will be done on earth. As humans we are "soul seeds," living beings encompassing in potential all the ranks of angels. The Son doesn't reply "I am the good gardener," seeing to our continued vertical growth, but "I AM the good shepherd." As our vertical guide He will also (horizontally) lead us to good pastures.

St. John agrees, and speaking of this aspect of the Word for this throat chakra "all things were made by it and without it was nothing made that was made"—in other "words,'" the whole of creation. Like begets like, whether or not it is obvious on the physical plane. Holding an acorn in my hand while eyeing the mighty oak from which it came, they seem very different, but add earth, water, air and warmth—and then time—and I will see they are identical. Comparing our own meager moral development to that of Jesus, it is right to hope His strength and example will continue in our own creative work, because this shepherd

also answers the essential questions for working in time: "Where am I from (from what or from whom am I descended?), and where will it lead (my future, and that of my children)?"

Marriage is the Church's sacrament, whereby the seed principle functions in human lives. If "the apple doesn't fall far from the tree" (physically and spiritually), it is this that is at work. "Like Father like Son," true in humans, has its heavenly archetype where the Father is the origin of the creation that the Son *speaks* into existence. Their oneness in the vertical is the guaranty of purity in the horizontal, and to speak (create) without it, outside of this union, will come from and lead to anger, both within what is created and the creator, just because of this disconnect.

Words can really hurt, and the Cardinal Sin for the Mars chakra is Wrath. Assembling them into thoughts (and systems of thought), can result in good or evil, and the art form for the chakra of speech is Sculpture. United with us from the cross, the Lord says "I thirst." On our behalf, He pleads that the waters above be reflected in the waters below in all our creating. Establishing this "blessed union" first, we will "sculpt" good creations, be they things, words, thoughts, or beings.

From the Mystery Prayer, "The will of the heavens no longer rules," and in such a place the perfect representative of heavenly will must surely die. But the good shepherd is one that will defend his flock unto death, and the stage of the Passion here is the Crucifixion. Frozen, alone and almost entirely forgotten, the creative force of this chakra (the Word) is rendered entirely without will, so He thirsts also that "Thy will be done on earth as it is in heaven," in the Our Father and from the Our Mother. "May the resurrection of Thy (Her) will renew eternal faith to the depths of physical substance." Every "atom" of the creation is to partake in the reunion (marriage) of their two wills.

The picture of stability this complete sacrifice of the will achieves is the walking on water, where the attraction of heaven is stronger than the pull of gravity. The "winds" of destiny and "waves" of upheaval are ineffective. They do not deter the Lord from finding and rescuing the ones seeking Him, and when He joins Himself to them, by "entering" the boat, both winds and waves are calmed. "It is I AM, be not afraid."

MERCURY: Wednesday, Solar plexus:

> Forgive us our debts, as we forgive our
> debtors
> ...Who implore Thee to forgive the sin of
> having forgotten Thee, and are ready to
> fight against temptation...
> Self-hood guilt to others attributed
> And this life was the light of humanity
> Healing of the Paralyzed Man
> I AM the Doorway, the entrance and the exit
> Crowning with Thorns
> Father, forgive them, for they know not what
> they do
> Let there be ensouled movement
> Dance
> Confession
> Greed

On the fifth day of creation the Father calls for ensouled movement. All of the "soul seeds" will be able to express themselves through action on the horizontal plane. Struggling to balance individuality with the outside world, in themselves and with others, they will surely be prone to unintentionally "bumping" into one another, a kind of spiritual precondition that will manifest in a million ways. Taking this into account, the petition from the Lord's Prayer, "Forgive us our debts, as we forgive our debtors," asks that the vertical will understand this and intercede in our private transgressions to the extent that we forgive those who are "bumping" into us.

The Son from the cross testifies that this is so, that we require this intercession and asks "Father forgive them, they know not what they do." Not just for the horrendous actions occurring, but for the state that leads them to it as well. They are murdering the sole remedy for their isolation, as love is the only way to reconnect our overly independent egos without constraint. This very human condition is pictured at the healing of the paraplegic who, having no resources of his own, no family or friends, can neither help himself nor ask for

help. Jesus asks him if he would like to be healed, and having waited there for thirty-eight years, this cannot simply mean the repairing of his limbs, but in the future for the man to redirect his will away from the isolating tendency (ego) that got him there, as witnessed by his lack of resources. "Sin no more," He advises, heals him and states, "I AM the doorway, the entrance and the exit." Christ Himself is the opening, built into us, that if we choose, allows us out of our selfishness, and into our neighbors's soul. The "price" of this liberation is the third Sacrament: Confession.

In the Mystery Prayer for this chakra we hear, "self-hood guilt to others attributed," an indication of just how much we "know not what we do." Karma, a moral reflex/judgement from the universe on our actions, determines our destiny. By choosing to reincarnate and work this through, we acknowledge this judgment. In the marvel of human oneness that is our pre-incarnation state we see the need to accept this, are even eager to "get what's coming to us," to atone and reestablish the moral balance we see from the spiritual world. Whereas on earth in our hyper-individualized state, we have forgotten this so completely that upon receiving a stroke of destiny we blame the one "bumping" into us as the cause of our situation. When we add the fact of karma it is simply the consequence of an action we initiated in a previous life, and should we include this in our assessment, we might begin to "know what we do." If we reverse this mis-attribution of what is really ours to others, we think that what really is theirs should be ours, and so the Cardinal Sin of Greed or Avarice.

The Our Mother prayer, having petitioned in the chakra above for forgiveness for forgetting Her very existence (and with that the fact of our essential brother/sisterhood) asks here that we be "ready to fight (this) temptation." If we truly "love our neighbors as ourselves," we cannot covet anything about them. We feel their success (and hardship) to be our own, not as in a tribe or clan but as individuals. By remembering our common spiritual Mother, our obligation to kindness—as in *kin*ship—we fight against the physical illusion of separateness. Joining this with karmic awareness, breeches will start to occur in the closed circle of "self-hood guilt" in which we find ourselves. Imagine a circle with a hundred perpendicular lines in it and you have a crown of thorns, the stage of the passion for this chakra.

"And life became the light of men," says the Prologue to the Gospel of John, and at the heart chakra above, "in it (the Word) was life." So instead of the fact of Christ's union with God, His function as creating all things, it is life that became our guiding principle (light). Life itself will show us the "meaning of life," and the more compassion and understanding enter into our *actions*, the less "bumping" will occur. By choosing love to coordinate our movements with those around us, the more it will become Dancing, the art form for the Solar-plexus.

THURSDAY: Jupiter, Brow:

Thy Kingdom come
May the breath from Thy awakening
    kingdom warm hearts that wander
    homeless
Man has severed himself from Thy Kingdom
The same was in the beginning with God
Healing of the Man Born Blind
I AM the Light of the World
Entombment
My God, My God, why have You forsaken
    Me?
Let the waters above be separated from the
    waters below
Painting
Ordination
Envy

On the second day of creation, the Father says "Let the waters above be separated from the waters below," to establish two levels or speeds of evolution, one completely unmanifested and one to create the manifestation. The Word replies, "I AM the light of the world," identifying Himself as the one thing that is true and good in both waters. He will create the world, manifest Himself in it, all the while remaining in complete connection with the unmanifested, His Father. This aspect of

Himself, the light, is what the opened eyes of the Man Born Blind will see, and we should acknowledge the truth that, as far as the upper waters, we are all born blind.

Envy is the cardinal sin associated with the brow chakra and here we see the vertical root to its horizontal manifestation. We long for that which once was ours but is no longer, a living connection with heaven. "Man has severed himself from Thy Kingdom," says the Prayer from the Mysteries. Jesus has united himself so completely with us that from the cross we hear that this is so, even for the Son of God: "Why have You forsaken Me?" St. John tells us that in the beginning these two waters were united, "The same was in the beginning with God," so it is right to feel this loss of connection, that we are in a sense abandoned.

But this cannot be our permanent condition because in spite of it, the Our Father asks here that "Thy kingdom come," that by keeping the first petition, by hallowing the name of the Father, the separation of the waters will be overcome, and their reuniting will see heaven established on earth. This new kingdom will include the Mother, and from her prayer we hear, "May the breath from Thy awakening kingdom warm hearts that wander homeless." Breathing is a living, rhythmic exchange, something new coming in when something old goes out. The homeless wandering of Cain, the pursuit of horizontal, masculine knowledge at the expense of vertical, feminine connectedness, is to be breathed out of our hearts and the coming kingdom is to be breathed into them.

This is the chakra associated with clairvoyance, or seeing into the upper waters, and the Sacrament is Ordination. The spiritual ideal of a priest is one who can see both horizontally and vertically and derives their authority solely "from above," and so in a sense, every clairvoyant that abides by this is "ordained." Since we all are not yet "priests," the art form here is the physical substitute, Painting, and a great painter is one who fills their representations with inspiration from the waters above.

The stage of the Passion here is Entombment, not only in the sense that our spiritual ability to see is locked up in our skulls, itself an image of death, but it is the Father who is active at this Jupiter chakra, and this is the planet of the Father. The will of Christ is to incarnate through the Baptism, to heal humanity by the teaching and cures, and to take their sins upon Himself in Gethsemane, with the consequent descent to Hell. The Son's will has been accomplished, and He rests in the earth, awaiting the verdict of His Father on His work. The Lord has been the subject and verb (word) of the five previous stages, but here the action is the Father's, and His judgement is shown through the Resurrection.

VENUS: Friday, Sacral:

> Lead us not into temptation
> ...and are ready to fight against temptation
>   that has led to Thy existence in darkness
> Witness egoity becoming free
> And the light shines in the darkness
> Healing of the Nobleman's Son
> I AM the Way, the Truth, and the Life
> Scourging
> Woman, behold thy son, son behold thy
>   Mother
> Let there be horizontal Heredity
> Poetry
> Confirmation
> Lust

"Let there be horizontal Heredity" sings the Father on the sixth day of creation. "Lead us not into temptation" petitions His Prayer. To forget the vertical in the process of procreation *is* the temptation. To concentrate only on the horizontal flow of heredity, a distortion of the Father-Son relationship, leads us to a different sort of strength. We begin to rely on and seek only this earthly power, that turns us into the children of our parents, forgetting our original function as daughters and sons of God. When we forget even this hereditary aspect as well, we are subject to the Cardinal Sin for this chakra, Lust.

A young man's thoughts about the girl next door in spring can be curtailed abruptly by just the sound of his mother's voice, because she is the vertical element in their hereditary relationship. Her natural perpendicularity causes shame

to arise naturally because the need to procreate is natural indeed. If forgetting heredity causes shame, then what will forgetting our heavenly inheritance entail? The Nobleman whose son is dying has been focused on his earthly lord (horizontal) to the detriment of his child's health (vertical). He changes perpendicularly the direction of his faith to Jesus, and the healing occurs. The Lord says "I AM the Way, the Truth and the Life," the directing force, the fact of our (vertical) Sonship, and the strength to maintain it in this horizontal aspect of human evolution. The healing demonstrates the absolute necessity of the vertical in life, and the connection to heaven that was vouchsafed in the Baptism is now recognized by the thinking human, and the Church calls this Sacrament Confirmation.

The words from the cross for this chakra, "Woman behold thy son, son behold thy Mother," tell us not only that Jesus wants the disciple there, St. John, to see to the earthly care of his mother Mary. Woman (horizontal, feminine, water), behold thy Son (vertical, masculine, fire), indicates the universal, spiritual need to re-establish this connection at the same time.

From the Passion, the Scourging is the price the Lord pays on our behalf. Corporal (bodily) punishment presumes that the horizontal blows (and this can be destiny as well as physical pain) will cause us to retreat (ascend) into the vertical. Here, the original "vertical" has descended to receive the blows that we have earned, and thereby create a connection to humanity, who must see His innocence as a "light shining in the darkness," from St. John.

With this light we "witness (completely earthly) egoity becoming free," from the Mystery Prayer.

In the Our Mother, the words here are connected to the line from the chakra above, Mercury, that we be "ready to fight the temptation (Venus) that has led to Thy (Her) existence in darkness." This is the "shade" of our materialism. That the universe is not alive, but a system of mechanical "laws," from conception in a mother's womb to the stars in their dances, is a fairly recent interpretation of things. For ten thousand years various cultures, regardless of sometimes very great differences between them, have known that this is *The* Mother, the living counterpart to *The* Father. That the dead concepts of science for a couple of centuries are the "real" ones just doesn't add up, and She must remain in what is darkness for the materialistic intellect, until we find another light with which to seek Her.

Another example of this light in action is in Poetry, the art form. The horizontal nature of a story presented in time is enlivened by the presence of a "spirit" in the rhyme. It adds harmony, rhythm and enlivens prose; a more spiritual language that speaks to the soul first and therefore spiritual truths can be shown without necessarily being understood, for example nursery rhymes and fairy tales. The oldest of humanity's stories are poems, "preserved" by this spirit, and if prose is talking, poetry is singing and singing lasts.

The Dead Speak

I am not on Earth as soul
but only in water, air, and fire;

In my fire I am in the planets
and the Sun.

In my Sun-being I am the
sky of the fixed stars—

I am not on the Earth as soul
but in Light, Word, and Life;

In my life I am within
the being of the Sun and the planets,
in the Spirit of Wisdom.

In my wisdom being I am
in the Spirit of Love.

—Rudolf Steiner
(New Year 1917/1918)

WORKING WITH THE
STAR WISDOM CALENDAR
Robert Powell, PhD

In taking note of the astronomical events listed in the Star Calendar, it is important to distinguish between long- and short-term astronomical events. Long-term astronomical events—for example, Pluto transiting a particular degree of the zodiac—will have a longer period of meditation than would the five days advocated for short-term astronomical events such as the New and Full Moon. The following describes, in relation to meditating on the Full Moon, a meditative process extending over a five-day period.

Sanctification of the Full Moon

As a preliminary remark, let us remind ourselves that the great sacrifice of Christ on the Cross—the Mystery of Golgotha—took place at Full Moon. As Christ's sacrifice took place when the Moon was full in the middle of the sidereal sign of Libra, the Libra Full Moon assumes special significance in the sequence of twelve (or thirteen) Full Moons taking place during the cycle of the year. In following this sequence, the Mystery of Golgotha serves as an archetype for *every* Full Moon, since each Full Moon imparts a particular spiritual blessing. Hence the practice described here as *Sanctification of the Full Moon* applies to every Full Moon. Similarly, there is also the practice of *Sanctification of the New Moon*, as described in *Hermetic Astrology, Volume 2: Astrological Biography,* chapter 10.

During the two days prior to the Full Moon, we can consider the focus of one's meditation to extend over these two days as *preparatory days,* immediately preceding the day of the Full Moon. These two days can be dedicated to spiritual reflection and detachment from everyday concerns as one prepares to become a vessel for the in-streaming light and love one will receive at the Full Moon, something that one can then impart further—for example, to help people in need, or to support Mother Earth in times of catastrophe. During these two days, it is helpful to hold an attitude of dedication and service and try to assume an attitude of receptivity that opens to what one's soul will receive and subsequently impart—an attitude conducive to making one a true *servant of the spirit.*

The day of the Full Moon is itself a day of *holding the sacred space.* In doing so, one endeavors to cultivate inner peace and silence, during which one attempts to contact and consciously hold the in-streaming blessing of the Full Moon for the rest of humanity. One can heighten this silent meditation by visualizing the zodiacal constellation–sidereal sign in which the Moon becomes full, since the Moon serves to reflect the starry background against which it appears.

If the Moon is full in Virgo, for example, it reminds us of the night of the birth of the Jesus child visited by the three magi, as described in the Gospel of St. Matthew. That birth occurred at the Full Moon in the middle of the sidereal sign of Virgo, and the three magi, who gazed up that evening to behold the Full Moon against the background of the stars of the Virgin, witnessed the soul of Jesus emerge from the disk of the Full Moon and descend toward Earth. They participated from afar, via the starry heavens, in the Grail Mystery of the holy birth.

By meditating on the Full Moon and opening oneself to receive the in-streaming blessing from the starry heavens, we can exercise restraint by avoiding the formulation of what will happen or what one might receive from the Full Moon. Moreover, we can also refrain from seeking tangible results or effects connected with our attunement to the Full Moon. Even if we observe only the date but not the exact moment when the Moon is full, it is helpful to find quiet time to reflect alone or to use the opportunity for deep meditation on the day of the Full Moon.

We can think of the two days following the Full Moon as a *time of imparting* what we have received from the in-streaming of the Moon's full disk against the background of the stars. It is now possible to turn our attention toward humanity and the world and endeavor to pass on any spiritual blessing we have received from the starry heavens. Thereby we can assist in the work of the spiritual world by transforming what we have received into goodwill and allowing it to flow wherever the greatest need exists.

It is a matter of *holding a sacred space* throughout the day of the Full Moon. This is an important time to still the mind and maintain inner peace. It is a time of spiritual retreat and contact with the spiritual world, of holding in one's consciousness

the archetype of the Mystery of Golgotha as a great outpouring of Divine Love that bridges Heaven and Earth. Prior to the day of the Full Moon, the two preceding days prepare the sacred space as a vessel to receive the heavenly blessing. The two days following the day of the Full Moon are a time to assimilate and distribute the spiritual transmission received into the sacred space we have prepared.

One can apply the process described here as a meditative practice in relation to the Full Moon to any of the astronomical events listed in *Star Wisdom,* especially as most of these *remember* significant Christ Events. Take note, however, whether an event is long-term or short-term and adjust the period of meditative practice accordingly.

> The stars once spoke to humanity.
> It is world destiny that they are silent now.
> To be aware of this silence
> Can bring pain to earthly humanity.
> But in the deepening silence
> There grows and ripens
> What humanity speaks to the stars.
> To be aware of this speaking
> Can become strength
> To spirit body.
>
> —RUDOLF STEINER,
> (for Marie Steiner, Christmas 1922)

SYMBOLS USED IN CHARTS

PLANETS		ZODIACAL SIGNS		ASPECTS	
⊕	Earth	♈	Aries (Ram)	☌	Conjunction 0°
☉	Sun	♉	Taurus (Bull)	⚹	Sextile 60°
☽	Moon	♊	Gemini (Twins)	□	Square 90°
☿	Mercury	♋	Cancer (Crab)	△	Trine 120°
♀	Venus	♌	Leo (Lion)	☍	Opposition 180°
♂	Mars	♍	Virgo (Virgin)		
♃	Jupiter	♎	Libra (Scales)		
♄	Saturn	♏	Scorpio (Scorpion)		
♅	Uranus	♐	Sagittarius (Archer)		
♆	Neptune	♑	Capricorn (Goat)		
♇	Pluto	♒	Aquarius (Water Carrier)		
		♓	Pisces (Fishes)		

OTHER

☊	Ascending (North) Node	☼	Sun Eclipse
☋	Descending (South) Node	☽	Moon Eclipse
P	Perihelion–Perigee	☿	Inferior Conjunction
A	Aphelion–Apogee	♀	Superior Conjunction
☊	Maximum Latitude	⚷	Chiron
☋	Minimum Latitude		

TIME

The information relating to daily geocentric and heliocentric planetary positions in the sidereal zodiac is tabulated in the form of an ephemeris for each month, in which the planetary positions are given at 0 hours Universal Time (UT) each day.

Beneath the geocentric and heliocentric ephemeris for each month, the information relating to planetary aspects is given in the form of an aspectarian, which lists the most important aspects—geocentric and heliocentric–hermetic—between the planets for the month in question. The day and the time of occurrence of the aspect on that day are indicated, all times being given in Universal Time (UT), which is identical to Greenwich Mean Time (GMT). For example, zero hours Universal Time is midnight GMT. This time system applies in Britain; however, when summer time is in effect, one hour must be added to all times.

In other time zones, the time must be adjusted according to whether it is ahead of or behind Britain. For example, in Germany, where the time is one hour ahead of British time, an hour must be added; when summer time is in effect in Germany, two hours have to be added to all times.

Using the calendar in the United States, do the following subtraction from all time indications according to time zone:

- Pacific Time subtract 8 hours
- Mountain Time subtract 7 hours
- Central Time subtract 6 hours
- Eastern Time subtract 5 hours

This subtraction will often change the date of an astronomical occurrence, shifting it back one day. Consequently, since most of the readers of this calendar live on the American Continent, astronomical occurrences during the early hours of day *x* are sometimes listed in the Commentaries as occurring on days *x–1/x*. For example, an eclipse occurring at 03:00 UT on the 12th is listed

as occurring on the 11–12th since in America it takes place on the 11th.[1]

SIMPLIFYING THE PROCEDURE

The preceding procedure can be greatly simplified. Here is an example for someone wishing to know the zodiacal locations of the planets on Christmas Day, December 25, 2018. Looking at the December ephemeris, it can be seen that Christmas Day falls on a Tuesday. In the upper tabulation, the geocentric planetary positions are given, with that of the Sun indicated in the first column, that of the Moon in the second column, and so on. The position of the Sun is listed as 8°07' Sagittarius.

For someone living in London, 8°07' Sagittarius is the Sun's position at midnight, December 24–25, 2017—noting that in London and all of the United Kingdom, the Time Zone applying there is that of Universal Time–Greenwich Mean Time (UT–GMT).

For someone living in Sydney, Australia, which on Christmas Day is eleven hours ahead of UT–GMT, 8°07' Sagittarius is the Sun's position at 11 a.m. on December 25.

For someone living in California, which is eight hours behind UT–GMT on Christmas Day, 8°07' Sagittarius is the Sun's position at 4 p.m. on **December 24**.

For the person living in California, therefore, it is necessary to look at the entries for **December 26** to know the positions of the planets on December 25. The result is:

For someone living in California, which is eight hours behind UT–GMT on Christmas Day, the Sun's position at 4 p.m. on December 25 is 9°08' Sagittarius and, by the same token, the Moon's position on Christmas Day at 4 p.m. on December 25 is 24°08' Pisces—these are the positions

---

1 See *General Introduction to the Christian Star Calendar: A Key to Understanding* for an in-depth clarification of the features of the calendar in *Star Wisdom,* including indications about how to work with it.

alongside December 26 at midnight UT–GMT— and eight hours earlier equates with 4 p.m. on December 25 in California.

From these examples it emerges that the **planetary positions as given in the ephemeris** can be utilized, but that according to the Time Zone one is in, **the time of day is different** and also for locations West of the United Kingdom **the date changes** (look at the date following the actual date).

Here is a tabulation in relation to the foregoing example of December 25 (Christmas Day).

UNITED KINGDOM, EUROPE, AND ALL LOCATIONS WITH TIME ZONES EAST OF GREENWICH

Look at what is given alongside December 25— these entries indicate the planetary positions at these times:

- 12:00 a.m. (midnight December 24–25) in London (UT–GMT)
- 01:00 a.m. in Berlin (CENTRAL EUROPEAN TIME, which is one hour ahead of UT–GMT)
- 11:00 a.m. in Sydney (AUSTRALIAN EASTERN DAYLIGHT TIME, which is eleven hours ahead of UT–GMT)

CANADA, USA, CENTRAL AMERICA, SOUTH AMERICA, AND ALL LOCATIONS WITH TIME ZONES WEST OF GREENWICH

Look at what is given alongside December 26— these entries indicate the planetary positions at these times:

- 7:00 p.m. in New York (EASTERN STANDARD TIME, which is five hours behind UT–GMT)
- 6:00 p.m. in Chicago (CENTRAL STANDARD TIME, which is six hours behind UT–GMT)
- 5:00 p.m. in Denver (MOUNTAIN STANDARD TIME, which is seven hours behind UT–GMT)
- 4:00 p.m. in San Francisco (PACIFIC STANDARD TIME, which is eight hours behind UT–GMT)

- **IF SUMMER TIME IS IN USE,** add **ONE HOUR**—FOR EXAMPLE:
- 8:00 p.m. in New York (EASTERN DAYLIGHT TIME, which is four hours behind UT–GMT)
- 7:00 p.m. in Chicago (CENTRAL DAYLIGHT TIME, which is five hours behind UT–GMT)
- 6:00 p.m. in Denver (MOUNTAIN DAYLIGHT TIME, which is six hours behind UT–GMT)
- 5:00 p.m. in San Francisco (PACIFIC DAYLIGHT TIME, which is seven hours behind UT–GMT)

Note that Daylight Time in the U.S. becomes permanent in 2023. Note, too, that in the preceding tabulation, the time given in Sydney on Christmas Day, December 25, is Daylight Time. Six months earlier, on June 25, for someone in Sydney they would look alongside the entry in the ephemeris for June 25 and would know that this applies (for them) to

- 10:00 a.m. in Sydney (AUSTRALIAN EASTERN TIME, which is ten hours ahead of UT–GMT).

In these examples, it is not just the position of the Sun that is referred to. The same applies to the zodiacal locations given in the ephemeris for *all* the planets, whether geocentric (upper tabulation) or heliocentric (lower tabulation). *All that is necessary to apply this method of reading the ephemeris is to know the Time Zone in which one is and to apply the number of hours difference from UT–GMT.*

The advantage of using the method described here is that it greatly simplifies reference to the ephemeris when studying the **zodiacal positions of the planets.** However, for applying the time indications listed under "Ingresses" or "Aspects" it is still necessary to add or subtract the time difference from UT–GMT as described in the above paragraph denoted.

COMMENTARIES AND EPHEMERIDES
JANUARY – DECEMBER 2023

Commentaries and Ephemerides by Joel Matthew Park featuring the visions of Anne Catherine Emmerich

I would like to extend my gratitude to my friend and colleague Julie Humphreys, who for the past five years committed herself to contributing stargazing and astronomical skywatch to *Star Wisdom* and its predecessor, the *Journal for Star Wisdom*. She has in one sense decided to step back from doing so, and in another, she carries on with it. She now offers a weekly "Stargram" by email. It is my hope and intention to send this out over the Sophia Foundation's new substack version of *Starlight*, the newsletter and journal of the Foundation.[1] You may get in touch with me at joelmpark77@gmail.com if you wish to contact Julie.

For this year's commentaries, I was given access to digital copies of the three volumes of *The Visions of Anne Catherine Emmerich* from my friend and colleague James Wetmore, who spent most of his adult life compiling them. This facilitated direct quotations from the text without the burden of transcription, as I was doing in prior years. Many thanks to Jim for making this text available to me!

Similar to last year in what follows, volume and page numbers refer to the three-volume set published as *The Visions of Anne Catherine Emmerich* (Angelico Press, 2015).

1   See https://starlightnewsletter.substack.com.

JANUARY 2023

January 1: Venus conjunct Pluto
November 23, 30: Healing on the Shore of the Lake, pp. 157–58, vol. II

Next morning the disciples brought him the news that Mary Cleophas was lying very ill at Peter's near Capernaum, that his mother entreated him to come to her soon, and that a great multitude of sick of whom many were from Nazareth, were awaiting his arrival. Jesus again taught and cured numbers on the shore of the lake. Many possessed were brought to him, and he delivered them. The crowd of people and the pressure of the throng were constantly on the increase, and no words can say how unweariedly Jesus labored and helped all in need.

That afternoon he and all his apostles rowed over to Bethsaida. Matthew had delivered the custom house to a man belonging to the fishery. Since his reception of John's baptism, he had carried on his business in an altogether blameless manner. The other publicans also were honest in their dealings and very liberal men, who gave large alms to the poor.

Judas is still good. He is uncommonly active and ready to render service, though in his distribution of alms somewhat close and calculating. A large number of Gentiles crossed the lake today. Those that were not going on further, to Capernaum for instance, left their camels and asses on rafts towed by the boats, or led them over the bridge that crossed the Jordan above the lake.

It was approaching four o'clock when Jesus reached Bethsaida, where Mary with Maroni and her son, who had been here for two days, were

SIDEREAL GEOCENTRIC LONGITUDES : JANUARY 2023 Gregorian at 0 hours UT

DAY	☉	☽	☊	☿	♀	♂	♃	♄	♅	♆	♇
1 SU	15 ♐ 13	8 ♈ 36	16 ♈ 41	28 ♐ 38R	2 ♑ 19	14 ♉ 0R	6 ♓ 8	27 ♑ 21	20 ♈ 5R	27 ♒ 49	2 ♑ 36
2 MO	16 15	21 11	16 42R	28 2	3 35	13 51	6 15	27 28	20 4	27 50	2 38
3 TU	17 16	3 ♉ 33	16 40	27 14	4 50	13 43	6 23	27 34	20 3	27 51	2 39
4 WE	18 17	15 45	16 36	26 16	6 5	13 35	6 30	27 40	20 2	27 52	2 41
5 TH	19 18	27 49	16 29	25 9	7 20	13 29	6 38	27 46	20 1	27 53	2 43
6 FR	20 19	9 ♊ 49	16 19	23 55	8 35	13 23	6 46	27 52	20 0	27 54	2 45
7 SA	21 20	21 44	16 7	22 37	9 50	13 18	6 54	27 58	19 59	27 55	2 47
8 SU	22 21	3 ♋ 38	15 54	21 16	11 5	13 13	7 2	28 5	19 59	27 56	2 49
9 MO	23 22	15 30	15 41	19 56	12 20	13 10	7 11	28 11	19 58	27 58	2 51
10 TU	24 24	27 23	15 28	18 39	13 35	13 7	7 19	28 17	19 57	27 59	2 53
11 WE	25 25	9 ♌ 18	15 17	17 27	14 50	13 5	7 28	28 24	19 56	28 0	2 55
12 TH	26 26	21 18	15 9	16 22	16 5	13 4	7 37	28 30	19 56	28 1	2 57
13 FR	27 27	3 ♍ 27	15 4	15 26	17 20	13 4D	7 46	28 37	19 55	28 3	2 59
14 SA	28 28	15 48	15 2	14 39	18 35	13 5	7 55	28 43	19 55	28 4	3 1
15 SU	29 29	28 26	15 2	14 1	19 50	13 6	8 4	28 50	19 54	28 5	3 3
16 MO	0 ♑ 30	11 ♎ 25	15 2	13 33	21 5	13 8	8 13	28 57	19 54	28 7	3 5
17 TU	1 31	24 50	15 2	13 15	22 20	13 11	8 23	29 3	19 54	28 8	3 7
18 WE	2 33	8 ♏ 44	14 59	13 6	23 35	13 14	8 32	29 10	19 53	28 10	3 9
19 TH	3 34	23 7	14 55	13 5D	24 50	13 18	8 42	29 17	19 53	28 11	3 11
20 FR	4 35	7 ♐ 57	14 47	13 13	26 5	13 23	8 52	29 24	19 53	28 13	3 13
21 SA	5 36	23 8	14 38	13 28	27 20	13 29	9 2	29 30	19 53	28 14	3 14
22 SU	6 37	8 ♑ 29	14 26	13 50	28 35	13 35	9 12	29 37	19 53	28 16	3 16
23 MO	7 38	23 50	14 14	14 18	29 49	13 42	9 22	29 44	19 53D	28 17	3 18
24 TU	8 39	8 ♒ 57	14 4	14 52	1 ♒ 4	13 50	9 33	29 51	19 53	28 19	3 20
25 WE	9 40	23 43	13 55	15 31	2 19	13 58	9 43	29 58	19 53	28 20	3 22
26 TH	10 41	8 ♓ 0	13 50	16 15	3 34	14 7	9 54	0 ♒ 5	19 53	28 22	3 24
27 FR	11 42	21 48	13 47	17 3	4 48	14 16	10 4	0 12	19 53	28 24	3 26
28 SA	12 43	5 ♈ 6	13 46	17 55	6 3	14 26	10 15	0 19	19 53	28 26	3 28
29 SU	13 44	18 0	13 46	18 50	7 18	14 37	10 26	0 26	19 54	28 27	3 30
30 MO	14 45	0 ♉ 32	13 46	19 48	8 32	14 49	10 37	0 33	19 54	28 29	3 32
31 TU	15 46	12 48	13 44	20 50	9 47	15 1	10 48	0 40	19 54	28 31	3 34

INGRESSES :

2 ☽ → ♉ 17: 4	☽ → ♒ 9:44
5 ☽ → ♊ 4:20	25 ♄ → ♒ 6:33
7 ☽ → ♋ 16:40	☽ → ♓ 10:27
10 ☽ → ♌ 5:17	27 ☽ → ♈ 14:41
12 ☽ → ♍ 17:13	29 ☽ → ♉ 22:57
15 ☽ → ♎ 2:56	
☉ → ♑ 12: 6	
17 ☽ → ♏ 9: 1	
19 ☽ → ♐ 11:12	
21 ☽ → ♑ 10:45	
23 ♀ → ♒ 3:25	

ASPECTS & ECLIPSES :

1 ♀ ☌ ♇ 5:19	10 ☽ ☍ ♄ 1:51	21 ☽ ☌ ♇ 15:50	29 ☉ □ ☊ 0:44
☽ ☌ ☊ 15:23	11 ♀ □ ☊ 7:46	☉ ☌ ☽ 20:52	☽ ☌ ♅ 3:35
☽ ☌ ♅ 21:51	12 ☽ ☍ ♆ 13:20	☽ ☌ P 20:59	31 ☽ ☌ ♂ 4:25
3 ☽ ☌ ♂ 19:46	13 ☽ ☍ ♃ 8:32	22 ☽ ⚼ ☊ 9: 9	
6 ☉ ☍ ☽ 23: 6	15 ♀ □ ♅ 1:19	♀ ☌ ♄ 22:11	
7 ☽ ☍ ☿ 1:34	☉ □ ☽ 2: 9	23 ☽ ☌ ♄ 9:23	
☉ ☋ ☿ 12:55	16 ☽ ☌ ☋ 6:32	☽ ☌ ♀ 10:18	
☽ ☍ ♇ 22:21	☽ ☍ ♅ 15:15	25 ☽ ☌ ♆ 7:41	
8 ☽ ☌ A 9:33	18 ☽ ☍ ♂ 7:37	26 ☽ ☌ ♃ 3:16	
☽ ☍ ♀ 16:51	☉ ☌ ♇ 14:38	28 ☉ □ ☽ 15:17	
9 ☽ ⚻ ☊ 0:20	20 ☽ ☌ ☿ 8:29	☽ ☌ ☊ 16: 2	

SIDEREAL HELIOCENTRIC LONGITUDES : JANUARY 2023 Gregorian at 0 hours UT

DAY	Sid. Time	☿	♀	⊕	♂	♃	♄	♅	♆	♇	Vernal Point
1 SU	6:41:34	10 ♉ 56	25 ♑ 46	15 ♊ 14	3 ♊ 2	17 ♓ 27	1 ♒ 13	22 ♈ 26	29 ♒ 37	3 ♑ 5	4 ♓ 56'21"
2 MO	6:45:30	17 13	27 21	16 15	3 31	17 32	1 15	22 27	29 37	3 6	4 ♓ 56'20"
3 TU	6:49:27	23 32	28 56	17 16	4 1	17 38	1 17	22 28	29 38	3 6	4 ♓ 56'20"
4 WE	6:53:24	29 51	0 ♒ 31	18 17	4 31	17 43	1 18	22 28	29 38	3 6	4 ♓ 56'20"
5 TH	6:57:20	6 ♊ 9	2 6	19 18	5 0	17 49	1 20	22 29	29 39	3 6	4 ♓ 56'20"
6 FR	7: 1:17	12 25	3 41	20 20	5 30	17 54	1 22	22 30	29 39	3 7	4 ♓ 56'20"
7 SA	7: 5:13	18 36	5 16	21 21	5 59	18 0	1 24	22 30	29 39	3 7	4 ♓ 56'20"
8 SU	7: 9:10	24 42	6 51	22 22	6 28	18 5	1 26	22 31	29 40	3 7	4 ♓ 56'20"
9 MO	7:13: 6	0 ♋ 41	8 26	23 23	6 58	18 11	1 28	22 32	29 40	3 8	4 ♓ 56'19"
10 TU	7:17: 3	6 32	10 1	24 24	7 27	18 16	1 30	22 32	29 40	3 8	4 ♓ 56'19"
11 WE	7:20:59	12 16	11 36	25 25	7 56	18 22	1 32	22 33	29 41	3 8	4 ♓ 56'19"
12 TH	7:24:56	17 50	13 11	26 26	8 26	18 27	1 34	22 34	29 41	3 8	4 ♓ 56'19"
13 FR	7:28:53	23 15	14 46	27 27	8 55	18 33	1 35	22 34	29 41	3 9	4 ♓ 56'19"
14 SA	7:32:49	28 30	16 21	28 29	9 24	18 38	1 37	22 35	29 42	3 9	4 ♓ 56'19"
15 SU	7:36:46	3 ♌ 35	17 57	29 30	9 53	18 44	1 39	22 36	29 42	3 9	4 ♓ 56'19"
16 MO	7:40:42	8 31	19 32	0 ♋ 31	10 22	18 49	1 41	22 36	29 43	3 10	4 ♓ 56'18"
17 TU	7:44:39	13 18	21 7	1 32	10 51	18 55	1 43	22 37	29 43	3 10	4 ♓ 56'18"
18 WE	7:48:35	17 55	22 42	2 33	11 20	19 0	1 45	22 38	29 43	3 10	4 ♓ 56'18"
19 TH	7:52:32	22 24	24 18	3 34	11 49	19 6	1 47	22 38	29 44	3 10	4 ♓ 56'18"
20 FR	7:56:28	26 43	25 53	4 35	12 18	19 11	1 49	22 39	29 44	3 11	4 ♓ 56'18"
21 SA	8: 0:25	0 ♍ 55	27 28	5 36	12 47	19 17	1 51	22 40	29 44	3 11	4 ♓ 56'18"
22 SU	8: 4:22	4 59	29 3	6 37	13 16	19 22	1 52	22 40	29 45	3 11	4 ♓ 56'18"
23 MO	8: 8:18	8 56	0 ♓ 39	7 38	13 44	19 28	1 54	22 41	29 45	3 12	4 ♓ 56'18"
24 TU	8:12:15	12 45	2 14	8 40	14 13	19 33	1 56	22 42	29 45	3 12	4 ♓ 56'17"
25 WE	8:16:11	16 29	3 50	9 41	14 42	19 39	1 58	22 42	29 46	3 12	4 ♓ 56'17"
26 TH	8:20: 8	20 6	5 25	10 42	15 10	19 44	2 0	22 43	29 46	3 12	4 ♓ 56'17"
27 FR	8:24: 4	23 38	7 0	11 43	15 39	19 50	2 2	22 44	29 47	3 13	4 ♓ 56'17"
28 SA	8:28: 1	27 4	8 36	12 44	16 8	19 55	2 4	22 44	29 47	3 13	4 ♓ 56'17"
29 SU	8:31:57	0 ♎ 26	10 11	13 45	16 36	20 1	2 6	22 45	29 47	3 13	4 ♓ 56'17"
30 MO	8:35:54	3 43	11 47	14 46	17 5	20 6	2 8	22 46	29 48	3 14	4 ♓ 56'17"
31 TU	8:39:51	6 57	13 22	15 46	17 33	20 12	2 9	22 46	29 48	3 14	4 ♓ 56'16"

INGRESSES :

3 ♀ → ♒ 16:16
4 ☿ → ♊ 0:33
8 ☿ → ♋ 21:15
14 ☿ → ♌ 6:59
15 ⊕ → ♋ 11:53
20 ☿ → ♍ 18:40
22 ♀ → ♓ 14:13
28 ☿ → ♎ 20:51

ASPECTS (HELIOCENTRIC +MOON(TYCHONIC)) :

2 ☽ ☌ ♅ 2:26	6 ☽ ☌ ☿ 10:52	13 ☿ ⚻ ☊ 1:20	☽ □ ♆ 10:46	25 ☽ ☌ ♆ 10: 3
☽ □ ♀ 13:39	☽ □ ♃ 16:24	☽ □ ♂ 11: 7	☿ ☍ ♀ 16:29	☽ ☌ ♀ 19: 2
☽ □ ♄ 19:32	☿ □ ♃ 21:37	14 ☽ ☍ ♃ 5:29	20 ☽ ☍ ♂ 7: 8	☿ ☍ ♃ 21:30
☿ ☌ P 21: 2	7 ☿ ☌ ⊕ 12:55	☿ ☍ ♄ 14:43	☿ ☍ ♆ 17:10	26 ☽ □ ♂ 12:48
3 ⊕ □ ♃ 9:21	☽ ☍ ♇ 22:58	15 ☽ □ ♇ 8:49	☽ □ ♃ 17:54	☽ ☌ ♃ 20:30
☿ □ ♆ 23:10	9 ☿ ☍ ♇ 9:57	16 ☽ ☍ ♅ 20: 4	21 ☽ ☌ ♇ 15:43	27 ☽ ☍ ☿ 4:23
⊕ ☌ P 23:35	☽ □ ♅ 14:12	17 ♀ ⚼ ☊ 10:42	22 ♀ ☌ ♆ 10:25	☽ □ ♇ 20:32
4 ♀ ☌ ♄ 12:19	10 ☽ ☍ ♄ 8:19	☽ □ ♄ 12: 0	☽ □ ♅ 22:11	29 ☽ ☌ ♅ 9: 2
☿ ☌ ♂ 19:13	11 ☽ ☍ ♀ 5:19	18 ⊕ ☍ ♇ 14:38	23 ☽ ☌ ♄ 12:46	☿ □ ♇ 20:19
5 ☽ □ ♆ 3:38	12 ☽ ☍ ♆ 16:36	☽ □ ☿ 22:17	24 ☿ □ ♂ 10:42	30 ☽ □ ♄ 3: 5
☽ ☌ ♂ 14:58	☿ □ ♅ 20:58	19 ☽ □ ♀ 2: 9	♃ ☌ P 22:11	

awaiting his coming along with others. Jesus took some refreshments, while Mary Cleophas's sons repaired at once to their sick mother. A crowd of people was assembled in front of Andrew's house, and Jesus taught and cured until after night had closed.

January 6: Full Moon Gemini

December 9–10, 29: Scattering Blossoms, p. 375, vol. I

When Jesus left the inn near Dibon, he started southward for Eleale about four hours distant, taking a road two hours farther to the southeast of the Jordan than that by which he had come thither from Bethabara. He arrived with about seven disciples, and put up with one of the elders of the synagogue.

When the sabbath began, he taught in the synagogue taking for his subject a parable upon the waving branches of a tree scattering around their blossoms and bearing no fruit. By this parable Jesus intended to rebuke the inhabitants, who for the most part had not become better after having received John's baptism. They allowed the blossoms of penance to be scattered by every wind without bearing fruit. Such were they here. Jesus chose this similitude because these people found their support chiefly in the cultivation of fruit. They had to carry it far away for sale, as no highroad passed near their isolated city. They were also largely engaged in coarse embroidery and the manufacture of covers.

Up to the present Jesus had met no contradiction. The people of Dibon and the country around loved him, and said that never before had they heard such a teacher. The old men always likened him to the prophets of whose teaching they had heard from their forefathers.

January 7: Inferior Conjunction Sun and Mercury

December 24, 29: Summons of Phillip, p. 382, vol. I

Jesus taught again, morning and afternoon, in the synagogue. After the close of the sabbath, Jesus went with his disciples into a little valley near the synagogue. It seemed intended for a promenade or a place of seclusion. There were trees in front of the entrance, as well as in the valley. The sons of Mary Cleophas, of Zebedee, and some others of the disciples were with him. But Philip, who was backward and humble, hung behind, not certain as to whether he should or should not follow. Jesus, who was going on before, turned his head and, addressing Philip, said: "Follow me!" at which words Philip went on joyously with the others. There were about twelve in the little band.

Jesus taught here under a tree, his subject being "Vocation and Correspondence." Andrew, who was full of zeal for his Master's interests, rejoiced at the happy impression made upon the disciples by the teaching of Jesus on the preceding sabbath. He saw them convinced that Jesus was the Messiah, and his own heart was so full that he lost no opportunity to recount to them again and again all that he had seen at Jesus' baptism, also the miracles he had wrought.

I heard Jesus calling heaven to witness that they should behold still greater things, and he spoke of his mission from his heavenly Father.

He alluded also to their own vocation, telling them to hold themselves in readiness. They would, he continued, have to forsake all when he called them. He would provide for them; they should suffer no want. They might still continue their customary occupations, because as the Passover was now approaching, he would have to discharge other affairs. But when he should call them, they should follow him immediately. The disciples questioned him unrestrainedly as to how they should manage with regard to their families. Peter, for instance, said that just at present he could not leave his old stepfather, who was also Philip's uncle. But Jesus relieved his anxiety by his answer, that he would not begin before the Passover feast; that only insofar as the heart was concerned, should they detach themselves from their occupations; that exteriorly they should continue them until he called them. In the meantime, however, they should take the necessary steps toward freeing themselves from their different avocations. Jesus then left the valley by the opposite end, and went to his mother's house, one of a row that stood between Capernaum and Bethsaida. His nearest relatives accompanied him, for their mothers also were with Mary.

January 18: Sun conjunct Pluto

December 1, 30: Second Raising of Salome, pp. 163–67, vol. II

When Jesus next day went down from the mountain to Capernaum, he found a crowd of people assembled to bid him welcome. He repaired to Peter's house near the city. It stood outside the gate to the right on entering the city from the valley. When it was known that Jesus and the disciples were in the house, a crowd soon gathered around him. The scribes and Pharisees also hastened out to hear him. The whole court around the open hall in which Jesus sat and taught with the disciples and scribes was full. He spoke of the Ten Commandments and, coming to the words recorded in the Gospel of the Sermon on the Mount: "You have heard that it was said to them of old: thou shalt not kill," he based upon them his instruction on the forgiveness of injuries and the love of one's enemies. Just at this moment a loud noise arose on the roof of the hall, and through the usual opening in the ceiling a paralytic on his bed was lowered by four men, who cried out: "Lord, have pity upon a poor sick man!"

He was let down by two cords into the midst of the assembly before Jesus. The friends of the sick man had tried in vain to carry him through the crowd into the courtyard, and had at last mounted the outside steps to the roof of the hall, whose trap door they opened. All eyes were fixed upon the invalid, and the Pharisees were vexed at what appeared to them a great misdemeanor, a piece of unheard-of impertinence. But Jesus, who was pleased at the faith of the poor people, stepped forward and addressed the paralytic, who lay there motionless: "Be of good heart, son, thy sins are forgiven thee!" words that were, as usual, particularly distasteful to the Pharisees. They thought within themselves: "That is blasphemy! Who but God can forgive sins?" Jesus saw their thoughts and said: "Wherefore have ye such thoughts of bitterness in your heart? Which is easier to say to the paralytic: Thy sins are forgiven thee; or to say: Arise, take up thy bed, and walk? But that you may know that the Son of Man has power on earth to forgive sins, I say to thee" (here Jesus turned to the paralytic): "Arise! Take up thy bed, and go into thy house!" And immediately the man arose cured, rolled up the coverlets of his bed, laid the laths of the frame together, took them under his arm and upon his shoulder, and accompanied by those that had brought him and some other friends went off singing canticles of praise while the whole multitude shouted for joy. The Pharisees, full of rage, slipped away, one by one. It was now the sabbath, and Jesus, followed by the multitude, repaired to the synagogue.

Jairus, the chief of the synagogue, was also present at that last miracle in the synagogue. He was very sad and full of remorse. His daughter was again near death, and truly a frightful death, as it had fallen upon her in punishment of her own and her parents' sins. Since the preceding sabbath she had lain ill of a fever. The mother and her sister together with Jairus' mother, who all lived in the same house, had, along with the daughter herself, taken Jesus' miraculous healing in a very frivolous way, without gratitude and without in any way altering their life. Jairus, weak and yielding, entirely under the control of his vain and beautiful wife, had let the women have their own way. Their home was the theater of female vanity, and all the latest pagan styles of finery were brought into requisition for their adornment. When the little girl was well again, these women laughed among themselves at Jesus and turned him into ridicule. The child followed their example. Until very recently she had retained her innocence, but now it was no longer so. A violent fever seized upon her. The burning and thirst that she had endured were something extraordinary; the last week was spent in a state of constant delirium, and she now lay near death. The parents suspected that it was a punishment of their frivolity, though they would not acknowledge it to themselves. At last, the mother became so ashamed and so frightened that she said to Jairus: "Will Jesus again have pity on us?" And she commissioned her husband once more humbly to implore his assistance. But Jairus was ashamed to appear again before the Lord, so he waited till the sabbath instructions were over. He had full faith that Jesus could help him at any time, if he would. He was too ashamed to be seen by the people again asking for help.

When Jesus was leaving the synagogue, a great crowd pressed around him, for there were many, both sick and well, who wanted to speak to him. Jairus approached with trouble on his countenance. He threw himself at Jesus' feet, and begged him again to have pity on his daughter whom he had left in a dying state. Jesus promised that he would return with him. And now there came someone from Jairus' house looking for him, because he stayed so long, and the mother of the girl thought that Jesus would not come. The messenger told Jairus that his daughter was already dead. Jesus comforted the father and told him to have confidence. It was already dark, and the crowd around Jesus was very great. Just then a woman afflicted with an issue of blood, taking advantage of the darkness, made her way through the crowd, leaning on the arms of her nurses. She dwelt not far from the synagogue. The women afflicted with the same malady, though not so grievously as herself, had told her of their own cure some hours earlier. They had that day at noon, when Jesus was passing in the midst of the crowd, ventured to touch his garments, and were thereby instantly cured. Their words roused her faith. She hoped in the dusk of evening and in the throng that would gather round Jesus on leaving the synagogue, to be able to touch him unnoticed. Jesus knew her thoughts and consequently slackened his pace. The nurses led her as close to him as possible. Standing near her were her daughter, her husband's uncle, and Lea. The sufferer knelt down, leaned forward supporting herself on one hand, and with the other reaching through the crowd she touched the hem of Jesus' robe. Instantly she felt that she was healed. Jesus at the same moment halted, glanced around at the disciples, and inquired, "Who hath touched me?"

To which Peter answered, "Thou askest, 'Who touched me?' The people throng and press upon thee, as thou seest!" But Jesus responded: "Someone hath touched me, for I know that virtue is gone out from me." Then he looked around and, as the crowd had fallen back a step, the woman could no longer remain hidden. Quite abashed, she approached him timidly, fell on her knees before him, and acknowledged in hearing of the whole crowd what she had done. Then she related how long she had suffered from an issue of blood, and that she believed herself healed by the touch of his garment. Turning to Jesus, she

begged him to forgive her. Then Jesus addressed to her these words: "Be comforted, my daughter, thy faith hath made thee whole! Go in peace, and remain free from thy infirmity!" and she departed with her friends.

She was thirty years old, very thin and pale, and was named Enue. Her deceased husband was a Jew. She had only one daughter, who had been taken charge of by her uncle. He had now come to the baptism, accompanied by his niece and a sister-in-law named Lea. The husband of the latter was a Pharisee and an enemy of Jesus. Enue had, in her widowhood, wished to enter into a connection that, to her rich relatives, appeared far below her position; therefore, they had opposed her.

Jesus with rapid steps accompanied Jairus to his house. Peter, James, John, Saturnin, and Matthew were with him. In the forecourt were again gathered the mourners and weepers, but this time they uttered no word of mockery, nor did Jesus say as he did before: "She is only sleeping," but passed on straight through the crowd. Jairus' mother, his wife, and her sister came timidly forth to meet him. They were veiled and in tears; their robes, the garments of mourning. Jesus left Saturnin and Matthew with the people in the forecourt, while, accompanied by Peter, James, and John, the father, the mother, and the grandmother, he entered the room in which the dead girl lay. It was a different room from the first time. Then she lay in a little chamber; now she was in the room behind the fireplace. Jesus called for a little branch from the garden and a basin of water, which he blessed. The corpse lay stiff and cold. It did not present so agreeable an appearance as on the former occasion. Then I had seen the soul hovering in a sphere of light close to the body, but this time I did not see it at all. On the former occasion, Jesus said: "She is sleeping," but now he said nothing. She was dead. With the little branch Jesus sprinkled her with the blessed water, prayed, took her by the hand, and said: "Little maid, I say to thee, arise!" As Jesus was praying, I saw the girl's soul in a dark globe approaching her mouth, into which it entered. She suddenly opened her eyes, obeyed the touch of Jesus' hand, arose and stepped from her couch. Jesus led her to her parents who, receiving her with hot tears and choking sobs, sank at Jesus' feet. He ordered them to give her something to eat, some bread and grapes. His order was obeyed. The girl ate and began to speak. Then Jesus earnestly exhorted the parents to receive the mercy of God thankfully, to turn away from vanity and worldly pleasure, to embrace the penance preached to them, and to beware of again compromising their daughter's life now restored for the second time. He reproached them with their whole manner of living, with the levity they had exhibited at the reception of the first favor bestowed upon them, and their conduct afterward, by which in a short time they had exposed their child to a much more grievous death than that of the body, namely, the death of the soul. The little girl herself was very much affected and shed tears. Jesus warned her against concupiscence of the eyes and sin. While she partook of the grapes and the bread that he had blessed, he told her that for the future she should no longer live according to the flesh, but that she should eat of the Bread of Life, the Word of God, should do penance, believe, pray, and perform works of mercy. The parents were very much moved and completely transformed. The father promised to break the bonds that bound him to worldliness, and to obey Jesus' orders, while the mother and the rest of the family, who had now come in, expressed their determination to reform their lives. They shed tears and gave thanks to Jesus. Jairus, entirely changed, immediately made over a great part of his possessions to the poor. The daughter's name was Salome.

As a crowd had gathered before the house, Jesus told Jairus that they should make no unnecessary reports concerning what had just taken place. He often gave this command to those whom he cured, and that for various reasons. The chief was that the divulging and boasting of such favors troubles the recollection of the soul and prevents its reflection upon the mercy of God. Jesus desired that the cured should enter into themselves instead of running about enjoying the new life that had been given them, and thereby falling an easy prey to sin. Another reason for enjoining silence was that Jesus wanted to impress upon the disciples the necessity of avoiding vainglory and of performing the good they did through love and for God alone. Sometimes

again, he made use of this prohibition in order not to increase the number of the inquisitive, the importunate, and the sick who came to him not by the impulse of faith. Many indeed came merely to test his power, and then they fell back into their sins and infirmities, as Jairus' daughter had done.

Jesus and his five disciples left Jairus' house by the rear, in order to escape the crowd that pressed around the door. The first miracle here was performed in clear daylight; that of today was after the sabbath and by the light of lamps. Jairus' house was in the northern part of the city. Jesus, on leaving it, turned to the northwest off toward the ramparts. Meanwhile two blind men with their guides were on the lookout for his coming. It seemed almost as if they scented his presence, for they followed after him, crying: "Jesus, thou Son of David, have pity on us!" At that moment Jesus went into the house of a good man who was devoted to him. The house was built in the rampart and had on the other side a door opening into the country beyond the city precincts. The disciples sometimes stopped at this house. Its owner was one of the guards in this section of the city. The blind men, however, still followed Jesus, and even into the house, crying in beseeching tones: "Have mercy on us, Son of David!" At last Jesus turned to them and said: "Do you believe that I can do this unto you?" and they answered: "Yea, Lord!" Then he took from his pocket a little flask of oil, or balsam, and poured some into a small dish, brown and shallow. Holding it and the flask in his left hand, with the right he put into the dish a little earth, mixed it up with the thumb and forefinger of the right hand, touched the eyes of the blind men with the same, and said: "May it be done unto you according to your desire!" Their eyes were opened, they saw, they fell on their knees and gave thanks. To them also Jesus recommended silence as to what had just taken place. This he did to prevent the crowd from following him and to avoid exasperating the Pharisees. The cries of the blind men as they followed him had, however, already betrayed his presence in this part of the country, and besides this, the two men could not forbear imparting their happiness to all whom they met. A crowd was in consequence soon gathered around Jesus.

Some people from the region of Sepphoris, distant relatives of Anne, brought hither a man possessed of a mute devil. His hands were bound, and they led him and pulled him along by cords tied around his body, for he was perfectly furious and oftentimes scandalous in his behavior. He was one of those Pharisees that had formed a committee to spy on the actions of Jesus. He was named Joas, and belonged to the number of those that had disputed with Jesus in an isolated school between Sepphoris and Nazareth. When Jesus returned from Nain, that is about fourteen days before, the demon seized upon Joas, because, silencing his own interior convictions, he had, through sheer adulation of the other Pharisees, joined in the calumnious cry against Jesus: "He is possessed by the devil! He runs like a madman about the country!" It was on the subject of divorce that Jesus had disputed with him at Sepphoris. The man was in grievous sin. As he was led up, he made an attempt to rush upon Jesus, but he, with a motion of the hand, commanded the devil to withdraw. The man shuddered, and a black vapor issued from his mouth. Then he sank on his knees before Jesus, confessed his sins, and begged forgiveness. Jesus pardoned him, and enjoined certain fasts and alms as a penance. He had likewise to abstain for a long time from several kinds of food of which the Jews were exceedingly fond, garlic for instance. The excitement produced by this cure was very great, for it was considered a most difficult thing to drive out mute devils. The Pharisees had already put themselves to much trouble on Joas's account. Were it not that he was brought by his friends, he never would have appeared before Jesus, for the Pharisees would not have permitted it. Now indeed were they indignant that one of their own number had been helped by Jesus and had openly avowed his sins, in which they themselves had had a share. As the cured man was returning to his home, the news of his deliverance was spread throughout Capernaum, and the people everywhere proclaimed that such wonders had never before been heard in Israel. But the Pharisees in their fury retorted: "By the prince of devils he casteth out devils."

Jesus now left the house by the back door, and with him the disciples. They went around to Peter's on the west side and a little distant from the city, and here Jesus spent the night.

During these days Jesus repeated to his disciples his testimony of John the Baptist. "He is," he said, "as pure as an angel. Nothing unclean has ever entered his mouth, nor has an untruth or anything sinful ever come forth from it." When the disciples asked Jesus whether John had long to live, Jesus answered that he would die when his time came, and that was not far off. This information made them very sad.

January 21: New Moon Capricorn

January 12, 31: Revelation of the Death of John the Baptist, pp. 209–10, vol. II

The next time that Jesus taught in the synagogue of Hebron the sacred edifice was thrown open on all sides, and near the entrance, placed in an elevated position, was a teacher's chair by which he stood. All the inhabitants of the city and numbers from the surrounding places were assembled, the sick lying on little beds or sitting on mats around the teacher's chair. The whole place was crowded. The festal arches were still standing and the scene was truly touching. The multitude seemed impressed and edified, and above all not a word of contradiction was heard. After the instruction Jesus cured the sick.

Jesus' discourse on this occasion was full of deep significance. The lessons from scripture were those referring to the Egyptian darkness, the institution of the paschal lamb, and the redeeming of the firstborn; there was also something from Jeremiah. Jesus gave a marvelously profound explanation of the ransom of the firstborn. I remember that he said, "When sun and moon are darkened, the mother brings the child to the temple to be redeemed." More than once he made use of the expression, "The obscuring of the sun and of the moon."

He referred to conception, birth, circumcision, and presentation in the temple as connected with darkness and light. The departure from Egypt, so full of mystery, was applied to the birth of humankind. He spoke of circumcision as an external sign that, like the obligation to ransom the firstborn, would one day be abolished. No one gainsaid Jesus; all his hearers were very quiet and attentive. He spoke likewise of Hebron and of Abraham, and came at last to Zechariah and John. He alluded to John's high dignity in terms more detailed and intelligible than ever before, namely, his birth, his life in the desert, his preaching of penance, his baptism, his faithful discharge of his mission as precursor, and lastly of his imprisonment. Then he alluded to the fate of the prophets and the high priest Zechariah, who had been murdered between the altar and the sanctuary, also the sufferings of Jeremiah in the dungeon at Jerusalem, and the persecutions endured by the others. When Jesus spoke of the murder of the first Zechariah between the temple and the altar, the relatives present thought of the sad fate of the Baptist's father, whom Herod had decoyed to Jerusalem and then caused to be put to death in a neighboring house. Jesus nevertheless had made no mention of this last fact. Zechariah was buried in a vault near his own house outside of Jutta.

As Jesus was thus speaking in an impressive and very significant manner of John and the death of the prophets, the silence throughout the synagogue grew more profound. All were deeply affected, many were shedding tears, and even the Pharisees were very much moved. Several of John's relatives and friends at this moment received an interior illumination by which they understood that the Baptist himself was dead, and they fainted away from grief. This gave rise to some excitement in the synagogue. Jesus quieted the disturbance by directing the bystanders to support those that had fainted, as they would soon revive; so they lay a few moments in the arms of their friends, while Jesus went on with his discourse.

To me there was something significant in the words, "Between the temple and the altar," as recorded of the murder of that first Zechariah. They might well be applied to John the Baptist's death since, in the life of Jesus, it also stood between the temple and the altar, for John died between the birth of Jesus and his sacrifice upon the altar of the cross. But this signification of the words did not present itself to Jesus' hearers. At the close of the instruction they who had fainted were conducted to their homes.

Besides Zechariah, John's cousin, Elizabeth had a niece, her sister's daughter, married here in Hebron. She had a family of twelve children, of whom some were daughters already grown. It was these and some others who had been so deeply affected. On leaving the synagogue Jesus went with young Zechariah and the disciples to the house of Elizabeth's niece, where he had not yet been. The holy women, however, had visited her several times before their departure. Jesus had engaged to sup with her this day, but it was a very sad meal.

Jesus was in a room with Peter, John, James Cleophas, Heliachim, Sadoch, Zechariah, Elizabeth's niece and her husband. John's relatives asked Jesus in a trembling voice: "Lord, shall we see John again?" They were in a retired room, the door locked, so that no one could disturb them. Jesus answered with tears: "No!" and spoke most feelingly, but in consoling terms, of John's death. When they sadly expressed their fear that the body would be ill treated, Jesus reassured them. He told them no, that the corpse was lying untouched, though the head had been abused and thrown into a sewer; but that, too, would be preserved and would one day come to light. He told them likewise that in some days Herod would leave Machaerus and the news of John's death would spread abroad; then they could take away the body. Jesus wept with his sorrowful listeners. They afterward partook of a repast that, on account of the retired situation of the apartment, the silence, the gravity, the great ardor and emotion of Jesus, made me think of the Last Supper.

I had on this occasion a vision of Mary's coming to present Jesus in the temple, which presentation took place on the forty-third day after his birth. The holy family, on account of a feast of three days, had to remain with the good people of the little inn outside the Bethlehem gate. Besides the usual offering of doves, Mary brought five little triangular plates of gold, gifts of the three kings, and several pieces of fine embroidered stuff as a present for the temple. The ass that he had pawned to one of his relatives, Joseph now sold to him. I am under the impression that the ass used by Jesus on Palm Sunday sprang from it.

January 22: Venus conjunct Saturn

July 10, 30: The Baptismal Well, pp. 470–71, vol. I

When morning dawned, Jesus joined the disciples, and they went back to the city together by a roundabout way on which were several huts. Invitations and instructions were given at these huts as at the other houses. Arrived at the city, Jesus and the disciples went to the residence of the governor, which stood in an open square, and there took some refreshment. The repast consisted of little rolls joined in pairs, and small fish with upright heads. These last were served in a many-colored, shining glass dish formed like a ship. Jesus laid one of the fishes on a roll before each of the disciples. All around the edge of the table were cavities hollowed out like plates, and into them the portions were put.

After the repast, Jesus gave an instruction in the hall opening on the court in presence of the governor and his household, all of whom were to be baptized. After that he went to the place of instruction outside the city where he found many already waiting for him, and there, too, he taught in preparation for baptism. The people in bands came and went by turns, proceeding from this place to the synagogue where they prayed, sprinkled their head with ashes, and did penance. They repaired afterward to the bathing garden near the "Place of Grace," where two by two they performed their ablutions in a bathhouse separated from each other by a curtain.

When the last band had left the place of instruction, Jesus and his disciples followed. The baptismal well was that into which the water from the arm of the Jordan flowed. The basin here, as in other places, was surrounded by a canal so broad as to afford a passage for two, and from it five conduits connected with the basin. These conduits could be opened or closed at pleasure, and at the side of each ran a path over the little canal. In the center of the basin rose a stake that, by a crosspiece that reached to the bank, could be made to open and close the basin.

This reservoir with its five canals had not been especially constructed for the baptism. The number five was a frequent recurrence in Palestine, and the five aqueducts leading to the pool of Bethesda, to John's fountain in the desert, to the baptismal well of Jesus, bore reference no doubt to the five sacred wounds, or to some other mystery of religion.

Jesus here gave instructions as an immediate preparation for baptism. The neophytes were clothed in long mantles, which they laid aside at the moment of stepping into the canal, retaining only the covering for the loins and the little scapular on the breast. Water from the basin had been let into the canal. On the pathways over it stood the baptizers and the sponsors. The water was thrice poured from a shallow dish over the head in the name of Jehovah and him whom he had sent. Four disciples baptized at the same time, two others imposing hands as sponsors. This ceremony, with the instructions of Jesus in preparation for it, lasted until evening. Many of the aspirants to baptism were not admitted to its reception.

FEBRUARY 2023

February 5: Full Moon Cancer

January 8, 30: Conversation with Virgin Mary, p. 393, vol. I

After the sabbath, Jesus returned to his mother, with whom he conversed alone far into the night. He spoke of his future movements: he would first go to the Jordan, then celebrate Passover at Jerusalem, afterward call his apostles, and make his public appearance. He predicted the persecution he should endure at Nazareth, alluded to his career after that, and explained in what way she and the other women should bear a part in it. There was at that time in Mary's house a woman already far advanced in years. She was the same poor widowed relative whom Anne had sent to Mary to take the place of a servant to her in the crib cave. She was now so old that Mary rather served her than she Mary.

February 10: Mercury conjunct Pluto

December 26, 30: Second Conversion of Magdalene, pp. 189–90, vol. II

Jesus, accompanied by six apostles and a number of the disciples, started from the inn at Dothaim for Azanoth. On the way, he met the holy women coming from Damna. Lazarus was among Jesus' companions on this occasion.

After Martha's departure, Magdalene was very much tormented by the devil, who wanted to prevent her going to Jesus' instruction. She would have followed his suggestions, were it not for some of her guests who had agreed to go with her to Azanoth, to witness what they called a great show. Magdalene and her frivolous, sinful companions rode on asses to the inn of the holy women near the baths of Bethulia. Magdalene's splendid seat, along with cushions and rugs for the others, followed packed on asses.

Next morning Magdalene, again arrayed in her most wanton attire and surrounded by her companions, made her appearance at the place of instruction, which was about an hour from the inn at which she was stopping. With noise and bustle, loud talk and bold staring about, they took their places under an open tent far in front of the holy women. There were some men of their own stamp in their party. They sat upon cushions and rugs and upholstered chairs, all in full view, Magdalene in front. Their coming gave rise to general whispering and murmurs of disapprobation, for they were even more detested and despised in these quarters than in Gabara. The Pharisees especially, who knew of her first remarkable conversion at Gabara and of her subsequent relapse into her former disorders, were scandalized and expressed their indignation at her daring to appear in such an assembly.

Jesus, after healing many sick, began his long and severe discourse. The details of his sermon I cannot now recall, but I know that he cried woe upon Capernaum, Bethsaida, and Chorazin. He said also that the Queen of Sheba had come from the South to hear the wisdom of Solomon, but here was one greater than Solomon. And lo, the wonder! Children that had never yet spoken, babes in their mothers' arms, cried out from time to time during the instruction: "Jesus of Nazareth! Holiest of prophets! Son of David! Son of God!" Which words caused many of the hearers, and among them Magdalene, to tremble with fear. Making allusion to Magdalene, Jesus said

that when the devil has been driven out and the house has been swept, he returns with six other demons, and rages worse than before. These words terrified Magdalene. After Jesus had in this way touched the hearts of many, he turned successively to all sides and commanded the demon to go out of all that sighed for deliverance from his thralldom, but that those who wished to remain bound to the devil should depart and take him along with them. At this command, the possessed cried out from all parts of the circle: "Jesus, thou Son of God!"—and here and there people sank to the ground unconscious.

Magdalene also, from her splendid seat upon which she had attracted all eyes, fell in violent convulsions. Her companions in sin applied perfumes as restoratives, and wanted to carry her away. Desiring to remain under the empire of the evil one, they were themselves glad to profit by the opportunity to retire from the scene. But just then some persons near her cried out: "Stop, Master! Stop! This woman is dying." Jesus interrupted his discourse to reply: "Place her on her chair! The death she is now dying is a good death, and one that will vivify her!" After some time another word of Jesus pierced her to the heart, and she again fell into convulsions, during which dark forms escaped from her. A crowd gathered round her in alarm, while her own immediate party tried once again to bring her to herself. She was soon able to resume her seat on her beautiful chair, and then she tried to look as if she had suffered only an ordinary fainting spell. She had now become the object of general attention, especially as many other possessed back in the crowd had, like her, fallen in convulsions, and afterward rose up freed from the evil one. But when for the third time Magdalene fell down in violent convulsions, the excitement increased, and Martha hurried forward to her. When she recovered consciousness, she acted like one bereft of her senses. She wept passionately and wanted to go to where the holy women were sitting. The frivolous companions with whom she had come hither held her back forcibly, declaring that she should not play the fool, and they at last succeeded in getting her down the mountain. Lazarus, Martha, and others who had followed her, now went forward and led her to the inn of the holy women. The crowd of worldlings who

COSMIC COMMUNION: STAR WISDOM, VOLUME 4

had accompanied Magdalene had already made their way off.

Before going down to his inn, Jesus healed many blind and sick. Later on, he taught again in the school, and Magdalene was present. She was not yet quite cured, but profoundly impressed, and no longer so wantonly arrayed. She had laid aside her superfluous finery, some of which was made of a fine scalloped material like pointed lace, and so perishable that it could be worn only once. She was now veiled. Jesus in his instruction appeared again to speak for her special benefit and, when he fixed upon her his penetrating glance, she fell once more into unconsciousness and another evil spirit went out of her. Her maids bore her from the synagogue to where she was received by Martha and Mary, who took her back to the inn. She was now like one distracted. She cried and wept. She ran through the public streets saying to all she met that she was a wicked creature, a sinner, the refuse of humanity. The holy women had the greatest trouble to quiet her. She tore her garments, disarranged her hair, and hid her face in the folds of her veil. When Jesus returned to his inn with the disciples and some of the Pharisees, and while they were taking some refreshments standing, Magdalene escaped from the holy women, ran with streaming hair and uttering loud lamentations, made her way through the crowd, cast herself at Jesus' feet, weeping and moaning, and asked if she might still hope for salvation. The Pharisees and disciples, scandalized at the sight, said to Jesus that he should no longer suffer this reprobate woman to create disturbance everywhere, that he should send her away once for all. But Jesus replied: "Permit her to weep and lament! Ye know not what is passing in her"—and he turned to her with words of consolation. He told her to repent from her heart, to believe and to hope, for that she should soon find peace. Then he bade her depart with confidence. Martha, who had followed with her maids, took her again to her inn. Magdalene did nothing but wring her hands and lament. She was not yet quite freed from the power of the evil one, who tortured and tormented her with the most frightful remorse and despair. There was no rest for her— she thought herself forever lost.

Upon her request, Lazarus went to Magdalum in order to take charge of her property, and to dissolve the ties she had there formed. She owned, near Azanoth and in the surrounding country, fields and vineyards that Lazarus, on account of her extravagance, had previously sequestered.

February 15: Venus conjunct Neptune
December 29, 30: Visiting Jonadab, p. 193–94, vol. II

Some Pharisees of Nazareth came to Jesus at Chisloth to invite him to his native city. Those Pharisees who, on a former occasion, wanted to hurl him from the rock, were no longer in Nazareth. The envoys told Jesus that he ought to go to his native city and there exhibit some of his signs and wonders. The people, they said, were eager to hear his doctrine; then, too, he could cure his fellow countrymen that were sick. But they laid down as a condition that he would not heal on the sabbath day. Jesus replied that he would go and keep the sabbath with them. He warned them, however, that they would be scandalized on his account, and as to the cures, he would condescend to their desires even if it proved to their own detriment. Upon receiving this answer, the Pharisees returned to Nazareth, whither Jesus soon followed with his disciples, whom he instructed on the way. It was noon when they arrived. Many from curiosity, others really well intentioned people, came forth from the city to meet him. They washed the feet of the newcomers and offered them some refreshments. Jesus had two disciples from Nazareth, Parmenas and Jonadab. With the widowed mother of the latter, Jesus and his companions took up their quarters. These disciples had been friends of Jesus in early youth, and had accompanied him on his first journey to Hebron after Joseph's death. He now employed them frequently in discharging commissions and errands of all kinds.

Jesus went to some sick who had implored his assistance. He knew that they believed in him and had need of his aid. But he passed by many who wanted only to test his power or who, under the pretence of a cure, were desirous only of getting a sight of him. An Essene youth, paralyzed on one side from his birth, was brought to

SIDEREAL GEOCENTRIC LONGITUDES : FEBRUARY 2023 Gregorian at 0 hours UT											
DAY	☉	☽	☊	☿	♀	♂	♃	♄	♅	♆	♇
1 WE	16 ♑ 47	24 ♉ 53	13 ♈ 39R	21 ♐ 54	11 ♒ 2	15 ♉ 13	11 ♓ 0	0 ♒ 47	19 ♈ 55	28 ♒ 33	3 ♑ 36
2 TH	17 48	6 ♊ 50	13 32	23 0	12 16	15 26	11 11	0 54	19 55	28 34	3 38
3 FR	18 49	18 44	13 21	24 8	13 31	15 40	11 22	1 2	19 56	28 36	3 40
4 SA	19 49	0 ♋ 36	13 8	25 19	14 45	15 54	11 34	1 9	19 56	28 38	3 42
5 SU	20 50	12 28	12 53	26 31	16 0	16 8	11 45	1 16	19 57	28 40	3 44
6 MO	21 51	24 22	12 38	27 45	17 14	16 23	11 57	1 23	19 58	28 42	3 45
7 TU	22 52	6 ♌ 20	12 24	29 1	18 28	16 39	12 9	1 30	19 59	28 44	3 47
8 WE	23 53	18 21	12 12	0 ♑ 18	19 43	16 55	12 21	1 38	19 59	28 46	3 49
9 TH	24 53	0 ♍ 29	12 3	1 36	20 57	17 11	12 33	1 45	20 0	28 48	3 51
10 FR	25 54	12 44	11 56	2 56	22 11	17 28	12 45	1 52	20 1	28 50	3 53
11 SA	26 55	25 10	11 53	4 17	23 26	17 46	12 57	1 59	20 2	28 52	3 55
12 SU	27 56	7 ♎ 50	11 52	5 40	24 40	18 3	13 9	2 6	20 3	28 54	3 57
13 MO	28 56	20 47	11 52D	7 3	25 54	18 22	13 22	2 14	20 4	28 56	3 58
14 TU	29 57	4 ♏ 6	11 53R	8 28	27 8	18 40	13 34	2 21	20 5	28 58	4 0
15 WE	0 ♒ 58	17 48	11 51	9 54	28 22	18 59	13 46	2 28	20 7	29 0	4 2
16 TH	1 58	1 ♐ 57	11 48	11 21	29 36	19 19	13 59	2 35	20 8	29 2	4 4
17 FR	2 59	16 31	11 42	12 48	0 ♓ 50	19 38	14 12	2 43	20 9	29 4	4 6
18 SA	3 59	1 ♑ 26	11 34	14 17	2 4	19 59	14 24	2 50	20 10	29 6	4 7
19 SU	5 0	16 36	11 24	15 47	3 18	20 19	14 37	2 57	20 12	29 8	4 9
20 MO	6 0	1 ♒ 50	11 13	17 18	4 32	20 40	14 50	3 4	20 13	29 10	4 11
21 TU	7 1	16 56	11 4	18 50	5 46	21 1	15 3	3 12	20 15	29 12	4 13
22 WE	8 1	1 ♓ 46	10 56	20 22	7 0	21 23	15 16	3 19	20 16	29 14	4 14
23 TH	9 2	16 11	10 51	21 56	8 13	21 45	15 29	3 26	20 18	29 17	4 16
24 FR	10 2	0 ♈ 8	10 49	23 31	9 27	22 7	15 42	3 33	20 19	29 19	4 18
25 SA	11 3	13 36	10 48D	25 6	10 41	22 30	15 55	3 41	20 21	29 21	4 19
26 SU	12 3	26 36	10 49	26 43	11 54	22 52	16 8	3 48	20 23	29 23	4 21
27 MO	13 3	9 ♉ 13	10 49	28 21	13 8	23 16	16 22	3 55	20 24	29 25	4 23
28 TU	14 4	21 32	10 49R	29 59	14 21	23 39	16 35	4 2	20 26	29 28	4 24

INGRESSES :	
1 ☽ → ♊ 10:14	19 ☽ → ♒ 21: 6
3 ☽ → ♋ 22:48	21 ☽ → ♓ 21: 6
6 ☽ → ♌ 11:18	23 ☽ → ♈ 23:45
7 ☿ → ♑ 18:30	26 ☽ → ♉ 6:23
8 ☽ → ♍ 23: 3	28 ☿ → ♒ 0:10
11 ☽ → ♎ 9:12	☽ → ♊ 16:47
13 ☽ → ♏ 16:41	
14 ☉ → ♒ 1:14	
15 ☽ → ♐ 20:44	
16 ♀ → ♓ 7:44	
17 ☽ → ♑ 21:42	

ASPECTS & ECLIPSES :		
3 ☽ ☍ ☿ 12: 7	☿ ☌ ♇ 17:10	19 ☽ ☌ P 9: 5
4 ☉ □ ♅ 2:48	12 ☽ ☌ ☋ 7:32	20 ☽ ☌ ♄ 1:59
☽ ☍ ♇ 6:17	☽ ☍ ♅ 22:41	☉ ☌ ☽ 7: 4
☽ ☌ A 8:44	13 ☉ □ ☽ 15:59	21 ☽ ☌ ♆ 19:51
5 ☽ N ☊ 0:49	15 ☽ ☍ ♂ 2: 4	☿ □ ♅ 22:20
♀ □ ♂ 3:27	♀ ☌ ♆ 12:31	22 ☽ ☌ ♀ 9:24
☉ ☍ ☽ 18:27	16 ☿ □ ☊ 7: 5	☽ ☌ ♃ 22:47
6 ☽ ☍ ♄ 14:14	☉ ☌ ♄ 16:47	24 ☽ ☌ ☊ 18:56
8 ☽ ☍ ♀ 3: 0	18 ☽ ☌ ♇ 4:16	25 ☽ ☌ ♅ 12:23
☽ ☍ ♆ 20:39	☽ S ☊ 15:52	27 ☉ □ ☽ 8: 4
10 ☽ ☍ ♃ 0: 1	☽ ☌ ☿ 22:34	28 ☽ ☌ ♂ 4:19

SIDEREAL HELIOCENTRIC LONGITUDES : FEBRUARY 2023 Gregorian at 0 hours UT											
DAY	Sid. Time	☿	♀	⊕	♂	♃	♄	♅	♆	♇	Vernal Point
1 WE	8:43:47	10 ♎ 6	14 ♓ 58	16 ♋ 47	18 ♊ 2	20 ♓ 17	2 ♒ 11	22 ♈ 47	29 ♒ 48	3 ♑ 14	4 ♓ 56'16"
2 TH	8:47:44	13 12	16 34	17 48	18 30	20 23	2 13	22 48	29 49	3 14	4 ♓ 56'16"
3 FR	8:51:40	16 14	18 9	18 49	18 58	20 28	2 15	22 48	29 49	3 15	4 ♓ 56'16"
4 SA	8:55:37	19 14	19 45	19 50	19 27	20 34	2 17	22 49	29 49	3 15	4 ♓ 56'16"
5 SU	8:59:33	22 12	21 21	20 51	19 55	20 39	2 19	22 50	29 50	3 15	4 ♓ 56'16"
6 MO	9: 3:30	25 7	22 56	21 52	20 23	20 45	2 21	22 50	29 50	3 16	4 ♓ 56'16"
7 TU	9: 7:26	28 0	24 32	22 52	20 51	20 50	2 23	22 51	29 51	3 16	4 ♓ 56'15"
8 WE	9:11:23	0 ♏ 51	26 8	23 53	21 20	20 56	2 25	22 52	29 51	3 16	4 ♓ 56'15"
9 TH	9:15:20	3 40	27 43	24 54	21 48	21 1	2 26	22 52	29 51	3 16	4 ♓ 56'15"
10 FR	9:19:16	6 28	29 19	25 55	22 16	21 7	2 28	22 53	29 52	3 17	4 ♓ 56'15"
11 SA	9:23:13	9 15	0 ♈ 55	26 55	22 44	21 12	2 30	22 54	29 52	3 17	4 ♓ 56'15"
12 SU	9:27: 9	12 2	2 31	27 56	23 12	21 18	2 32	22 54	29 52	3 17	4 ♓ 56'15"
13 MO	9:31: 6	14 47	4 7	28 57	23 40	21 23	2 34	22 55	29 53	3 18	4 ♓ 56'15"
14 TU	9:35: 2	17 32	5 43	29 57	24 8	21 29	2 36	22 56	29 53	3 18	4 ♓ 56'15"
15 WE	9:38:59	20 17	7 18	0 ♌ 58	24 36	21 34	2 38	22 56	29 53	3 18	4 ♓ 56'14"
16 TH	9:42:55	23 1	8 54	1 59	25 4	21 40	2 40	22 57	29 54	3 18	4 ♓ 56'14"
17 FR	9:46:52	25 46	10 30	2 59	25 32	21 45	2 42	22 58	29 54	3 19	4 ♓ 56'14"
18 SA	9:50:49	28 31	12 6	4 0	25 59	21 51	2 43	22 58	29 55	3 19	4 ♓ 56'14"
19 SU	9:54:45	1 ♐ 17	13 42	5 0	26 27	21 56	2 45	22 59	29 55	3 19	4 ♓ 56'14"
20 MO	9:58:42	4 3	15 18	6 1	26 55	22 2	2 47	23 0	29 55	3 20	4 ♓ 56'14"
21 TU	10: 2:38	6 51	16 55	7 1	27 23	22 7	2 49	23 0	29 56	3 20	4 ♓ 56'14"
22 WE	10: 6:35	9 39	18 31	8 2	27 50	22 13	2 51	23 1	29 56	3 20	4 ♓ 56'13"
23 TH	10:10:31	12 29	20 7	9 2	28 18	22 18	2 53	23 2	29 56	3 20	4 ♓ 56'13"
24 FR	10:14:28	15 21	21 43	10 3	28 46	22 24	2 55	23 2	29 57	3 21	4 ♓ 56'13"
25 SA	10:18:24	18 14	23 19	11 3	29 13	22 29	2 57	23 3	29 57	3 21	4 ♓ 56'13"
26 SU	10:22:21	21 9	24 55	12 4	29 41	22 35	2 59	23 4	29 57	3 21	4 ♓ 56'13"
27 MO	10:26:18	24 7	26 32	13 4	0 ♋ 9	22 40	3 1	23 4	29 58	3 22	4 ♓ 56'13"
28 TU	10:30:14	27 7	28 8	14 4	0 36	22 46	3 2	23 5	29 58	3 22	4 ♓ 56'13"

INGRESSES :
7 ☿ → ♏ 16:52
10 ♀ → ♈ 10:13
14 ⊕ → ♌ 1: 2
18 ☿ → ♐ 12:52
26 ♂ → ♋ 16:30
28 ☿ → ♑ 22:40

ASPECTS (HELIOCENTRIC +MOON(TYCHONIC)) :				
1 ☽ □ ♆ 9:51	6 ☽ □ ☿ 1:57	13 ☽ ☍ ♅ 3:53	19 ☽ □ ♅ 10: 3	☽ □ ♄ 12: 4
2 ☽ □ ♀ 22:39	☽ ☍ ♄ 16: 3	☽ □ ♄ 21:20	20 ☽ ☌ ♄ 1:31	28 ☽ □ ♆ 16:44
3 ☽ ☌ ♂ 0:30	♂ □ ♃ 22:55	15 ☽ ☌ ☿ 5:17	21 ☽ ☌ ♆ 20:59	
☽ □ ♃ 3:33	⊕ □ ♅ 23:27	☽ □ ♆ 20:33	22 ☽ □ ☿ 16:13	
♀ □ ♂ 17:30	8 ☿ □ ♄ 13:25	☿ ☌ A 21:38	23 ☽ ☌ ♃ 10:29	
4 ☽ ☍ ♇ 5:22	☽ ☍ ♆ 22:45	16 ⊕ ☍ ♄ 16:47	☽ □ ♂ 21:31	
☿ □ ⊕ 7:16	10 ☽ ☍ ♃ 16:20	17 ☽ □ ♃ 8:32	24 ☽ □ ♇ 5:39	
♀ ☌ ♃ 13: 2	☽ □ ♂ 19: 8	☽ ☍ ♂ 15: 0	♀ ☌ ♅ 19:58	
5 ☿ ☍ ♅ 5:12	11 ☽ ☍ ♀ 12:32	18 ☽ ☌ ♇ 2:59	25 ☽ ☌ ♅ 17:23	
☿ ☌ ☋ 11: 3	☽ □ ♇ 15:26	☿ □ ♆ 12: 6	☽ ☌ ♀ 20:24	
☽ □ ♅ 20:54	12 ♀ □ ♇ 11:39	☽ □ ♀ 18:54	26 ☿ □ ♃ 11:58	

him. He implored Jesus to cure him, and he did so on the street, as also two blind men. Then he entered certain houses wherein he cured many aged sick people, men and women. Some of them were afflicted with edema in its worst form; one woman in particular was frightfully swollen. Jesus cured, altogether, fifteen people. After that he went to the synagogue where also some sick were gathered; but he passed without curing them, and celebrated the sabbath without interruption. The reading for this sabbath was about God's speaking to Moses in Egypt, also some chapters from Ezekiel.

February 16: Sun conjunct Saturn

June 23, 31: On Samuel, pp. 405–07, vol. II

That evening Jesus closed the sabbath exercises in the synagogue. He had repaired thither with the apostles and disciples some time before the usual hour, that all might hear what he had to say to his followers and thereby understand that he had no need to teach in secret. In this instruction, he warned them against the Pharisees and false prophets, commanded them to be vigilant, explained the parable of the good and watchful servants and contrasted it with that of the slothful. As Peter during the discourse asked whether his words were meant for all his hearers or only for the disciples, Jesus now addressed himself to him. He spoke to him as if he were the master of the house, the overseer of the servants. He extolled the good householder, and at the same time condemned severely the negligent one that fulfilled not his duty.

Jesus continued to teach until the Pharisees came to close the sabbath, and when he wanted to give place to them, they very courteously addressed him with, "Rabbi, do thou explain the lesson," and laid the roll of scriptures before him. Thereupon Jesus taught, in a manner most impressive, upon Samuel's abdication of the judicial office. He quoted the words used by him on that occasion: "I am old and gray-headed"; and explained them in such a way that the Pharisees could plainly see that he was applying them to himself. He said something to this effect: "Ye have had me a long time among you, and ye are tired of me! Ye are constantly renewing your accusations, but I am always the same."

Samuel's questions to the people, "Have I committed this or that injustice against you? Have I taken any man's oxen or ass? Have I oppressed anyone?" Jesus cited as those of God and the sent of God, and the explanation that he gave of them pointed most clearly to those doctors and Pharisees who could not venture to put similar questions to the people. The clamoring of the Israelites after a king by whom, like the pagan nations, they wanted to be ruled, and their rejection of Judges, signified, Jesus said, their perverse expectation of a worldly kingdom, of a king and a Messiah surrounded by magnificence, with whom they could pass their lives in splendor and enjoyment; a Messiah who, instead of expiating their sins and disorders by his own labors, sufferings, penance, and satisfaction, would envelop them together with their filth and vices in his own rich mantle of royalty, and even reward them for their crimes.

That Samuel did not cease to pray for the nation and that by his prayer he caused thunder and lightning in the sky above them, Jesus explained as an effect of God's compassion for the good; and he assured them that the sent of God, whom instead of receiving they would reject, would likewise implore his Father's mercy for them until the end. The rain and thunder granted to prayer, Jesus explained as the signs and wonders that were to attend upon the sent of God to rouse and convert the good. They and their king, as Samuel had said, would find favor with God if they walked before him who would not reject them. Then Jesus declared to them that the righteous would receive justice and the grace of knowledge, but against the wicked, Samuel would rise up in judgment. Jesus afterward referred to David and his anointing as king in opposition to Saul, to the separation of the good from the bad, and to the destruction of Saul and his family.

The Pharisees took care not to contradict Jesus in the synagogue, that they might not (as was always the case on such occasions) be put to shame before the people. They had, however, resolved beforehand to attack him at the entertainment to which they had invited him along with the apostles and a part of the disciples. It was given in an open hall of the house belonging to the ruler of the synagogue, and there were at least twenty Pharisees present. Before taking their places at table, one of them put a large wash basin before Jesus, asking whether he did not want to wash, and he went on talking of the holy old customs and commandments of the Israelites, and called upon Jesus and his followers to observe them. But Jesus repulsed him. He told him that he saw through his trick, and wanted no water from him. When at table, they began to dispute with him upon the discourse he had delivered that day. But he convicted and confounded them in such a manner that many of them became perfectly furious, and several others were so frightened and touched that during the disputation, which they carried on walking up and down, twelve of them withdrew from their obstinate colleagues. Thus was the number of Jesus' enemies decreased.

One of the young men of Nazareth who had so often, but vainly, petitioned to be received among the disciples, here presented himself again before Jesus with the question: "Master, what must I do to possess eternal life?" Thereupon followed the scene recorded in the Gospel, and Jesus recounted the story of the compassionate Samaritan. Meanwhile the Pharisees reproached Jesus for not receiving the young man among his disciples. It was, they said, because the youth was well educated, and Jesus knew that he could not silence him so easily as he could the others. They again accused the disciples of irregular conduct, of uncleanliness, of stripping the wheat ears on the sabbath, of gathering fruit on the wayside, of eating out of time, of ill breeding, and of many other similar things. They reproached Peter in particular with being a wrangler and quarreler like his father. Jesus defended the disciples. They might indeed be joyful, he said, as long as the Bridegroom was with them. After these words he withdrew, passing through the beautiful cemetery near the synagogue that lay in the direction of Jairus' house, and thence by the land route to Bethsaida. He prayed alone until after midnight, when he retired to his mother's. The Pharisees had hired the rabble to throw stones after the disciples, but God protected them. They knew not where Jesus had gone.

The Jews that had emigrated from Cyprus to Palestine lived at first in caves, but by degrees their settlement became a city, which received the name of Eleutheropolis. It was situated west of Hebron and not far from the well of Samson. More than once the Jews sought to destroy the little colony, but after every attack of the kind, the inhabitants again returned. The caves lay under the city, so that in times of persecution the inhabitants could take refuge in them. In the first attack, which was made at the time of the stoning of St. Stephen, when the colony between Ophel and Bethany was destroyed, Mercuria lost her life. The people of this colony often went to the Cenacle and to the church at the pool of Bethesda, to carry thither their offerings and contributions, and at the destruction of Ophel they fled to Eleutheropolis. Joseph Barsabbas, son of Mary Cleophas and her second husband Sabbas, became the first bishop of that city, and there during a persecution he was crucified on a tree.

February 20: New Moon Aquarius
January 22, 30: Feast of the New Moon, pp. 397–98, vol. I

The next day was the first Feast of the New Moon (close of the month of Tebeth/start of the month of Shebat), and I saw that the serving class and civil functionaries in Jerusalem had a holiday. It was kept as a festival of joy, a day of rest, consequently there was no baptizing on it.

The flags for the Feast of the New Moon were waving from long flagstaffs on the roof of the synagogue. Large knots were made at intervals on the staves between which the folds of the streamers opened in the breeze. The number of knots signified to those at a distance what month had just begun. Such flags were unfurled also as signals of victory or of danger.

MARCH 2023

March 2: Venus conjunct Jupiter
May 24, 32: Walking through the Pharisees, p. 470, vol. II

Jesus remained these four days in Bethjesimoth. The Pharisees tried to prevent him from going into the synagogue, but Jesus walked through them and entered the holy building, where he taught in parables.

Mercury conjunct Saturn

June 9, 32: Confronting the Pharisees, p. 473, vol. II

About one hundred Pharisees from various places came to Jericho. Together with the local Pharisees, they questioned Jesus. Jesus replied with such powerful words that they were reduced to silence.

The disciples, on the contrary, were anxious and dissatisfied on account of Jesus' so unconcernedly exposing himself to the snares that the enraged Pharisees, of whom almost a hundred were gathered here from different parts of the country, sought to prepare for him. They sent messengers to Jerusalem to consult as to how they could take him into custody. The apostles, too, were in a certain dread, as if they thought that Jesus laid himself open to danger and treated with the people rather rashly. Once I saw Jesus surrounded by a great crowd seeking his help, and among them were some sick that had caused themselves to be carried to him. The disciples meanwhile kept at a distance. The palsied woman with the issue of blood whom he had already sent away more than once had caused herself to be carried to the bath of purification, or expiation, with which was connected the forgiveness of sin. She crept afterward to Jesus and touched the hem of his robe. He instantly stood still, looked after her, and healed her. The woman arose, thanked her benefactor, and returned cured to her home in the city. Jesus then taught upon persevering and repeated prayer. He said that one should never desist from his entreaties. I was thinking meantime of the great charity of the good people who had brought the woman so long a distance, carrying her here and there after the Lord, and begging the disciples to inform them whither he was going next, that they might procure for her a good place. Owing to the nature of her sickness, which was regarded as unclean, she could not rest anywhere and everywhere. She had to solicit her cure for eight days long.

March 7: Full Moon Leo

February 7, 30: Raising of the Daughter of Jairus the Essene, p. 402, vol. I

Then he passed through Aruma where he had before been. Jairus, a descendant of the Essene Chariot, dwelt in the neighboring and somewhat despised place, Phasael. He had some time previously begged Jesus to cure his sick daughter, and Jesus had promised to do so, though not just then. Although his daughter was dead, Jairus now dispatched a messenger to meet him and remind him of his promise. Jesus sent his disciples on ahead after appointing a certain place [in Jezreel] where they should again meet him, and he himself accompanied Jairus' messenger back to Phasael.

When he entered the house of Jairus, the daughter lay wrapped in the winding sheet ready for burial, her weeping friends around her. Jesus ordered the neighbors to be called in, and the winding sheet and linens to be loosened. Then taking the dead girl by the hand, he commanded her to arise. She did so, and stood before him. She was about sixteen years old and not good. She had no love for her father, although he prized her above all things. He was charitable and pious, and shrank not from communication with the poor and despised. That was a source of vexation to his daughter. Jesus roused her from death both of soul and body. She reformed and, sometime after, joined the holy women. Jesus warned those present not to speak of the miracle they had witnessed. It was through the same desire of secrecy that he had not allowed the disciples to accompany him. This was not the Jairus of Capernaum whose daughter also was, at a later period, raised from the dead by Jesus.

March 15: Sun conjunct Neptune

January 13, 30: Baptizing, pp. 394, vol. I

From Hay, Jesus departed for John's former baptismal place, on the Jordan three hours from Jericho. Andrew and many of the disciples had come about an hour's distance to meet him. Several of John's disciples, some also from Nazareth, were here. Some of them went on ahead to the little village of Ono, about an hour's distance from the place of baptism, and gave notice that Jesus

SIDEREAL GEOCENTRIC LONGITUDES : MARCH 2023 Gregorian at 0 hours UT

DAY	☉	☽	☊	☿	♀	♂	♃	♄	♅	♆	♇
1 WE	15 ♒ 4	3 ♊ 37	10 ♈ 47R	1 ♒ 39	15 ♓ 35	24 ♉ 3	16 ♓ 48	4 ♒ 9	20 ♈ 28	29 ♒ 30	4 ♑ 26
2 TH	16 4	15 33	10 43	3 19	16 48	24 27	17 2	4 17	20 30	29 32	4 27
3 FR	17 4	27 25	10 36	5 1	18 1	24 51	17 15	4 24	20 32	29 34	4 29
4 SA	18 5	9 ♋ 16	10 28	6 44	19 14	25 16	17 29	4 31	20 34	29 36	4 30
5 SU	19 5	21 9	10 18	8 28	20 28	25 40	17 42	4 38	20 36	29 39	4 32
6 MO	20 5	3 ♌ 7	10 8	10 12	21 41	26 6	17 56	4 45	20 38	29 41	4 33
7 TU	21 5	15 12	9 58	11 58	22 54	26 31	18 10	4 52	20 40	29 43	4 35
8 WE	22 5	27 23	9 49	13 45	24 7	26 56	18 24	4 59	20 42	29 45	4 36
9 TH	23 5	9 ♍ 44	9 43	15 33	25 20	27 22	18 37	5 6	20 44	29 48	4 38
10 FR	24 5	22 13	9 39	17 23	26 32	27 48	18 51	5 13	20 46	29 50	4 39
11 SA	25 5	4 ♎ 54	9 38	19 13	27 45	28 14	19 5	5 20	20 49	29 52	4 40
12 SU	26 5	17 46	9 38D	21 4	28 58	28 41	19 19	5 27	20 51	29 54	4 42
13 MO	27 5	0 ♏ 53	9 39	22 57	0 ♈ 11	29 7	19 33	5 34	20 53	29 57	4 43
14 TU	28 4	14 16	9 41	24 51	1 23	29 34	19 47	5 41	20 56	29 59	4 45
15 WE	29 4	27 56	9 41	26 45	2 36	0 ♊ 1	20 1	5 48	20 58	0 ♓ 1	4 46
16 TH	0 ♓ 4	11 ♐ 56	9 41R	28 41	3 48	0 29	20 15	5 55	21 0	0 4	4 47
17 FR	1 4	26 14	9 38	0 ♓ 38	5 1	0 56	20 29	6 2	21 3	0 6	4 48
18 SA	2 4	10 ♑ 48	9 34	2 36	6 13	1 24	20 43	6 8	21 5	0 8	4 50
19 SU	3 3	25 33	9 29	4 34	7 25	1 51	20 57	6 15	21 8	0 10	4 51
20 MO	4 3	10 ♒ 23	9 24	6 34	8 37	2 19	21 11	6 22	21 11	0 13	4 52
21 TU	5 3	25 10	9 19	8 34	9 49	2 48	21 26	6 29	21 13	0 15	4 53
22 WE	6 2	9 ♓ 46	9 15	10 34	11 1	3 16	21 40	6 35	21 16	0 17	4 54
23 TH	7 2	24 4	9 13	12 35	12 13	3 44	21 54	6 42	21 18	0 19	4 55
24 FR	8 1	7 ♈ 59	9 12	14 36	13 25	4 13	22 8	6 49	21 21	0 22	4 56
25 SA	9 1	21 29	9 12D	16 37	14 37	4 42	22 23	6 55	21 24	0 24	4 58
26 SU	10 0	4 ♉ 34	9 14	18 38	15 49	5 11	22 37	7 2	21 27	0 26	4 59
27 MO	11 0	17 17	9 16	20 38	17 0	5 40	22 51	7 8	21 29	0 28	5 0
28 TU	11 59	29 40	9 17	22 36	18 12	6 9	23 6	7 14	21 32	0 31	5 1
29 WE	12 59	11 ♊ 49	9 17	24 34	19 23	6 39	23 20	7 21	21 35	0 33	5 2
30 TH	13 58	23 47	9 17R	26 30	20 34	7 9	23 35	7 27	21 38	0 35	5 2
31 FR	14 57	5 ♋ 41	9 15	28 23	21 46	7 38	23 49	7 33	21 41	0 37	5 3

INGRESSES :

3 ☽ → ♋ 5:14	17 ☽ → ♑ 6:15
5 ☽ → ♌ 17:45	19 ☽ → ♒ 7:11
8 ☽ → ♍ 5: 6	21 ☽ → ♓ 7:53
10 ☽ → ♎ 14:46	23 ☽ → ♈ 10: 8
12 ♀ → ♈ 20:29	25 ☽ → ♉ 15:31
☽ → ♏ 22:24	28 ☽ → ♊ 0:38
14 ♆ → ♓ 10:29	30 ☽ → ♋ 12:31
♂ → ♊ 22:52	31 ☿ → ♈ 20:55
15 ☽ → ♐ 3:34	
☉ → ♓ 22:22	
16 ☿ → ♓ 16:12	

ASPECTS & ECLIPSES :

2 ♀ ☌ ♃ 5:34	11 ☽ ☌ ☋ 8:51	☽ ☌ ♇ 14:12	☽ ☌ ♅ 23:50
☿ ☌ ♄ 14:33	12 ☽ ☍ ♅ 5:41	☽ S ☊ 22: 0	28 ☿ ☌ ♃ 6:49
3 ☽ ☍ ♇ 14:21	15 ♂ □ ♆ 0: 0	19 ☽ ☌ P 15: 2	☽ ☌ ♂ 13:18
☽ ☌ A 18: 3	☉ □ ☽ 2: 7	☽ ☌ ♄ 17:26	29 ☉ □ ☽ 2:31
4 ☽ N ☊ 2:23	☽ ☍ ♂ 3:44	20 ♀ ☌ ☊ 14:29	30 ♀ ☌ ♅ 22:23
6 ☽ ☍ ♄ 3:17	☉ ☌ ♆ 23:47	21 ☽ ☌ ♆ 8:19	☽ ☍ ♇ 22:44
☽ ☍ ☿ 16:31	16 ☿ ☌ ♆ 17:16	☉ ☌ ☽ 17:22	31 ☽ N ☊ 7:12
7 ☉ ☍ ☽ 12:39	☉ □ ♂ 18: 8	22 ☽ ☌ ☿ 1:32	☽ ☌ A 11:13
8 ☽ ☍ ♆ 4:38	♀ □ ♇ 19:53	☽ ☌ ♃ 20:15	
9 ☽ ☍ ♃ 17:26	17 ☿ □ ♂ 4:47	24 ☽ ☌ ☊ 2: 7	
10 ☽ ☍ ♀ 9: 5	☉ S☌ ☿ 10:43	☽ ☌ ♀ 10:29	

SIDEREAL HELIOCENTRIC LONGITUDES : MARCH 2023 Gregorian at 0 hours UT

DAY	Sid. Time	☿	♀	⊕	♂	♃	♄	♅	♆	♇	Vernal Point
1 WE	10:34:11	0 ♑ 10	29 ♈ 44	15 ♌ 4	1 ♋ 4	22 ♓ 51	3 ♒ 4	23 ♈ 6	29 ♒ 59	3 ♑ 22	4 ♓ 56'12"
2 TH	10:38: 7	3 16	1 ♉ 20	16 5	1 31	22 57	3 6	23 6	29 59	3 22	4 ♓ 56'12"
3 FR	10:42: 4	6 26	2 57	17 5	1 59	23 2	3 8	23 7	29 59	3 23	4 ♓ 56'12"
4 SA	10:46: 0	9 39	4 33	18 5	2 26	23 8	3 10	23 8	0 ♓ 0	3 23	4 ♓ 56'12"
5 SU	10:49:57	12 56	6 10	19 5	2 53	23 13	3 12	23 8	0 0	3 23	4 ♓ 56'12"
6 MO	10:53:53	16 17	7 46	20 5	3 21	23 19	3 14	23 9	0 0	3 24	4 ♓ 56'12"
7 TU	10:57:50	19 42	9 22	21 5	3 48	23 24	3 16	23 10	0 1	3 24	4 ♓ 56'12"
8 WE	11: 1:47	23 13	10 59	22 5	4 15	23 30	3 18	23 10	0 1	3 24	4 ♓ 56'11"
9 TH	11: 5:43	26 49	12 36	23 5	4 43	23 35	3 19	23 11	0 1	3 24	4 ♓ 56'11"
10 FR	11: 9:40	0 ♒ 30	14 12	24 5	5 10	23 41	3 21	23 12	0 2	3 25	4 ♓ 56'11"
11 SA	11:13:36	4 18	15 49	25 5	5 37	23 46	3 23	23 12	0 2	3 25	4 ♓ 56'11"
12 SU	11:17:33	8 11	17 25	26 5	6 4	23 52	3 25	23 13	0 3	3 25	4 ♓ 56'11"
13 MO	11:21:29	12 12	19 2	27 5	6 32	23 57	3 27	23 14	0 3	3 26	4 ♓ 56'11"
14 TU	11:25:26	16 19	20 39	28 5	6 59	24 3	3 29	23 15	0 3	3 26	4 ♓ 56'11"
15 WE	11:29:22	20 34	22 15	29 5	7 26	24 8	3 31	23 15	0 4	3 26	4 ♓ 56'11"
16 TH	11:33:19	24 56	23 52	0 ♍ 5	7 53	24 14	3 33	23 16	0 4	3 26	4 ♓ 56'10"
17 FR	11:37:16	29 27	25 29	1 4	8 20	24 19	3 35	23 17	0 4	3 27	4 ♓ 56'10"
18 SA	11:41:12	4 ♓ 7	27 6	2 4	8 47	24 25	3 37	23 17	0 5	3 27	4 ♓ 56'10"
19 SU	11:45: 9	8 54	28 42	3 4	9 14	24 30	3 38	23 18	0 5	3 27	4 ♓ 56'10"
20 MO	11:49: 5	13 51	0 ♊ 19	4 3	9 41	24 36	3 40	23 19	0 6	3 28	4 ♓ 56'10"
21 TU	11:53: 2	18 57	1 56	5 3	10 8	24 41	3 42	23 19	0 6	3 28	4 ♓ 56'10"
22 WE	11:56:58	24 12	3 33	6 3	10 35	24 47	3 44	23 20	0 6	3 28	4 ♓ 56'10"
23 TH	12: 0:55	29 37	5 10	7 2	11 2	24 52	3 46	23 21	0 7	3 28	4 ♓ 56' 9"
24 FR	12: 4:51	5 ♈ 10	6 47	8 2	11 29	24 58	3 48	23 21	0 7	3 29	4 ♓ 56' 9"
25 SA	12: 8:48	10 51	8 24	9 1	11 56	25 3	3 50	23 22	0 7	3 29	4 ♓ 56' 9"
26 SU	12:12:45	16 41	10 1	10 1	12 23	25 9	3 52	23 23	0 8	3 29	4 ♓ 56' 9"
27 MO	12:16:41	22 39	11 38	11 0	12 50	25 14	3 54	23 23	0 8	3 30	4 ♓ 56' 9"
28 TU	12:20:38	28 43	13 15	12 0	13 17	25 20	3 56	23 24	0 8	3 30	4 ♓ 56' 9"
29 WE	12:24:34	4 ♉ 52	14 52	12 59	13 43	25 25	3 57	23 25	0 9	3 30	4 ♓ 56' 9"
30 TH	12:28:31	11 6	16 30	13 58	14 10	25 31	3 59	23 25	0 9	3 30	4 ♓ 56' 8"
31 FR	12:32:27	17 24	18 7	14 58	14 37	25 36	4 1	23 26	0 10	3 31	4 ♓ 56' 8"

INGRESSES :

1 ♀ → ♉ 3:57
4 ♆ → ♓ 21: 6
9 ☿ → ♒ 20:45
15 ⊕ → ♍ 22:10
17 ☿ → ♓ 2:51
19 ♀ → ♊ 19:12
23 ☿ → ♈ 1:42
28 ☿ → ♉ 5: 3

ASPECTS (HELIOCENTRIC +MOON(TYCHONIC)) :

1 ☿ ☍ ♂ 8: 9	7 ☿ □ ♅ 23:43	♀ ☌ ☊ 17:35	♀ □ ♆ 20:33	☽ □ ♄ 22:40
2 ☿ ☌ ♇ 0:48	8 ☿ S ☊ 2:12	15 ☽ □ ♆ 3:40	21 ☽ ☌ ♆ 8: 3	♀ □ ⊕ 23:52
☽ □ ♃ 15: 4	☽ ☍ ♆ 5: 8	☿ □ ♀ 14:49	☽ □ ♀ 12:26	27 ☿ ☌ ♅ 2:58
3 ♀ □ ♄ 2:52	10 ☽ ☍ ♃ 2:48	⊕ ☍ ♆ 23:47	22 ☿ ☌ ♃ 2:37	☿ ☌ ☊ 3:34
☽ ☌ ♂ 9:37	☿ ☌ ♄ 18:16	16 ☽ □ ♃ 20:48	23 ☽ ☌ ♃ 1:22	28 ☽ □ ♆ 0:54
☽ ☍ ♇ 12: 5	☽ □ ♇ 21:13	17 ☿ ☌ ♆ 3:14	☽ ☌ ☿ 15:43	☿ □ ♄ 20:26
4 ☽ ☍ ☿ 1: 3	11 ☽ □ ♂ 1:24	☿ ☍ ⊕ 10:43	☽ □ ♇ 16: 8	29 ☽ ☌ ♀ 7: 3
5 ☽ □ ♅ 4: 0	12 ☽ ☍ ♅ 10: 2	☽ ☌ ♇ 11:56	☿ □ ♇ 16:46	30 ☽ □ ♃ 3:29
6 ☽ ☍ ♄ 0:13	13 ☽ □ ♄ 4:39	☽ ☍ ♂ 20:36	24 ☽ □ ♂ 6:21	☽ ☍ ♇ 19:37
♂ ☍ ♇ 2:31	14 ☽ □ ☿ 5:16	18 ☽ □ ♅ 20:20	25 ☽ ☌ ♅ 3:24	31 ☽ ☌ ♂ 18:47
☽ □ ♀ 10:41	☽ ☍ ♀ 12:46	19 ☽ ☌ ♄ 13: 6	☿ □ ♂ 4:50	☿ ☌ P 20:21

would there celebrate the sabbath and cure the sick. They told the people that Jesus was continuing John's work and teaching, and that openly and effectively he perfected that for which John had laid the foundation. Outside of Ono and about one half hour from the baptismal place there was a private inn for Jesus' accommodation. Lazarus had purchased it for him and had placed there a man to see to the cooking, though Jesus usually took his meals cold. This inn served him as a stopping place when in that part of the country, and from it he went around to the neighboring villages teaching and baptizing.

March 16: Mercury conjunct Neptune
February 4, 30: New Year's Fruit Festival, p. 401, vol. I

After that began the preparations for the new year's fruit festival. Throughout the day, Jesus taught in Ono concerning the threefold meaning of the approaching feast: firstly, it commemorated the rising of the sap in the trees; secondly, because today tithes of all the fruits were offered; and lastly, it was a feast of thanksgiving for the fertility of the soil.

March 17: Superior conjunction Sun and Mercury
March 4, 30: Protecting the Ships at Sea, p. 412, vol. I

Jesus performed no cures here, and held himself very much aloof; still, on the sabbath he preached in the synagogue and went to an inn nearby for his meals. He visited many private individuals and families, principally Essenes, however, whom he exhorted and consoled, for many of the wicked inhabitants ridiculed and slandered them, on account of their affection for him. Jesus told several of those that lived in the environs, as also some of his own relatives, not to follow him just then, but to remain his friends in secret, and to continue their good works until the end of his career. His relatives did much good here and contributed also to the support of the blessed Virgin, to whom they sent all kinds of necessaries. I saw Jesus conversing with these different families in so affectionate and intimate a way that I have no words to describe it. His deportment, so full of love, touched me to tears.

That night I saw something else that appeared to me surprising and inexpressibly affecting. There happened on that night a great windstorm in the Holy Land, and I saw Jesus with many others in prayer. He prayed with outstretched hands that danger might be averted. Then I had a glance at the Sea of Galilee, which was lashed by the tempest, the ships of Peter, Andrew, and Zebedee being in distress. The apostles were, as I saw, asleep in Bethany, their servants alone being on the ships. And lo! As Jesus stood praying, I saw an apparition of him there upon the ships, now on one, now on the other, and then again upon the raging billows. It was as if he were laboring among them, holding back the vessels, warding off the danger. He was not there in person, for I did not see him going, but he stood above the sufferers, he hovered on the waves. The sailors did not see him, for it was his spirit assisting them in prayer. Nobody knew anything about his being there, though he was really helping them. Perhaps the sailors believed in him and called on him for help.

March 20: Venus conjunct Node
March 10, 33: Centurion Cornelius, p. 4, vol. III

During these days, three young men came to Lazarus at Bethany from the Chaldean city of Sikdor, and he procured them quarters at the disciples' inn. These youths were very tall and slight, very handsome and active, and much nobler in figure than the Jews. Jesus spoke only a few words to them. He directed them to the centurion of Capernaum, who had been a pagan like themselves, and who would instruct them. Then I saw the youths with the centurion, who was relating to them the cure of his servant. He told them that through shame of the idols that were in his house, and because it was just the time at which the pagan carnival was celebrated, he had begged Jesus, the Son of God, not to enter into his idolatrous household. Five weeks before the Jewish Feast of Easter, the pagans celebrated their carnival, during which they gave themselves up to all kinds of infamous practices. The centurion Cornelius after his conversion gave all his metallic idols in alms to the poor, or to make sacred vessels for the temple. The three Chaldeans returned from Capernaum to Bethany and thence back to Sikdor, where they gathered together the other converts, and with them and their treasures went to join King Mensor.

March 21: New Moon Pisces

February 21, 30: From Jezreel to Shunem, pp. 406–07, vol. I

From Jezreel Jesus went one hour and a half southward to a field in a valley, two hours long and as many broad, wherein were numerous orchards surrounded by low hedges. It was an uncommonly productive and charming fruit region. There were numerous tents here standing in couples at different intervals, and occupied by people from Shunem who guarded and gathered in the fruit. I think it was a kind of service that they were obliged to take turns in rendering. About four occupied one tent. The women dwelt together apart from the men, for whom they did the cooking. Jesus instructed these people under a tent. There were here most beautiful springs and abundant streams, which flowed into the Jordan. The principal source came from Jezreel. It formed in the valley a charming spring, over which a kind of chapel was built. From this spring house the stream divided into several others throughout the valley, united with other waters, and at last emptied into the Jordan. There were about thirty custodians whom Jesus instructed, the women remaining at some distance. He taught of the slavery of sin, from which they should free themselves. They were inexpressibly rejoiced and touched that he had come to them. He was so loving and courteous to these poor people that I had to shed tears myself over it. They set fruit before Jesus and the disciples, of which they ate. In some parts of the valley the fruit was already ripe, in others the trees were only in blossom. There were some brown fruits like figs, but growing in clusters like grapes, also yellow plants from which they prepared a kind of pap. In this valley rises Mount Gilboa, and here also was Saul slain in battle against the Philistines.

In the evening Jesus went through Jezreel and about three hours further to Shunem, an open place on a hill. Some of the disciples had gone on before, in order to make arrangements with the landlord of the inn at the entrance of the city. The fertile valley through which Jesus had just passed lay to the south of Jezreel. He went through a part of Jezreel without attracting notice, and then turned northward toward Shunem. Near this city, that is, at a distance of one to two hours, are two others, one of which Jesus had passed on his way from Chisloth-Tabor to Jezreel.

The inhabitants of Shunem depended upon weaving for their livelihood. They wove narrow edging of twisted silk, plain or interspersed with flowers. Shunem did not lie in the valley of Esdrelon, but rather where the mountains took their rise.

March 28: Mercury conjunct Jupiter

March 6, 30: Three Rich Youths, p. 413, vol. I

The three rich youths of Nazareth who had once before vainly proffered their petition to him to be received as disciples came to him again, reiterating their request. They almost knelt to him, but he sent them away after pointing out certain conditions that had to be fulfilled before he would allow them to join his disciples. Jesus knew well that their views were wholly terrestrial, and that they could not understand him. They wanted to follow him because they saw in him a philosopher, a learned Rabbi. After a time spent in his school, they could, as they thought, shine with a more brilliant reputation and do honor to their city Nazareth. They were besides somewhat vexed at seeing him giving the preference to the poor sons of Nazareth rather than to themselves.

Until far into the night I saw Jesus with the old Essene, Eliud of Nazareth. The holy man looked as if he would soon die of old age. He was no longer able for much, indeed he was almost bedridden. Jesus leaned on his arm at the bedside and talked with him. Eliud was entirely absorbed in God.

March 30: Venus conjunct Uranus

July 26, 32: Raising of Lazarus, pp. 478–79, vol. II

It seems to me that it was very early in the morning when Jesus went with the apostles to the tomb. Mary, Lazarus' sisters, and others, in all about seven women, were likewise there, as also a crowd of people that was constantly on the increase. Indeed, the throng presented somewhat the appearance of a tumult, as upon the day of Christ's crucifixion. They proceeded along a road upon either side of which was a thick, green hedge, then passed through a gate, after which about a quarter of an hour's distance brought them to the walled-in cemetery of Bethany. From the gate of the cemetery a road led right and left around a hill through which ran a vault. The latter was divided by railings into compartments, and the opening at the end was closed by a grate. One could, from the entrance, see through the whole length of the vault and the green branches of the trees waving outside the opposite end. Light was admitted from openings above.

Lazarus' tomb was the first on the right of the entrance to the vault, down into which some steps led. It was a four-cornered, oblong cave, about three feet in depth, and covered with a flat stone. In it lay the corpse in a lightly woven coffin, and around it in the tomb there was room for one to walk. Jesus with some of the apostles went down into the vault, while the holy women, Magdalene, and Martha remained standing in the doorway. But the crowd pressed around so that many people climbed up on the roof of the vault and the cemetery walls in order to see. Jesus commanded the apostles to raise the stone from the grave. They did so, rested it against the wall, and then removed a light cover or door that closed the tomb below that stone. It was at this point of the proceedings that Martha said: "Lord, by this time he stinketh, for he is now of four days." After that they took the lightly woven cover from the coffin, and disclosed the corpse lying in its winding sheet. At that instant Jesus raised his eyes to heaven, prayed aloud, and called out in a strong voice: "Lazarus, come forth!" At this cry, the corpse arose to a sitting posture. The crowd now pressed with so much violence that Jesus ordered them to be driven outside the walls of the cemetery. The apostles, who were standing in the tomb by the coffin, removed the handkerchief from Lazarus' face, unbound his hands and feet, and drew off the winding sheet. Lazarus, as if waking from lethargy, rose from the coffin and stepped out of the grave, tottering and looking like a phantom. The apostles threw a mantle around him. Like one

walking in sleep, he approached the door, passed the Lord and went out to where his sisters and the other women had stepped back in fright as before a ghost.

Without daring to touch him, they fell prostrate on the ground. At the same instant, Jesus stepped after him out of the vault and seized him by both hands, his whole manner full of loving earnestness.

And now all moved on toward Lazarus' house. The throng was great. But a certain fear prevailed among the people; consequently, the procession formed by Lazarus and his friends was not impeded in its movements by the crowd that followed. Lazarus moved along more like one floating than walking, and he still had all the appearance of a corpse. Jesus walked by his side, and the rest of the party followed sobbing and weeping around them in silent, frightened amazement. They reached the old gate, and went along the road bordered by verdant hedges to the avenue of trees from which they had started. The Lord entered it with Lazarus and his followers, while the crowd thronged outside, clamoring and shouting.

At this moment Lazarus threw himself prostrate on the earth before Jesus, like one about to be received into a religious order. Jesus spoke some words, and then they went on to the house, about a hundred paces distant.

Jesus, the apostles, and Lazarus were alone in the dining hall. The apostles formed a circle around Jesus and Lazarus, who was kneeling before the Lord. Jesus laid his right hand on his head and breathed upon him seven times. The Lord's breath was luminous. I saw a dark vapor withdrawing as it were from Lazarus, and the devil under the form of a black winged figure, impotent and wrathful, clearing the circle backward and mounting on high. By this ceremony, Jesus consecrated Lazarus to his service, purified him from all connection with the world and sin, and strengthened him with the gifts of the Holy Spirit. He made him a long address in which he told him that he had raised him to life that he might serve him, and that he would have to endure great persecution on the part of the Jews.

Up to this time, Lazarus was in his grave clothes, but now he retired to lay them aside and put on his own garments. It was at this moment that his sisters and friends embraced him for the first time, for before this there was something so corpse-like about him that it inspired terror. I saw meanwhile that Lazarus' soul, during the time of its separation from his body, was in a place peaceful and painless, lighted by only a glimmering twilight, and that while there he related to the just, Joseph, Joachim, Anne, Zechariah, John, and so on, how things were going with the Redeemer on earth.

By the Savior's breathing upon him, Lazarus received the seven gifts of the Holy Spirit and was perfectly freed from connection with earthly things. He received those gifts before the apostles, for he had by his death become acquainted with great mysteries, had gazed upon another world. He had actually been dead, and he was now born again. He could therefore receive those gifts. Lazarus comprises in himself a deep significance and a profound mystery.

And now a meal was ready, and all reclined at table, upon which were many dishes and little jugs. A man served. After the meal the women entered, but remained at the lower end of the hall, to hear the teachings of Jesus. Lazarus was sitting next to him. There was a frightful noise around the house, for many had come out from Jerusalem, even the guards, and were now besetting the house. But Jesus sent the apostles out to drive off both people and guards. Jesus continued his instruction till after lamplight, and told the disciples that he was going next morning with two apostles to Jerusalem. When they placed before him the danger attending such a step, he replied that he would not be recognized, that he would not go openly. I saw them afterward taking a little sleep, leaning around against the wall.

APRIL 2023

April 6: Full Moon Virgo
March 7–8, 30: Festival of Purim,
pp. 413–14, vol. I

At the commencement of the Festival of Purim, a musical instrument, which stood on three feet, was again played on the roof of the synagogue.

It was hollow with pipes running through it, the ends extending both above and below. By pushing the pipes in and out, the music was produced. Children also were playing on harps and flutes. Today in commemoration of Esther, the women and young maidens enjoyed certain rights and privileges in the synagogue. They were not separated from the men, they could even approach where the priests were. There was a procession in the synagogue of children dressed fancifully, some in white, others in red. Then a maiden entered wearing around her neck an ornament somewhat frightful looking. It was a blood-red circle around her throat, as if she had been beheaded, and from it hung on her white garments, numerous knots of blood-red threads like so many streaks of blood from the wounded neck. She wore a magnificent mantle borne by train bearers, and appeared to be enacting the principal part in some drama. Children and maidens followed her. She wore a high, pointed ornament on the forepart of her head and a long veil. In her hand she carried something, whether a sword or a scepter, I do not know. She was tall, and a maiden of great beauty. I do not know for certain what distinguished character she represented. It might, I think, have been Esther, or again, Judith, though not that Judith who slew Holofernes, for there was with her a maiden, who carried a beautiful basket containing presents for the chief priest. She presented to him many precious little shields, such as the priests wore sometimes on the forehead or the breast. In one corner of the synagogue, concealed by a curtain, lay upon a bed of state the effigy of a man, whose head the maiden struck off and took to the chief priest. Then, making use of the privilege granted to females on that day, she rebuked the priests for the principal faults they had committed during the year. That done, she withdrew. This privilege to rebuke the priests belonged to the women on certain other feasts also.

In the synagogue they read in turn from separate rolls the Book of Esther, Jesus also taking his turn to read. The Jews, especially the children, had little wooden tablets with hammers. When they pulled a string, the hammer struck a name inscribed on the tablet, while at the same time holders uttered some words. They did this as often as the name of Aman was pronounced.

There were also great banquets. Jesus was present at that given to the priests in the grand public hall. The adornments of this feast were similar to those of the Feast of Tabernacles. There were numbers of wreaths, roses as large as one's head, pyramids made up entirely of flowers, and quantities of fruit. A whole lamb was on the table, and I gazed in wonder at the magnificence of the plates, glasses, and dishes. There was one kind of dish, many-colored and transparent, like precious stones. They looked as if formed of interwoven threads of colored glass. There was today a great exchange of gifts, consisting principally of jewels and handsome articles of apparel, such as robes, maniples, veils for the head, and sashes trimmed with tassels. Jesus, too, was presented with a holiday robe trimmed in like manner. But he would not keep it; he passed it to another. Many others likewise bestowed their presents on the poor, who were very bountifully remembered that day.

After the banquet, Jesus and his disciples walked with the priests to the pleasure gardens, and the beautifully adorned teaching places near Nazareth. They had with them three rolls of writings, and I saw again the Book of Esther, out of which they read in turn. Crowds of youths and maidens followed them, but the latter listened to the discourse only at a distance. I saw also on that day men going around and taking up a tax.

Mercury conjunct Node

April 14, 33: The Night before the Communion of Fish, pp. 400–03, vol. III

Before going to the sea, the holy apostles went over the Way of the Cross to Mount Calvary, and thence to Bethany, from which place they took with them some disciples. They went by different routes and in several companies to the Sea of Galilee. Peter went with John, James the Greater, Thaddeus, Nathaniel, John Mark, and Silas, seven in all, to Tiberias, leaving Samaria to the left. All chose routes remote from cities. They went to a fishery outside Tiberias, which Peter had held on lease, but that was now rented by another man, a widower with two sons. They took a repast with this man, and I heard Peter saying that he had not fished here for three years.

They went aboard two ships, one somewhat larger and better than the other. They gave to Peter the choice of the former, into which he mounted with Nathaniel, Thomas, and one of the fisherman's servants. In the second ship were John, James, John Mark, and Silas. Peter would not suffer another to row. He wanted to do it himself. Although so distinguished by Jesus, he was exceedingly humble and modest, especially before Nathaniel, who was polished and educated.

They sailed about the whole night with torches, casting the nets here and there between the two ships, but always drawing them in empty. At intervals they prayed and sang psalms. When day was beginning to dawn, the ships approached the opposite side of the mouth of the Jordan, on the eastern shore of the sea. The apostles were worn out and wanted to cast anchor. They had laid aside their garments while fishing, retaining only a linen bandage and a little mantle. When about resuming their clothing preparatory to taking a little rest, they saw a figure standing behind the reeds on the shore. It was Jesus. He cried out: "Children, have you any meat?" They answered: "No!" Then he cried out again, telling them to cast the net to the west of Peter's ship. They did it, and John had to sail round to the other side of the ship. And now the net was so heavily filled that John recognized Jesus, and called to Peter across the silent deep: "It is the Lord!" At these words Peter instantly girded his coat about him, leaped into the water, and waded through the reeds to the shore where Jesus was standing. But John pushed on in a boat, very light and narrow, that was fastened to his ship.

Two of this kind were hooked together. They pushed one before the other, and crossed over it to land. It held only one man, and was needed only for shallow water near the land.

While the apostles were on the sea fishing, I saw the Savior floating out of the valley of Jehosaphat and surrounded by many souls of the ancient patriarchs whom he had freed from Limbo, also by others that had been banished to different places, caves, swamps, and deserts. During the whole period of these forty days, I saw Jesus, when not among the disciples, with the holy souls. They were principally from Adam and Eve down to Noah, Abraham, and other

SIDEREAL GEOCENTRIC LONGITUDES : APRIL 2023 Gregorian at 0 hours UT

DAY	☉	☽	☊	☿	♀	♂	♃	♄	⚷	♆	♇
1 SA	15 ♓ 57	17 ♋ 33	9 ♈ 13R	0 ♈ 14	22 ♈ 57	8 ♊ 8	24 ♓ 3	7 ♒ 40	21 ♈ 44	0 ♓ 40	5 ♑ 4
2 SU	16 56	29 28	9 9	2 2	24 8	8 38	24 18	7 46	21 47	0 42	5 5
3 MO	17 55	11 ♌ 30	9 6	3 47	25 19	9 8	24 32	7 52	21 50	0 44	5 6
4 TU	18 54	23 41	9 2	5 28	26 29	9 39	24 47	7 58	21 53	0 46	5 7
5 WE	19 53	6 ♍ 4	8 59	7 5	27 40	10 9	25 1	8 4	21 56	0 48	5 7
6 TH	20 52	18 39	8 57	8 37	28 51	10 40	25 16	8 10	21 59	0 51	5 8
7 FR	21 51	1 ♎ 27	8 56	10 5	0 ♉ 1	11 10	25 30	8 16	22 2	0 53	5 9
8 SA	22 50	14 28	8 56D	11 28	1 12	11 41	25 45	8 22	22 5	0 55	5 10
9 SU	23 49	27 43	8 57	12 45	2 22	12 12	25 59	8 28	22 8	0 57	5 10
10 MO	24 48	11 ♏ 10	8 58	13 57	3 32	12 43	26 14	8 34	22 12	0 59	5 11
11 TU	25 47	24 50	8 59	15 4	4 42	13 14	26 28	8 39	22 15	1 1	5 12
12 WE	26 46	8 ♐ 41	9 0	16 4	5 52	13 45	26 42	8 45	22 18	1 3	5 12
13 TH	27 45	22 43	9 1	16 59	7 2	14 16	26 57	8 51	22 21	1 5	5 13
14 FR	28 44	6 ♑ 54	9 1R	17 47	8 12	14 48	27 11	8 56	22 24	1 8	5 13
15 SA	29 42	21 12	9 0	18 30	9 21	15 19	27 26	9 2	22 28	1 10	5 14
16 SU	0 ♈ 41	5 ♒ 35	8 59	19 6	10 31	15 51	27 40	9 7	22 31	1 12	5 14
17 MO	1 40	19 57	8 58	19 36	11 40	16 23	27 55	9 12	22 34	1 14	5 15
18 TU	2 39	4 ♓ 16	8 58	19 59	12 49	16 54	28 9	9 18	22 38	1 16	5 15
19 WE	3 37	18 25	8 57	20 17	13 58	17 26	28 23	9 23	22 41	1 18	5 15
20 TH	4 36	2 ♈ 22	8 57	20 28	15 7	17 58	28 38	9 28	22 44	1 20	5 16
21 FR	5 35	16 2	8 57D	20 33	16 16	18 30	28 53	9 33	22 48	1 22	5 16
22 SA	6 33	29 23	8 57	20 32R	17 25	19 2	29 7	9 38	22 51	1 24	5 16
23 SU	7 32	12 ♉ 24	8 57	20 26	18 34	19 35	29 21	9 43	22 54	1 26	5 17
24 MO	8 30	25 6	8 57	20 14	19 42	20 7	29 36	9 48	22 58	1 27	5 17
25 TU	9 29	7 ♊ 31	8 57R	19 57	20 50	20 40	29 50	9 53	23 1	1 29	5 17
26 WE	10 27	19 42	8 57	19 35	21 58	21 12	0 ♈ 5	9 58	23 4	1 31	5 17
27 TH	11 26	1 ♋ 43	8 57	19 9	23 6	21 45	0 19	10 2	23 8	1 33	5 17
28 FR	12 24	13 37	8 57	18 39	24 14	22 17	0 33	10 7	23 11	1 35	5 18
29 SA	13 22	25 30	8 57D	18 7	25 22	22 50	0 47	10 12	23 15	1 37	5 18
30 SU	14 21	7 ♌ 27	8 58	17 31	26 29	23 23	1 2	10 16	23 18	1 39	5 18

INGRESSES :

2	☽ → ♌	1: 3	22 ☽ → ♉ 1: 7
4	☽ → ♍	12:17	24 ☽ → ♊ 9:23
6	☽ → ♎	21:18	25 ♃ → ♈ 16:24
	♀ → ♉	23:33	26 ☽ → ♋ 20:33
9	☽ → ♏	4: 6	29 ☽ → ♌ 9: 3
11	☽ → ♐	8:59	
13	☽ → ♑	12:20	
15	☉ → ♈	7: 9	
	☽ → ♒	14:41	
17	☽ → ♓	16:49	
19	☽ → ♈	19:53	

ASPECTS & ECLIPSES :

2	☽ ☌ ♀	16:43	12	☽ ☍ ☿	9: 1	☽ ☌ ☊	11:29
3	☿ □ ♆	18:51	13	☉ □ ☽	9:10	☉ □ ♄	16:20
4	☽ ☍ ♆	13:49		☽ ☌ ♇	21: 9	21 ☽ ☌ ⚷	8: 4
6	☽ ☍ ☽	4:33	14	☽ ⚷ ☊	3:32	☽ ☌ ⚷	12: 8
	☿ ☌ ☊	5:19		♀ □ ♇	16:37	23 ☽ ☌ ♇	12:42
	☽ ☍ ♃	12:41	16	☽ ☌ P	2:22	24 ☉ ☌ ☊	11: 9
7	☽ ☌ ♅	13:51		☽ ☌ ♄	5:56	26 ☽ ☌ ♂	3: 7
	☽ ☍ ♇	17:51	17	☽ ☌ ♆	18:56	27 ☽ ☍ ♀	7:11
8	☽ ☍ ♄	13:54	19	☽ ☌ ♃	17:25		
	☽ ☍ ♀	9: 8	20	☉ ☌ ☽	4:11	☉ □ ☽	21:18
9	☽ ☍ ♂	9: 8				28 ☽ ☌ A	6:47
11	☉ ☌ ♃	22: 5		☉ ☽ AT	4:16	30 ☉ □ ⚷ 2:20
						☽ ☍ ♄	5:40

SIDEREAL HELIOCENTRIC LONGITUDES : APRIL 2023 Gregorian at 0 hours UT

DAY	Sid. Time	☿	♀	⊕	♂	♃	♄	⚷	♆	♇	Vernal Point
1 SA	12:36:24	23 ♉ 43	19 ♊ 44	15 ♍ 57	15 ♋ 4	25 ♓ 42	4 ♒ 3	23 ♈ 27	0 ♓ 10	3 ♑ 31	4 ♓ 56' 8"
2 SU	12:40:20	0 ♊ 2	21 21	16 56	15 31	25 47	4 5	23 27	0 10	3 31	4 ♓ 56' 8"
3 MO	12:44:17	6 20	22 58	17 55	15 57	25 53	4 7	23 28	0 11	3 32	4 ♓ 56' 8"
4 TU	12:48:14	12 35	24 36	18 55	16 24	25 58	4 9	23 29	0 11	3 32	4 ♓ 56' 8"
5 WE	12:52:10	18 46	26 13	19 54	16 51	26 4	4 11	23 29	0 11	3 32	4 ♓ 56' 8"
6 TH	12:56: 7	24 52	27 50	20 53	17 17	26 9	4 13	23 30	0 12	3 32	4 ♓ 56' 7"
7 FR	13: 0: 3	0 ♋ 51	29 28	21 53	17 44	26 15	4 14	23 31	0 12	3 33	4 ♓ 56' 7"
8 SA	13: 4: 0	6 42	1 ♋ 5	22 52	18 10	26 20	4 16	23 31	0 13	3 33	4 ♓ 56' 7"
9 SU	13: 7:56	12 25	2 42	23 50	18 37	26 26	4 18	23 32	0 13	3 33	4 ♓ 56' 7"
10 MO	13:11:53	17 59	4 20	24 49	19 4	26 31	4 20	23 33	0 13	3 34	4 ♓ 56' 7"
11 TU	13:15:49	23 24	5 57	25 48	19 30	26 37	4 22	23 33	0 14	3 34	4 ♓ 56' 7"
12 WE	13:19:46	28 39	7 34	26 47	19 57	26 42	4 24	23 34	0 14	3 34	4 ♓ 56' 7"
13 TH	13:23:43	3 ♌ 45	9 12	27 45	20 24	26 48	4 26	23 35	0 14	3 34	4 ♓ 56' 6"
14 FR	13:27:39	8 40	10 49	28 44	20 50	26 53	4 28	23 35	0 15	3 35	4 ♓ 56' 6"
15 SA	13:31:36	13 27	12 27	29 43	21 17	26 59	4 30	23 36	0 15	3 35	4 ♓ 56' 6"
16 SU	13:35:32	18 4	14 4	0 ♎ 42	21 43	27 4	4 32	23 37	0 15	3 35	4 ♓ 56' 6"
17 MO	13:39:29	22 32	15 42	1 41	22 10	27 10	4 33	23 37	0 16	3 36	4 ♓ 56' 6"
18 TU	13:43:25	26 51	17 19	2 39	22 36	27 15	4 35	23 38	0 16	3 36	4 ♓ 56' 6"
19 WE	13:47:22	1 ♍ 3	18 57	3 38	23 3	27 21	4 37	23 39	0 17	3 36	4 ♓ 56' 6"
20 TH	13:51:18	5 7	20 34	4 37	23 29	27 26	4 39	23 39	0 17	3 36	4 ♓ 56' 6"
21 FR	13:55:15	9 3	22 12	5 35	23 56	27 32	4 41	23 40	0 17	3 37	4 ♓ 56' 5"
22 SA	13:59:12	12 53	23 49	6 34	24 22	27 37	4 43	23 41	0 18	3 37	4 ♓ 56' 5"
23 SU	14: 3: 8	16 36	25 27	7 32	24 48	27 43	4 45	23 41	0 18	3 37	4 ♓ 56' 5"
24 MO	14: 7: 5	20 13	27 4	8 31	25 15	27 48	4 47	23 42	0 18	3 38	4 ♓ 56' 5"
25 TU	14:11: 1	23 45	28 42	9 29	25 41	27 54	4 49	23 43	0 19	3 38	4 ♓ 56' 5"
26 WE	14:14:58	27 11	0 ♌ 20	10 28	26 8	27 59	4 51	23 43	0 19	3 38	4 ♓ 56' 5"
27 TH	14:18:54	0 ♎ 33	1 57	11 26	26 34	28 5	4 52	23 44	0 19	3 38	4 ♓ 56' 5"
28 FR	14:22:51	3 50	3 35	12 25	27 1	28 10	4 54	23 45	0 20	3 39	4 ♓ 56' 4"
29 SA	14:26:47	7 3	5 12	13 23	27 27	28 16	4 56	23 45	0 20	3 39	4 ♓ 56' 4"
30 SU	14:30:44	10 12	6 50	14 21	27 53	28 21	4 58	23 46	0 20	3 39	4 ♓ 56' 4"

INGRESSES :

1	☿ → ♊	23:52
6	☿ → ♋	20:33
	♀ → ♋	8: 0
12	☿ → ♌	6:16
15	⊕ → ♎	6:56
18	☿ → ♍	17:55
25	♀ → ♌	19:12
26	☿ → ♎	20: 3

ASPECTS (HELIOCENTRIC +MOON(TYCHONIC)) :

1	☽ ☐ ⚷	11:54	7	☽ ☐ ♆	3:53	13	☽ ☌ ♄	3:19	⊕ □ ♃	23:17	24	☽ □ ♆ 9:59
2	☿ ☍ ♆	0:31		☿ ☍ ♆	10:59		☽ □ ♃	6:58	19	☽ ☌ ♂	15:24	26 ☿ ☍ ♇ 5:49
	☽ ☐ ♄	9:15	8	☽ ☌ ♇	6:59		☽ □ ♀	18:23	20	☽ ☍ ♃	2: 9	☽ ☐ ♃ 16:39
4	☽ ☐ ♆	12:39		☽ ☍ ⚷	16:27	14	☽ □ ♀	7:26		♂ ☍ ⚷	9:28	☽ □ ♄ 20:45
	♀ □ ♃	21:37	9	☽ □ ♄	11:49	15	☽ ☍ ♂	0: 7	21	☽ ☐ ♀	12:32	27 ☽ ☍ ♆ 3:52
5	☿ □ ⊕	5:13		☽ ☍ ♀	12:37		☽ □ ⚷	4: 0		☽ ☍ ⚷	13:40	☿ □ ♆ 22:37
6	☽ ☐ ♀	5:12	10	☽ ☌ ♄	5: 7		☽ □ ♇	22:14	22	☽ ☍ ♄	9:47	28 ♀ ☍ ♇ 20:27
	☽ ☐ ♃	14:13	11	☿ ☍ ♆	0:37	17	☽ ☌ ♂	6:12		♀ ☍ ⚷	21:50	29 ☽ ☌ ♂ 4: 3
	☿ ☌ ♀	16:16		☿ □ ♄	0:41		♀ ☌ P	16:39		☿ ☌ ♀	11: 2	☽ ☍ ♄ 19: 1
	☽ ☐ ♀	19:46		☽ □ ♆	9:23		☽ ☍ ♀	17:16	23	☿ ☌ ♀	11: 2	☽ ☍ ♂ 22:33
	☽ ☐ ☿	21:57		⊕ □ ♃	22: 5	18	☿ □ ♆	19:29		♂ ☍ ⚷	16:37	

ancient leaders of the people. He went over all places remarkable in his life, showing them all things, and instructing them upon what he had done and suffered for them, whereby they became indescribably quickened and through gratitude purified. He taught them, in a certain measure at this time, the mysteries of the New Testament, by which they were released from their fetters. I saw him with them in Nazareth, in the crib cave and Bethlehem, and in every place in which anything remarkable had happened to him. One could distinguish, by a certain weakness or vigor in the appearance of the souls, whether they animated men or women when on earth. I saw them in long, narrow garments that fell around them in shining folds, and floated behind in a long train. Their hair did not look like ordinary hair, but like rays of light, each of which signified something. The beards of the men were composed of similar rays. Though not distinguished by any external sign, yet I recognized the kings, and especially the priests that from the time of Moses had anything to do with the Ark of the Covenant. In the journeys of the Savior, I always saw them floating around him, so that here, too, the spirit of order reigned in everything. The movements of these apparitions were exceedingly graceful and dignified. They seemed to float along, not exactly in an upright position, but inclining gently forward. They did not touch the earth like bodies that have weight, but appeared to hover just above the ground.

I saw the Lord arrive at the sea in company with these souls while the apostles were still fishing. Back of a little mound on the shore there was a hollow in which was a covered fireplace, for the use of the shepherds, perhaps. I did not see Jesus kindling a fire, catching a fish, or getting one in any other way. Fire and fish and everything necessary appeared at once in presence of the souls as soon as ever it entered into the Lord's mind that a fish should here be prepared for eating. How it happened, I cannot say.

The spirits of the patriarchs had a share in this fish and in its preparation. It bore some signification relative to the Church Suffering, to the souls undergoing purification. They were in this meal bound to the Church Militant by visible ties. In the eating of this fish, Jesus gave the apostles an idea of the union existing between the Church Suffering and the Church Militant. Jonah in the fish was typical of Jesus' stay in the lower world. Outside the hut was a beam that served for a table.

I saw all this before Jesus crossed the mound and went down to the sea. Peter did not swim, he waded through the water. The bottom could be seen, although the water was tolerably deep. Peter was already standing by Jesus when John came up. Those on the ship now began to cry to them to help draw in the net. Jesus told Peter to go bring in the fish. They drew the net to land, and Peter emptied it on the shore. In it were one hundred and fifty-three different kinds of fishes. This number signified that of the new believers who were to be gained at Thebez. There were on the ships several people in the employ of the fishermen of Tiberias, and they took charge of the ships and the fish, while the apostles and disciples went with Jesus to the hut whither he invited them to come and eat. When they entered, the spirits of the patriarchs had vanished. The apostles were very much surprised to see the fire and a fish, not of their own catching, also bread and honeycakes. The apostles and disciples reclined by the beam while Jesus played the host. He handed to each on a little roll a portion of the fish from the pan. I did not see that the fish became less. He gave to them also of the honeycakes and then reclined with them at table and ate. All this took place very quietly and solemnly.

Thomas was the third of those that had on the ship a perception of Jesus' presence. But they were all timid and frightened, for Jesus was more spirit-like than before, and the whole meal and the hour had in them something full of mystery. No one dared ask a question. A feeling of holy awe stole over them and gave rise to solemn silence. Jesus was wrapped in a mantle, his wounds not visible.

After the meal, I saw Jesus and the apostles rise from table. They walked up and down the shore, and at last stood still while Jesus solemnly addressed Peter: "Simon, son of John, lovest thou me more than these?" Peter timidly answered. "Yea, Lord, thou knowest that I love thee!" Jesus said to him: "Feed my lambs!" And at the same instant I saw a vision of the church and the Chief Pastor. I saw him teaching and guiding the first Christians, and I saw the baptizing and cleansing of the new Christians, who appeared like so many tender lambs.

After a pause, Jesus again said to Peter: "Simon, son of John, lovest thou me?" (They were walking all the time, Jesus occasionally turning and pausing while they regarded him with attention). Peter very timidly and humbly, for he was thinking of his denial, again answered: "Yea, Lord, thou knowest that I love thee!" Jesus again addressed him solemnly: "Feed my sheep!" Again, I had a vision of the rising church and her persecutions. I saw the chief Bishop gathering together the numerous scattered Christians, protecting them, providing them with shepherds, and governing them.

After another pause and still walking, Jesus said once more: "Simon, son of John, lovest thou me?" I saw that Peter grew troubled at the thought that Jesus asked him so often, as if he doubted his love. It reminded him of his thrice-repeated denial, and he answered: "Lord, thou knowest all things, thou knowest that I love thee!" I saw that John was thinking: "Oh, what love must Jesus have, and what ought a shepherd to have, since he thrice questions Peter, to whom he confides his flock, concerning his love!" Jesus again said: "Feed my sheep! Amen, amen, I say to thee: when thou wast younger, thou didst gird thyself, and didst walk where thou wouldst. But when thou shalt be old, thou shalt stretch forth thy hands, and another shall gird thee, and lead thee whither thou wouldst not. Follow me!"

Jesus turned again to go on. John walked with him, for Jesus was saying something to him alone, but what it was I could not hear. I saw that Peter, noticing this, asked the Lord while pointing to John: "Lord, what will become of this man?" Jesus, to rebuke his curiosity, answered: "If I will have him to remain till I come, what is it to thee? Follow thou me!" And Jesus turning again, they went forward.

When Jesus said for the third time: "Feed my sheep!" and that Peter would in his old age be bound and led away, I had a vision of the spreading church. I saw Peter in Rome bound and crucified, also the martyrdom of the saints. Peter, too, had a vision of his own martyrdom and of John's future sufferings. While Jesus was predicting his death to Peter, the latter glanced at John and very naturally thought: "Shall not this man whom Jesus loves so dearly be crucified like him?" Putting the question to Jesus, he was answered with a rebuke. I had at this moment a vision of John's death in Ephesus. I saw him stretch himself out in his grave, address some words to his disciples, and die. After his death I saw his body no longer on earth, but in a place as resplendent as the sun off toward the southeast, and it seemed as if John here received something from above that he transmitted to the earth. I became aware also that some understand these words of Jesus falsely and think they mean: "I will that he *so* remain," or "If I will that he *so* remain." But they mean: "If I will that he *remains*." They therefore that heard these words thought that John would not die. But he did die. I had on this occasion, as I have said, a vision of his death and his subsequent sojourn.

The apostles and disciples went on a little farther with Jesus, who was instructing them upon their future conduct. He then vanished before them eastward of the sea toward Gerasa and they returned to Tiberias, though not by a route that would lead them past the place in which Jesus had given them to eat.

Of the fish that the apostles caught, none were used at that meal. When Jesus said that they should bring them ashore, Peter threw them in rows at Jesus' feet, that they might be numbered. By this it was acknowledged that they had caught the fish not by themselves and for themselves, but by his miraculous power and for him. When the fish were deposited on the shore, Jesus said to the apostles: "Come and eat!" and conducted them over the little hill, or mound, where the sea could no longer be seen, to the mud hut over the furnace. Jesus did not at once place himself at table, but went to the pan and brought to each a portion of fish on a piece of bread. He blessed the portions and they shone with light. The honeycakes were not in the pan. They were already prepared, and lay in a pile one above the other. Jesus distributed them, and when all were served, he, too, ate with them. There was only one fish in the pan, but it was larger than any they had caught. There was some mystery connected with this meal. The presence of the souls of the patriarchs and others, their participation in the preparation of the meal, and the subsequent call of Peter, gave me to understand that in this spiritual meal the Church Suffering, the holy souls, should be committed to Peter's care, should be incorporated with the Church Militant, and the Church Triumphant, in short, that they should occupy a third place in the church as a whole. I cannot explain how this was to be done, but I had in vision this intimate conviction. It was in reference to this also that Jesus closed with the prophecy of Peter's death and John's future.

April 11: Sun conjunct Jupiter

April 15–16, 31: Invitation to the Sermon on the Mount, p. 347, vol. II

Jesus journeyed on, teaching through the country of Galilee, and dispatched a large number of the elder disciples to invite the people to an instruction to be given on the mountain beyond Gabara. It was to begin on the following Wednesday and last several days. I heard the day indicated differently, but I knew that the coming Wednesday was meant.

A great many of the disciples rowed across the lake to the country of the Gergeseans, to Dalmanutha, and into the Decapolis. They were commissioned to invite all, for Jesus would not be with them much longer, and they were to bring back as many with them as they could. About forty disciples went on this mission. Jesus kept with him the apostles, as well as the disciples that had last returned, all of whom he continued to instruct. He went with them to Tarichea at the southern extremity of the lake. The journey to Tarichea could not be made along the lakeshore, for at two hours' distance from that place rose steep cliffs that extended off to the lake. Jesus went around Tarichea to the west, and crossed over a bridge to a place that seemed to be one of the environs of the city. The bridge spanned the stone dam, which extended from Tarichea to the spot at which the Jordan flowed out of the lake. Near the bridge ran two rows of houses. Before reaching them, Jesus had to pass the abode of the lepers, where he had wrought some cures the preceding year. Being informed of his approach, these cured came out to thank him, while others, who had come hither since his last visit, now cried to him for help and he healed them. When arrived at the houses mentioned above, many sick were presented to him. They had been rowed across the lake from Dalmanutha. Jesus helped them. That dam, along with most of the houses, was overturned by the earthquake at Jesus' death. They were abandoned and never rebuilt, since the lakeshore was much changed by the catastrophe. Tiberias was in reality only half a city, being quite unfinished on one side.

April 20: New Moon Aries

March 22, 30: Feast of the New Moon, p. 418, vol. I

Accompanied by Lazarus and Saturnin, he visited the homes of several poor, pious sick people of the working class in Bethany, and cured about six of them. Some were lame, some dropsical, and others afflicted with melancholy. Jesus commanded those that he cured to go outdoors and sit in the sun. Up to this time there was very little excitement about Jesus in Bethany, and even these cures produced none. The presence of Lazarus, for whom they felt great reverence, kept the enthusiasm of the people in check.

That evening, upon which began the first day of the month Nisan, there was a feast celebrated in the synagogue. It appeared to be the Feast of the New Moon, for there was a kind of illumination in the synagogue. There was a disc like the moon that, during the recitation of prayers, shone with ever-increasing brilliancy, owing to the lights lit one after another by a man behind it.

April 24: Sun conjunct Node

March 27, 33: On the End of Days, pp. 14–15, vol. III

Early on the following day Jesus returned to the resting place on the Mount of Olives, and again spoke of the destruction of Jerusalem, illustrating with the similitude of a fig tree that was there standing. He said that he had already been betrayed, though the traitor had not yet mentioned his name, and had merely made the offer to betray him. The Pharisees desired to see the traitor again, but he, Jesus, wanted him to be converted, to repent, and not to despair. Jesus said all this in vague, general terms, to which Judas listened with a smile.

Jesus exhorted the apostles not to give way to their natural fears upon what he had said to them, namely, that they would all be dispersed; they should not forget their neighbor and should not allow one sentiment to veil, to stifle another; and here he made use of the similitude of a mantle. In general terms he reproached some of them for murmuring at Magdalene's anointing. Jesus probably said this in reference to Judas's first definitive step toward his betrayal, which had been taken just after that action of hers—also, as a gentle warning to him for the future, since it would be after Magdalene's last anointing that he would carry out his treacherous design. That some others were scandalized at Magdalene's prodigal expression of love arose from their erroneous severity and parsimony. They regarded this anointing as a luxury so often abused at worldly feasts, while overlooking the fact that such an action performed on the Holy of Holies was worthy of the highest praise.

Jesus told them, moreover, that he would only twice again teach in public. Then, speaking of the end of the world and the destruction of Jerusalem, he gave them the signs by which they should know that the hour of his departure was near. There would be, he said, a strife among them as to which should be the greatest, and that would be a sign that he was about to leave them. He signified to them also that one of them would deny him, and he told them that he said all these things to them that they might be humble and watch over themselves. He spoke with extraordinary love and patience.

About noon Jesus taught in the temple, his subject being the ten virgins, the talents entrusted, and he again inveighed severely against the Pharisees. He repeated the words of the murdered prophets, and several times upbraided the Pharisees for their wicked designs. He afterward told the apostles and disciples that even where there was no longer hope of improvement, words of warning must not be withheld.

When Jesus left the temple, a great number of pagans from distant parts approached him. They had not, indeed, heard his teaching in the temple, since they had not dared to set foot therein; but through the sight of his miracles, his triumphal entrance on Palm Sunday, and all the other wonders that they had heard of him, they wanted to be converted. Among them were some Greeks. Jesus directed them to the disciples, a few of whom he took with him to the Mount of Olives where, in a public inn formerly used by strangers only, they lodged for the night.

MAY 2023

May 1: Inferior Conjunction Sun and Mercury
April 2, 31: The Day before the Transfiguration, pp. 339–40

From the inn near Hadad-Rimmon, Jesus went with some of the disciples eastward to Chisloth-Tabor, which lay at the foot of Tabor toward the south, about three hours from Rimon. On the way thither he was joined, from time to time, by the disciples that were returning from their mission. At Chisloth another great multitude of travelers who had come from Jerusalem again gathered around him. He taught, and then healed the sick. In the afternoon he sent the disciples right and left around the mountain, to teach and to cure. Taking with him Peter, John, and James the Greater, he proceeded up the mountain by a footpath. They spent nearly two hours in ascent, for Jesus paused frequently at the different caves and places made memorable by the sojourn of the prophets. There he explained to them manifold mysteries and united with them in prayer. They had no provisions, for Jesus had forbidden them to bring any, saying that they should be satiated to overflowing. The view from the summit of the mountain extended far and wide. On it was a large open place surrounded by a wall and shade trees. The ground was covered with aromatic herbs and sweet-scented flowers. Hidden in a rock was a reservoir, which upon the turning of a spigot poured forth water sparkling and very cold. The apostles washed Jesus' feet and then their own, and refreshed themselves. Then Jesus withdrew with them into a deep grotto behind a rock that formed, as it were, a door to the cave. It was like the grotto on the Mount of Olives, to which Jesus so often retired to pray, and from it a descent led down into a vault.

Jesus here continued his instructions. He spoke of kneeling to pray, and told them that they should henceforth pray earnestly with hands raised on high. He taught them also the Lord's Prayer, interspersing the several petitions with verses from the Psalms; and these they recited half kneeling, half sitting around him in a semi-circle. Jesus knelt opposite to them, leaning on a projecting rock, and from time to time interrupted the prayer with instructions wonderfully profound and sweet upon the mysteries of Creation and Redemption. His words were extraordinarily loving, like those of one inspired, and the disciples were wholly inebriated by them. In the beginning of his instruction, he had said that he would show them who he was, they should behold him glorified, that they might not waver in faith when his enemies would mock and maltreat him, when they should behold him in death shorn of all glory.

The sun had set and it was dark, but the apostles had not remarked the fact, so entrancing were Jesus' words and bearing. He became brighter and brighter, and apparitions of angelic spirits hovered around him. Peter saw them, for he interrupted Jesus with the question: "Master, what does this mean?" Jesus answered: "They serve me!" Peter, quite out of himself, stretched forth his hands, exclaiming: "Master, are we not here? We will serve thee in all things!" Jesus began again his instructions, and along with the angelic apparitions flowed alternate streams of delicious perfumes, of celestial delights and contentment over the apostles. Jesus, meantime, continued to shine with ever-increasing splendor, until he became as if transparent. The circle around them was so lighted up in the darkness of night that each little plant could be distinguished on the green sod as if in clear daylight. The three apostles were so penetrated, so ravished that, when the light reached a certain degree, they covered their heads, prostrated on the ground, and there remained lying.

It was about twelve o'clock at night when I beheld this glory at its height. I saw a shining pathway reaching from heaven to earth and, on it, angelic spirits of different choirs, all in constant movement. Some were small, but of perfect form; others were merely faces peeping forth from the glancing light; some were in priestly garb, while others looked like warriors. Each had some special characteristic different from that of the others, and from each radiated some special refreshment, strength, delight, and light. They were in constant action, constant movement.

The apostles lay, ravished in ecstasy rather than in sleep, prostrate on their faces. Then I saw three shining figures approaching Jesus in the light. Their coming appeared perfectly natural. It was like that of one who steps from the darkness of night into a place brilliantly illuminated. Two of them appeared in a more definite form, a form more like the corporeal. They addressed Jesus and conversed with him. They were Moses and Elijah. The third apparition spoke no word. It was more ethereal, more spiritual. That was Malachi.

I heard Moses and Elijah greet Jesus, and I heard him speaking to them of his Passion and of Redemption. Their being together appeared perfectly simple and natural. Moses and Elijah did not look aged nor decrepit as when they left the earth. They were, on the contrary, in the bloom of youth. Moses—taller, graver, and more majestic than Elijah—had on his forehead something like two projecting bumps. He was clothed in a long garment. He looked like a resolute man, like one that could govern with strictness, though at the same time he bore the impress of purity, rectitude, and simplicity. He told Jesus how rejoiced he was to see him who had led himself and his people out of Egypt; and who was now once more about to redeem them. He referred to the numerous types of the Savior in his own time, and uttered deeply significant words upon the paschal lamb and the Lamb of God. Elijah was quite the opposite of Moses. He appeared to be more refined, more lovable, of a sweeter disposition. But both Elijah and Moses were very dissimilar from the apparition of Malachi, for in the former one could trace something human, something earthly in form and countenance; yes, there was even a family likeness between them. Malachi, however, looked quite different. There was in his appearance something supernatural. He looked like an angel, like the personification of strength and repose. He was more tranquil, more spiritual than the others.

Jesus spoke with them of all the sufferings he had endured up to the present, and of all that still

SIDEREAL GEOCENTRIC LONGITUDES : MAY 2023 Gregorian at 0 hours UT											
DAY	☉	☽	☊	☿	♀	♂	♃	♄	♅	♆	♇
1 MO	15 ♈ 19	19 ♌ 31	8 ♈ 58	16 ♈ 53R	27 ♉ 37	23 ♊ 56	1 ♈ 16	10 ♒ 20	23 ♈ 22	1 ♓ 40	5 ♑ 18
2 TU	16 17	1 ♍ 46	8 59	16 15	28 44	24 29	1 30	10 25	23 25	1 42	5 18R
3 WE	17 15	14 16	8 59	15 36	29 51	25 2	1 44	10 29	23 28	1 44	5 18
4 TH	18 14	27 3	9 0	14 58	0 ♊ 57	25 35	1 59	10 33	23 32	1 45	5 18
5 FR	19 12	10 ♎ 8	9 0R	14 20	2 4	26 8	2 13	10 37	23 35	1 47	5 18
6 SA	20 10	23 32	9 0	13 44	3 10	26 42	2 27	10 41	23 39	1 49	5 17
7 SU	21 8	7 ♏ 12	8 59	13 10	4 16	27 15	2 41	10 45	23 42	1 50	5 17
8 MO	22 6	21 7	8 58	12 39	5 22	27 48	2 55	10 49	23 46	1 52	5 17
9 TU	23 4	5 ♐ 13	8 56	12 11	6 28	28 22	3 9	10 53	23 49	1 54	5 17
10 WE	24 2	19 26	8 54	11 46	7 34	28 55	3 23	10 56	23 53	1 55	5 17
11 TH	25 0	3 ♑ 42	8 53	11 26	8 39	29 29	3 37	11 0	23 56	1 57	5 16
12 FR	25 58	17 58	8 52	11 10	9 44	0 ♋ 2	3 51	11 3	24 0	1 58	5 16
13 SA	26 56	2 ♒ 12	8 52D	10 58	10 49	0 36	4 5	11 7	24 3	2 0	5 16
14 SU	27 54	16 20	8 52	10 50	11 54	1 10	4 19	11 10	24 7	2 1	5 16
15 MO	28 52	0 ♓ 21	8 54	10 47	12 58	1 44	4 32	11 13	24 10	2 3	5 15
16 TU	29 50	14 13	8 55	10 49D	14 2	2 18	4 46	11 17	24 14	2 4	5 15
17 WE	0 ♉ 48	27 55	8 56	10 55	15 6	2 52	5 0	11 20	24 17	2 6	5 14
18 TH	1 45	11 ♈ 25	8 56R	11 6	16 10	3 26	5 14	11 23	24 20	2 7	5 14
19 FR	2 43	24 42	8 55	11 21	17 14	4 0	5 27	11 26	24 24	2 8	5 14
20 SA	3 41	7 ♉ 45	8 53	11 41	18 17	4 34	5 41	11 28	24 27	2 10	5 13
21 SU	4 39	20 34	8 50	12 5	19 20	5 8	5 54	11 31	24 31	2 11	5 13
22 MO	5 37	3 ♊ 9	8 46	12 34	20 22	5 42	6 8	11 34	24 34	2 12	5 12
23 TU	6 34	15 29	8 41	13 6	21 25	6 17	6 21	11 36	24 38	2 13	5 11
24 WE	7 32	27 38	8 37	13 43	22 27	6 51	6 35	11 39	24 41	2 15	5 11
25 TH	8 30	9 ♋ 38	8 33	14 23	23 28	7 25	6 48	11 41	24 45	2 16	5 10
26 FR	9 27	21 32	8 30	15 7	24 30	8 0	7 1	11 43	24 48	2 17	5 10
27 SA	10 25	3 ♌ 25	8 29	15 55	25 31	8 34	7 14	11 45	24 51	2 18	5 9
28 SU	11 23	15 20	8 28D	16 46	26 31	9 9	7 28	11 48	24 55	2 19	5 8
29 MO	12 20	27 23	8 29	17 41	27 32	9 44	7 41	11 49	24 58	2 20	5 7
30 TU	13 18	9 ♍ 39	8 31	18 39	28 32	10 18	7 54	11 51	25 1	2 21	5 7
31 WE	14 15	22 12	8 32	19 41	29 31	10 53	8 7	11 53	25 5	2 22	5 6

INGRESSES :	
1 ☽ → ♍ 20:34	19 ☽ → ♉ 9:41
3 ♀ → ♊ 3:22	21 ☽ → ♊ 17:57
4 ☽ → ♎ 5:27	24 ☽ → ♋ 4:42
6 ☽ → ♏ 11:24	26 ☽ → ♌ 17: 6
8 ☽ → ♐ 15: 9	29 ☽ → ♍ 5: 9
10 ☽ → ♑ 17:46	31 ♀ → ♋ 11:35
11 ♂ → ♋ 22:13	☽ → ♎ 14:37
12 ☽ → ♒ 20:16	
14 ☽ → ♓ 23:24	
16 ☉ → ♉ 4:15	
17 ☽ → ♈ 3:41	

ASPECTS & ECLIPSES :			
1 ☉ ɣ ☿ 23:26	10 ☽ ☍ ♂ 16:37	☽ ☌ ♅ 23:27	☽ ☍ ♄ 16:51
☽ ☍ ♆ 23:52	11 ☽ ☌ ♇ 2:38	19 ☉ ☌ ☽ 15:52	28 ☉ □ ♄ 10:45
4 ☽ ☍ ♃ 9:15	☽ ☌ P 5:23	21 ♂ ☍ ♇ 3: 2	29 ☽ ☍ ♆ 9:45
♀ □ ♆ 17:47	☽ □S ☊ 8:41	23 ♂ □ ♃ 5:11	
☽ ☌ ☋ 21:56	12 ☉ □ ☽ 14:27	☽ ☌ ♀ 12:44	
5 ☽ ☍ ☿ 7:14	13 ☽ ☌ ♄ 15:10	24 ☽ ☍ ♇ 15: 2	
☽ ☍ PN17:23	15 ☽ ☌ ♆ 2:55	☽ ☌ ♂ 19:19	
☉ ☍ ☽ 17:32	17 ☽ ☌ ♃ 12:46	☽ N□ ☊ 21:49	
6 ☽ ☍ ♅ 0:12	☽ ☌ ☊ 19:34	26 ☽ ☌ A 1:34	
9 ☽ ☍ ♀ 2:18	☽ ☌ ☿ 23:25	♂ □ ☊ 20: 6	
☉ ☌ ♅ 19:53	18 ♃ □ ♇ 0:48	27 ☉ □ ☽ 15:21	

SIDEREAL HELIOCENTRIC LONGITUDES : MAY 2023 Gregorian at 0 hours UT											
DAY	Sid. Time	☿	♀	⊕	♂	♃	♄	♅	♆	♇	Vernal Point
1 MO	14:34:41	13 ♎ 18	8 ♌ 27	15 ♎ 19	28 ♋ 20	28 ♓ 27	5 ♒ 0	23 ♈ 47	0 ♓ 21	3 ♑ 40	4 ♓ 56' 4"
2 TU	14:38:37	16 21	10 5	16 18	28 46	28 32	5 2	23 47	0 21	3 40	4 ♓ 56' 4"
3 WE	14:42:34	19 20	11 42	17 16	29 12	28 38	5 4	23 48	0 22	3 40	4 ♓ 56' 4"
4 TH	14:46:30	22 18	13 20	18 14	29 39	28 43	5 6	23 49	0 22	3 40	4 ♓ 56' 4"
5 FR	14:50:27	25 13	14 57	19 12	0 ♌ 5	28 49	5 8	23 49	0 22	3 41	4 ♓ 56' 3"
6 SA	14:54:23	28 5	16 34	20 10	0 31	28 54	5 10	23 50	0 23	3 41	4 ♓ 56' 3"
7 SU	14:58:20	0 ♏ 56	18 12	21 8	0 57	29 0	5 11	23 51	0 23	3 41	4 ♓ 56' 3"
8 MO	15: 2:16	3 46	19 49	22 7	1 24	29 5	5 13	23 51	0 23	3 42	4 ♓ 56' 3"
9 TU	15: 6:13	6 34	21 27	23 5	1 50	29 11	5 15	23 52	0 24	3 42	4 ♓ 56' 3"
10 WE	15:10:10	9 21	23 4	24 3	2 16	29 16	5 17	23 53	0 24	3 42	4 ♓ 56' 3"
11 TH	15:14: 6	12 7	24 41	25 1	2 42	29 22	5 19	23 53	0 24	3 42	4 ♓ 56' 3"
12 FR	15:18: 3	14 53	26 19	25 59	3 9	29 27	5 21	23 54	0 25	3 43	4 ♓ 56' 3"
13 SA	15:21:59	17 38	27 56	26 57	3 35	29 33	5 23	23 55	0 25	3 43	4 ♓ 56' 2"
14 SU	15:25:56	20 22	29 33	27 54	4 1	29 38	5 25	23 55	0 26	3 43	4 ♓ 56' 2"
15 MO	15:29:52	23 7	1 ♍ 11	28 52	4 27	29 44	5 27	23 56	0 26	3 44	4 ♓ 56' 2"
16 TU	15:33:49	25 52	2 48	29 50	4 54	29 49	5 29	23 57	0 26	3 44	4 ♓ 56' 2"
17 WE	15:37:45	28 37	4 25	0 ♏ 48	5 20	29 55	5 30	23 57	0 27	3 44	4 ♓ 56' 2"
18 TH	15:41:42	1 ♐ 23	6 2	1 46	5 46	0 ♈ 0	5 32	23 58	0 27	3 44	4 ♓ 56' 2"
19 FR	15:45:39	4 9	7 39	2 44	6 12	0 6	5 34	23 59	0 27	3 45	4 ♓ 56' 2"
20 SA	15:49:35	6 56	9 16	3 42	6 39	0 11	5 36	24 0	0 28	3 45	4 ♓ 56' 1"
21 SU	15:53:32	9 45	10 53	4 39	7 5	0 17	5 38	24 0	0 28	3 45	4 ♓ 56' 1"
22 MO	15:57:28	12 35	12 30	5 37	7 31	0 22	5 40	24 1	0 28	3 46	4 ♓ 56' 1"
23 TU	16: 1:25	15 26	14 7	6 35	7 57	0 28	5 42	24 2	0 29	3 46	4 ♓ 56' 1"
24 WE	16: 5:21	18 20	15 44	7 33	8 23	0 33	5 44	24 2	0 29	3 46	4 ♓ 56' 1"
25 TH	16: 9:18	21 15	17 21	8 30	8 50	0 38	5 46	24 3	0 30	3 46	4 ♓ 56' 1"
26 FR	16:13:14	24 13	18 58	9 28	9 16	0 44	5 48	24 4	0 30	3 47	4 ♓ 56' 1"
27 SA	16:17:11	27 13	20 35	10 26	9 42	0 49	5 50	24 4	0 30	3 47	4 ♓ 56' 0"
28 SU	16:21: 8	0 ♑ 16	22 12	11 23	10 8	0 55	5 51	24 5	0 31	3 47	4 ♓ 56' 0"
29 MO	16:25: 4	3 23	23 48	12 21	10 34	1 0	5 53	24 6	0 31	3 48	4 ♓ 56' 0"
30 TU	16:29: 1	6 32	25 25	13 18	11 1	1 6	5 55	24 6	0 31	3 48	4 ♓ 56' 0"
31 WE	16:32:57	9 45	27 2	14 16	11 27	1 11	5 57	24 7	0 32	3 48	4 ♓ 56' 0"

INGRESSES :
4 ♂ → ♌ 19:36
6 ☿ → ♏ 16: 3
14 ♀ → ♍ 6:35
16 ⊕ → ♏ 4: 2
17 ☿ → ♐ 12: 2
♃ → ♈ 23:45
27 ☿ → ♑ 21:52

ASPECTS (HELIOCENTRIC +MOON(TYCHONIC)) :				
1 ☽ ☍ ♆ 21:15	☽ □ ♀ 21:29	♀ ☍ ♆ 12:56	21 ☽ □ ♆ 18:52	28 ☿ □ ♃ 5: 9
☿ ☌ ⊕ 23:26	8 ☿ □ ♄ 12:36	☿ ☌ A 20:49	☿ □ ♀ 22:31	29 ☿ ☌ ♇ 3:12
4 ☽ ☍ ♃ 3: 6	☽ □ ♆ 15:49	15 ☽ ☌ ♆ 0: 8	22 ⊕ □ ♄ 1:14	☽ ☍ ♆ 6:10
☿ ☌ ☋ 10:14	9 ♀ N□ ☊ 5:36	☽ ☍ ♀ 1:36	☽ □ ♀ 20:55	30 ♂ ☌ A 22:43
☽ □ ♇ 12:13	⊕ ☍ ♅ 19:53	17 ☽ ☌ ♃ 3:33	☽ ☍ ☿ 23:52	31 ☽ ☌ ♀ 10:23
☿ ☍ ♅ 12:31	10 ☽ □ ♃ 16:39	☽ □ ♇ 10:19	24 ☽ □ ♃ 5:50	☽ ☍ ♃ 16:57
6 ☽ ☍ ♅ 0:32	11 ☽ ☌ ♇ 0: 0	♂ ☍ ♄ 10:24	☽ ☍ ♇ 12:14	☽ □ ♇ 21:39
☽ ☌ ☿ 10:11	12 ☽ □ ♅ 9:59	☿ □ ♆ 15:56	25 ⊕ □ ♂ 14:50	
☽ □ ♂ 12:43	13 ☽ ☍ ♂ 2:25	18 ☽ ☌ ♅ 22:41	26 ☽ □ ♅ 5: 5	
☽ □ ♄ 20:29	☽ ☌ ♄ 5:24	19 ☽ □ ♄ 20: 0	27 ☽ ☍ ♄ 4:52	
7 ☿ □ ♂ 0: 9	14 ☽ □ ☿ 8:34	☽ □ ♂ 21:52	☽ ☌ ♂ 13: 9	

awaited him. He related the history of his Passion in detail, point by point. Elijah and Moses frequently expressed their emotion and joy. Their words were full of sympathy and consolation, of reverence for the Savior, and of the uninterrupted praises of God. They constantly referred to the types of the mysteries of which Jesus was speaking, and praised God for having from all eternity dealt in mercy toward his people. But Malachi kept silence.

The disciples raised their heads, gazed long upon the glory of Jesus, and beheld Moses, Elijah, and Malachi. When in describing his Passion Jesus came to his exaltation on the cross, he extended his arms at the words: "So shall the Son of Man be lifted up!" His face was turned toward the south, he was entirely penetrated with light, and his robe flashed with a bluish white gleam. He, the prophets, and the three apostles—all were raised above the earth.

And now the prophets separated from Jesus, Elijah and Moses vanishing toward the east, Malachi westward into the darkness. Then Peter, ravished with joy, exclaimed: "Master, it is good for us to be here! Let us make here three tabernacles: one for thee, one for Moses, and one for Elijah!" Peter meant that they had need of no other heaven, for where they were was so sweet and blessed. By the tabernacles, he meant places of rest and honor, the dwellings of the saints. He said this in the delirium of his joy, in his state of ecstasy, without knowing what he was saying.

When they had returned to their usual waking state, a cloud of white light descended upon them, like the morning dew floating over the meadows. I saw the heavens open above Jesus and the vision of the most holy Trinity, God the Father seated on a throne. He looked like an aged priest, and at his feet were crowds of angels and celestial figures. A stream of light descended upon Jesus, and the apostles heard above them, like a sweet, gentle sighing, a voice pronouncing the words: "This is my beloved Son in whom I am well pleased. Hear ye him!"

Fear and trembling fell upon them. Overcome by the sense of their own human weakness and the glory they beheld, they cast themselves face downward on the earth. They trembled in the presence of Jesus, in whose favor they had just heard the testimony of his heavenly Father.

May 5: Full Moon Libra

April 6, 30: Overturning the Tables in the Temple, p. 423, vol. I

At daybreak they went up to the temple, which was lighted by numerous lamps, and to which the people were already flocking from all parts with their offerings. Jesus took his stand in one of the courts with his disciples, and there taught. A crowd of vendors had again pressed into the court of the suppliants and even into that of the women. They were scarcely two steps from the worshippers. As they still came crowding in, Jesus bade the newcomers to keep back, and those that had already taken their position to withdraw. But they resisted, and called upon the guard nearby for help. The latter, not venturing to act of themselves, reported what was taking place to the Sanhedrin. Jesus, meantime, persisted in his command to the vendors to withdraw. When they boldly refused, he drew from the folds of his robe a cord of twisted reeds or slender willow branches and pushed up the ring that held the ends confined, whereupon one half of it opened out into numerous threads like a whip. With this he rushed upon the vendors, overthrew their tables, and drove back those that resisted, while the disciples, pressing on right and left, shoved his opponents away. And now came a crowd of priests from the Sanhedrin and summoned Jesus to say who had authorized him to behave so in that place. Jesus answered that, although the holy mystery had been taken away from the temple, yet it had not ceased to be a sacred place and one to which the prayer of so many just was directed. It was not a place for usury, fraud, and for low and noisy traffic. Jesus having alleged the commands of his Father, they asked him who was his Father. He answered that he had no time then to explain that point to men, and even if he did they would not understand. Saying that, he turned away from them and continued his chase of the vendors.

Two companies of soldiers now arrived on the spot, but the priests did not dare to take action against Jesus. They themselves were ashamed of having tolerated such an abuse. The crowd gathered around declared Jesus in the right, and the soldiers even lent a hand to remove the vendors' stands and to clear away the overturned tables and wares. Jesus and the disciples drove the vendors to the exterior court, but those that were modestly selling doves, little rolls, and other needful refreshments in the recesses of the wall around the inner court, he did not molest. After that he and his followers went to the court of Israel. It may have been between seven and eight in the morning when all this took place.

On the evening of this day, a kind of procession went out along the valley of Kidron, to cut the first fruits of the harvest.

May 9: Sun conjunct Uranus

August 3, 30: Healing of the Nobleman's Son, pp. 1–2, vol. II

From Nain, Jesus, leaving Nazareth on the left, journeyed past Tabor to Cana, where he put up near the synagogue with a doctor of the Law. The forecourt of the house was soon full of people who had anticipated his coming from Engannim, and were here awaiting him. He had been teaching the whole morning, when a servant of the centurion of Capernaum with several companions mounted on mules arrived. He was in a great hurry and wore an air of anxiety and solicitude. He vainly sought on all sides to press his way through the throng around Jesus, but could not succeed. After several fruitless attempts, he began to cry out lustily: "Venerable Master, let thy servant approach thee! I come as the messenger of my lord of Capernaum. In his name and as the father of his son, I implore thee to come with me at once, for my son is very sick and nigh unto death." Jesus appeared not to hear him; but encouraged at seeing that some were directing Jesus' attention to him, the man again sought to press through the crowd. But not succeeding, he cried out anew: "Come with me at once, for my son is dying!" When he cried so impatiently, Jesus turned his head toward him and said loud enough for the people to hear: "If you see not signs and wonders, you do not believe. I know your case well. You want to boast of a miracle and glory over the Pharisees, though you have the same need of being humbled as they. My mission is not to work miracles in order to further your designs. I stand in no need of your approbation. I shall reserve my miracles until it is my Father's will that I should

perform them, and I shall perform them when my mission calls for it!" Thus, Jesus went on for a long time, humbling the man before all the people. He said that that man had been waiting long for him to cure his son, that he might boast of it before the Pharisees. But miracles, Jesus continued, should not be desired in order to triumph over others, and he exhorted his hearers to believe and be converted.

The man listened to Jesus' reproaches without being at all disturbed. Not at all diverted from his design, he again tried to approach nearer, crying out: "Of what use is all that, Master? My son is in the agony of death! Come with me at once, he may perhaps be already dead!" Then Jesus said to him: "Go, thy son liveth!" The man asked: "Is that really true?" Jesus answered: "Believe me, he has in this very hour been cured." Thereupon the man believed and, no longer importuning Jesus to accompany him, mounted his mule and hastened back to Capernaum.

I saw this man not as invested with the royal commission, but as himself the father of the sick boy. He was the chief officer of the centurion of Capernaum. The latter had no children, but had long desired to have one. He had, consequently, adopted as his own a son of this his confidential servant and his wife. The boy was now fourteen years old. The man came in quality of messenger, though he was himself the true father and almost indeed the master. I saw the whole affair, all the circumstances were clear to me. It was perhaps on account of them that Jesus permitted the man to importune him so long. The details I have just given were not publicly known.

The boy had long sighed after Jesus. The sickness was at first slight and the desire for Jesus' presence arose from the feeling entertained against the Pharisees. But for the last fourteen days, the case becoming aggravated, the boy had constantly said to his physicians: "All these medicines do me no good. Jesus, the prophet of Nazareth, alone can help me!" When the danger had become imminent, messages had been dispatched to Samaria by means of the holy women, while Andrew and Nathaniel had been sent to Engannim; and at last the father and steward himself rode to Cana, where he found Jesus. Jesus had delayed to grant his prayer in order to punish what was evil in his intentions.

It was a day's journey from Cana to Capernaum, but the man rode with such speed that he reached home before night. A couple of hours from Capernaum, some of his servants met him and told him that the boy was cured. They had come after him to tell him that if he had not found Jesus, he should give himself no further trouble, for the boy had been suddenly cured at the seventh hour. Then he repeated to them the words of Jesus. They were filled with astonishment, and hurried home with him. I saw the centurion Zorobabel and the boy coming to the door to meet him. The boy embraced him. He repeated all that Jesus had said, the servants that accompanied him confirming his words. There was great joy, and I saw a feast made ready. The youth sat between his adopted father and his real father, the mother being nearby. He loved his real father as much as he did the supposed one, and the former exercised great authority in the house.

After Jesus had dismissed the man of Capernaum, he cured several sick persons, who had been brought into a court of the house. There were some possessed among them, though not of the vicious kind. The possessed were often brought to Jesus' instructions. At first sight of him, they fell into frightful raging and threw themselves on the ground, but as soon as he commanded them to be at peace, they became quiet. After some time, however, they seemed no longer able to restrain themselves, and began again to move convulsively. Jesus made them a sign with his hand, and they again recovered themselves. The instruction over, he commanded Satan to go out of them. They lay, as was usual on such occasions, for about two minutes as if unconscious, and then, coming to themselves, thanked Jesus joyfully, not exactly knowing what had happened to them. There are such good, possessed people of whom the demon has taken possession by no fault of their own. I cannot clearly explain it, but I saw on this occasion, as well as upon others, how it happens that a guilty person may, by the mercy and long-sufferance of God, be spared, while Satan takes possession of one of his weak, innocent relatives. It is as if the innocent took upon himself a part of the other's punishment. I cannot make it clear, but it is certain that we are all members of one body. It is as if a healthy member, in consequence of a secret, intimate bond between them, suffers for another that is not sound. Such were the possessed of this place. The wicked are much more terrible and they cooperate with Satan, but the others merely suffer the possession and are meanwhile very pious.

Jesus afterward taught in the synagogue. There were present from Nazareth several doctors of the Law, and they invited him to return with them. They said that his native city was ringing with the great miracles he had wrought in Judea, Samaria, and Engannim; that he knew very well the opinion prevalent in Nazareth that whoever had not studied in the school of the Pharisees could not know much; therefore, they desired him to come and teach them better. They thought by these arguments to seduce Jesus. But he replied that he would not yet go to Nazareth, and that when he did, they would not obtain what they were now demanding.

After the instruction in the synagogue, Jesus was present at a great feast in the house of the father of the bride of Cana. The bride and bridegroom with the widowed aunt of the latter were there. Nathaniel the bridegroom had joined Jesus as a disciple on his coming to Cana, and had helped to keep order during the instruction and the curing of the sick. The bridegroom and bride dwelt alone. They carried on no housekeeping, for they received their meals from the parents of the latter. Her father limped a little. They were good people. Cana was a clean, beautiful city on a lofty plateau. Several highways ran through it, and one straight to Capernaum, about seven hours distant. The road inclined a little before reaching Capernaum.

After the feast, Jesus returned to his abode and again healed several sick persons who were patiently awaiting him. He did not always cure in the same way. Sometimes it was by a word of command, sometimes he laid his hands upon the sick, again he bowed himself over them, again he ordered them to bathe, and sometimes he mixed dust with his saliva and smeared their eyes with it. To some he gave admonitions, to others he declared their sins, and others again he sent away without being cured.

May 19: New Moon Taurus

April 21, 30: John Returns to Ainon, p. 424, vol. I

Jesus traveled northward through Samaria to the southern end of the Sea of Galilee. He crossed over to the east side of the Jordan and journeyed south of Succoth to the region of Ainon, where John the Baptist had first started baptizing. John himself had now returned to this first place of baptism. Jesus taught some of John's disciples during these days, but he did not meet John.

May 21: Mars opposite Pluto

April 30, 31: Conversation with Mercuria, pp. 362–64, vol. II

Next morning Jesus delivered, on the open square near the baptismal well, a lengthy instruction to both Jews and pagans. He taught of the harvest, the multiplication of the grain, the ingratitude of humankind who receive the greatest wonders of God so indifferently, and predicted for these ingrates the fate of the chaff and weeds, namely, to be cast into the fire. He said also that from one seed corn a whole harvest was gathered, that all things came forth from One, almighty God, the Creator of heaven and earth, the Father and Supporter of all men, who would reward their good works and punish their evil ones. He showed them also how men, instead of turning to God the Father, turn to creatures, to lifeless blocks.

They pass coldly by the wonders of God, while they gaze in astonishment at the specious though paltry works of men, even rendering honor to miserable jugglers and sorcerers. Here Jesus took occasion to speak of the pagan gods, the ridiculous ideas entertained of them, the confusion existing in those ideas, the service rendered them, and all the cruelties related of them. Then he spoke of some of these gods individually, asking such questions as these: "Who is this god? Who is that other? Who was his father?" etc. To these questions he himself gave the answers, exposing in them the confused genealogies and families of their pagan divinities and the abominations connected with them, all which facts could be found, not in the kingdom of God, but only in that of the father of lies. Finally, he mentioned and analyzed the various and contradictory attributes of these gods.

Although Jesus spoke in so severe and conclusive a manner, still his instruction was so agreeable, so suggestive of good thoughts to his hearers, that it could rouse no displeasure. His teaching against paganism was much milder here in Salamis than it was wont to be in Palestine. He spoke, too, of the vocation of the Gentiles to the kingdom of God and said that many strangers from the east and from the west would get possession of the thrones intended for the children of the house, since the latter cast salvation far from them.

During a pause in the instruction, Jesus took a mouthful to eat and drink, and the people discussed among themselves what they had just heard. Meanwhile some pagan philosophers drew near to Jesus and questioned him upon some points not understood by them, also about something that had been transmitted to them by their ancestors as coming from Elijah, who had been in these parts. Jesus gave them the desired information, and then began teaching upon baptism, also of prayer, referring for his text to the harvest and their own daily bread.

Many of the pagans received most salutary impressions from Jesus' instructions and were led to reflections productive of fruit. But others, finding his words not to their liking, took their departure.

And now I saw a great number of Jews baptized at the baptismal well, the waters of which Jesus blessed. Three at a time stood round one basin. The water in the ditches reached as high as the calf of the leg.

Jesus afterward went with his followers and some of the doctors to the separate Jewish city, about one half hour to the north. He was followed by many of his late audience, and he continued to speak with several little groups. The route led over some more elevated places below which lay meadows and gardens. Here and there were rows of trees, and again some solitary ones, high and dense, up which the traveler might climb and find a shady seat. The view extended far around on several little localities and fields of golden wheat. Sometimes the road ran along broad, naked walls of rock, in which whole rows of cells had been hewn out for the field laborers.

Outside the Jewish city stood a fine inn and pleasure garden. Here Jesus' own party entered, while he bade the rest of his escort return to their homes. The disciples washed Jesus' feet, then one another's, let down their garments, and followed their Master into the Jewish city. During the foot washing, I saw near the inn on one side of the highroad that ran along the city, long, light buildings like sheds, in which were a great number of Jewish women and maidservants busied in selecting, arranging, and carefully preserving the fruits that female slaves, or domestics, carried thither in baskets from the gardens around. The fruits were of all kinds, large and small, also berries. They separated the good from the bad, made all kinds of divisions, and even laid some wrapped in cotton on shelves one over another. Others were engaged in picking and packing cotton. I noticed all the housewives lowering their veils as soon as the men appeared on the highroad. The sheds were divided into several compartments. They looked to me like a general fruitery, where the portion intended for the tithes and that for alms were laid aside. It was a very busy scene.

Jesus went with his party to the dwelling of the rabbis near the synagogue. The eldest rabbi received him courteously, though with a tinge of stiff reserve in his manner. He offered him the customary refreshments, and said a few words upon his visit to the island and his far-famed reputation, etc. Jesus' arrival having become known, several invalids implored his help, whereupon, accompanied by the rabbis and the disciples, he visited them in their homes and cured many lame and paralyzed. The latter, with their families, followed him out of their houses, and proclaimed his praise. But he silenced them and bade them go back. On the streets he was met by mothers and their children, whom he blessed. Some carried sick children to him, and he cured them.

And so passed the afternoon away till evening, when Jesus accompanied the rabbis to an entertainment in his honor, which entertainment was likewise connected with the beginning of the harvest. The poor and the laboring people were fed at it, a custom that drew from Jesus words of commendation. They were brought from the fields in bands and seated at long tables, like benches of stone, and there served with various foods. Jesus, from time to time, waited on them himself with the disciples, and instructed them in short sentences and parables. Several of the Jewish doctors were present at the entertainment; but on the whole this company was not so well disposed, not so sincere as the Jews around Jesus' inn near Salamis. There was a tinge of pharisaism about them and, after they had become heated, they gave utterance to some offensive remarks. They asked whether he could not conveniently remain longer in Palestine, what was the real object of his visit to them, whether he intended to stay any time among them, and ended by suggesting that he should create no disturbance in Cyprus. They likewise touched upon diverse points of his doctrine and manner of acting, which the Pharisees of Palestine were in the habit of rehearsing. Jesus answered them as he usually did on similar occasions, with more or less severity according to the measure of their own civility. He told them that he had come to exercise the works of mercy as the Father in heaven willed him to do. The conversation was very animated. It gave Jesus an opportunity for delivering a stern lecture in which, while commending their goodness to the poor and whatever else was praiseworthy in them, he denounced their hypocrisy. It was already late when Jesus left with his followers. The rabbis bore him company as far as the city gate.

When Jesus had returned to the inn with the disciples, a pagan came to him and begged him to go with him to a certain garden a few steps distant, where a person in distress was waiting to implore his assistance. Jesus went with the disciples to the place indicated. There he saw standing between the walls on the road a pagan lady, who inclined low before him. He ordered the disciples to fall back a little, and then questioned the woman as to what she wanted. She was a very remarkable person, perfectly destitute of instruction, quite sunk in paganism, and wholly given up to its abominable service. One glance from Jesus had cast her into disquiet, and roused in her the feeling that she was in error, but she was without simple faith, and had a very confused manner of accusing herself. She told Jesus that she had heard of his having helped Magdalene, as also the woman afflicted with an issue of blood, of whom the latter had merely touched the hem of his garment. She begged Jesus to cure and instruct her, but then again, she said perhaps he could not cure her as she was not, like the woman with the issue, physically sick. She confessed that she was married and had three children, but that one, unknown to her husband, had been begotten in adultery. She had also intercourse with the Roman commandant. When Jesus, on the preceding day, visited the last named, she had watched him from a window and saw a halo of light around his head, which sight very powerfully impressed her. She at first thought that her emotion sprang from love for Jesus, and the idea caused her anguish so intense that she fell to the ground unconscious. When returned to herself, her whole life, her whole interior passed before her in so frightful a manner that she entirely lost her peace of mind. She then made inquiries about Jesus, and learned from some Jewish women of Magdalene's cure, also that of Enue of Caesarea-Philippi, the woman afflicted with the issue of blood. She now implored Jesus to heal her if he possibly could. Jesus told her that the faith of that afflicted woman was simple; that, in the firm belief that if she could touch only the seam of his garment she would be cured, she had approached him stealthily and her faith had saved her.

The silly woman again asked Jesus how he could have known that Enue touched him and that he healed her. She did not comprehend Jesus or his power, although she heartily longed for his assistance. Jesus rebuked her, commanded her to renounce her shameful life, and told her of God the Almighty and of his commandment: "Thou shalt not commit adultery." He placed before her all the abominations of the debauchery (against which her nature itself revolted) practiced in the impure service of her gods; and he met her with words so earnest and so full of mercy that she retired weeping and penetrated with sorrow. The lady's name was Mercuria. She was tall, and about thirty-five years old. She was enveloped in a white mantle, long and flowing in the back but rather shorter in front, which formed a cap around the head. Her other garments also were white, though with colored borders. The materials in which the pagan women dressed were so soft

and clung so closely to the form that the latter could readily be traced by the eye.

JUNE 2023

June 1: Jupiter conjunct Node
July 5, 31: In Salcha, p. 465 vol. II

This morning Jesus visited the huts of some of the shepherds, teaching and consoling them. He then went to Salcha, arriving there around midday. He was solemnly received at the city gate by the teachers and children in procession, and he taught in the synagogue, taking for the subject of his discourse the testimony rendered by John. Many of his hearers were baptized and cured. The children received his blessing.

June 4: Full Moon Scorpio
May 6, 30: Controversy around Baptism, p. 459, vol. I

After leaving the third place of baptism near Ono, Jesus crossed the Jordan and went to the second place of baptism near Gilgal. Many people were baptized there during this period by Andrew, Saturnin, Peter, and James the brother of John (John 3:22). John the Baptist remained at the first place of baptism near Ainon (John 3:23). Several of John's disciples traveled down the Jordan to join Jesus, and a controversy arose between these disciples of John and one who had been baptized by Jesus' disciples —a controversy concerning the difference between the baptisms with regard to purification (John 3:25). Furthermore, as Jesus now had so many disciples, John's remaining disciples complained that everyone was going over to Jesus (John 3:26). John's reply that he had come to bear witness as the forerunner of the Messiah is reported in John 3:26–36. All of these events—the controversy, the testimony of John the Baptist, the multitude that flocked to be baptized by Jesus' disciples —aroused fresh excitement among the Pharisees. They dispatched letters to the elders of all the synagogues in the land, directing them to take Jesus and his disciples into custody.

Mercury conjunct Uranus

August 21, 32: Beehive and Vineyard,
pp. 488–89

On the mountain near this place, Sichar-Kedar, there were whole rows of beehives. The declivity of the mountain was terraced, and on the terraces resting against the mountain stood numerous square, flat-roofed beehives about seven feet in height, the upper part ornamented with knobs. They were placed in several rows, one above the other. They were not rounded in the back, but pointed like a roof, and they could be opened from top to bottom on the shelf side. The whole apiary was enclosed by a fine trellis of woven reeds. Between these stacks of hives there were steps leading up to the terraces, and to the railings on either side bushes bearing white blossoms and berries were trained. One could mount from terrace to terrace, upon each of which were similar arrangements for bees.

When Jesus was asked by the people whence he had come he invariably answered in parables, to which they gave simple-hearted credence. Under the bower of the public house, he delivered an instruction, in which he related the parable of the king's son who came to discharge all the debts of his subjects. His hearers took the parable in its literal sense and rejoiced greatly over what it promised. Jesus then turned to the parable of the debtor who, after having obtained a delay for the payment of his own great debt, insisted upon bringing before the judge the man that owed him a trifle. He told them also that his father had given him a vineyard that had to be cultivated and pruned, and that he was looking for laborers to replace the useless, lazy servants whom he was going to chase away, and who were fitting images of the branches they had neglected to prune. Then he explained to them the cutting away of the vinestock, spoke of the quantity of useless wood and foliage, and of the small number of grapes. To this he compared the hurtful elements that had, through sin, entered into man. These, he said, should be cut off and destroyed by the exercise of mortification in order that fruit might be produced. This led to some words on marriage and its precepts, as well as upon the modesty and propriety to be observed in it, after which he returned to the vine and told the

people that they, too, ought to cultivate it. They replied quite innocently that the country was not adapted to vine culture. But Jesus responded that they ought to plant it on that side of the mountain occupied by the apiary, for that was an excellent exposure for it, and then he related a parable treating of bees. The people expressed their readiness to labor in his vineyard, if he would allow them. But he told them that he had to go and discharge the debts, that he had to see that the true vine was put into the wine press, in order to produce a life-giving wine, and to teach others how to cultivate and prepare the same. The simple-hearted people were troubled at the thought of his going away, and implored him to remain with them. But he consoled them by saying that if they believed him, he would send them one who would make them laborers in his vineyard. I saw that the inhabitants of this little place were afterward baptized by Thaddeus, and that all emigrated during a persecution.

Jesus recalled none of the prophecies, performed no miracles in this place. In spite of their moral disorders, these people were simple and childlike. Married couples living apart were again united by Jesus, and he explained to the man who, after having married five sisters was now about to espouse the sixth, that such unions were unlawful.

June 5: Venus opposite Pluto

April 22, 31: In the Mountains of Garisima,
p. 350, vol. II

After that he went with them from four to six hours northwest from Garisima to the mountains of a very retired region, and there they passed the night. Herds of asses and camels, and flocks of sheep were grazing off in the valleys on the west side of the lofty mountain range that ran through the heart of the country. The valleys here run in a zigzag direction, like the plant known as the common club moss, or wolf's claw. There were a great many palm trees in this wilderness, also a kind of tree whose interlaced branches fell to the earth, and under which one could creep as into a hut. The shepherds of the region used to take shelter under them. Jesus and the disciples spent most of the night in prayer and instruction. Jesus repeated many of the directions he had given

SIDEREAL GEOCENTRIC LONGITUDES : JUNE 2023 Gregorian at 0 hours UT

DAY	☉	☽	☊	☿	♀	♂	♃	♄	♅	♆	♇
1 TH	15 ♉ 13	5 ♎ 5	8 ♈ 33	20 ♈ 45	0 ♋ 31	11 ♋ 28	8 ♈ 20	11 ♒ 55	25 ♈ 8	2 ♓ 23	5 ♑ 5R
2 FR	16 10	18 21	8 33R	21 53	1 29	12 3	8 33	11 56	25 11	2 24	5 4
3 SA	17 8	2 ♏ 1	8 31	23 4	2 28	12 38	8 45	11 58	25 15	2 25	5 4
4 SU	18 5	16 3	8 27	24 18	3 26	13 12	8 58	11 59	25 18	2 26	5 3
5 MO	19 3	0 ♐ 24	8 22	25 34	4 23	13 47	9 11	12 1	25 21	2 27	5 2
6 TU	20 0	14 58	8 16	26 54	5 20	14 22	9 23	12 2	25 24	2 28	5 1
7 WE	20 57	29 38	8 10	28 16	6 17	14 57	9 36	12 3	25 28	2 28	5 0
8 TH	21 55	14 ♑ 17	8 4	29 42	7 13	15 32	9 49	12 4	25 31	2 29	4 59
9 FR	22 52	28 48	8 0	1 ♉ 10	8 9	16 8	10 1	12 5	25 34	2 30	4 58
10 SA	23 50	13 ♒ 8	7 58	2 41	9 4	16 43	10 13	12 6	25 37	2 31	4 57
11 SU	24 47	27 13	7 58D	4 14	9 58	17 18	10 26	12 6	25 40	2 31	4 56
12 MO	25 44	11 ♓ 3	7 58	5 51	10 52	17 53	10 38	12 7	25 43	2 32	4 55
13 TU	26 42	24 38	8 0	7 30	11 46	18 29	10 50	12 8	25 47	2 32	4 54
14 WE	27 39	7 ♈ 58	8 0R	9 12	12 39	19 4	11 2	12 8	25 50	2 33	4 53
15 TH	28 36	21 5	7 59	10 57	13 31	19 39	11 14	12 8	25 53	2 33	4 52
16 FR	29 34	4 ♉ 0	7 56	12 44	14 22	20 15	11 26	12 8	25 56	2 34	4 51
17 SA	0 ♊ 31	16 44	7 51	14 34	15 13	20 50	11 37	12 9	25 59	2 34	4 50
18 SU	1 28	29 16	7 43	16 26	16 4	21 26	11 49	12 9R	26 2	2 35	4 49
19 MO	2 26	11 ♊ 38	7 34	18 21	16 53	22 1	12 1	12 9	26 5	2 35	4 48
20 TU	3 23	23 51	7 24	20 18	17 42	22 37	12 12	12 8	26 8	2 36	4 46
21 WE	4 20	5 ♋ 54	7 14	22 18	18 30	23 13	12 24	12 8	26 11	2 36	4 45
22 TH	5 18	17 51	7 5	24 20	19 18	23 48	12 35	12 8	26 13	2 36	4 44
23 FR	6 15	29 43	6 57	26 23	20 4	24 24	12 46	12 7	26 16	2 37	4 43
24 SA	7 12	11 ♌ 34	6 51	28 29	20 50	25 0	12 58	12 7	26 19	2 37	4 42
25 SU	8 9	23 27	6 48	0 ♊ 36	21 35	25 36	13 9	12 6	26 22	2 37	4 40
26 MO	9 7	5 ♍ 28	6 47	2 44	22 18	26 12	13 20	12 5	26 25	2 37	4 39
27 TU	10 4	17 41	6 47D	4 54	23 1	26 48	13 30	12 4	26 27	2 37	4 38
28 WE	11 1	0 ♎ 12	6 47	7 4	23 43	27 24	13 41	12 3	26 30	2 37	4 37
29 TH	11 58	13 5	6 47R	9 15	24 24	28 0	13 52	12 2	26 33	2 38	4 35
30 FR	12 55	26 23	6 46	11 26	25 4	28 36	14 2	12 1	26 35	2 38	4 34

INGRESSES :

2 ☽ → ♏ 20:30	23 ☽ → ♌ 0:34
4 ☽ → ♐ 23:20	24 ☿ → ♊ 17:13
7 ☽ → ♑ 0:36	25 ☽ → ♍ 13: 6
8 ☿ → ♉ 5: 3	27 ☽ → ♎ 23:37
9 ☽ → ♒ 1:59	30 ☽ → ♏ 6:21
11 ☽ → ♓ 4:46	
13 ☽ → ♈ 9:36	
15 ☽ → ♉ 16:31	
16 ☉ → ♊ 10:59	
18 ☽ → ♊ 1:24	
20 ☽ → ♋ 12:12	

ASPECTS & ECLIPSES :

1 ☽ ☍ ♃ 6: 2	☽ ⊓S ☊ 13:52	16 ☽ ☌ ☿ 19:11	26 ☉ □ ☽ 7:48
☽ ☌ ☋ 6:20	8 ☽ ☍ ♂ 2: 9	18 ☉ ☌ ☽ 4:36	♂ □ ♅ 9:20
♃ ☌ ☊ 23:57	♀ □ ☊ 20:38	19 ☉ □ ♆ 4: 2	28 ☽ ☌ ☋ 12:22
2 ☽ ☍ ☿ 6:51	9 ☽ ☌ ♄ 22:14	20 ☽ ☍ ♇ 21:41	29 ☽ ☍ ♃ 1:27
☽ ☍ ♅ 12: 8	10 ☉ □ ☽ 19:30	21 ☽ ⊓N ☊ 2:36	30 ☽ ☍ ♅ 0:21
4 ☉ ☍ ☽ 3:40	11 ☽ ☌ ♆ 9: 8	22 ☽ ☌ ♀ 3: 6	
☿ ☌ ♅ 19:47	♀ □ ♃ 15:38	☽ ☌ ♂ 12:40	
5 ♀ ☍ ♇ 15:58	14 ☽ ☌ ☊ 0: 3	☽ ☌ A 18:27	
6 ☽ ☌ P 23: 8	☽ ☌ ♃ 5:39	24 ☽ ☍ ♄ 1: 6	
7 ☽ ☌ ♇ 8:46	15 ☽ ☌ ♅ 8:53	25 ☽ ☍ ♆ 18:20	
☽ ☍ ♀ 11:37	☿ □ ♄ 16: 8	☿ □ ♆ 22:39	

SIDEREAL HELIOCENTRIC LONGITUDES : JUNE 2023 Gregorian at 0 hours UT

DAY	Sid. Time	☿	♀	⊕	♂	♃	♄	♅	♆	♇	Vernal Point
1 TH	16:36:54	13 ♑ 2	28 ♍ 38	15 ♏ 13	11 ♌ 53	1 ♈ 17	5 ♒ 59	24 ♈ 8	0 ♓ 32	3 ♑ 48	4♓56' 0"
2 FR	16:40:50	16 23	0 ♎ 15	16 11	12 19	1 22	6 1	24 8	0 32	3 49	4♓56' 0"
3 SA	16:44:47	19 49	1 51	17 8	12 45	1 28	6 3	24 9	0 33	3 49	4♓56' 0"
4 SU	16:48:43	23 20	3 28	18 6	13 12	1 33	6 5	24 10	0 33	3 49	4♓55'59"
5 MO	16:52:40	26 56	5 4	19 3	13 38	1 39	6 7	24 10	0 34	3 50	4♓55'59"
6 TU	16:56:37	0 ♒ 38	6 41	20 1	14 4	1 44	6 9	24 11	0 34	3 50	4♓55'59"
7 WE	17: 0:33	4 25	8 17	20 58	14 30	1 50	6 10	24 12	0 34	3 50	4♓55'59"
8 TH	17: 4:30	8 19	9 53	21 55	14 56	1 55	6 12	24 12	0 35	3 50	4♓55'59"
9 FR	17: 8:26	12 20	11 30	22 53	15 23	2 1	6 14	24 13	0 35	3 51	4♓55'59"
10 SA	17:12:23	16 27	13 6	23 50	15 49	2 6	6 16	24 14	0 35	3 51	4♓55'59"
11 SU	17:16:19	20 42	14 42	24 48	16 15	2 12	6 18	24 14	0 36	3 51	4♓55'58"
12 MO	17:20:16	25 5	16 18	25 45	16 41	2 17	6 20	24 15	0 36	3 52	4♓55'58"
13 TU	17:24:12	29 36	17 54	26 42	17 8	2 23	6 22	24 16	0 36	3 52	4♓55'58"
14 WE	17:28: 9	4 ♓ 16	19 30	27 40	17 34	2 28	6 24	24 16	0 37	3 52	4♓55'58"
15 TH	17:32: 6	9 4	21 6	28 37	18 0	2 34	6 26	24 17	0 37	3 52	4♓55'58"
16 FR	17:36: 2	14 1	22 42	29 34	18 26	2 39	6 28	24 18	0 38	3 53	4♓55'58"
17 SA	17:39:59	19 7	24 18	0 ♐ 32	18 52	2 45	6 30	24 18	0 38	3 53	4♓55'58"
18 SU	17:43:55	24 23	25 54	1 29	19 19	2 50	6 31	24 19	0 38	3 53	4♓55'57"
19 MO	17:47:52	29 47	27 30	2 26	19 45	2 56	6 33	24 20	0 39	3 54	4♓55'57"
20 TU	17:51:48	5 ♈ 20	29 6	3 23	20 11	3 1	6 35	24 20	0 39	3 54	4♓55'57"
21 WE	17:55:45	11 2	0 ♏ 41	4 21	20 37	3 7	6 37	24 21	0 39	3 54	4♓55'57"
22 TH	17:59:41	16 52	2 17	5 18	21 4	3 12	6 39	24 22	0 40	3 54	4♓55'57"
23 FR	18: 3:38	22 50	3 53	6 15	21 30	3 18	6 41	24 22	0 40	3 55	4♓55'57"
24 SA	18: 7:35	28 54	5 28	7 13	21 56	3 23	6 43	24 23	0 40	3 55	4♓55'57"
25 SU	18:11:31	5 ♉ 4	7 4	8 10	22 23	3 29	6 45	24 24	0 41	3 55	4♓55'56"
26 MO	18:15:28	11 18	8 39	9 7	22 49	3 34	6 47	24 24	0 41	3 56	4♓55'56"
27 TU	18:19:24	17 35	10 15	10 4	23 15	3 40	6 49	24 25	0 42	3 56	4♓55'56"
28 WE	18:23:21	23 54	11 50	11 1	23 41	3 45	6 50	24 26	0 42	3 56	4♓55'56"
29 TH	18:27:17	0 ♊ 13	13 26	11 59	24 8	3 51	6 52	24 26	0 42	3 56	4♓55'56"
30 FR	18:31:14	6 31	15 1	12 56	24 34	3 56	6 54	24 27	0 43	3 57	4♓55'56"

INGRESSES :

1 ♀ → ♎ 20:16
5 ☿ → ♒ 19:58
13 ☿ → ♓ 2: 4
16 ⊕ → ♐ 10:46
19 ☿ → ♈ 0:56
20 ♀ → ♏ 13:39
24 ☿ → ♉ 4:19
28 ☿ → ♊ 23: 9

ASPECTS (HELIOCENTRIC +MOON(TYCHONIC)) :

1 ☽ □ ☿ 19:19	☿ ☌ ♄ 10:58	☽ □ ♇ 16:34	☽ ☍ ♇ 19:59	☽ ☍ ♆ 14:28
2 ☽ ☍ ♅ 10:15	☽ □ ♀ 15:54	15 ☽ ☍ ♀ 0: 2	21 ☽ □ ☿ 20: 5	27 ☿ ☌ P 19:38
♀ ☍ ♃ 17:46	8 ☽ □ ♅ 16:22	☽ ☌ ♅ 5:54	22 ☽ □ ♅ 13:10	☿ □ ♂ 23: 8
3 ☽ □ ♄ 6:58	9 ☽ ☌ ♄ 12:25	16 ☽ □ ♄ 4:37	23 ☿ ☌ ☊ 2:50	28 ☽ ☍ ♃ 6:44
☽ □ ♂ 19: 0	☿ ☍ ♂ 19:54	17 ♀ ☍ ♅ 0: 3	☿ ☌ ♅ 6: 9	☽ □ ♇ 7: 2
4 ☿ ⊓S ☊ 1:23	10 ☽ ☍ ♂ 4:40	⊕ □ ♆ 2:39	☽ □ ♀ 9:44	29 ☿ □ ♆ 1:50
♀ □ ♇ 5:19	☽ ☌ ☿ 7:59	☽ □ ♂ 4:13	☽ ☍ ♄ 14: 9	☽ ☍ ♅ 20:33
☿ □ ♅ 5:34	11 ☽ ☌ ♆ 5:48	18 ☽ □ ♆ 2:38	24 ♀ □ ♄ 19: 8	30 ♃ □ ♇ 3:13
5 ☽ □ ♆ 0:15	12 ☿ □ ⊕ 4:32	19 ☿ ☌ ♃ 13:53	☽ ☌ ♂ 21:44	☽ □ ♄ 18:25
7 ☽ □ ♃ 3:37	13 ☿ ☌ ♆ 5:14	☿ □ ♇ 17:49	25 ☿ □ ♄ 6:33	
☽ ☌ ♇ 6:52	☽ ☌ ♃ 13:59	20 ☽ □ ♃ 18:22	☿ ☍ ♀ 10:23	

when first sending them out upon their earlier missions. I was especially struck on hearing that they were to possess no private purse. That was to be confided to their superior, one of whom was appointed for every ten. Jesus indicated to them the signs by which they might recognize the places in which they could effect some good, told them to shake the dust from their shoes before those that were ill disposed, and instructed them as to how they should justify themselves when placed under arrest. They were not to be disturbed as to what they should answer, for words would then be put into their mouths, nor were they to be afraid, since their lives would not be in any danger.

I saw here and there around this region men with long staves and iron hoes. They were guarding the herds against the attacks of wild animals that came up from the seacoast.

June 18: New Moon Gemini
May 31, 29: The Family of Lazarus, pp. 294–96, vol. I

In Bethany Jesus visited Lazarus, who looked much older than Jesus; he appeared to me to be fully eight years his senior. Lazarus had large possessions, landed property, gardens, and many servants. Martha had her own house, and another sister named Mary, who lived entirely alone, had also her separate dwelling. Magdalene lived in her castle at Magdala. Lazarus was already long acquainted with the holy family. He had at an early period aided Joseph and Mary with large alms and, from first to last, did much for the community. The purse that Judas carried and all the early expenses, he supplied out of his own wealth. From Bethany Jesus went to the temple in Jerusalem.

The father of Lazarus was named Zarah, or Zerah, and was of very noble Egyptian descent. He had dwelt in Syria, on the confines of Arabia, where he held a position under the Syrian king; but for services rendered in war, he received from the Roman emperor property near Jerusalem and in Galilee. He was like a prince, and was very rich. He had acquired still greater wealth by his wife Jezebel, a Jewess of the sect of the Pharisees. He became a Jew, and was pious and strict according to the Pharisaical laws. He owned part of the city on Mount Zion, on the side upon which the brook near the height on which the temple stands flows through the ravine. But the greater part of this property he had bequeathed to the temple, retaining, however, in his family some ancient privilege on its account. This property was on the road by which the apostles went up to the Cenacle, but the Cenacle itself formed no longer a part of it. Zarah's castle in Bethany was very large. It had numerous gardens, terraces, and fountains, and was surrounded by double ditches. The prophecies of Anna and Simeon were known to the family of Zarah, who were waiting for the Messiah. Even in Jesus' youth they were acquainted with the holy family, just as pious, noble people are wont to be with their humble, devout neighbors.

The parents of Lazarus had in all fifteen children, of whom six died young. Of the nine that survived, only four were living at the time of Christ's teaching. These four were: Lazarus; Martha, about two years younger; Mary, looked upon as a simpleton, two years younger than Martha; and Mary Magdalene, five years younger than the simpleton. The simpleton is not named in scripture, not reckoned among the Lazarus family; but she is known to God. She was always put aside in her family, and lived altogether unknown.

Magdalene, the youngest child, was very beautiful and, even in her early years, tall and well developed, like a girl of more advanced age. She was full of frivolity and seductive art. Her parents died when she was only seven years old. She had no great love for them even from her earliest age, on account of their severe fasts. Even as a child she was vain beyond expression, given to petty thefts, proud, self-willed, and a lover of pleasure. She was never faithful, but clung to whatever flattered her the most. She was, therefore, extravagant in her pity when her sensitive compassion was aroused, and kind and condescending to all that appealed to her senses by some external show. Her mother had had some share in Magdalene's faulty education, and that sympathetic softness the child had inherited from her.

Magdalene was spoiled by her mother and her nurse. They showed her off everywhere, caused her cleverness and pretty little ways to be admired, and sat much with her dressed up at the window. That window-sitting was the chief cause of her ruin. I saw her at the window and on the terraces of the house upon a magnificent seat of carpets and cushions, where she could be seen in all her splendor from the street. She used to steal sweetmeats and take them to other children in the garden of the castle. Even in her ninth year she was engaged in love affairs.

With her developing talents and beauty increased also the talk and admiration they excited. She had crowds of companions. She was taught, and she wrote love verses on little rolls of parchment. I saw her while so engaged counting on her fingers. She sent these verses around, and exchanged them with her lovers. Her fame spread on all sides, and she was exceedingly admired.

But I never saw that she either really loved or was loved. It was all, on her part at least, vanity, frivolity, self-adoration, and confidence in her own beauty. I saw her a scandal to her brother and sisters whom she despised and of whom she was ashamed on account of their simple life.

When the patrimony was divided, the castle of Magdala fell by lot to Magdalene. It was a very beautiful building. Magdalene had often gone there with her family when she was a very young child, and she had always entertained a special preference for it. She was only about eleven years old when, with a large household of servants, men and maids, she retired thither and set up a splendid establishment for herself.

Magdala was a fortified place, consisting of several castles, public buildings, and large squares of groves and gardens. It was eight hours east of Nazareth, about three from Capernaum, one and a half from Bethsaida toward the south, and about a mile from the Sea of Galilee. It was built on a slope of the mountain and extended down into the valley that stretches off toward the lake and around its shores. One of those castles belonged to Herod. He possessed a still larger one in the fertile region of Galilee. Some of his soldiers were stationed in Magdala, and they contributed their share to the general demoralization. The officers were on intimate terms with Magdalene. There were, besides the troops, about two hundred people in Magdala, chiefly officials, master builders, and servants. There was no synagogue in the place; the people went to the one at Bethsaida.

The castle of Magdala was the highest and most magnificent of all; from its roof one could see across the Sea of Galilee to the opposite shore. Five roads led to Magdala, and on every one at one half-hour's distance from the well-fortified place stood a tower built over an arch. It was like a watchtower whence could be seen far into the distance. These towers had no connection with one another; they rose out of a country covered with gardens, fields, and meadows. Magdalene had menservants and maids, fields and herds, but a very disorderly household; all went to rack and ruin.

Through the wild ravine at the head of which Magdala lay far up on the height, flowed a little stream to the lake. Around its banks was a quantity of game, for from the three deserts contiguous to the valley the wild beasts came down to drink. Herod used to hunt here. He had also near his castle in the country of Galilee a park filled with game.

The country of Galilee began between Tiberias and Tarichea, about four hours' distance from Capernaum; it extended from the sea three hours inland and to the south around Tarichea to the mouth of the Jordan. The rising valley with the baths near Bethulia, artificially formed from a brook nearby, lay contiguous to this region, and was watered by streams flowing to the sea. This brook formed in its course several artificial lakes and waterfalls in different parts of the beautiful district that consisted entirely of gardens, villas, castles, parks, walks, orchards, and vineyards. The whole year round found it teeming with blossoms and fruits. The rich ones of the land, and especially of Jerusalem, had here their villas and gardens.

Every portion was under cultivation, or laid off in pleasure grounds, groves, and verdant labyrinths, and adorned with walks winding around pyramidal hillocks. There were no large villages in this part of the country. The permanent residents were mostly gardeners and custodians of the property, also shepherds whose herds consisted of fine sheep and goats. There were besides all kinds of rare animals and birds under their care. No street ran through Magdala, but two roads from the sea and from the Jordan met here.

JULY 2023

July 1: Superior Conjunction Sun and Mercury
June 1, 31: In Misael, p. 393, vol. II

To the north of the suburb and on a declivity halfway up the height lay the beautiful pleasure garden of Misael, commanding a magnificent view of the gulf. Higher up on the hill one could see the pond, or swamp, of Cendevia and Libnath, the "City of Waters," which was an hour and a half distant. It was nearer the sea—which here makes a bend into the land—than Misael, which was a couple of hours from the sea. Debbaseth was five hours to the east of the Kishon, and Nazareth about seven. Jesus walked in the garden with his disciples and related the parable of a fisherman that went out to sea to fish, and took five hundred and seventy fishes. He told them that an experienced fisherman would put into pure water the good fish found in bad, that like Elijah he would purify the springs and wells, that he would remove good fish from bad water, where the fish of prey would devour them, and that he would make for them new spawning ponds in better water. Jesus introduced into the parable also the accident that had happened on the sandbank to those that, out of self-will, had not followed the master of the vessels. The Cypriotes who had followed Jesus could not restrain their tears when they heard him speak of the laborious task of transporting fish from bad to good water. Jesus mentioned clearly and precisely the number "five hundred and seventy good fish" that had been saved, and said that that was indeed enough to pay for the labor.

He spoke of Cyprus to the Levites, who rejoiced that Jews from that country were coming hither. Many were coming also from Ptolemais, and would pass this way. There was question of measures to be taken. Jesus spoke of the danger that threatened them there, whereupon the Levites asked anxiously whether the pagans of their country would ever become so powerful as to prove dangerous. Jesus answered by an allusion to the judgment that was to fall upon the whole country, the danger that threatened himself, and the chastisement that would overtake Jerusalem. His hearers were unable to comprehend how he could again return to Jerusalem. But he said that he had still much to do before the consummation of his labors.

The Syrophoenician from Ornithopolis sent hither by some of the disciples little golden bars and plates of the same metal chained together. She was desirous to send one of her ships to Cyprus, in order to facilitate Mercuria's flight from the island.

July 3: Full Moon Sagittarius
June 12, 32: Raising the Daughter of a Shepherd, pp. 473–74, vol. II

He next went in the direction of Samaria. Not far from one of the little villages along the highroad, about a hundred paces to one side, there stood a tent in which ten lepers were lying in beds. As Jesus was passing, the lepers came out and cried to him for help. Jesus stood still, but the disciples went on. The lepers, entirely enveloped in their mantles, approached —some quickly, others slowly, as their strength permitted—and stood in a circle around Jesus. He touched each one separately, directed them to present themselves to the priests, and went on his way. One of the lepers, a Samaritan and the most active of the ten, went along the same road with two of the disciples, but the others took different routes. These were not cured all at once; although able to walk, they were not made perfectly clean till about an hour afterward.

Soon after this last encounter, a father from a shepherd village a quarter of an hour to the right of the road came to meet Jesus and begged him to go back with him to the village, for his little daughter was lying dead. Jesus went with him at once, and on the way was overtaken by the cured Samaritan who, touched by his perfect cure, had hurried back to thank his benefactor. He cast himself at the feet of Jesus, who said: "Were not ten made clean? And where are the nine? Is not one found among them to return and give glory to God, but only this stranger? Arise, go thy way! Thy faith hath made thee whole!" This man later on became a disciple. Peter, John, and James the Greater were with Jesus at this time. The little girl, who was about seven years old, was already four days dead. Jesus laid one hand on her head, the other on her breast, and raising his eyes to heaven prayed, whereupon the child rose up alive. Then

SIDEREAL GEOCENTRIC LONGITUDES: JULY 2023 Gregorian at 0 hours UT

DAY	☉	☽	☊	☿	♀	♂	♃	♄	⛢	♆	♇
1 SA	13 ♊ 53	10 ♏ 10	6 ♈ 42R	13 ♊ 37	25 ♋ 43	29 ♋ 12	14 ♈ 13	12 ♒ 0R	26 ♈ 38	2 ♓ 38R	4 ♑ 33R
2 SU	14 50	24 24	6 36	15 48	26 20	29 48	14 23	11 59	26 41	2 38	4 31
3 MO	15 47	9 ♐ 3	6 27	17 58	26 56	0 ♌ 24	14 33	11 57	26 43	2 37	4 30
4 TU	16 44	23 58	6 18	20 7	27 31	1 0	14 44	11 56	26 46	2 37	4 29
5 WE	17 41	9 ♑ 2	6 8	22 15	28 5	1 36	14 54	11 54	26 48	2 37	4 27
6 TH	18 38	24 4	5 59	24 22	28 38	2 13	15 4	11 52	26 51	2 37	4 26
7 FR	19 36	8 ♒ 55	5 52	26 28	29 9	2 49	15 13	11 50	26 53	2 37	4 25
8 SA	20 33	23 29	5 47	28 32	29 38	3 25	15 23	11 49	26 55	2 37	4 23
9 SU	21 30	7 ♓ 41	5 44	0 ♋ 35	0 ♌ 6	4 2	15 33	11 47	26 58	2 36	4 22
10 MO	22 27	21 31	5 44	2 36	0 33	4 38	15 42	11 45	27 0	2 36	4 20
11 TU	23 24	4 ♈ 59	5 44	4 35	0 58	5 15	15 51	11 42	27 2	2 36	4 19
12 WE	24 22	18 8	5 44	6 33	1 21	5 51	16 1	11 40	27 5	2 36	4 18
13 TH	25 19	1 ♉ 0	5 42	8 29	1 43	6 28	16 10	11 38	27 7	2 35	4 16
14 FR	26 16	13 39	5 37	10 22	2 3	7 4	16 19	11 35	27 9	2 35	4 15
15 SA	27 13	26 6	5 30	12 14	2 21	7 41	16 28	11 33	27 11	2 34	4 13
16 SU	28 11	8 ♊ 24	5 20	14 4	2 37	8 18	16 36	11 30	27 13	2 34	4 12
17 MO	29 8	20 34	5 7	15 53	2 51	8 54	16 45	11 28	27 15	2 33	4 11
18 TU	0 ♋ 5	2 ♋ 37	4 54	17 39	3 3	9 31	16 53	11 25	27 17	2 33	4 9
19 WE	1 2	14 34	4 40	19 23	3 13	10 8	17 2	11 22	27 19	2 32	4 8
20 TH	2 0	26 27	4 27	21 2	3 21	10 45	17 10	11 19	27 21	2 32	4 6
21 FR	2 57	8 ♌ 17	4 17	22 47	3 27	11 22	17 18	11 16	27 23	2 31	4 5
22 SA	3 54	20 7	4 9	24 25	3 31	11 59	17 26	11 13	27 25	2 30	4 3
23 SU	4 52	2 ♍ 0	4 3	26 2	3 32	12 36	17 34	11 10	27 27	2 30	4 2
24 MO	5 49	14 0	4 0	27 37	3 31R	13 13	17 41	11 7	27 28	2 29	4 1
25 TU	6 46	26 11	3 59	29 11	3 28	13 50	17 49	11 3	27 30	2 28	3 59
26 WE	7 43	8 ♎ 28	3 59	0 ♌ 42	3 22	14 27	17 56	11 0	27 32	2 27	3 58
27 TH	8 41	21 28	3 59	2 12	3 14	15 4	18 3	10 57	27 33	2 27	3 56
28 FR	9 38	4 ♏ 43	3 57	3 39	3 3	15 41	18 10	10 53	27 35	2 26	3 55
29 SA	10 35	18 27	3 53	5 5	2 50	16 18	18 17	10 50	27 36	2 25	3 53
30 SU	11 33	2 ♐ 41	3 47	6 28	2 35	16 55	18 24	10 46	27 38	2 24	3 52
31 MO	12 30	17 23	3 38	7 50	2 17	17 33	18 30	10 42	27 39	2 23	3 51

INGRESSES :

```
 2 ♂→♌  8: 2      ☉→♋  21:50
   ☽→♐  9:14   20 ☽→♌   7:11
 4 ☽→♑  9:37   22 ☽→♍  19:58
 6 ☽→♒  9:32   25 ☽→♎   7:24
 8 ☽→♓ 10:56      ☿→♌  12:53
   ☿→♋ 17: 5   27 ☽→♏  15:33
   ♀→♌ 18:21   29 ☽→♐  19:32
10 ☽→♈ 15: 2   31 ☽→♑  20: 9
12 ☽→♉ 22: 6
15 ☽→♊  7:34
15 ☽→♊ 18:46
```

ASPECTS & ECLIPSES :

```
 1 ☉☌☿   5: 4  10 ☉☐☽   1:46  20 ☽☌A   6:52      ☉☌☽  22: 5
 2 ♀☐⛢  14:30      ♀☌♃  20:44      ☽☌♀  14: 7  26 ☽☌♃  17:37
 3 ☽☐Ω  11:37  11 ☽☌Ω   1:21      ♂☌⛢  20:38  27 ☽☌♄  11: 9
   ☽☍♄  16:48      ☽☐Ω  13:59  21 ☽☍♂   6: 1      ♀☌♂  15:14
 4 ☽☌♆  16:44      ☽☐♃  20: 2      ☽☌♂   6:34  28 ♆☐Ω  23: 8
   ☽☿Ω  19:26  12 ☽☌⛢  16:40  22 ☉☍♀   3:46
   ☽☌P  22:17  17 ♀☐♃  12:47      ☉☐☽   5:23
 6 ☽☍♀   7:36      ☉☌♃  18:30  23 ☽☍♆   0:59
   ☽☌♂  13:40  18 ☽☍♀   3: 4      ♆☐Ω  15:20
 7 ☽☌♄   4:46      ☽⛢Ω   4:29      ♀☐⛢  21:37
   ☽☌♀  15:21  19 ☽☍♀  11:21  25 ☽☌♇  15: 5
```

SIDEREAL HELIOCENTRIC LONGITUDES :   JULY 2023 Gregorian at 0 hours UT

DAY	Sid. Time	☿	♀	⊕	♂	♃	♄	⛢	♆	♇	Vernal Point
1 SA	18:35:10	12 ♊ 46	16 ♏ 36	13 ♐ 53	25 ♌ 0	4 ♈ 2	6 ♒ 56	24 ♈ 28	0 ♓ 43	3 ♉ 57	4 ♓ 55'56"
2 SU	18:39: 7	18 57	18 12	14 50	25 27	4 7	6 58	24 28	0 43	3 57	4 ♓ 55'56"
3 MO	18:43: 4	25 3	19 47	15 47	25 53	4 12	7 0	24 29	0 44	3 58	4 ♓ 55'55"
4 TU	18:47: 0	1 ♋ 1	21 22	16 45	26 20	4 18	7 2	24 30	0 44	3 58	4 ♓ 55'55"
5 WE	18:50:57	6 52	22 57	17 42	26 46	4 23	7 4	24 30	0 44	3 58	4 ♓ 55'55"
6 TH	18:54:53	12 35	24 33	18 39	27 12	4 29	7 6	24 31	0 45	3 58	4 ♓ 55'55"
7 FR	18:58:50	18 9	26 8	19 36	27 39	4 34	7 8	24 32	0 45	3 59	4 ♓ 55'55"
8 SA	19: 2:46	23 33	27 43	20 33	28 5	4 40	7 10	24 32	0 46	3 59	4 ♓ 55'55"
9 SU	19: 6:43	28 48	29 18	21 31	28 32	4 45	7 11	24 33	0 46	3 59	4 ♓ 55'55"
10 MO	19:10:39	3 ♌ 53	0 ♐ 53	22 28	28 58	4 51	7 13	24 34	0 46	4 0	4 ♓ 55'54"
11 TU	19:14:36	8 49	2 28	23 25	29 24	4 56	7 15	24 34	0 46	4 0	4 ♓ 55'54"
12 WE	19:18:33	13 35	4 3	24 22	29 51	5 2	7 17	24 35	0 47	4 0	4 ♓ 55'54"
13 TH	19:22:29	18 11	5 38	25 19	0 ♍ 17	5 7	7 19	24 36	0 47	4 0	4 ♓ 55'54"
14 FR	19:26:26	22 39	7 13	26 17	0 44	5 13	7 21	24 36	0 48	4 1	4 ♓ 55'54"
15 SA	19:30:22	26 59	8 48	27 14	1 10	5 18	7 23	24 37	0 48	4 1	4 ♓ 55'54"
16 SU	19:34:19	1 ♍ 10	10 23	28 11	1 37	5 24	7 25	24 38	0 48	4 1	4 ♓ 55'54"
17 MO	19:38:15	5 13	11 58	29 8	2 3	5 29	7 27	24 39	0 49	4 2	4 ♓ 55'53"
18 TU	19:42:12	9 10	13 33	0 ♑ 6	2 30	5 35	7 29	24 39	0 49	4 2	4 ♓ 55'53"
19 WE	19:46: 8	12 59	15 8	1 3	2 57	5 40	7 31	24 40	0 49	4 2	4 ♓ 55'53"
20 TH	19:50: 5	16 42	16 43	2 0	3 23	5 46	7 32	24 41	0 50	4 2	4 ♓ 55'53"
21 FR	19:54: 2	20 19	18 18	2 57	3 50	5 51	7 34	24 41	0 50	4 3	4 ♓ 55'53"
22 SA	19:57:58	23 51	19 53	3 55	4 16	5 57	7 36	24 42	0 51	4 3	4 ♓ 55'53"
23 SU	20: 1:55	27 17	21 28	4 52	4 43	6 2	7 38	24 43	0 51	4 3	4 ♓ 55'52"
24 MO	20: 5:51	0 ♎ 38	23 2	5 49	5 10	6 8	7 40	24 43	0 51	4 4	4 ♓ 55'52"
25 TU	20: 9:48	3 55	24 37	6 47	5 36	6 13	7 42	24 44	0 52	4 4	4 ♓ 55'52"
26 WE	20:13:44	7 8	26 12	7 44	6 3	6 19	7 44	24 45	0 52	4 4	4 ♓ 55'52"
27 TH	20:17:41	10 17	27 47	8 41	6 30	6 24	7 46	24 46	0 52	4 5	4 ♓ 55'52"
28 FR	20:21:37	13 23	29 22	9 39	6 56	6 29	7 48	24 46	0 53	4 5	4 ♓ 55'52"
29 SA	20:25:34	16 26	0 ♑ 57	10 36	7 23	6 35	7 50	24 47	0 53	4 5	4 ♓ 55'52"
30 SU	20:29:31	19 25	2 32	11 33	7 50	6 40	7 52	24 47	0 54	4 5	4 ♓ 55'52"
31 MO	20:33:27	22 23	4 6	12 31	8 16	6 46	7 53	24 48	0 54	4 6	4 ♓ 55'52"

INGRESSES :

```
 3 ☿→♋ 19:51
 9 ☿→♌  5:35
   ♀→♐ 10:36
12 ⊕→♑  8:14
15 ☿→♍ 17:15
17 ⊕→♉ 21:39
23 ☿→♎ 19:23
28 ♀→♑  9:38
```

ASPECTS (HELIOCENTRIC +MOON(TYCHONIC)) :

```
 1 ☿☍⊕   5: 4   6 ☽☐☿   0:44      ☽☌♂  23:55      ☽☐♃   5:58      ☿☌♃  17:35
   ☽☌♀  12:18     ☽☌♄  21: 4   12 ☽☌⛢  11:59   19 ☽☐⛢  20:24      ☽☍♃  19:30
 2 ☽☌♂   1:46   7 ☿⛢Ω  23:56   13 ☽☐♄  11:58   20 ☿☐♀   0: 8      ☽☌☿  20: 8
   ☽☐♇  10:25   8 ☽☌♄   4:27   14 ☽☍♆   3:30      ☽☍♄  22:32   26 ☿☐⊕   6:25
 4 ♀☌⛢   6:52     ☽☐♂   7:47   15 ☽☐♂   2:35   22 ☿☍♂   3:29   27 ☽☍♇   6: 2
   ☿☌♆  12: 0     ☽☍♀   7:57      ☽☍♄   9: 8      ☽☍♂  21:40   28 ☽☐♄   5:28
   ☿☐♃  13:34     ☽☐♀   7:58      ☽☌♂  10:13   23 ☽☌♂   5:39   29 ☽☍♆  21: 1
   ☿☌♀  15:56     ☽☌♃  12:13      ♀☍♃  21:55   24 ☽☐♄   8:28   30 ☽☐⊕   8:45
   ☽☐♃  16:34   9 ☿☐♆  22:16   16 ☿☌♂   2:56      ☽☐♀  20:29      ♀☍♇  23:46
   ☽☍♆  18:25  10 ☿☍♄  16:17      ☽☍♀   4:29   25 ☿☐♀   1: 3   31 ☿⛢Ω   9:33
 5 ⊕☌A  14:32     ☽☐♀  22:13   18 ☽☍♆   2:50      ☽☐♀  15:14      ☿☍⛢  20: 0
```

Jesus told the apostles that even so should they do in his name. The child's father had strong faith, and full of confidence he had awaited Jesus' coming. His wife wanted him to send word to Jesus, but he was full of hope and waited until he came. Soon after, he gave up his business to another and, when his wife died after Jesus' death, he became a disciple and acquired a distinguished name. The little girl restored to life likewise became very pious.

July 10: Mercury opposite Pluto
June 16, 29: Wedding in Dothan, p. 297, vol. I

I saw all the wedding ceremonies as at Cana. Jesus attended the wedding in Dothaim, speaking at the celebration in a friendly manner. Jesus was like an honored stranger at the feast. Afterward, he addressed some words of wisdom to the bride and groom, who later, after the resurrection, joined the community of Christians. He spoke wisely and graciously, giving the bride and groom good advice.

July 17: New Moon Gemini
June 8, 31: In Maroni's Garden, p. 396, vol. II

Jesus visited several people in Nain and then went to Maroni's garden. Here he gave the holy women advice about their inner life and their work serving the community of Christians. When on the sabbath Jesus repaired to the synagogue, he did not go to the teacher's chair, but stood with his disciples in the place in which traveling teachers were accustomed to stand. But after bidding him welcome and the prayers being said, the rabbis constrained him to take his place before the open rolls of scripture and to read therefrom. The sabbath lesson treated of the Levites, the murmuring of the people, the quails sent by God, and the punishment that befell Miriam; and from the prophet Zechariah, some passages referring to the vocation of the Gentiles and to the Messiah. Jesus' words were severe. He said that the pagans would occupy in the Messiah's kingdom the places of the obdurate Jews. Of the Messiah, he said that they would not recognize him as such, for he would be totally different from what they expected. Among the Pharisees were three more insolent than the others; they

had been on the commission at Capernaum. The cure of the Pharisee at Thaanach had vexed them exceedingly, and they said that Jesus had effected it merely so that the Pharisees of that place might connive at his doings. They recommended him to be quiet and not to disturb the sabbath with his cures. It would be just as well for him, they said, to go back whence he came and to forbear creating any excitement. Jesus replied that he would fulfill the duties of his mission, journeying and teaching until his hour had arrived. The Pharisees gave no entertainment to Jesus in Nain. They were full of spite against him, because his doctrine and charity drew after him all the poor, the miserable and the simple-hearted, whom their own severity alienated.

July 20: Mars opposite Saturn
February 14, 30: In Gennabris, p. 403, vol. I

The place of baptism near Ono was guarded in turn by the inhabitants. Jesus taught in Gennabris and cured some raging possessed. A road for traffic ran through the city. The inhabitants were not so docile as those nearer the lake. Although they did not openly contradict Jesus, yet many received his teaching coldly.

Besides the future apostles, Jonathan, Peter's half-brother, was also in Gennabris. The other apostles had scattered around Capernaum and Bethsaida relating all that they had seen and heard of Jesus.

July 22: Sun opposite Pluto
May 29, 29: Jesus Begins His Travels, p. 292–94, vol. I

Jesus went through Nazareth in going from Capernaum to Hebron, passing through the indescribably beautiful country of Galilee and by the hot baths of Emmaus. These baths were on the declivity of a mountain, about an hour further on from Magdala in the direction of Tiberias.

The meadows were covered with very high, thick grass, and on the declivity stood the houses and tents between rows of fig trees, date palms, and orange trees. The road was crowded, for a kind of national feast was going on. Men and women in separate groups were playing for wagers, the prize consisting of fruit. There

Jesus saw Nathaniel, called also Chased, standing among the men under a fig tree. Just at the moment when Nathaniel was struggling against a sensual temptation that had seized him and was glancing over at the women's game, Jesus passed and cast upon him a warning look. Without knowing Jesus, Nathaniel was deeply moved by his glance, and thought: "That man has a sharp eye." He felt that Jesus was more than an ordinary man. He became conscious of his guilt, entered into himself, overcame the temptation, and from that time kept a stricter guard over his senses. I think I saw there, also, Naphtali, known as Bartholomew, and that a glance from Jesus touched him also.

July 27: Mercury conjunct Venus

July 13, 32: Teaching on the Good Samaritan and the Lost Coin, p. 475, vol. II

During these days Jesus taught concerning the good Samaritan (Luke 10:30–37) and the lost coin (Luke 15:8–10). He also healed the sick and blessed many children.

AUGUST 2023

August 1: Full Moon Capricorn

July 3, 30: In the Court of Simeon's Mansion, p. 465, vol. I

In the court of the large mansion belonging to Simeon, there was a round, shallow basin from which the water overflowed into a surrounding trench. Here, too, the water was not good; it had a bad taste. Jesus blessed it, casting into it at the same time salt in lumps like stones. In this region there was a whole mountain formed of salt.

In that basin, which had previously been drained and cleansed, the baptism of about thirty persons took place. The master of the house with all the males of his household, some other Jews of the place, many of the pagans that had lately been with Jesus, and some of the slaves from the huts, were baptized. These last Jesus had on several different occasions instructed when returned from their work. The pagans were the last to be baptized. They had to prepare themselves for the

ceremony by certain purifications. Jesus poured from a flask into the baptismal basin some of the Jordan water, which the disciples always carried with them, and then he blessed it. The trench around the basin was filled high enough for the neophytes to stand in it up to the knees in water.

Before administering baptism, Jesus prepared the aspirants by a long instruction. These latter wore long, gray mantles with hoods over the head, something like the mantles worn in prayer. When about to step into the trench around the basin, they laid aside the mantle. Their loins were covered, as also the back and breast, while from the shoulders fell a little open mantle like a scapular. A disciple laid one hand upon the shoulder of the neophyte, the other upon his head. The baptizer, in the name of the Most High, poured over his head several times from a flat shell water dipped from the basin. First Andrew baptized, then Peter, who was afterward relieved by Saturnin. The pagans were baptized last. The ceremony, including the preparations, continued until near evening.

When the people had retired, Jesus and the disciples left the place separately. They met again on the road and went eastward toward Adama on Lake Merom, resting by night in the beautiful high grass under the trees.

August 2: Mercury opposite Saturn

January 5, 31: Reproached by Pharisees, pp. 203–04, vol. II

It was about six hours from Ozensara to Beth-Horon. At some distance from the latter place, John and Peter went on ahead, leaving Jesus to follow alone. The Egyptian disciples, along with the son of Johanna Chusa, came to meet Jesus here. They brought news that the holy women were celebrating the sabbath in Machmas, which was situated in a narrow defile four hours to the north of this place. Machmas was the place at which Jesus in his twelfth year withdrew from his parents and returned to the temple. Here it was that Mary missed him and thought that he had gone on to Gophna. Not finding him at this latter place, she was filled with anxious solicitude, and made her way back to Jerusalem.

There was in Beth-Horon a Levitical school, with whose teacher the holy family was

COSMIC COMMUNION: STAR WISDOM, VOLUME 4

acquainted. Anne and Joachim had lodged with him on the occasion of their taking Mary to the temple; and when returning to Nazareth as Joseph's bride, Mary had again stopped at his house. Several of the disciples from Jerusalem had come hither with Joseph of Arimathea's nephews at the time of Jesus' arrival: Jesus went to the synagogue where, amid the contradictions and objections of the Pharisees, he explained the scripture appointed for that sabbath. The instruction over, he cured the sick at the inn, among them several women afflicted with an issue of blood, and blessed some sick children. The Pharisees had invited him to a dinner, and when they found him so tardy in coming, they went to call him. All things, they said, had their time and so had these cures. The sabbath belonged to God, and he had now done enough. Jesus responded: "I have no other time and no other measure than the will of the heavenly Father." When he had finished curing, he accompanied the disciples to the dinner.

During the meal the Pharisees addressed to him all kinds of reproaches; among others they alleged that he allowed women of bad repute to follow him about. These men had heard of the conversion of Magdalene, of Mara the Suphanite, and of the Samaritan. Jesus replied: "If ye knew me, ye would speak differently. I am come to have pity on sinners." He contrasted external ulcers, which carry off poisonous humors and are easily healed, with internal ones that, though full of loathsome matter, do not affect the appearance of the individual so afflicted.

August 13: Inferior Conjunction Sun and Venus
March 20–21, 33: Cursing of the Fig Tree, Magdalene's Last Anointing, pp. 9–11, vol. III

As Jesus next day was going to Jerusalem with the apostles, he was hungry, but it seemed to me that it was after the conversion of the Jews and the accomplishment of his own mission. He sighed for the hour when his Passion would be over, for he knew its immensity and dreaded it in advance. He went to a fig tree on the road and looked up at it. When he saw no fruit, but only leaves upon it, he cursed it that it should wither and never more bear fruit. And thus, did he say, would it happen to those that would not

acknowledge him. I understood that the fig tree signified the Old Law; the vine, the New. On the way to the temple, I saw a heap of branches and garlands from yesterday's triumph. In the outer portico of the temple, many vendors had again established themselves. Some of them had, on their backs, cases, or boxes that they could unfold and that they placed on a pedestal. The latter they carried along with them. When folded, it was like a walking stick. I saw lying on the tables heaps of pence, bound together in different ways by little chains, hooks, and cords, so as to form various figures. Some were yellow; others, white, brown, and variegated. I think they were pieces of money intended for ornamental pendants. I saw also numbers of cages with birds, standing one above another and, in one of the porticos, there were calves and other cattle. Jesus ordered the dealers to be off, and as they hesitated to obey, he doubled up a cincture like a whip and drove them from side to side and beyond the precincts of the temple.

While Jesus was teaching, some strangers of distinction from Greece dispatched their servants from the inn to ask Philip how they could converse with the Lord without mingling with the crowd. Philip passed the word to Andrew, who in turn transmitted it to the Lord. Jesus replied that he would meet them on the road between the city gate and the house of John Mark when he should have left the temple to return to Bethany. After this interruption, Jesus continued his discourse. He was very much troubled and when, with folded hands, he raised his eyes to heaven, I saw a flash of light descend upon him from a resplendent cloud, and heard a loud report. The people glanced up frightened, and began to whisper to one another, but Jesus went on speaking. This was repeated several times, after which I saw Jesus come down from the teacher's chair, mingle with the disciples in the crowd, and leave the temple.

When Jesus taught, the disciples threw around him a white mantle of ceremony that they always carried with them; and when he left the teacher's chair, they took it off so that, clothed like the others, he could more easily escape the notice of the crowd. Around the teacher's chair were three platforms, one above the other, each enclosed by a balustrade, which was ornamented

SIDEREAL GEOCENTRIC LONGITUDES : AUGUST 2023 Gregorian at 0 hours UT

DAY	☉	☽	☊	☿	♀	♂	♃	♄	⛢	♆	♇
1 TU	13 ♋ 27	2 ♑ 26	3 ♈ 28R	9 ♌ 10	1 ♌ 57R	18 ♌ 10	18 ♈ 37	10 ♒ 39R	27 ♈ 41	2 ♓ 22R	3 ♑ 49R
2 WE	14 25	17 42	3 18	10 27	1 35	18 47	18 43	10 35	27 42	2 21	3 48
3 TH	15 22	2 ♒ 59	3 8	11 43	1 11	19 25	18 49	10 31	27 43	2 20	3 46
4 FR	16 20	18 6	3 0	12 56	0 44	20 2	18 55	10 27	27 45	2 19	3 45
5 SA	17 17	2 ♓ 55	2 55	14 7	0 16	20 40	19 1	10 23	27 46	2 18	3 44
6 SU	18 14	17 20	2 52	15 16	29 ♋ 46	21 17	19 6	10 19	27 47	2 17	3 42
7 MO	19 12	1 ♈ 17	2 51	16 22	29 14	21 55	19 12	10 15	27 48	2 16	3 41
8 TU	20 9	14 49	2 51D	17 26	28 41	22 32	19 17	10 11	27 49	2 15	3 40
9 WE	21 7	27 56	2 51R	18 27	28 7	23 10	19 22	10 7	27 50	2 14	3 38
10 TH	22 4	10 ♉ 43	2 50	19 26	27 32	23 48	19 27	10 3	27 51	2 13	3 37
11 FR	23 2	23 13	2 46	20 21	26 55	24 25	19 32	9 59	27 52	2 12	3 36
12 SA	23 59	5 ♊ 31	2 40	21 14	26 19	25 3	19 37	9 54	27 53	2 10	3 34
13 SU	24 57	17 39	2 31	22 4	25 42	25 41	19 41	9 50	27 54	2 9	3 33
14 MO	25 55	29 40	2 21	22 50	25 4	26 19	19 45	9 46	27 55	2 8	3 32
15 TU	26 52	11 ♋ 35	2 9	23 33	24 27	26 57	19 49	9 41	27 55	2 7	3 30
16 WE	27 50	23 28	1 57	24 12	23 50	27 34	19 53	9 37	27 56	2 5	3 29
17 TH	28 48	5 ♌ 19	1 45	24 47	23 14	28 12	19 57	9 33	27 57	2 4	3 28
18 FR	29 45	17 10	1 36	25 18	22 38	28 50	20 0	9 28	27 57	2 3	3 27
19 SA	0 ♌ 43	29 2	1 29	25 45	22 4	29 29	20 4	9 24	27 58	2 1	3 25
20 SU	1 41	10 ♍ 59	1 24	26 8	21 31	0 ♍ 7	20 7	9 19	27 58	2 0	3 24
21 MO	2 39	23 2	1 22	26 25	20 59	0 45	20 10	9 15	27 59	1 59	3 23
22 TU	3 36	5 ♎ 16	1 22D	26 38	20 29	1 23	20 12	9 10	27 59	1 57	3 22
23 WE	4 34	17 44	1 22	26 45	20 0	2 1	20 15	9 6	27 59	1 56	3 20
24 TH	5 32	0 ♏ 32	1 23	26 47R	19 33	2 39	20 17	9 1	28 0	1 54	3 19
25 FR	6 30	13 42	1 23R	26 43	19 9	3 18	20 20	8 57	28 0	1 53	3 18
26 SA	7 28	27 19	1 21	26 33	18 46	3 56	20 22	8 52	28 0	1 52	3 17
27 SU	8 25	11 ♐ 24	1 17	26 18	18 26	4 34	20 23	8 47	28 0	1 50	3 16
28 MO	9 23	25 57	1 12	25 56	18 8	5 13	20 25	8 43	28 0	1 49	3 15
29 TU	10 21	10 ♑ 52	1 5	25 29	17 52	5 51	20 26	8 38	28 0	1 47	3 14
30 WE	11 19	26 4	0 57	24 55	17 39	6 30	20 28	8 34	28 0R	1 46	3 13
31 TH	12 17	11 ♒ 21	0 50	24 16	17 28	7 8	20 29	8 29	28 0	1 44	3 12

INGRESSES :

2	☽ → ♒ 19:18	21	☽ → ♎ 13:43
4	☽ → ♓ 19:13	23	☽ → ♏ 23: 1
5	♀ → ♋ 13: 2	26	☽ → ♐ 4:37
6	☽ → ♈ 21:45	28	☽ → ♑ 6:34
9	☽ → ♉ 3:50	30	☽ → ♒ 6:11
11	☽ → ♊ 13:11		
14	☽ → ♋ 0:40		
16	☽ → ♌ 13:13		
18	☉ → ♌ 6: 5		
19	☽ → ♍ 1:56		
	♂ → ♍ 19:49		

ASPECTS & ECLIPSES :

1	☽ □s ☊	1:37		☽ ☌ ☊	2:44		☽ ☌ A	11:39	27	☉ ☍ ♄	8:27
	☽ ☌ ♇	2:11	8	☽ ☌ ♃	8: 9	17	☽ ☍ ♄	8:30	28	☽ □s ☊	8:26
	☉ ☍ ☽	18:30		☉ □ ☽	10:27	18	☽ ☌ ☿	17: 7		☽ ☌ ♇	11:47
2	☿ ☍ ♄	2:16		☽ ☌ ⛢	23:49	19	☽ ☌ ♂	0:56	29	☽ ☍ ♀	10:55
	☽ ☌ P	5:43	9	♀ □ ⛢	11: 8		☽ ☍ ♆	6: 0	30	☽ ☌ P	15:40
	☽ ☍ ♀	21:14	13	☉ ☌ ♀	11:14	21	☽ ☌ ☋	16:22		☽ ☌ ♄	19:31
3	☽ ☌ ♄	11:51	14	☽ □N ☊	5:18	22	♀ □ ♃	12:15	31	☉ ☍ ☽	1:34
	☽ ☍ ☿	15: 1		☽ ☍ ♇	7:44		♂ ☍ ♆	20:47		☽ ☍ ☿	19:27
4	☽ ☍ ♂	3:13	16	☽ ☌ ♀	0:42	23	☽ ☍ ♃	4:46			
	☽ ☌ ♆	22:59		☉ □ ⛢	2:32		☽ ☍ ⛢	19:17			
7	☉ □ ♃	0: 1		☉ ☌ ☽	9:37	24	☉ □ ☽	9:56			

SIDEREAL HELIOCENTRIC LONGITUDES : AUGUST 2023 Gregorian at 0 hours UT

DAY	Sid. Time	☿	♀	⊕	♂	♃	♄	⛢	♆	♇	Vernal Point
1 TU	20:37:24	25 ♎ 17	5 ♑ 41	13 ♑ 28	8 ♍ 43	6 ♈ 51	7 ♒ 55	24 ♈ 49	0 ♓ 54	4 ♑ 6	4 ♓ 55'51"
2 WE	20:41:20	28 10	7 16	14 25	9 10	6 57	7 57	24 49	0 55	4 6	4 ♓ 55'51"
3 TH	20:45:17	1 ♏ 1	8 51	15 23	9 37	7 2	7 59	24 50	0 55	4 6	4 ♓ 55'51"
4 FR	20:49:13	3 51	10 26	16 20	10 4	7 8	8 1	24 51	0 55	4 7	4 ♓ 55'51"
5 SA	20:53:10	6 39	12 1	17 17	10 31	7 13	8 3	24 51	0 56	4 7	4 ♓ 55'51"
6 SU	20:57: 6	9 26	13 36	18 15	10 58	7 19	8 5	24 52	0 56	4 7	4 ♓ 55'51"
7 MO	21: 1: 3	12 12	15 11	19 12	11 24	7 24	8 7	24 53	0 56	4 8	4 ♓ 55'51"
8 TU	21: 5: 0	14 57	16 45	20 10	11 51	7 30	8 9	24 53	0 57	4 8	4 ♓ 55'50"
9 WE	21: 8:56	17 42	18 20	21 7	12 18	7 35	8 11	24 54	0 57	4 8	4 ♓ 55'50"
10 TH	21:12:53	20 27	19 55	22 5	12 45	7 41	8 13	24 55	0 58	4 8	4 ♓ 55'50"
11 FR	21:16:49	23 12	21 30	23 2	13 12	7 46	8 14	24 55	0 58	4 9	4 ♓ 55'50"
12 SA	21:20:46	25 57	23 5	24 0	13 39	7 52	8 16	24 56	0 58	4 9	4 ♓ 55'50"
13 SU	21:24:42	28 42	24 40	24 58	14 6	7 57	8 18	24 57	0 59	4 9	4 ♓ 55'50"
14 MO	21:28:39	1 ♐ 28	26 15	25 55	14 33	8 3	8 20	24 57	0 59	4 10	4 ♓ 55'50"
15 TU	21:32:35	4 14	27 50	26 53	15 0	8 8	8 22	24 58	0 59	4 10	4 ♓ 55'49"
16 WE	21:36:32	7 1	29 25	27 50	15 28	8 14	8 24	24 59	1 0	4 10	4 ♓ 55'49"
17 TH	21:40:29	9 50	1 ♒ 0	28 48	15 55	8 19	8 26	24 59	1 0	4 10	4 ♓ 55'49"
18 FR	21:44:25	12 40	2 35	29 46	16 22	8 24	8 28	25 0	1 0	4 11	4 ♓ 55'49"
19 SA	21:48:22	15 32	4 10	0 ♒ 44	16 49	8 30	8 30	25 1	1 1	4 11	4 ♓ 55'49"
20 SU	21:52:18	18 25	5 45	1 41	17 16	8 35	8 32	25 1	1 1	4 11	4 ♓ 55'49"
21 MO	21:56:15	21 21	7 20	2 39	17 43	8 41	8 34	25 2	1 2	4 12	4 ♓ 55'49"
22 TU	22: 0:11	24 19	8 55	3 37	18 11	8 46	8 36	25 3	1 2	4 12	4 ♓ 55'48"
23 WE	22: 4: 8	27 19	10 30	4 35	18 38	8 52	8 37	25 3	1 2	4 12	4 ♓ 55'48"
24 TH	22: 8: 4	0 ♑ 22	12 5	5 32	19 5	8 57	8 39	25 4	1 3	4 12	4 ♓ 55'48"
25 FR	22:12: 1	3 28	13 40	6 30	19 33	9 3	8 41	25 5	1 3	4 13	4 ♓ 55'48"
26 SA	22:15:58	6 38	15 16	7 28	20 0	9 8	8 43	25 5	1 3	4 13	4 ♓ 55'48"
27 SU	22:19:54	9 51	16 51	8 26	20 27	9 14	8 45	25 6	1 4	4 13	4 ♓ 55'48"
28 MO	22:23:51	13 9	18 26	9 24	20 55	9 19	8 47	25 7	1 4	4 14	4 ♓ 55'48"
29 TU	22:27:47	16 30	20 1	10 22	21 22	9 25	8 49	25 7	1 4	4 14	4 ♓ 55'48"
30 WE	22:31:44	19 56	21 36	11 20	21 50	9 30	8 51	25 8	1 5	4 14	4 ♓ 55'47"
31 TH	22:35:40	23 27	23 12	12 18	22 17	9 36	8 53	25 9	1 5	4 14	4 ♓ 55'47"

INGRESSES :

2	☿ → ♏ 15:22
13	☿ → ♐ 11:20
16	♀ → ♒ 8:51
18	⊕ → ♒ 5:54
23	☿ → ♑ 21: 7

ASPECTS (HELIOCENTRIC +MOON(TYCHONIC)) :

1	☽ ☌ ♇	2:37		☽ ☌ ♃	10:50		♀ ☌ ⊕	11:14	21	♀ ☌ ♄	18:56	28	☽ ☌ ♇	13:22
	☽ ☌ ♀	5:44	8	♀ ☌ A	1: 2		☿ □ ♆	19:51		☽ □ ♇	21:55		☽ □ ♃	21:39
	☽ □ ♃	7: 1		☽ □ ♀	3:59	14	☽ ☍ ♇	9: 2	22	☽ ☍ ♃	6:51	29	☽ ☌ ☿	11:31
	♀ □ ♃	18:49		☽ ☌ ⛢	18:23		☽ □ ♃	16:58	23	☽ ☍ ⛢	13:49		☽ □ ⛢	22:32
2	☽ □ ⛢	11:10	9	☽ □ ♄	19:14	16	☽ □ ⛢	3: 3	24	☽ □ ♄	14:55	30	♀ □s ☊	3:16
	☽ □ ☿	20:12	10	☿ ☌ A	20: 7		☽ ☍ ♀	13:54		☽ □ ♀	23:56		☽ ☌ ♄	20: 6
3	☽ ☌ ♄	7:54		☽ ☍ ☿	23:56	17	☽ ☍ ♄	6:19	25	☿ ☌ ♇	5:38	31	☿ □s ☊	0:36
4	☽ ☌ ♆	20:43	11	☽ □ ♆	15: 4	19	☽ ☍ ♆	3:59	26	☽ □ ♆	6:27		☿ □ ⛢	11:24

with carving and, I think, molding. There were all sorts of brown heads and knobs on them. I saw no carved images in the temple, although there were various kinds of ornamentation: vines, grapes, animals for sacrifice, and figures like swathed infants, such as I used to see Mary embroidering.

It was still bright daylight when Jesus and his followers reached the neighborhood of John Mark's house. Here the Greeks stepped up, and Jesus spoke to them some minutes. The strangers had some women with them, but they remained standing back. These people were converted. They were among the first to join the disciples at Pentecost and to receive baptism.

Full of trouble, Jesus went back with the apostles to Bethany for the sabbath. While he was teaching in the temple, the Jews had been ordered to keep their houses closed, and it was forbidden to offer him or his disciples any refreshment. On reaching Bethany, they went to the public house of Simon, the healed leper, where a meal awaited them. Magdalene, filled with compassion for Jesus' fatiguing exertions, met the Lord at the door. She was clothed in a penitential robe and girdle, her flowing hair concealed by a black veil. She cast herself at his feet and with her hair wiped from them the dust, just as one would clean the shoes of another. She did it openly before all, and many were scandalized at her conduct.

After Jesus and the disciples had prepared themselves for the sabbath, that is, put on the garments prescribed and prayed under the lamp, they stretched themselves at table for the meal. Toward the end of it, Magdalene, urged by love, gratitude, contrition, and anxiety, again made her appearance. She went behind the Lord's couch, broke a little flask of precious balm over his head and poured some of it upon his feet, which she again wiped with her hair. That done, she left the dining hall. Several of those present were scandalized, especially Judas, who excited Matthew, Thomas, and John Mark to displeasure. But Jesus excused her, on account of the love she bore him. She often anointed him in this way. Many of the facts mentioned only once in the Gospels happened frequently.

The meal was followed by prayer, after which the apostles and disciples separated. Judas, full of chagrin, hurried back to Jerusalem that night. I saw him, torn by envy and avarice, running in the darkness over the Mount of Olives, and it seemed as if a sinister glare surrounded him, as if the devil were lighting his steps. He hurried to the house of Caiaphas, and spoke a few words at the door. He could not stay long in any one place. Thence he ran to the house of John Mark. The disciples were wont to lodge there, so Judas pretended that he had come from Bethany for that purpose. This was the first definite step in his treacherous course.

When, on the following morning, Jesus was going from Bethany to Jerusalem with some of his disciples, they found the fig tree that Jesus had cursed entirely withered, and the disciples wondered at it. I saw John and Peter halting on the roadside near the tree. When Peter showed his astonishment, Jesus said to them: "If ye believe, ye shall do still more wonderful things. Yea, at your word mountains will cast themselves into the sea" (Mark 11:20–25). He continued his instruction on this object, and said something about the signification of the fig tree.

A great many strangers were gathered in Jerusalem, and both morning and evening, preaching and divine service went on in the temple. Jesus taught in the interim. He stood when preaching, but if anyone wanted to put a question to him, he sat down while the questioner rose.

During his discourse today, some priests and scribes stepped up to him and inquired by what right he acted as he did. Jesus answered: "I, too, shall ask you something; and when you answer me, I shall tell you by what authority I do these things" (Matt. 21:23–32). Then he asked them by what authority John had baptized, and when they would not answer him, he replied that neither would he tell them by what authority he acted.

In his afternoon instruction, Jesus introduced the similitude of the vine dresser, also that of the cornerstone rejected by the builders (Matt. 21:33–46). In the former, he explained that the murdered vine dresser typified himself, and the murderers, the Pharisees. Thereupon these last-named became so exasperated that they would willingly have arrested him then and there but they dared not, as they saw how all the people clung to him. They determined, however, to set five of their confidential followers, who were relatives of some of the disciples, to spy on him, and they gave them orders to try to catch him by captious questions. These five men were some of them followers of the Pharisees; others, servants of Herod.

As Jesus was returning toward evening to Bethany, some kindhearted people approached him on the road and offered him something to drink. He passed the night at the disciples' inn near Bethany.

August 16: New Moon Cancer
July 19, 30: John the Baptist's Arrest, pp. 477–80, vol. I

I saw Jesus conversing with Mary alone. She was weeping at the thought of his exposing himself to danger by going to Jerusalem. He comforted her, telling her that she must not be anxious, that he would accomplish his mission, and that the sorrowful days had not yet come. He encouraged her to persevere in prayer and exhorted the others to refrain from all comments and judgments upon John's imprisonment and the action of the Pharisees against himself, for such proceedings on their part would only increase the danger— adding that the Pharisees' manner of acting was permitted by divine Providence, though they were thereby working out their own destruction.

Some mention was made of Magdalene also. Jesus again told them to pray for her and think of her kindly, for she would soon be converted and become so good as to be an example for many.

That morning, Jesus went to Bethany with Lazarus and about five of the disciples belonging to Jerusalem. It was the beginning of the Feast of the New Moon, and I saw floating from the synagogues of Capernaum and other places long streamers of knotted drapery and festoons of fruit on the principal houses.

August 22: Mars opposite Neptune
July 21, 29: Early Travels, p. 302, vol. I

When he left this place, he went northward to the country that John had first visited on leaving the desert. It was a little sheep-rearing place. Naomi and her daughter Ruth dwelt there a long time. Naomi had so good a name among the people that she is still spoken of in those parts. Later she removed to Bethlehem. The Lord taught very zealously here. The time approached for him to retrace his steps southward and thence to Samaria for his baptism. Jacob also owned fields up here. Through this place ran a little river, back of which far up in the desert lay John's spring. From this spring the road became very steep, reminding me of what Adam and Eve took when driven from Paradise. It led down to the battlefield of Ezekiel. On Adam and Eve's route, the trees became smaller and smaller and quite misshapen until, at last, they reached a desolate region where grew some miserable bushes. Paradise was as high above the earth as is the sun. After the Fall it disappeared behind a mountain that seemed to rise before it.

The Savior, on his return from the shepherds' country to Sarepta, followed the route trodden by the prophet Elijah when going from the brook Kerith to Sarepta. Jesus taught here and there as he journeyed on, passing by Sidon.

August 27: Sun opposite Saturn
November 30, 29: Ministered unto by Angels, pp. 370–71, vol. I

At the same moment I beheld myriads of angels draw near to Jesus, bend low before him, take him up as if in their hands, float down gently with him to the rock, and into the grotto in which the forty-day fast had been begun. There were twelve angelic spirits who appeared to be the leaders, and a definite number of assistants. I cannot now remember distinctly, but I think it was seventy-two, and I feel that the whole vision was symbolical of the apostles and the disciples. And now was held in the grotto a grand celebration, one of triumph and thanksgiving, and a banquet was made ready. The interior of the grotto was adorned by the angels with garlands of vine leaves from which depended a victor's crown, likewise of leaves, over the head of Jesus. The preparations were made rapidly, though with marvelous order and magnificence. All was resplendent, all was symbolical. Whatever was needed appeared instantly at hand and in its proper place.

Next came the angels bearing a table, small at first but that quickly increased in size, laden with celestial fare. The food and vessels were such as

I have always seen on the heavenly tables, and I saw Jesus, the twelve chief spirits, and also the others partaking of refreshment. But there was no eating by the mouth, though still a real participation, a passing of the essence of the fruits into the partakers. All was spiritual. It was as if the interior signification of the aliments entered into the participants, bearing with it refreshment and strength. But it is inexpressible.

At one end of the table stood a large, shining chalice with little cups around it, the whole similar to what I have always seen in my visions of the institution of the blessed sacrament. But this that I now saw was immaterial, was larger. There was also a plate with thin disks of bread. I saw Jesus pouring something from the large chalice into the cups and dipping morsels of bread into it, which morsels and cups the angels took and carried away. With this the vision ended and Jesus, going out from the grotto, went down toward the Jordan.

The angels that ministered unto Jesus appeared under different forms and seemed to belong to different hierarchies. Those that, at the close of the banquet, bore away the cups of wine and morsels of bread, were clothed in priestly raiment. I saw at the instant of their disappearance all kinds of supernatural consolation descending upon the friends of Jesus, those of his own time and those of after ages. I saw Jesus appearing in vision to the blessed Virgin then at Cana, to comfort and strengthen her. I saw Lazarus and Martha wonderfully touched, while their hearts grew warm with the love of Jesus. I saw Mary the Silent actually fed with the gifts from the table of the Lord. The angel stood by her while she, like a child, received the food. She had been a witness of all the temptations and sufferings of Jesus. Her whole life was one of vision and suffering through compassion, therefore such supernatural favors caused her no astonishment. Magdalene, too, was wonderfully agitated. She was at the time busied with finery for some amusement. Suddenly anxiety about her life seized upon her, and a longing rose in her soul to be freed from the chains that bound her. She cast the finery from her hands, but was laughed at by those around her. I saw many of the future apostles consoled, their hearts filled with heavenly desires. I saw Nathaniel in his home thinking of all that

he had heard of Jesus, of the deep impression he had made upon him, and of how he had cast it out of his mind. Peter, Andrew, and all the others were, as I saw, strengthened and consoled. This was a most wonderful vision.

During Jesus' fast, Mary resided in the house near Capernaum, and had to listen to all kinds of speeches about her divine Son. They said that he went wandering about, no one knew where; that he neglected her; that after the death of Joseph it was his duty to undertake some business for his mother's support, etc. Throughout the whole country, the talk about Jesus was rife at this time, for the wonders attendant on his baptism, the testimony rendered by John, and the accounts of his scattered disciples had been everywhere noised abroad. Only once after this, and that was before his Passion, at the resurrection of Lazarus, were reports of Jesus so widespread and active. The blessed Virgin was grave and recollected, for she was never without the internal vision of Jesus, whose actions she contemplated and whose sufferings she shared.

Toward the close of the forty days, Mary went to Cana, in Galilee, and stopped with the parents of the bride of Cana, people of distinction who appeared to be of the first rank. Their beautiful mansion stood in the heart of the clean and well-built city. A street ran through the middle of it, I think a continuation of the highroad from Ptolomais; one could see it descending toward Cana from a higher level. This city was not so irregularly and unevenly built as many others of Palestine. The bridegroom was almost of the same age as Jesus and he managed his mother's household with the cleverness of an old married man. The parents of the young people consulted the blessed Virgin upon all the affairs of their children and showed her everything.

John was at this time constantly occupied in administering baptism. Herod did his best to procure a visit from him, and he likewise sent messengers to draw him out on the subject of Jesus. But John paid very little attention to him, and went on repeating his old testimony of Jesus. From Jerusalem also, messengers were again sent to call him to account concerning Jesus and himself. John answered as usual that he had never laid eyes on him when he began his own career, but that he had been sent to prepare for him the way.

Following Jesus' baptism, John taught that, through that baptism and the descent of the Holy Spirit upon him, water had been sanctified and out of it much evil had been cast. Jesus' baptism had been like an exorcism of the water. Jesus had suffered himself to be baptized in order to sanctify water. John's baptism had in consequence become purer and holier. It was for this end that Jesus was baptized in a separate basin. The water sanctified by contact with his divine Person had then been conducted to the Jordan and into the public pool of baptism, and of it also Jesus and his disciples had taken some for baptism in distant towns and villages.

August 31: Full Moon Aquarius

August 2, 30: Meeting the Widow Maroni in Nain, p. 497, vol. I

The widow of Nain, the sister of the wife of James the Greater, had been informed by Andrew and Nathaniel of Jesus' near approach, and she was awaiting his arrival. With another widow she now went out to the inn to welcome him. They cast themselves veiled at his feet. The widow of Nain begged Jesus to accept the offer of the other good widow, who wished to put all she possessed into the treasury of the holy women for the maintenance of the disciples and for the poor, whom she herself also wanted to serve. Jesus graciously accepted her offer, while he instructed and consoled her and her friend. They had brought some provisions for a repast, which along with a sum of money they handed over to the disciples. The latter was sent to the women at Capernaum for the common treasury.

Jesus took some rest here with the disciples. He had on the preceding day taught in Engannim with indescribable effort and had cured the sick, after which he had journeyed thence to Nain, a distance of about seven hours. The widow, lately introduced to Jesus, told him of another woman named Mary who likewise desired to give what she possessed for the support of the disciples. But Jesus replied that she should keep it till later when it would be more needed. This woman was an adulteress, and had been, on account of her infidelity, repudiated by her husband, a rich Jew of Damascus. She had heard of Jesus' mercy to sinners, was very much touched, and had no other

desire than to do penance and be restored to grace. She had visited Martha, with whose family she was distantly related, had confessed her transgression to her and begged her to intercede for her with the mother of Jesus. She gave over to her also a part of her wealth. Martha, Johanna Chusa, and Veronica, full of compassion for the sinner, interested themselves in her case, and took her at once to Mary's dwelling at Capernaum. Mary looked at her gravely and allowed her to stand for a long time at a distance. But the woman supplicated with burning tears and vehement sorrow: "O Mother of the prophet! Intercede for me with thy Son, that I may find favor with God!" She was possessed by a mute devil and had to be guarded, for in her paroxysms she could not cry for help and the devil drove her into fire or water. When she came again to herself, she would lie in a corner weeping piteously. Mary sent in behalf of the unhappy creature a messenger to Jesus, who replied that he would come in good time and heal her.

SEPTEMBER 2023

September 6: Inferior Conjunction Sun and Mercury

August 24, 30: Herod and John, pp. 28–29, vol. II

That evening Jesus put up near Gennabris in another farmhouse, and taught again of the grain of mustard seed. The master of the house complained to him of a neighbor who for a long time had encroached upon his field and in many ways infringed his rights. Jesus went to the field with the owner, that he might point out to him the injury done. As the present state of affairs had lasted some time, the damage was considerable, and the owner complained that he could not do anything with the trespasser. Jesus asked whether he still had sufficient for the support of himself and his family. The man answered, yes, that he enjoyed competency. Upon hearing this, Jesus told him that he had lost nothing, since properly speaking nothing belongs to us, and so long as we have sufficient to support life, we have enough. The owner of the field should resign still more to his importunate neighbor, in order to satisfy the latter's greed after earthly goods. All that one cheerfully gives up here below for the sake of peace, will be restored to him in the kingdom of his Father. That hostile neighbor, viewed from his own standpoint, acted rightly, for his kingdom was of this world, and he sought to increase in earthly goods. But in Jesus' kingdom, he should have nothing. The owner of the field should take a lesson from his neighbor in the art of enriching himself, and should strive to acquire possessions in the kingdom of God. Jesus drew a similitude from a river that wore away the land on one side and deposited the debris on the other. The whole discourse was something like that upon the unjust steward, in which worldly artifice and earthly greed after enrichment should furnish an example for one's manner of acting in spiritual affairs. Earthly riches were contrasted with heavenly treasures. Some points of the instruction seemed a little obscure to me, though to the Jews, on account of their notions, their religion, and the standpoint from which they viewed things, all was quite plain and intelligible. To them all was symbolical.

The field in which lay Joseph's well was in this neighborhood, and Jesus took occasion from the circumstance just related to refer to a somewhat similar struggle recorded in the Old Testament. Abraham had given far more land to Lot than the latter had demanded. After relating the fact, Jesus asked what had become of Lot's posterity, and whether Abraham had not recovered full propriety. Ought we not to imitate Abraham? Was not the kingdom promised to him, and did he not obtain it? This earthly kingdom, however, was merely a symbol of the kingdom of God, and Lot's struggle against Abraham was typical of the struggle of man with man. But, like Abraham, man should aim at acquiring the kingdom of God. Jesus quoted the text of holy scripture in which the strife alluded to is recorded, and continued to talk of it and of the kingdom before all the harvest laborers.

The unjust husbandman likewise was present with his followers. He listened in silence and at a distance. He had engaged his friends to interrupt Jesus from time to time with all kinds of captious questions. One of them asked him what would be the end of his preaching, what would come of it all. Jesus answered so evasively that they could make nothing out of his words. They were, however, something to this effect: If his preaching seemed too long to some, to others it was short. He spoke in parables of the harvest, of sowing, of reaping, of separating the tares from the good grain, of the bread and nourishment of eternal life, etc. The good husbandman, the host of Jesus, listened to his teaching with a docile heart. He ceased to accuse his enemy, later on gave over all he possessed into the treasury of the rising church, and his sons joined the disciples.

There was much talk here of the Herodians. The people complained of their spying into everything. They had recently accused and arrested here at Dothaim and also in Capernaum several adulterers, and taken them to Jerusalem where they were to be judged. The people of Dothaim were well pleased that such persons should be removed from among them, but the feeling of being continually watched was very distasteful to them. Jesus spoke of the Herodians with perfect freedom. He told the people to beware of sin, also of hypocrisy and criticizing others. One should confess his own delinquencies before sitting in judgment upon his neighbor. Then Jesus painted the ordinary manner of acting among the Herodians, applying to them the passage from the prophet Isaiah read in the synagogue on the preceding sabbath, which treats of mute dogs that do not bark, that do not turn away from evil, and that tear men in secret. He reminded them that those adulterers were delivered over to justice while Herod, the patron of their accusers, lived in the open commission of the same crime, and he gave them signs by which they might recognize the Herodians.

There were in several of the huts nearby some men who had received injuries during their labor. Jesus visited them, cured the poor creatures, and told them to go to the instruction and resume their work. They did so, singing hymns of praise.

Jesus sent some shepherds from Dothaim to Machaerus with directions to John's disciples to induce the people to disperse, for their rebellion, he said, might render John's imprisonment more rigorous, or even give occasion for his death.

SIDEREAL GEOCENTRIC LONGITUDES : SEPTEMBER 2023 Gregorian at 0 hours UT											
DAY	☉	☽	☊	☿	♀	♂	♃	♄	♅	♆	♇
1 FR	13 ♌ 15	26 ♒ 33	0 ♈ 45R	23 ♌ 32R	17 ♋ 19R	7 ♍ 47	20 ♈ 29	8 ♒ 25R	28 ♈ 0R	1 ♓ 42R	3 ♑ 11R
2 SA	14 13	11 ♓ 30	0 41	22 44	17 13	8 26	20 30	8 20	28 0	1 41	3 10
3 SU	15 11	26 4	0 40	21 51	17 9	9 4	20 30	8 16	28 0	1 39	3 9
4 MO	16 9	10 ♈ 11	0 40D	20 56	17 8	9 43	20 31	8 11	27 59	1 38	3 8
5 TU	17 7	23 50	0 41	19 58	17 9D	10 22	20 31R	8 7	27 59	1 36	3 7
6 WE	18 6	7 ♉ 3	0 42	19 0	17 12	11 1	20 30	8 2	27 59	1 35	3 6
7 TH	19 4	19 53	0 43R	18 2	17 18	11 40	20 30	7 58	27 58	1 33	3 5
8 FR	20 2	2 ♊ 22	0 42	17 5	17 26	12 18	20 30	7 54	27 58	1 31	3 4
9 SA	21 0	14 37	0 39	16 12	17 36	12 57	20 29	7 49	27 57	1 30	3 3
10 SU	21 59	26 40	0 35	15 23	17 48	13 36	20 28	7 45	27 57	1 28	3 2
11 MO	22 57	8 ♋ 36	0 29	14 39	18 2	14 15	20 27	7 41	27 56	1 26	3 1
12 TU	23 55	20 29	0 23	14 2	18 19	14 55	20 25	7 36	27 55	1 25	3 1
13 WE	24 54	2 ♌ 19	0 16	13 33	18 37	15 34	20 24	7 32	27 55	1 23	3 0
14 TH	25 52	14 11	0 10	13 12	18 57	16 13	20 22	7 28	27 54	1 22	2 59
15 FR	26 50	26 5	0 5	12 59	19 19	16 52	20 20	7 24	27 53	1 20	2 58
16 SA	27 49	8 ♍ 4	0 1	12 56D	19 42	17 31	20 18	7 19	27 52	1 18	2 58
17 SU	28 47	20 10	29 ♓ 59	13 2	20 8	18 11	20 15	7 15	27 51	1 17	2 57
18 MO	29 46	2 ♎ 23	29 58D	13 18	20 35	18 50	20 13	7 11	27 50	1 15	2 56
19 TU	0 ♍ 45	14 47	29 59	13 43	21 3	19 30	20 10	7 7	27 49	1 13	2 56
20 WE	1 43	27 24	0 ♈ 1	14 17	21 33	20 9	20 7	7 3	27 48	1 12	2 55
21 TH	2 42	10 ♏ 17	0 2	15 0	22 5	20 48	20 4	7 0	27 47	1 10	2 55
22 FR	3 40	23 29	0 3	15 51	22 38	21 28	20 0	6 56	27 46	1 8	2 54
23 SA	4 39	7 ♐ 2	0 4R	16 50	23 12	22 8	19 57	6 52	27 45	1 7	2 54
24 SU	5 38	20 57	0 3	17 56	23 48	22 47	19 53	6 48	27 44	1 5	2 53
25 MO	6 37	5 ♑ 15	0 1	19 8	24 25	23 27	19 49	6 45	27 42	1 3	2 53
26 TU	7 35	19 52	29 ♓ 58	20 26	25 3	24 7	19 45	6 41	27 41	1 2	2 52
27 WE	8 34	4 ♒ 45	29 56	21 50	25 42	24 46	19 41	6 38	27 40	1 0	2 52
28 TH	9 33	19 46	29 53	23 18	26 23	25 26	19 36	6 34	27 38	0 58	2 51
29 FR	10 32	4 ♓ 46	29 51	24 50	27 4	26 6	19 32	6 31	27 37	0 57	2 51
30 SA	11 31	19 36	29 50	26 26	27 47	26 46	19 27	6 28	27 36	0 55	2 51

INGRESSES :

1 ☽ → ♓ 5:30	20 ☽ → ♏ 4:52
3 ☽ → ♈ 6:36	22 ☽ → ♐ 11:37
5 ☽ → ♉ 11: 5	24 ☽ → ♑ 15:15
7 ☽ → ♊ 19:24	25 ☊ → ♓ 9:19
10 ☽ → ♋ 6:40	26 ☽ → ♒ 16:22
12 ☽ → ♌ 19:17	28 ☽ → ♓ 16:21
15 ☽ → ♍ 7:51	30 ☽ → ♈ 17: 4
16 ☊ → ♓ 7:58	
17 ☽ → ♎ 19:20	
18 ☉ → ♍ 5:45	
19 ☊ → ♈ 15:20	

ASPECTS & ECLIPSES :

1 ☽ ☌ ♆ 8:12	13 ☽ ☍ ♄ 10:29	24 ☽ S ☊ 15:18
☽ ☍ ♂ 18:48	☽ ☌ ☿ 22: 3	☽ ☌ ♇ 20: 3
3 ☽ ☌ ☊ 7:43	15 ☉ ☌ ☽ 1:38	26 ☽ ☍ ♀ 8:46
4 ☽ ☌ ♃ 18: 4	☽ ☍ ♆ 10:29	27 ☽ ☌ ♄ 2:59
5 ☽ ☌ ♅ 7:26	16 ☽ ☌ ♂ 19:51	28 ☽ ☌ P 0:49
6 ☉ ☌i ☿ 11: 8	17 ♀ □ ♃ 6: 8	☽ ☍ ☿ 6:17
☉ □ ☽ 22:19	☽ ☌ ☋ 19:17	☽ ☌ ♆ 17:53
10 ☽ N ☊ 7:46	19 ☽ ☍ ♃ 10:14	29 ☉ ☍ ☽ 9:56
☽ ☍ ♇ 12:45	☉ ☍ ♆ 11:26	♀ □ ♅ 17:50
11 ☽ ☌ ♀ 19:30	20 ☽ ☍ ♅ 0:45	30 ☽ ☍ ♂ 12:18
12 ☽ ☌ A 15:12	22 ☉ □ ☽ 19:30	☽ ☌ ☊ 16:47

SIDEREAL HELIOCENTRIC LONGITUDES : SEPTEMBER 2023 Gregorian at 0 hours UT											
DAY	Sid. Time	☿	♀	⊕	♂	♃	♄	♅	♆	♇	Vernal Point
1 FR	22:39:37	27 ♑ 3	24 ♒ 47	13 ♒ 16	22 ♍ 45	9 ♈ 41	8 ♒ 55	25 ♈ 9	1 ♓ 6	4 ♑ 15	4 ♓ 55'47"
2 SA	22:43:33	0 ♒ 45	26 22	14 14	23 12	9 47	8 57	25 10	1 6	4 15	4 ♓ 55'47"
3 SU	22:47:30	4 33	27 57	15 12	23 40	9 52	8 58	25 11	1 6	4 15	4 ♓ 55'47"
4 MO	22:51:27	8 27	29 33	16 10	24 7	9 57	9 0	25 11	1 7	4 16	4 ♓ 55'47"
5 TU	22:55:23	12 28	1 ♓ 8	17 8	24 35	10 3	9 2	25 12	1 7	4 16	4 ♓ 55'47"
6 WE	22:59:20	16 36	2 44	18 6	25 3	10 8	9 4	25 13	1 7	4 16	4 ♓ 55'46"
7 TH	23: 3:16	20 51	4 19	19 4	25 30	10 14	9 6	25 14	1 8	4 16	4 ♓ 55'46"
8 FR	23: 7:13	25 14	5 54	20 2	25 58	10 19	9 8	25 14	1 8	4 17	4 ♓ 55'46"
9 SA	23:11: 9	29 45	7 30	21 1	26 26	10 25	9 10	25 15	1 8	4 17	4 ♓ 55'46"
10 SU	23:15: 6	4 ♓ 25	9 5	21 59	26 54	10 30	9 12	25 16	1 9	4 17	4 ♓ 55'46"
11 MO	23:19: 2	9 14	10 41	22 57	27 22	10 36	9 14	25 16	1 9	4 17	4 ♓ 55'46"
12 TU	23:22:59	14 11	12 16	23 56	27 49	10 41	9 16	25 17	1 10	4 18	4 ♓ 55'46"
13 WE	23:26:56	19 18	13 52	24 54	28 17	10 47	9 18	25 18	1 10	4 18	4 ♓ 55'45"
14 TH	23:30:52	24 33	15 27	25 52	28 45	10 52	9 20	25 18	1 10	4 18	4 ♓ 55'45"
15 FR	23:34:49	29 58	17 3	26 51	29 13	10 58	9 21	25 19	1 11	4 19	4 ♓ 55'45"
16 SA	23:38:45	5 ♈ 32	18 39	27 49	29 41	11 3	9 23	25 20	1 11	4 19	4 ♓ 55'45"
17 SU	23:42:42	11 14	20 14	28 48	0 ♎ 9	11 8	9 25	25 20	1 11	4 19	4 ♓ 55'45"
18 MO	23:46:38	17 4	21 50	29 46	0 37	11 14	9 27	25 21	1 12	4 19	4 ♓ 55'45"
19 TU	23:50:35	23 2	23 25	0 ♓ 45	1 5	11 19	9 29	25 22	1 12	4 20	4 ♓ 55'45"
20 WE	23:54:31	29 6	25 1	1 44	1 34	11 25	9 31	25 22	1 12	4 20	4 ♓ 55'45"
21 TH	23:58:28	5 ♉ 16	26 37	2 42	2 2	11 30	9 33	25 23	1 13	4 20	4 ♓ 55'44"
22 FR	0: 2:25	11 30	28 13	3 41	2 30	11 36	9 35	25 24	1 13	4 21	4 ♓ 55'44"
23 SA	0: 6:21	17 47	29 48	4 40	2 58	11 41	9 37	25 24	1 14	4 21	4 ♓ 55'44"
24 SU	0:10:18	24 6	1 ♈ 24	5 38	3 26	11 47	9 39	25 25	1 14	4 21	4 ♓ 55'44"
25 MO	0:14:14	0 ♊ 26	3 0	6 37	3 55	11 52	9 41	25 26	1 14	4 21	4 ♓ 55'44"
26 TU	0:18:11	6 43	4 36	7 36	4 23	11 58	9 42	25 26	1 15	4 22	4 ♓ 55'44"
27 WE	0:22: 7	12 58	6 12	8 35	4 52	12 3	9 44	25 27	1 15	4 22	4 ♓ 55'44"
28 TH	0:26: 4	19 9	7 48	9 33	5 20	12 9	9 46	25 28	1 15	4 22	4 ♓ 55'43"
29 FR	0:30: 0	25 14	9 24	10 32	5 48	12 14	9 48	25 28	1 16	4 23	4 ♓ 55'43"
30 SA	0:33:57	1 ♋ 13	11 0	11 31	6 17	12 19	9 50	25 29	1 16	4 23	4 ♓ 55'43"

INGRESSES :

1 ☿ → ♒ 19:10
4 ♀ → ♓ 6:50
9 ☿ → ♓ 1:16
15 ☿ → ♈ 0: 8
16 ♂ → ♎ 16: 1
18 ⊕ → ♓ 5:33
20 ☿ → ♉ 3:31
23 ♀ → ♈ 2:54
24 ☿ → ♊ 22:22
29 ☿ → ♋ 19: 5

ASPECTS (HELIOCENTRIC +MOON(TYCHONIC)) :

1 ☽ ☌ ♆ 7:14	8 ☽ □ ♀ 7:54	16 ☿ ☌ ♃ 23:37	21 ☿ □ ♄ 16:35	26 ☿ □ ⊕ 3:57
2 ☽ ☍ ♂ 19:52	9 ☿ ☌ ♆ 7:12	17 ☽ ☍ ♀ 0:10	22 ☽ □ ♆ 13:47	☽ □ ♅ 9: 1
3 ☽ □ ♇ 13:49	10 ☽ □ ♂ 0:28	☽ ☌ ♂ 20:25	23 ☿ ☌ P 18:51	27 ☽ ☌ ♄ 8: 0
☽ ☌ ♃ 23:36	☽ ☍ ♇ 15:17	18 ☽ □ ♇ 3:46	24 ☽ □ ♀ 19:48	28 ☽ ☌ ♆ 18:23
4 ☿ ☌ ♄ 3:24	11 ☽ □ ♃ 4: 2	☽ ☍ ♃ 17:17	☽ □ ♂ 21:42	30 ☿ ☍ ♇ 12:57
♀ ☌ ♆ 23:42	☿ ☌ ♀ 10:28	19 ☿ ☌ ☊ 2: 2	☽ ☌ ♇ 22:31	♀ ☌ ♃ 21:11
5 ☽ ☌ ♅ 2:26	12 ☽ □ ♅ 9:44	☿ ☌ ♅ 9:16	25 ☿ □ ♆ 3: 5	☿ □ ♂ 22:38
6 ☽ □ ♄ 3:44	13 ☽ ☍ ♄ 14: 9	⊕ ☌ ♆ 11:10	☽ □ ♃ 10:59	
☿ ☌ ⊕ 11: 8	14 ☿ ☍ ♂ 20:25	☽ ☍ ♅ 20: 9	♀ ☍ ♂ 19:28	
7 ☽ □ ☿ 2:48	15 ☽ ☍ ♆ 10:13	20 ☽ ☍ ☿ 6: 7	♀ □ ♇ 20:26	
☽ □ ♆ 21:35	☿ □ ♇ 18:48	☽ □ ♄ 22:37	♂ □ ♇ 22:48	

Herod and his wife were in Machaerus. I saw that Herod caused the Baptist to be summoned to his presence in a grand hall near the prison. There he was seated surrounded by his guard, many officers, doctors of the Law, and numerous Herodians and Sadducees. John was led through a passage into the hall and placed in the midst of guards before the large, open doors. I saw Herod's wife insolently and scornfully sweeping past John as she entered the hall and took an elevated seat. Her physiognomy was different from that of most Jewish women. Her whole face was sharp and angular, even her head was pointed, and her countenance was in constant motion. She had developed a very beautiful figure, and in her dress she was loud and extreme, also very tightly laced. To every chaste mind she must have been an object of scandal, as she did everything in her power to attract all eyes upon her.

Herod began to interrogate John, commanding him to tell him in plain terms what he thought of Jesus who was making such disturbance in Galilee. Who was he? Was he come to deprive him (Herod) of his authority? He (Herod) had heard indeed that he (John) had formerly announced Jesus, but he had paid little attention to the fact. Now, however, John should disclose to him his candid opinion on the subject, for that man (Jesus) held wondrous language on the score of a kingdom, and uttered parables in which he called himself a king's son, etc., although he was only the son of a poor carpenter. Then I heard John in a loud voice, and as if addressing the multitude, giving testimony to Jesus. He declared that he himself was only to prepare his ways; that compared with him, he was nobody; that never had there been a man, not even among the prophets, like unto Jesus, and never would there be one; that he was the Son of the Father; that he was the Christ, the King of Kings, the Savior, the Restorer of the kingdom; that no power was superior to his; that he was the Lamb of God who was to bear the sins of the world, etc. So spoke John of Jesus, crying in a loud voice, calling himself his precursor, the preparer of his ways, his most insignificant servant. It was evident that his words were inspired. His whole bearing was stamped with the supernatural, so much so that

Herod, becoming terrified, stopped his ears. At last, he said to John, "Thou knowest that I wish thee well. But thou dost excite sedition against me amongst the people by refusing to acknowledge my marriage. If thou wilt moderate thy perverse zeal and recognize my union as lawful before the people, I shall set thee free, and thou canst go around teaching and baptizing." Thereupon, John again raised his voice vehemently against Herod, rebuking his conduct before all the assistants, and saying to him: "I know thy mind! I know that thou recognizest the right and tremblest before the judgment! But thou hast sunk thy soul in guilty pleasures, thou liest bound in the snares of debauchery!" The rage of the wife at these words is simply indescribable, and Herod became so agitated that he hastily ordered John to be led away. He gave directions for him to be placed in another cell that, having no communication outside, would prevent his being heard by the people.

Herod was induced to hold that judicial examination because of his anxiety, excited by the tumult raised by the aspirants to baptism and the news brought him by the Herodians of the wonders wrought by Jesus.

The whole country was discussing the execution in Jerusalem of certain adulterers from Galilee who had been denounced by the Herodians. They dwelt upon the fact that sinners in humble life were brought to justice while the great ones went free; and that the accusers themselves, the Herodians, were adherents of the adulterous Herod who had imprisoned John for reproaching him with his guilt. Herod became dispirited. I saw the execution of the adulterers mentioned above. Their crimes were read to them, and then they were thrust into a dungeon in which was a small pit. They were placed at its edge. They fell upon a knife, which cut off their heads. In a vault below waited some jailers to drag away the lifeless trunks. It was some kind of a machine into which the condemned were precipitated. It was in this same place that James the Greater was executed at a later period.

September 15: New Moon Leo

August 17, 30: Healing Many in Bethsaida, pp. 19–20, vol. II

Jesus went from Peter's dwelling over the mountain ridge to the north side of Bethsaida. The whole road was full of sick, pagans and Jews, separate however, the leprous far removed from all others. There were blind, lame, mute, deaf, paralytic, and an exceedingly large number of dropsical Jews. The ceremony of curing was performed with the greatest order and solemnity. The people had already been two days here, and the disciples of the place—Andrew, Peter, and the others whom Jesus had notified of his coming—had arranged them comfortably in the nooks, retired and shady, and the little gardens on the road. Jesus instructed and admonished the sick, who were carried or led and ranged around him in groups. Some desired to confess their sins to him, and he stepped with them to a more retired spot. They sank on their knees before him, confessing and weeping. Among the pagans were some that had committed murder and robbery on their journeys. Jesus passed by some, leaving them lying unnoticed for a time while he turned to others; but afterward coming back to them, he exclaimed: "Rise! Thy sins are forgiven thee!" Among the Jews were adulterers and usurers. When Jesus saw in them proofs of repentance, he imposed on them a penance, repeated some prayers with them, laid his hands upon them, and cured them. He commanded many to purify themselves in a bath. Some of the pagans he ordered to receive baptism or to join their converted brethren in Upper Galilee. Band after band passed before him, and the disciples preserved order.

Jesus went through Bethsaida also. It was crowded with people, as if upon a great pilgrimage. He cured here in the different inns and along the streets. Refreshments had been prepared in Andrew's house. I saw some children there: Peter's stepdaughter and some other little girls of about ten years, two others between eight and ten, and Andrew's little son who wore a yellow tunic with a girdle. There were also some females of advanced age. All were standing on a kind of covered porch outside the house, speaking of the prophet, asking whether he would soon come, and running from side to side to see whether he was in sight. They had assembled here in order to get a glimpse of him, though ordinarily the children were kept under greater restraint. At last Jesus passed, turned his head toward them, and gave them his blessing. I saw him going again to Peter's and curing many. He cured about one hundred on that day, pardoned their sins, and pointed out to them what they should do in the future.

I saw again that Jesus exercised many different manners of curing, and that probably he did so in order to instruct the disciples as to how they should act, also the ministers of the church till the end of time. All the actions of Jesus, even his sufferings, appeared to be of a purely human nature. There were no sudden, no magical transformations in the cures he wrought. I saw in them a certain transition from sickness to health analogous to the nature of the malady and the sins that had given rise to it. I saw stealing upon those over whom he prayed or upon whom he laid his hand a certain stillness and inward recollection, which lasted for some moments, when they rose up as if from a slight swoon, cured. The lame rose without effort and cast themselves cured at his feet, though their full strength and agility returned to some only after a few hours, to others not for days. I saw some sick of edema who could totter toward him without assistance, and others who had to be carried. He generally laid his hand on their head and stomach and pronounced some words, after which they at once arose and walked. They felt quite relieved, the water passing from them in perspiration. The leprous, on being cured, immediately lost the scales of their disease, though still retaining the red scars. They that recovered sight, speech, or hearing, had at first a feeling of strangeness in the use of those senses. I saw some swollen with gout cured. Their pains left them, and they could walk, but the swelling did not go down at once, though it disappeared very soon. Convulsions were cured immediately and fevers vanished at his word, though their victims did not instantly become strong and vigorous. They were like drooping plants regaining freshness in the rain. The possessed usually sank into a short swoon from which they recovered with a calm expression of countenance and quite worn out, though freed from the evil one. All was conducted quietly and methodically. Only for unbelievers and the malevolent had the miracles of Jesus anything frightful in them.

The pagans present on this occasion had been influenced to come chiefly by people that had been to the baptism and teaching of John, and by other pagans from Upper Galilee where Jesus had formerly taught and cured.

Some had already received John's baptism, and some had not. Jesus did not order them to be circumcised. When questioned on this point, he instructed them upon the circumcision of the heart and the senses, and taught them how to mortify themselves. He spoke to them of charity, temperance, frugality, ordered them to keep the Ten Commandments, taught them some parts of a prayer like the petitions of the Lord's Prayer, and promised to send them his disciples.

September 19: Sun opposite Neptune

July 18, 30: Discussing John's Imprisonment, p. 477, vol. I

During these days, I saw him again in various little places among the shepherds healing and exhorting, also in Gath-Hepher, Jonas's birthplace, and where some of his own relatives lived. He wrought cures in this latter place also, and then toward evening went as far as Capernaum.

How indefatigable was Jesus! With what ardor he inspired the disciples and apostles! At first, they were often overcome by fatigue; but now what a difference! The disciples while traveling along the highways went forward to meet some and to hunt up the others, to instruct them themselves or invite them to attend Jesus' instructions.

Lazarus, Obed, Joseph of Arimathea's nephews, the bridegroom of Cana, and some other disciples, had arrived at Mary's house near Capernaum. There were present also about seven women, relatives and friends, awaiting the return of Jesus. They went in and out the house and gazed along the road, to catch the first sight of him. And now came some of John's disciples with the news of their master's imprisonment, which filled the hearts of the little company with anxiety. The disciples then went on to meet Jesus, with whom they came up not far from Capernaum,

and made known to him their errand. He consoled them, and continued his way to his mother alone. He had sent his disciples on in advance. Lazarus came out to meet him, and washed his feet in the vestibule.

When Jesus entered the apartment, the men bowed low before him. He greeted them, and went up to his mother, to whom he stretched out his hands. She, too, most lovingly and humbly inclined to him. There was no rushing into each other's arms; their meeting was full of tender and ingenuous reserve, which touched all present and made upon them the holiest impression. Then Jesus turned toward the other women, who lowered their veils and sank on their knees before him. He was accustomed to give his blessing at such meetings and leave-takings.

I saw now a repast made ready, and the men reclining around the table, the women at one end sitting cross-legged. They spoke indignantly of John's imprisonment, but Jesus rebuked them. He said that they should not be angry and pass sentence upon it, for that it had to be. Were John not removed from the scene, he himself would not be able to begin his work and go to Bethany. Then he told them of the people among whom he had been. Of Jesus' coming, none knew excepting those present and the confidential disciples. Jesus slept with the other guests in a side building. He appointed the disciples to meet him after the next sabbath at a house, high and solitary, in the neighborhood of Beth-Horon.

September 29: Full Moon Pisces

September 8–9, 32: Jesus Reaches the Tent City, pp. 495–96, vol. II

When Jesus with the three youths left Kedar, Nazor, the ruler of the synagogue (who traced his origin up to Tobias), Salathiel, Eliud, and the youth Titus accompanied him a good part of the way. They crossed the river and passed through the pagan quarter of the city, in which just at that time a pagan feast was being celebrated and sacrifice was being offered in front of the temple. The road ran first eastward and then to the south through a plain that lay between two high mountain ridges, sometimes over heaths, again over yellow or white sand, and sometimes over white pebbles. At last, they reached a large, open tract of country covered with verdure, in which stood a great tent among the palm trees, and around it many smaller ones. Here Jesus blessed and took leave of his escort, and then continued his journey awhile longer toward the tent city of the star worshippers. The day was on its decline when he arrived at a beautiful well in a hollow. It was surrounded by a low embankment, and near it was a drinking ladle. The Lord drank, and then sat down by the well. The youths washed his feet and he, in turn, rendered them the same service. All was done with childlike simplicity, and the sight was extremely touching. The plain was covered with palm trees, meadows, and at a considerable distance apart there were groups of tents. A tower, or terraced pyramid of pretty good size, still not higher than an ordinary church, arose in the center of the district. Here and there some people made their appearance and from a distance gazed at Jesus in surprise not unmingled with awe, but no one approached him.

Not far from the well stood the largest of the tent houses. It was surmounted by several spires, and consisted of many stories and apartments connected together by partitions, some grated, others merely of canvas. The upper part was covered with skins. Altogether it was very artistically made and very beautiful. From this tent castle five men came forth bearing branches, and turned their steps in the direction of Jesus. Each carried in his hand a branch of a different kind of fruit: One had little yellow leaves and fruit, another was covered with red berries, a third was a palm branch, one bore a vine branch full of leaves, and the fifth carried a cluster of grapes. From the waist to the knees, they wore a kind of woolen tunic slit at the sides, and on the upper part of the body a jacket wide and full, made of some kind of transparent, woolen stuff, with sleeves that reached about halfway to the elbow. They were of fair complexion, had a short, black beard, and long, curling hair. On their head was a sort of spiral cap from which hung many lappets around their temples. They approached Jesus and his companions with a friendly air, saluted them and, while presenting to them the branches they held in their hands, invited them to accompany them back to the tent. The vine branch was presented to Jesus, the one who acted as guide carrying a similar one. On entering the tent Jesus and his companions were made to sit upon cushions trimmed with tassels, and fruit was presented to them. Jesus uttered only a few words. The guests were then led through a tent corridor lined with sleeping chambers containing couch beds, and furnished with high cushions, to that part of the tent in which was the dining hall. In the center of the hall rose the pillar that supported the tent; and around it were twined garlands of leaves and fruits, vine branches, apples, and clusters of grapes—all so natural in appearance that I cannot say whether they really were natural or only painted. Here the attendants drew out a little oval table about as high as a footstool. It was formed of light leaves that could be opened quickly and its feet separated into two supports. They spread under it a colored carpet upon which were representations of men like themselves, and placed upon it cups and other table furniture. The tent was hung with tapestry, so that no part of the canvas itself could be seen.

When Jesus and the young disciples stretched themselves on the carpet around the table, the men in attendance brought cakes, scooped out in the middle, all kinds of fruits, and honey. The attendants themselves sat on low, round folding stools, their legs crossed. Between their feet they stood a little disk supported on a long leg, and on the disk they laid their plate. They served their guests themselves by turns, the servants remaining outside the tent with everything that was necessary. I saw them going to another tent and bringing thence birds, which had been roasted on a spit in the kitchen. This last-named apartment consisted merely of a mud hut in which was an opening in the roof to let out the smoke from the fire on the hearth. The birds were served up in quite a remarkable manner. They were (but I know not how it was done) covered with their feathers, and looked just as if they were alive. The meal over, the guests were escorted by five men to their sleeping rooms, and there the latter were quite amazed at seeing Jesus washing the youths' feet, which service they rendered him in return. Jesus explained to them its signification, and they resolved to practice in future the same act of courtesy.

When the five men took leave of Jesus and his young companions, they all left the tent together.

They wore mantles longer behind than before, with a broad flap hanging from the back of the neck. They proceeded to a temple that was built in the shape of a large four-cornered pyramid, not of stone but of very light materials such as wood and skins. There was a flight of outside steps from base to summit. It was built in a hollow that rose in terraces and was surrounded by steps and parapets. The circular enclosure was cut through by entrances to the different parts of the temple, and the entrances themselves were screened by light, ornamental hedges. Several hundred people were already assembled in the enclosure. The married women were standing back of the men; the young girls, back of them; and last of all, the children. On the steps of the pyramidal temple were illuminated globes that flashed and twinkled just like the stars of heaven, but I do not know how that was effected. They were regularly arranged, in imitation of certain constellations. The temple was full of people. In the center of the building rose a high column from which beams extended to the walls and up into the summit of the pyramid, bearing the lights by which the exterior globes were lighted. The light inside the temple was very extraordinary. It was like twilight, or rather moonlight. One seemed to be gazing up into a sky full of stars. The moon likewise could be seen, and far up in the very center of all blazed the sun. It was a most skillfully executed arrangement, and so natural that it produced upon the beholder an impression of awe, especially when he beheld by the dim light of the lower part of the temple the three idols that were placed around that central column. One was like a human being with a bird's head and a great, crooked beak. I saw the people offering to it in sacrifice all kinds of foods. They crammed into its enormous bill birds and similar things that fell down into its body and out again. Another of these idols had a head almost like that of an ox, and was seated like a human being in a squatting posture. They laid birds in its arms, which were outstretched as if to receive an infant. In it was a fire into which, through the holes made for that purpose, the worshippers cast the flesh of animals that had been slaughtered and cut up on the sacrificial table in front of it. The smoke escaped through a pipe sunk in the earth and communicating with the outer air. No

flames were to be seen in the temple, but the horrible idols shone with a reddish glare in the dim light. During the ceremony, the multitude around the pyramid chanted in a very remarkable manner. Sometimes a single voice was heard, and then again, a powerful chorus, the strains suddenly changing from plaintive to exultant; and when the moon and different stars shone out, they sent up shouts of enthusiastic welcome. I think this idolatrous celebration lasted till sunrise.

OCTOBER 2023

October 2: Mercury opposite Neptune
August 9, 32: Teaching in Kedar,
pp. 485–86, vol. II

The next day he gave an instruction at the fountain. The men and women sat at his feet, and he pressed the children to his breast. He told them about Zacchaeus climbing up the fig tree, of his leaving all and following him; of him who in the temple had said: "I thank God that I am not like the publican"; and lastly, of that other who, striking his breast, said, "Lord, be merciful to me, a poor sinner!" The inhabitants of Kedar became very fond of Jesus and thought no harm of him. They begged him to stay with them till the next sabbath and then teach again in their school, and when they asked him about Jesus of Nazareth, he related to them many things of him and his doctrine.

October 4: Mars opposite Node
September 24, 32: Visiting Theokeno with
Mensor, p. 504, vol. II

Jesus requested Mensor to conduct him at once to Theokeno, whose rooms were in the trellised basement near the little garden. He was resting on a cushioned couch, and he took part in the meal that was served up in dishes of surpassing beauty. The food dishes were prepared very elegantly. Herbs, fine and delicate, were arranged on the plates to represent little gardens. The cups were of gold. Among the fruits was one particularly remarkable. It was yellow, ribbed, very large, and crowned by a tuft of leaves. The

SIDEREAL GEOCENTRIC LONGITUDES : OCTOBER 2023 Gregorian at 0 hours UT

DAY		☉	☽	☊	☿	♀	♂	♃	♄	♅	♆	♇
1	SU	12 ♍ 30	4 ♈ 10	29 ♓ 50	28 ♌ 4	28 ♋ 31	27 ♍ 26	19 ♈ 22R	6 ♒ 24R	27 ♈ 34R	0 ♓ 53R	2 ♑ 50R
2	MO	13 28	18 21	29 50	29 44	29 15	28 6	19 17	6 21	27 32	0 52	2 50
3	TU	14 27	2 ♉ 6	29 51	1 ♍ 27	0 ♌ 1	28 46	19 11	6 18	27 31	0 50	2 50
4	WE	15 27	15 25	29 52	3 10	0 48	29 26	19 6	6 15	27 29	0 49	2 50
5	TH	16 26	28 20	29 53	4 55	1 35	0 ♎ 6	19 0	6 12	27 28	0 47	2 50
6	FR	17 25	10 ♊ 54	29 54	6 41	2 23	0 47	18 54	6 9	27 26	0 45	2 49
7	SA	18 24	23 10	29 54R	8 27	3 13	1 27	18 48	6 6	27 24	0 44	2 49
8	SU	19 23	5 ♋ 14	29 53	10 13	4 2	2 7	18 42	6 4	27 22	0 42	2 49
9	MO	20 22	17 9	29 53	12 0	4 53	2 47	18 36	6 1	27 20	0 41	2 49
10	TU	21 22	29 0	29 51	13 46	5 45	3 28	18 30	5 59	27 19	0 39	2 49
11	WE	22 21	10 ♌ 51	29 50	15 32	6 37	4 8	18 23	5 56	27 17	0 38	2 49
12	TH	23 20	22 45	29 49	17 18	7 30	4 49	18 17	5 54	27 15	0 36	2 49D
13	FR	24 20	4 ♍ 45	29 49	19 3	8 23	5 29	18 10	5 52	27 13	0 35	2 49
14	SA	25 19	16 54	29 48	20 48	9 17	6 10	18 3	5 49	27 11	0 33	2 49
15	SU	26 18	29 12	29 48	22 33	10 12	6 51	17 56	5 47	27 9	0 32	2 49
16	MO	27 18	11 ♎ 42	29 48D	24 17	11 8	7 31	17 49	5 45	27 7	0 30	2 49
17	TU	28 17	24 24	29 48	26 0	12 4	8 12	17 42	5 44	27 5	0 29	2 50
18	WE	29 17	7 ♏ 19	29 49	27 43	13 0	8 53	17 34	5 42	27 3	0 28	2 50
19	TH	0 ♎ 16	20 28	29 48R	29 25	13 57	9 34	17 27	5 40	27 0	0 26	2 50
20	FR	1 16	3 ♐ 52	29 48	1 ♎ 6	14 55	10 15	17 19	5 38	26 58	0 25	2 50
21	SA	2 16	17 30	29 48	2 47	15 53	10 56	17 12	5 37	26 56	0 23	2 50
22	SU	3 15	1 ♑ 22	29 48	4 27	16 51	11 37	17 4	5 36	26 54	0 22	2 51
23	MO	4 15	15 29	29 48D	6 7	17 50	12 18	16 56	5 34	26 52	0 21	2 51
24	TU	5 15	29 48	29 48	7 46	18 50	12 59	16 48	5 33	26 49	0 19	2 51
25	WE	6 14	14 ♒ 16	29 49	9 24	19 50	13 40	16 41	5 32	26 47	0 18	2 52
26	TH	7 14	28 51	29 49	11 2	20 50	14 21	16 33	5 31	26 45	0 17	2 52
27	FR	8 14	13 ♓ 25	29 50	12 39	21 51	15 2	16 25	5 30	26 43	0 16	2 53
28	SA	9 14	27 55	29 50	14 16	22 52	15 44	16 17	5 29	26 40	0 14	2 53
29	SU	10 14	12 ♈ 13	29 50R	15 52	23 54	16 25	16 8	5 29	26 38	0 13	2 54
30	MO	11 14	26 15	29 49	17 28	24 56	17 6	16 0	5 28	26 35	0 12	2 54
31	TU	12 14	9 ♉ 58	29 48	19 3	25 58	17 48	15 52	5 27	26 33	0 11	2 55

INGRESSES :

2	☿ → ♍	3:43	19	☿ → ♎	8:17
	☽ → ♉	20:17		☽ → ♐	17: 7
	♀ → ♌	23:29	21	☽ → ♑	21:38
4	♂ → ♎	20:12	24	☽ → ♒	0:20
5	☽ → ♊	3: 8	26	☽ → ♓	1:54
7	☽ → ♋	13:32	28	☽ → ♈	3:28
10	☽ → ♌	2: 1	30	☽ → ♉	6:29
12	☽ → ♍	14:31			
15	☽ → ♎	1:32			
17	☽ → ♏	10:27			
18	☉ → ♎	17:22			

ASPECTS & ECLIPSES :

2	☽ ☌ ♃	1:35		☽ ☌ ♀	14:44	20	☉ S☌ ☿	5:36		♂ ☍ ♃	16: 1
	☿ ☍ ♆	15:39	12	☽ ☍ ♆	15:42	21	☿ □ ♇	0:46		☽ ☍ P	20:12
	☽ ☌ ♅	15:55	14	☽ ☌ ☿	8:56		☉ □ ♇	14: 3		☉ ☍ ☽	20:22
4	♂ ☍ ☊	16: 4		☉ ☌ ☽	17:54		☽ S ☊	21:18	29	☿ ☍ ♃	3:43
6	☉ □ ☽	13:46		☉ ● A	17:58	22	☽ ☌ ♇	2:31		☽ ☌ ♃	6:35
7	☽ N ☊	13:19	15	☽ ☌ ☋	1:10		☉ □ ☽	3:28		☽ ☍ ☿	6:59
	☽ ☍ ♇	19:10		☽ ☌ ♂	15:34	24	☽ ☌ ♄	9:33		☽ ☍ ♂	7:29
9	♂ □ ♇	0:56	16	☽ ☍ ♃	11:29	25	☽ ☍ ♀	9:50		☿ ☌ ♂	14:20
10	☽ ☌ A	3:27	17	☽ ☍ ♅	4:59	26	☽ ☌ ♆	2:21	30	☽ ☌ ♅	0:34
	♀ ☍ ♄	6: 9	18	☉ ☍ ☊	12:45		☽ ☌ P	2:54			
	☽ ☍ ♄	14: 5	19	☿ ☍ ☊	5:33	28	☽ ☌ ☊	3:12			

SIDEREAL HELIOCENTRIC LONGITUDES : OCTOBER 2023 Gregorian at 0 hours UT

DAY		Sid. Time	☿	♀	⊕	♂	♃	♄	♅	♆	♇	Vernal Point
1	SU	0:37:54	7 ♋ 3	12 ♈ 36	12 ♓ 30	6 ♎ 45	12 ♈ 25	9 ♒ 52	25 ♈ 30	1 ♓ 16	4 ♑ 23	4 ♓ 55'43"
2	MO	0:41:50	12 46	14 12	13 29	7 14	12 30	9 54	25 30	1 17	4 23	4 ♓ 55'43"
3	TU	0:45:47	18 19	15 48	14 28	7 43	12 36	9 56	25 31	1 17	4 24	4 ♓ 55'43"
4	WE	0:49:43	23 43	17 24	15 27	8 11	12 41	9 58	25 32	1 18	4 24	4 ♓ 55'43"
5	TH	0:53:40	28 58	19 0	16 26	8 40	12 47	10 0	25 32	1 18	4 24	4 ♓ 55'42"
6	FR	0:57:36	4 ♌ 2	20 36	17 25	9 9	12 52	10 2	25 33	1 18	4 25	4 ♓ 55'42"
7	SA	1: 1:33	8 57	22 12	18 24	9 37	12 58	10 4	25 34	1 19	4 25	4 ♓ 55'42"
8	SU	1: 5:29	13 43	23 48	19 23	10 6	13 3	10 5	25 34	1 19	4 25	4 ♓ 55'42"
9	MO	1: 9:26	18 20	25 24	20 23	10 35	13 9	10 7	25 35	1 19	4 25	4 ♓ 55'42"
10	TU	1:13:23	22 47	27 1	21 22	11 4	13 14	10 9	25 36	1 20	4 26	4 ♓ 55'42"
11	WE	1:17:19	27 6	28 37	22 21	11 33	13 20	10 11	25 36	1 20	4 26	4 ♓ 55'42"
12	TH	1:21:16	1 ♍ 17	0 ♉ 13	23 21	12 2	13 25	10 13	25 37	1 20	4 26	4 ♓ 55'41"
13	FR	1:25:12	5 21	1 49	24 20	12 31	13 30	10 15	25 38	1 21	4 27	4 ♓ 55'41"
14	SA	1:29: 9	9 17	3 26	25 19	13 0	13 36	10 17	25 38	1 21	4 27	4 ♓ 55'41"
15	SU	1:33: 5	13 6	5 2	26 19	13 29	13 41	10 19	25 39	1 22	4 27	4 ♓ 55'41"
16	MO	1:37: 2	16 49	6 39	27 18	13 58	13 47	10 21	25 40	1 22	4 27	4 ♓ 55'41"
17	TU	1:40:58	20 25	8 15	28 18	14 27	13 52	10 23	25 40	1 22	4 28	4 ♓ 55'41"
18	WE	1:44:55	23 57	9 52	29 17	14 57	13 58	10 25	25 41	1 23	4 28	4 ♓ 55'41"
19	TH	1:48:52	27 23	11 28	0 ♈ 17	15 26	14 3	10 27	25 42	1 23	4 28	4 ♓ 55'41"
20	FR	1:52:48	0 ♎ 44	13 5	1 17	15 55	14 9	10 29	25 42	1 23	4 29	4 ♓ 55'40"
21	SA	1:56:45	4 1	14 41	2 16	16 25	14 14	10 30	25 43	1 24	4 29	4 ♓ 55'40"
22	SU	2: 0:41	7 14	16 18	3 16	16 54	14 20	10 32	25 44	1 24	4 29	4 ♓ 55'40"
23	MO	2: 4:38	10 23	17 54	4 16	17 23	14 25	10 34	25 45	1 24	4 29	4 ♓ 55'40"
24	TU	2: 8:34	13 28	19 31	5 15	17 53	14 30	10 36	25 45	1 25	4 30	4 ♓ 55'40"
25	WE	2:12:31	16 31	21 8	6 15	18 22	14 36	10 38	25 46	1 25	4 30	4 ♓ 55'40"
26	TH	2:16:27	19 30	22 44	7 15	18 52	14 41	10 40	25 47	1 26	4 30	4 ♓ 55'40"
27	FR	2:20:24	22 28	24 21	8 15	19 22	14 47	10 42	25 47	1 26	4 31	4 ♓ 55'39"
28	SA	2:24:21	25 22	25 58	9 14	19 51	14 52	10 44	25 48	1 26	4 31	4 ♓ 55'39"
29	SU	2:28:17	28 15	27 35	10 14	20 21	14 58	10 46	25 49	1 27	4 31	4 ♓ 55'39"
30	MO	2:32:14	1 ♏ 6	29 11	11 14	20 51	15 3	10 48	25 49	1 27	4 31	4 ♓ 55'39"
31	TU	2:36:10	3 55	0 ♊ 48	12 14	21 21	15 9	10 50	25 50	1 27	4 32	4 ♓ 55'39"

INGRESSES :

5	☿ → ♌	4:51
11	☿ → ♍	16:32
	♀ → ♉	20:42
18	⊕ → ♈	17:10
19	☿ → ♎	18:42
29	☿ → ♏	14:42
30	♀ → ♊	12: 2

ASPECTS (HELIOCENTRIC +MOON(TYCHONIC)) :

1	☽ □ ♇	0:22	5	☽ □ ♆	5:35	13	☽ ☌ ☿	1:45	21	☿ □ ♇	3:27		☿ ☌ ♂	17:49
	☽ ☍ ♂	4:29	7	☿ ☍ ♄	5:31	15	☽ □ ♇	10: 8	22	☽ ☌ ♇	5:19	26	☽ ☌ ♆	4:14
	☽ □ ☿	8: 7		☽ ☍ ♇	22:22		♂ ☍ ♃	12:25		☽ □ ☿	12:54	27	☿ ☌ ☋	8:52
	☽ ☌ ♃	13:58	8	☽ □ ♂	10:11	16	☽ ☍ ♃	3:59		☽ □ ♃	22:11	28	☿ ☍ ♅	3:32
	☽ ☌ ♀	15:59		☽ □ ♃	15:50		☽ ☌ ♂	4:30	23	☽ □ ♂	3:19		☽ □ ♇	11: 1
	☿ □ ♃	22:53	9	♀ ☌ ♅	2:40	17	☽ ☍ ♅	2:23		⊕ □ ♇	5:36	29	☽ ☌ ♃	4:40
2	☿ □ ♀	8:33		☽ □ ♅	17: 5	18	☽ ☍ ♀	5:19		☽ □ ♅	17:14		☽ ☍ ♂	14:20
	☽ ☌ ♅	12:24		☽ □ ♀	19:19		☽ □ ♄	5:41	24	☿ ☍ ♃	8:22		☽ ☌ ♅	23:14
3	☽ □ ♄	14: 3	10	☽ ☍ ♄	22:39		♀ □ ♄	8:24		☽ ☌ ♄	17:58	30	☽ ☍ ☿	10:35
	☿ N ☊	23:11	12	☿ ☍ ♆	0:18	19	☽ □ ♆	19:36	25	♀ ☌ ☊	10:21	31	☽ □ ♄	1:32
4	☿ □ ♅	8:12		☽ ☍ ♆	17:12	20	☿ ☍ ⊕	5:36		☽ □ ♀	12:42		♀ □ ♆	9:43

honeycombs were especially fine. Jesus ate only some bread and fruit, and drank from a cup that had never before been used. This was the first time that I saw him eating with pagans. I saw him teaching here whole days at a time, and but seldom taking a mouthful.

He taught during that meal and, at last, told his hosts that he was not an envoy of the Messiah, but the Messiah himself. On hearing this, they fell prostrate on the ground in tears. Mensor especially wept with emotion. He could not contain himself for love and reverence, and was unable to conceive how Jesus could have condescended to come to him. But Jesus told him that he had come for the pagans as well as for the Jews, that he was come for all who believed in him. Then they asked him whether it was not time for them to abandon their country and follow him at once to Galilee, for, as they assured him, they were ready to do so. But Jesus replied that his kingdom was not of this world, and that they would be scandalized, that they would waver in faith if they should see how he would be scorned and maltreated by the Jews. These words they could not comprehend, and they inquired how it could be that things could go so well with the bad while the good had to suffer so much. Jesus then explained to them that they who enjoy on earth have to render an account hereafter, and that this life is one of penance.

The kings had some knowledge of Abraham and David; and when Jesus spoke of his ancestors, they produced some old books and searched in them to see whether they, too, could not claim descent from the same race. The books were in the form of tablets opening out in a zigzag form, like sample patterns. These pagans were so childlike, so desirous of doing all that they were told. They knew that circumcision had been prescribed to Abraham, and they asked the Lord whether they, too, should obey this part of the Law. Jesus answered that it was no longer necessary, that they had already circumcised their evil inclinations, and that they would do so still more. Then they told him that they knew something of Melchizedek and his sacrifice of bread and wine, and said that they, too, had a sacrifice of the same kind, namely, a sacrifice of little leaves and some kind of a green liquor. When they offered it they spoke some words like these: "Whoever eats me and is devout, shall have all kinds of felicity." Jesus told them that Melchizedek's sacrifice was a type of the most holy Sacrifice, and that he himself was the Victim. Thus, though plunged in darkness, these pagans had preserved many forms of truth.

Either the night that preceded Jesus' coming or what followed, I cannot now say which, all the paths and avenues to a great distance around the tent castle were brilliantly illuminated. Transparent globes with lights in them were raised on poles, and every globe was surmounted by a little crown that glistened like a star.

October 10: Venus opposite Saturn

December 5, 30: Healing Two Possessed Youths, p. 169, vol. II

On the following day Jesus climbed the mountain, and encountered two Jewish youths who had come from Gergesa to meet him. They were possessed by the devil. They were not furious, though the attacks of the evil one were frequent, and they roved restlessly about. When Jesus some time before had crossed the Jordan from Tarichea and passed Gerasa, these young men were not yet possessed. They had then come out to meet him and begged to be received among his disciples, but Jesus sent them away. Now again, after Jesus had delivered them, they desired to be received by him. They told him that the misfortune from which he had just freed them never would have overtaken them if he had yielded to their first request. Jesus exhorted them to amendment of life, and bade them return home and announce by what means their deliverance had been effected. The youths obeyed. As Jesus went along, pausing here and there to teach before the huts and homes of the shepherds, many possessed and simpletons ran hiding behind the hedges and hills, crying after him and making signs for him to keep off and not disturb their peace. But Jesus called them to him, and delivered them. Many of those thus freed cried out, imploring him not to drive them into the abyss! Some of the apostles also performed cures by the imposition of hands, and engaged the people to repair to the mountain beyond Magdala to the south, where Jesus was going to deliver an instruction.

October 14: New Moon Virgo (Annular Solar Eclipse)

September 16, 30: Gifts from Abigail, p. 54, vol. II

Abigail was held in esteem by the inhabitants of Betharamphtha. She sent gifts down from her castle to the Jews for the more honorable entertainment of Jesus and his disciples. On the first of the month of Tisri the new year was celebrated, which fact was announced from the roof of the synagogue by all kinds of musical instruments, among them harps and a number of large trumpets with several mouthpieces. I saw again one of those wonderful instruments I had formerly seen on the synagogue of Capernaum. It was filled with wind by means of a bellows. All the houses and public buildings were adorned on this feast day with flowers and fruit. The different classes of people had different customs. During the night many persons, most of them women clothed in long garments and holding lighted lanterns, prayed upon the tombs. I saw, too, that all the inhabitants bathed, the women in their houses and the men at the public baths. The married men bathed separate from the youths, as also the elder women from the maidens. As bathing was very frequent among the Jews and water not abundant, they made use of it sparingly. They lay on their back in tubs and, scooping up the water in a shell, poured it over themselves; it was often more like a washing than a bath. They performed their ablutions today at the baths outside the city, in water perfectly cold. Mutual gifts were interchanged, the poor being largely remembered. They commenced by giving them a good entertainment, and on a long rampart were deposited numerous gifts for them, consisting of food, raiment, and covers. Every one that received presents from his friends bestowed a part of them upon the poor. The Rechabites present superintended and directed all things. They saw what each one gave to the poor and how it was distributed. They kept three lists, in which they secretly recorded the generosity of the donors. One of these lists was called the Book of Life; another, the Middle Way; and the third, the Book of Death. It was customary for the Rechabites to exercise all such offices, while in the temple they were gatekeepers, treasurers, and above all, chanters. This last office they fulfilled on today's feast. Jesus also received presents in Betharamphtha of clothing, covers, and money, all of which he caused to be distributed among the poor.

October 18: Sun opposite Node

October 8, 32: Reprimanding Mozian's Idolatry, p. 515, vol. II

The name of this city was Mozin, or Mozian. It was a sacerdotal city, but sunk deep in idolatry. Jesus did not enter the temple. I saw him teaching a crowd of people on a graded hill surrounded by a wall. It was in front of the temple and near a fountain. He reproved them severely for having fallen into idolatry even more deeply than their neighbors, showed them the abominations of their worship, and told them that they had abandoned the Law. I heard him referring to the destruction of the temple in the time of their forefathers, and speaking of Nebuchadnezzar and Daniel. He said that they should separate the believing from the spiritually blind, for there were some good souls among them, and to these he indicated whither they should go. Many of the others were stiff-necked. There was one point that they would not understand, and that was the necessity for abolishing polygamy. The women dwelt in a street to themselves at the extreme end of the city, to which, however, there was communication by shaded walks. They seemed to be held in great contempt, and after a certain age the young girls dared not appear in public. No woman of this place saw Jesus. Only the boys were present with the men.

Jesus used severe words toward these people. They were, he said, so blinded, so obstinate, that when the apostle that he was going to send would make his appearance, he would find them unprepared for baptism. Jesus would not remain longer with them. As he was leaving the city, a procession of young girls met him at the gate, chanting hymns of praise in his honor. They wore white pantalets, had garlands around their arms and necks, and flowers in their hands.

From Mozian, Jesus went with his companions across a large field to a village of pastoral tents. He sat down near the fountain, the disciples washed his feet, and some men of the place approached with the branch of welcome and gave him a glad reception. They were clad in long garments, more like Abraham than any others I had yet seen, and they possessed an astronomical pyramid. I saw no idols. These people appeared to be pure star worshippers and to belong to that race of whom some had accompanied the kings to Bethlehem. They appeared to me to be only a little band of shepherds, of whom the superior alone had a permanent dwelling. Jesus ate bread and fruit in his house standing, and drank out of a special vessel. He afterward taught at the well. When he was leaving them, the people threw themselves across his path and entreated him to remain with them.

October 19: Mercury opposite Node

September 24, 32: Visiting Theokeno with Mensor, p. 504, vol. II (see entry for Oct. 4)

October 20: Superior Conjunction Sun and Mercury

October 9, 30: Messenger of Cyrinus, pp. 74, vol. II

Next morning Jesus went from house to house, exhorting the people to turn away from their avarice and love of gain, and engaging them to attend the instruction to be given in the synagogue. He saluted all with a congratulatory word on the close of the feast. The people of Ophra were so usurious and unpolished that they were held in the same low esteem as the publicans. But they had now improved a little. That afternoon the branches of which the tabernacles had been formed were brought processionally by the boys to the square in front of the synagogue, there piled in a heap, and burned. The Jews watched with interest the rising of the flames, presaging from their various movements good or bad fortune. Jesus preached afterward in the synagogue, taking for his subjects the happiness of Adam, his Fall, the Promise, and some passages from Joshua. He spoke also of too great solicitude for the things of life, of the lilies that do not spin, of the ravens that do not sow, etc., and brought forward examples in the person of Daniel and Job. They, he said, were men of piety, engrossed in occupations, but still without worldly solicitude.

Jesus was not entertained *gratis* in Ophra. The disciples had to pay all expenses at the inn. While he and they were still there a man from Cyprus came to see him. He had been to see John at Machaerus, ten hours from Ophra, and had been conducted hither by a servant of Zorobabel, the centurion of Capernaum. He had been commissioned by an illustrious man of Cyprus to bring him some reliable news of Jesus, also of John, of whom he had heard so much.

The messenger did not tarry long at Ophra. He left as soon as he had executed his commission, for a ship was in waiting to carry him home. He was a pagan, but of a most amiable and humble disposition. The centurion's servant had, at his request, conducted him from Capernaum to John, at Machaerus, and from the latter to Jesus, at Ophra. Jesus conversed with him a long time, and the disciples put in writing before his departure all that he desired to know. One of the ancestors of his master had been king of Cyprus. He had received many Jews fleeing from persecution and had even entertained them at his own table. This work of mercy bore its fruit in one of his descendants, obtaining for him the grace to believe in Jesus Christ. In this vision I had a glimpse of Jesus retiring after the coming Passover to Tyre and Sidon, and thence sailing over to the island of Cyprus to announce his doctrine.

October 28: Mars opposite Jupiter

September 14, 29: Refusing Three Youths, p. 320, vol. I

On the following day, the three youths went again to Jesus and begged once more to be accepted. They promised him perfect obedience and faithful service. But Jesus again dismissed them, and I saw that their inability to seize the meaning of his refusal troubled him. He spoke then with his nine disciples who, by his directions, were to go first to a certain place and afterward to John. On the subject of those whom he had dismissed, Jesus said that they desired to follow him for the sake of what they might gain, that they were not willing to give all for love. But that they, the disciples, sought for nothing, consequently they had been received. He spoke again in significant and beautiful terms of the baptism, telling them to go over to Capernaum and say to his mother that he was going to the baptism. He charged them like-wise to speak to the disciples, John, Peter, and Andrew about John (the Baptist) and say to the last named that he (Jesus) was coming.

Full Moon Aries

October 7, 32: Crossing the River Tigris, pp. 514–15, vol. II

On the evening of the second day of their departure from Sikdor, I saw Jesus and the disciples drawing near to a city outside of which rose a hill covered with circular gardens. Most of them had a fountain in the center and were planted with fine ornamental trees and shrubbery. The way taken by the Lord ran toward the south: Babylon lay to the north. It seemed as if one would have to descend a mountainous country to reach Babylon, which lay far below. The city was built on the river Tigris, which flowed through it. Jesus entered quietly and without pausing at the gates. It was evening, but few of the inhabitants were to be seen, and no one troubled himself about him. Soon, however, I saw several men in long garments, like those worn by Abraham, and with scarfs wound round their head, coming to meet him and inclining low before him. One of them extended toward him a short, crooked staff. It was made of reed, something like that afterward presented to Christ in derision, and was called the staff of peace. The others, two by two, held across the street a strip of carpet upon which Jesus walked. When he stepped from the first to the second, the former was raised and spread before the latter to be again in readiness for use, and so on. In this way they reached a courtyard, over whose grated entrance with its idols waved a standard upon which was represented the figure of a man holding a crooked staff like that presented to Jesus. The standard was the standard of peace. They led the Lord through a building from whose gallery floated another standard. It appeared to be the temple, for all around the interior stood veiled idols and in the center was another veiled in the same way, the veil being gathered above it to form a crown. The Lord did not pause here, but proceeded through a corridor, on either side of which were sleeping apartments. At last he and his attendants reached a little enclosed garden planted with delicate bushes and aromatic shrubs, its walks paved in ornamental figures with different kinds of colored stone. In the center rose a fountain under a little temple open on all sides, and here the Lord and the disciples sat down. In answer to Jesus' request, the idolaters brought some water in a basin. The Lord first blessed it, as if to annul the pagan benediction, and then the disciples washed his feet and he theirs, after which they poured what remained into the fountain. The pagans then conducted the Lord into an open hall adjoining, in which a meal had been prepared: large yellow, ribbed apples and other kinds of fruit; honeycombs; bread in the form of thin cakes, like waffles; and something else in little, square morsels. The table upon which they were spread was very low. The guests ate standing. Jesus' coming had been announced to these people by the priests of the neighboring city. They had in consequence expected him the whole day and at last received him with so much solemnity. Abraham also had received a staff of welcome such as had been presented to Jesus.

October 29: Mercury opposite Jupiter

October 3, 30: Talking with Mara the Suphanite, pp. 70–71, vol. II

Before Jesus again left Ainon with his disciples, he had an interview with Mara the Suphanite in her own house. He gave her salutary advice. Mara was entirely changed. She was full of love, zeal, humility, and gratitude; she busied herself with the poor and the sick. When journeying after her cure through Ramoth and Basan, Jesus had sent a disciple to Bethany to inform the holy women of it and of her reconciliation, in consequence of which announcement Veronica, Johanna Chusa, and Martha had been to visit her.

On his departure from Ainon, Jesus received rich presents from Mara and many other people, all of which were at once distributed to the poor. The gateway by which he left the city was decorated with an arch of flowers and garlands. The assembled crowd saluted him with songs of praise, and he was met outside the city by women and children who presented him with wreaths. This was one of the customs at the Feast of Tabernacles. Many of the citizens accompanied him beyond the city limits. For two hours his road ran to the south, through the valley of the Jordan, and on this side of the river. Then it wound for about half an hour to the west, then turned again to the south and led to the city of Akrabis, which was situated upon a ridge of the mountain.

Jesus was received in ceremony outside of Akrabis, for the inhabitants were expecting his coming. The tabernacles of green branches were ranged for some distance beyond the city, and into one of the largest and most beautiful they conducted Jesus for the customary washing of feet and offering of refreshments. Akrabis was rather a large place, about two hours from the Jordan. It had five gates, and was traversed by the highway between Samaria and Jericho. Travelers in this direction had to pass through Akrabis, consequently it was well supplied with provisions and other necessaries. Outside the gate at which Jesus arrived were inns for the accommodation of caravans. Tabernacles were erected before each of the five gates, for each quarter of the city had its own gate.

Mercury conjunct Mars

June 18, 31: On the Sea of Galilee, p. 403, vol. II

The next day he went with the apostles and disciples down to the ships. Peter's large boat and that of Jesus were bound together at some distance from the shore. They allowed them to float on the water without oar or rudder, for Jesus wanted to converse with the disciples undisturbed by the crowd. It was a beautiful day. They had stretched the sails overhead for shade, and they did not return till evening. Peter was very eager to talk, and he related with a certain complacency how much good they had effected. Jesus turned to him, and bade him to be silent. Peter, who so loved his Lord, immediately held his peace, and saw with regret that he had again been too ardent. Judas was vehemently desirous of praise, though he had not the candor to let it appear. He was on his guard more, however, that he might not be put to shame than that he might not sin.

When I consider the life of Jesus and his traveling about with his apostles and disciples, the certain conviction often forces itself upon me that, if he came now amongst us, he would encounter difficulties still greater than in his own day. How freely could he and his followers then go around teaching and healing! Apart from the Pharisees, thoroughly hardened and vainglorious as they were, no one put obstacles in his way. Even the Pharisees themselves knew not on what ground they stood with him. They did indeed know that the time of the Promise had come in which the prophecies were to be fulfilled, and they saw in him something irresistible, something holy and wonderful. How often have I seen them seated consulting the Prophets and the ancient commentaries upon them! But never would they yield assent to what they read, for they expected a Messiah very different from Jesus. They thought that he would be their friend, one of their own sect, and still they did not venture to decide upon Jesus. Even many of the disciples thought that he must certainly possess some secret power, a connection with some nation or king. They fancied that he would one day mount the throne of Jerusalem, the holy king of a holy people, that then they themselves would hold desirable positions in his kingdom and would also become holy and wise. Jesus allowed them to indulge these thoughts for a while. Others looked upon the affair in a more spiritual sense, though not going so far as to the humiliation of the crucifixion. But very few acted through childlike, holy love and the inspiration of the Holy Spirit.

NOVEMBER 2023

November 3: Sun opposite Jupiter

September 30, 30: Feast of Tabernacles, pp. 67–68, vol. II

Next morning Jesus cured several sick persons, and taught in the synagogue. He also taught in a place to which those pagans that had received baptism and those still in expectation of the same were admitted. In his latter instruction he spoke so feelingly, so naturally, of the lost son, that one would have thought him the father who had found his son. He stretched out his arms, exclaiming: "See! See! He returns! Let us make ready a feast for him!" It was so natural that the people looked around, as if all that Jesus was

SIDEREAL GEOCENTRIC LONGITUDES : NOVEMBER 2023 Gregorian at 0 hours UT											
DAY	☉	☽	☊	☿	♀	♂	♃	♄	♅	♆	♇
1 WE	13 ♎ 14	23 ♉ 18	29 ♓ 46R	20 ♎ 38	27 ♌ 1	18 ♎ 29	15 ♈ 44R	5 ♒ 27R	26 ♈ 31R	0 ♓ 10R	2 ♑ 55
2 TH	14 14	6 ♊ 16	29 44	22 12	28 4	19 11	15 36	5 27	26 28	0 9	2 56
3 FR	15 14	18 53	29 42	23 46	29 8	19 52	15 28	5 27	26 26	0 8	2 57
4 SA	16 14	1 ♋ 13	29 41	25 19	0 ♍ 11	20 34	15 20	5 26	26 23	0 7	2 57
5 SU	17 14	13 18	29 40	26 52	1 16	21 16	15 12	5 26D	26 21	0 6	2 58
6 MO	18 14	25 14	29 41D	28 25	2 20	21 57	15 3	5 27	26 19	0 5	2 59
7 TU	19 14	7 ♌ 5	29 41	29 57	3 25	22 39	14 55	5 27	26 16	0 4	3 0
8 WE	20 14	18 56	29 43	1 ♏ 29	4 30	23 21	14 47	5 27	26 14	0 3	3 0
9 TH	21 14	0 ♍ 52	29 45	3 0	5 35	24 3	14 39	5 28	26 11	0 2	3 1
10 FR	22 15	12 56	29 46	4 31	6 41	24 45	14 31	5 28	26 9	0 1	3 2
11 SA	23 15	25 13	29 47	6 2	7 47	25 27	14 23	5 29	26 6	0 0	3 3
12 SU	24 15	7 ♎ 45	29 47R	7 32	8 53	26 9	14 15	5 30	26 4	29 ♒ 59	3 4
13 MO	25 16	20 33	29 46	9 2	9 59	26 51	14 7	5 30	26 1	29 59	3 5
14 TU	26 16	3 ♏ 37	29 43	10 32	11 6	27 33	13 59	5 31	25 59	29 58	3 6
15 WE	27 17	16 58	29 39	12 1	12 13	28 15	13 52	5 32	25 56	29 57	3 7
16 TH	28 17	0 ♐ 33	29 35	13 30	13 20	28 58	13 44	5 34	25 54	29 56	3 8
17 FR	29 18	14 19	29 30	14 58	14 27	29 40	13 36	5 35	25 51	29 56	3 9
18 SA	0 ♏ 18	28 15	29 26	16 26	15 35	0 ♏ 22	13 29	5 36	25 49	29 55	3 10
19 SU	1 19	12 ♑ 17	29 23	17 53	16 42	1 5	13 22	5 38	25 46	29 54	3 11
20 MO	2 19	26 24	29 22	19 20	17 50	1 47	13 14	5 39	25 44	29 54	3 12
21 TU	3 20	10 ♒ 33	29 22D	20 46	18 58	2 30	13 7	5 41	25 41	29 53	3 13
22 WE	4 20	24 43	29 23	22 12	20 7	3 12	13 0	5 43	25 39	29 53	3 14
23 TH	5 21	8 ♓ 52	29 24	23 36	21 15	3 55	12 53	5 45	25 36	29 52	3 15
24 FR	6 21	22 58	29 25	25 0	22 24	4 37	12 46	5 47	25 34	29 52	3 17
25 SA	7 22	6 ♈ 59	29 25R	26 23	23 33	5 20	12 39	5 49	25 31	29 52	3 18
26 SU	8 23	20 52	29 23	27 45	24 42	6 3	12 33	5 51	25 29	29 51	3 19
27 MO	9 23	4 ♉ 34	29 19	29 6	25 51	6 46	12 26	5 53	25 27	29 51	3 20
28 TU	10 24	18 1	29 13	0 ♐ 25	27 1	7 28	12 20	5 56	25 24	29 51	3 22
29 WE	11 25	1 ♊ 12	29 6	1 43	28 10	8 11	12 14	5 58	25 22	29 50	3 23
30 TH	12 26	14 6	28 58	2 58	29 20	8 54	12 8	6 1	25 19	29 50	3 24

INGRESSES :	
1 ☽ → ♊ 12:18	☉ → ♏ 16:51
3 ♀ → ♍ 19:41	18 ☽ → ♑ 3: 0
☽ → ♋ 21:36	20 ☽ → ♒ 6: 6
6 ☽ → ♌ 9:38	22 ☽ → ♓ 8:57
7 ☿ → ♏ 0:44	24 ☽ → ♈ 12: 0
8 ☽ → ♍ 22:16	26 ☽ → ♉ 15:57
11 ♆ → ♒ 4:48	27 ☿ → ♐ 16:24
☽ → ♎ 9:12	28 ☽ → ♊ 21:47
13 ☽ → ♏ 17:23	30 ♀ → ♎ 13:47
15 ☽ → ♐ 23: 2	
17 ♂ → ♏ 11:22	

ASPECTS & ECLIPSES :			
3 ☉ ☍ ♃ 5: 1	11 ☽ ☌ ☋ 8:48	20 ☉ □ ☽ 10:48	☉ ☍ ☽ 9:15
☽ N ☊ 21: 0	♂ ☍ ♅ 21: 8	☽ ☌ ♄ 15:43	☿ □ ♆ 13:33
♀ ☍ ♆ 22:13	12 ☽ ☍ ♃ 12: 7	21 ☽ ☌ P 20:13	29 ☽ ☍ ☿ 1: 2
4 ☽ ☍ ♇ 3:26	13 ☉ ☌ ☽ 9:26	22 ☽ ☌ ♆ 8:44	♀ ☍ ☊ 17:14
☿ ☍ ♅ 16: 5	☽ ☍ ♅ 10: 4	23 ☉ □ ♄ 9:46	
5 ☉ □ ☽ 8:35	☽ ☌ ♂ 12:17	☽ ☍ ♀ 22:56	
6 ☽ ☍ ♄ 20:41	☉ ☍ ♅ 17:18	24 ☽ ☌ ☊ 11: 1	
☽ ☌ A 21:28	14 ☽ ☌ ☿ 14: 2	25 ☽ ☌ ♃ 9:41	
8 ☽ ☍ ♆ 22:20	18 ☽ S ☊ 2: 1	♂ □ ♄ 16:56	
9 ☽ ☌ ♀ 10:21	☉ ☌ ♂ 5:40	26 ☽ ☌ ♅ 8: 1	
10 ☿ □ ♄ 15: 6	☽ ☌ ♇ 8:25	27 ☽ ☍ ♂ 4: 6	

SIDEREAL HELIOCENTRIC LONGITUDES : NOVEMBER 2023 Gregorian at 0 hours UT											
DAY	Sid. Time	☿	♀	⊕	♂	♃	♄	♅	♆	♇	Vernal Point
1 WE	2:40: 7	6 ♏ 44	2 ♊ 25	13 ♈ 14	21 ♎ 50	15 ♈ 14	10 ♒ 52	25 ♈ 51	1 ♓ 28	4 ♑ 32	4 ♓ 55'39"
2 TH	2:44: 3	9 30	4 2	14 14	22 20	15 19	10 53	25 51	1 28	4 32	4 ♓ 55'39"
3 FR	2:48: 0	12 17	5 39	15 14	22 50	15 25	10 55	25 52	1 28	4 33	4 ♓ 55'38"
4 SA	2:51:56	15 2	7 16	16 14	23 20	15 30	10 57	25 53	1 29	4 33	4 ♓ 55'38"
5 SU	2:55:53	17 47	8 53	17 14	23 50	15 36	10 59	25 53	1 29	4 33	4 ♓ 55'38"
6 MO	2:59:50	20 32	10 30	18 14	24 21	15 41	11 1	25 54	1 30	4 33	4 ♓ 55'38"
7 TU	3: 3:46	23 16	12 7	19 15	24 51	15 47	11 3	25 55	1 30	4 34	4 ♓ 55'38"
8 WE	3: 7:43	26 1	13 44	20 15	25 21	15 52	11 5	25 55	1 30	4 34	4 ♓ 55'38"
9 TH	3:11:39	28 46	15 21	21 15	25 51	15 58	11 7	25 56	1 31	4 34	4 ♓ 55'38"
10 FR	3:15:36	1 ♐ 32	16 58	22 15	26 21	16 3	11 9	25 57	1 31	4 35	4 ♓ 55'37"
11 SA	3:19:32	4 19	18 36	23 16	26 52	16 8	11 11	25 57	1 31	4 35	4 ♓ 55'37"
12 SU	3:23:29	7 6	20 13	24 16	27 22	16 14	11 13	25 58	1 32	4 35	4 ♓ 55'37"
13 MO	3:27:25	9 55	21 50	25 16	27 53	16 19	11 15	25 59	1 32	4 35	4 ♓ 55'37"
14 TU	3:31:22	12 45	23 27	26 17	28 23	16 25	11 16	25 59	1 32	4 36	4 ♓ 55'37"
15 WE	3:35:19	15 36	25 4	27 17	28 54	16 30	11 18	26 0	1 33	4 36	4 ♓ 55'37"
16 TH	3:39:15	18 30	26 42	28 18	29 24	16 36	11 20	26 1	1 33	4 36	4 ♓ 55'37"
17 FR	3:43:12	21 26	28 19	29 18	29 55	16 41	11 22	26 1	1 34	4 37	4 ♓ 55'37"
18 SA	3:47: 8	24 23	29 56	0 ♉ 18	0 ♏ 26	16 47	11 24	26 2	1 34	4 37	4 ♓ 55'36"
19 SU	3:51: 5	27 24	1 ♋ 34	1 19	0 56	16 52	11 26	26 3	1 34	4 37	4 ♓ 55'36"
20 MO	3:55: 1	0 ♑ 27	3 11	2 20	1 27	16 57	11 28	26 3	1 35	4 37	4 ♓ 55'36"
21 TU	3:58:58	3 34	4 48	3 20	1 58	17 3	11 30	26 4	1 35	4 38	4 ♓ 55'36"
22 WE	4: 2:54	6 43	6 26	4 21	2 29	17 8	11 32	26 5	1 35	4 38	4 ♓ 55'36"
23 TH	4: 6:51	9 57	8 3	5 21	3 0	17 14	11 34	26 5	1 36	4 38	4 ♓ 55'36"
24 FR	4:10:48	13 14	9 41	6 22	3 31	17 19	11 36	26 6	1 36	4 38	4 ♓ 55'36"
25 SA	4:14:44	16 36	11 18	7 22	4 2	17 25	11 38	26 7	1 36	4 39	4 ♓ 55'35"
26 SU	4:18:41	20 2	12 56	8 23	4 33	17 30	11 40	26 7	1 37	4 39	4 ♓ 55'35"
27 MO	4:22:37	23 33	14 33	9 24	5 4	17 36	11 41	26 8	1 37	4 39	4 ♓ 55'35"
28 TU	4:26:34	27 9	16 11	10 25	5 35	17 41	11 43	26 9	1 38	4 40	4 ♓ 55'35"
29 WE	4:30:30	0 ♒ 51	17 48	11 25	6 7	17 46	11 45	26 9	1 38	4 40	4 ♓ 55'35"
30 TH	4:34:27	4 39	19 26	12 26	6 38	17 52	11 47	26 10	1 38	4 40	4 ♓ 55'35"

INGRESSES :
9 ☿ → ♐ 10:40
17 ♂ → ♏ 4: 2
⊕ → ♉ 16:40
18 ♀ → ♋ 0:53
19 ☿ → ♑ 20:27
28 ☿ → ♒ 18:31

ASPECTS (HELIOCENTRIC +MOON(TYCHONIC)) :				
1 ☽ □ ♆ 15: 1	8 ☽ □ ☿ 18:33	16 ☽ □ ♆ 1:46	☿ ☍ ♀ 19:31	☿ □ ♅ 17:20
☽ ☌ ♀ 19:12	9 ☽ ☍ ♆ 1:17	17 ☽ ☌ ☿ 15:34	22 ☽ ☌ ♆ 11:39	28 ♀ ☌ P 9:35
2 ☿ □ ♄ 12: 6	♂ ☍ ♅ 3:57	18 ☽ ☍ ♀ 3:17	24 ☽ □ ♇ 19:58	♀ □ ♃ 23:34
3 ⊕ ☌ ♃ 4:46	☿ □ ♆ 23:50	⊕ ☍ ♂ 5:40	25 ☿ □ ♃ 5:55	29 ☽ □ ♆ 0:47
4 ☽ ☍ ♇ 6:34	10 ☽ □ ♀ 9: 8	☽ ☌ ♇ 10:54	☽ □ ♀ 8:24	⊕ □ ♄ 8:11
5 ☽ □ ♃ 4:37	11 ☽ □ ♇ 17:58	19 ☽ □ ♃ 7:51	☽ ☌ ♃ 18: 6	30 ☿ □ ♂ 14: 8
☽ □ ♂ 22: 7	12 ☽ ☍ ♃ 16: 4	☽ □ ♅ 23:25	☽ □ ☿ 22: 3	
6 ☽ □ ♅ 1:21	13 ☽ ☍ ♅ 10: 2	20 ☽ □ ♂ 8:53	26 ☽ ☌ ♅ 9:10	
♂ ☌ ☋ 15:39	☽ ☌ ♂ 14: 3	♀ ☍ ♇ 21:19	☿ S ☊ 23:57	
☿ ☌ A 19:28	⊕ ☌ ♅ 17: 2	21 ☽ ☌ ♄ 1:36	27 ☽ ☍ ♂ 0:56	
7 ☽ ☍ ♄ 8: 4	14 ☽ □ ♄ 13:51	☿ ☌ ♇ 8: 9	☽ □ ♄ 12:41	

saying were a reality. When he mentioned the calf that the father had slaughtered for the newly found son, his words were full of mysterious significance. It was as if he said: "But what would not be the love that would lead the heavenly Father to give his own Son as a sacrifice, to save his lost children." The instruction was addressed principally to penitents, to the baptized, and to the pagans present, who were depicted as the lost son returning to his home. All were excited to joy and mutual charity. The fruit of Jesus' teaching was soon apparent at the celebration of the Feast of Tabernacles, in the good will and hospitality shown by the Jews to their pagan brethren. In the afternoon Jesus with his disciples and a crowd of the inhabitants took a walk outside the city and along by the Jordan, through the beautiful meadows and flowery fields in which the tents of the pagans stood. The parable they had just heard, that of the prodigal son, formed the subject of conversation, and all were cheerful and happy, full of love toward one another.

The exercises of the sabbath were today brought to a close at an earlier hour than usual. Jesus again taught and cured some sick before its close. Then all went out of the city, or rather to a quarter somewhat remote, for it was built very irregularly, the streets broken up by open squares and gardens. And now was celebrated a great feast. The tabernacles were arranged in three rows and adorned with flowers, green branches, all kinds of devices formed of fruit, streamers, and innumerable lamps. The middle row was occupied by Jesus, the disciples, the priests, and the chief men of the city disposed in numerous groups. In one of the side rows were the women, and in the other the school children, the youths, and the maidens forming three distinct bands. The teachers sat with their pupils, and every class had its own chanters. Soon the children, crowned with flowers, surrounded the tables with flutes and chimes and harps, playing and singing. I saw also that the men held in one hand palm branches on which were little tinkling bells, and branches of willow with fine, narrow leaves, also the branches of a kind of bush such as we cultivate in pots. It was myrtle. In the other they held the beautiful yellow Etrog apple.

They waved their branches as they sang. This was done three times: at the commencement, in the middle, and at the end of the feast. That kind of apple is not indigenous to Palestine; it comes from a warmer clime. It may indeed be found here and there in the sunny regions, but it is not so vigorous nor does it ripen to maturity. It was transported hither by caravans from warm countries. The fruit is yellow and like a small melon; it has a little crown on top, is ribbed and somewhat flat. The pulp in the center of the fruit is streaked with red, and in it closely packed together are five little kernels, but no seed vessel. The stalk is rather curved, and the blossoms form a large, white cluster like our elderberry. The branches below the large leaves strike root again in the earth, whence new ones spring up and thus an arbor is formed. The fruit rises from the axil of the leaves.

The pagans also took part in this feast. They, too, had their tabernacles of green branches, and those that had received baptism took their places next to the Jews, by whom they were cordially and hospitably entertained. All were still influenced by the impressions received at the instruction upon the prodigal son. The meal lasted until late into the night. Jesus went up and down along the tables instructing the guests, and wherever anything was needed supplying the want through one of the disciples. Joyous sounds of conversation and merriment arose from all sides, occasionally interrupted by prayer and canticles. The whole place was ablaze with lights. The roofs of Ainon were covered with tents and tabernacles, and there the occupants of the houses slept at night. In the tabernacles outside the city many poor people and servants, after the feast was over and all had gone to rest, passed the night as guards.

Venus opposite Neptune

June 5, 31: The Pharisee of Thaanach, p. 394, vol. II

Jesus meanwhile, with about ten of his disciples, among them Saturnin, went on to the Levitical city of Thaanach, where he was received by the elders of the synagogue. The Pharisees here, though not open enemies of Jesus, yet were cunning and on the watch to catch him in his speech. I saw that by their own equivocal language. They said that he would undoubtedly visit their sick, and asked him whether he would extend that same charity to a man who had been in Capernaum, and who was now in a very suffering state. They thought that Jesus would refuse to see the latter, who had shown himself one of his bitterest opponents in Capernaum. His present sickness, a very singular one indeed, they supposed to be a punishment for his conduct on that occasion. He hiccoughed and vomited continually, the upper part of his body was constantly convulsed, and he was visibly pining away. He was a man between thirty and forty, and had a wife and children. When Jesus went to see him, he asked him whether he believed that he could help him. The poor man, quite dejected and ashamed of his former conduct, answered: "Yes, Lord! I do believe!" Then Jesus laid one hand on his head and the other on his breast, prayed over him, and commanded him to rise and take some nourishment. The man arose, and with tears thanked Jesus, as did likewise his wife and children. Jesus addressed some gracious and comforting words to them, but made not the slightest allusion to the man's proceedings against himself. That evening when the Pharisees beheld the cured man appear in the synagogue, they completely renounced all desire to contradict Jesus in his speech. He taught of the accomplishment of the prophecies; of John the Baptist, the precursor of the Messiah, and of the Messiah himself. His words were so significant that his hearers might readily conclude that he was alluding to himself.

November 4: Mercury opposite Uranus
February 7, 31: Conferring Power on the Disciples, pp. 306–07, vol. II

On this journey Jesus further instructed the twelve and the disciples exactly how to proceed in the future when healing the sick and exorcising the possessed, as he himself did in such cases. He imparted to them the power and the courage always to effect, by imposition of hands and anointing with oil, what he himself could do. This communication of power took place without the imposition of hands, though not without a substantial transmission. They stood around Jesus, and I saw rays darting toward them of different colors, according to the nature of the gifts received and the peculiar disposition of each recipient. They exclaimed: "Lord, we feel ourselves endued with strength! Thy words are truth and life!" And now each knew just what he had to do in every case in order to effect a cure. There was no room left for either choice or reflection.

November 11: Mars opposite Uranus
October 22, 30: Instructions to Obed, p. 82, vol. II

A fast day commemorative of the putting out of Zedekiah's eyes by Nebuchadnezzar having begun, Jesus preached in the fields among the shepherds, also at Abraham's well. He spoke of the kingdom of God, declaring that it would pass from the Jews to the Gentiles, the latter of whom would even attain preeminence over the former. Obed afterward remarked to Jesus that if he preached to the Gentiles in that strain, they might possibly become proud. Jesus replied very graciously, and explained that it was just on account of their humility that they should reach the first place. He warned Obed and his people against the feeling of conscious rectitude and self-complacency to which they were predisposed. They in a measure distinguished themselves from their neighbors, and on account of their well-regulated life, their temperance, and the fruits of salvation amassed thereby, they esteemed themselves good and pleasing in the sight of God. Such sentiments might very easily end in pride. To guard against such a consequence, Jesus related the parable of the day laborers. He instructed the women also in their own separate pleasure garden, in which was a beautiful bower. To them he related the parable of the wise and the foolish virgins. While so engaged, Jesus stood, and they sat around him in a terraced circle, one above another. They sat on the ground with one knee slightly raised, and on it resting their hands. All the women on such occasions wore long mantles or veils that covered them completely; the rich had fine, transparent ones, while those of the poor were, of course, thick stuff. At first these veils were worn closed, but during the sermon they were opened for the sake of comfort.

About thirty men were here baptized. Most of them were servants and people from a distance who had come hither after John's imprisonment.

Jesus took a walk with the people through the vineyards, the fruits of which were ripening for the second time that year.

November 13: New Moon Libra

October 15, 30: Outer Form and Inner Spirit, p. 78, vol. II

After Jesus had earnestly addressed the Pharisees once more—telling them that they had lost the spirit of their religion, that they now held only to empty forms and customs that the devil had nevertheless managed to fill with himself, as they might see if they looked around at the pagans—he left Aruma and went to the city of Thanat-Shiloh, outside of which stood one of the inns established by Lazarus. He instructed the men and women he found working on the immense corn ricks in the field. He introduced parables into his discourse related to agriculture and the various kinds of land. These people were slaves and followers of the Samaritan creed.

Sun opposite Uranus

January 26–27, 30: Where the "Good Samaritan" Occurred, pp. 398–99, vol. I

Jesus, with most of his disciples, passed through Bethagla to Adummin, a place hidden away in a frightfully wild, mountainous region, broken by innumerable ravines. The road running along by the rocks was in some places so narrow that even an ass could scarcely tread it. It was about three hours from Jericho, in a district so retired on the boundary between Benjamin and Judah that I never before noticed it. It was wonderfully steep. It was a refugial city for murderers and other malefactors, who found here protection from capital punishment. They were either kept in custody until they reformed or employed in the quarries and in the most painful field labors. The place received on this account the appellation "The path of the red, the bloody." This city of refuge was in existence even before David's time. During the first persecution of the community after Jesus' death, it came to an end. Later on, a convent was built there to serve as a stronghold, or fortress, for the first religious guardians of the Holy Sepulcher. The people subsisted by the culture of the vine and other fruits. It was a

frightful wilderness, consisting chiefly of naked rocks, which sometimes toppled from their base, carrying down with them the clinging vines.

The road proper from Jericho to Jerusalem did not run through Adummin, but westward of it, on which side there was no access to the city. But that from Bethagla to Adummin was intersected by another running from the shepherd valley to Jericho, and at about one half-hour's distance from Adummin. Near this crossroad was a very narrow and dangerous pass, designated by a stone as the spot where long before had really happened the fact upon which Jesus based the parable of the good Samaritan and the man that had fallen among robbers. As Jesus was approaching Adummin, he turned a little out of the way with his disciples, to give an instruction on that memorable spot. Seated on the stone chair and surrounded by the disciples and the people of the immediate neighborhood, he taught, taking for his text the incident just quoted. He celebrated the sabbath in Adummin and taught in the synagogue, relating a parable that referred to the advantages offered to malefactors by the refugial city, all which he applied to the grace of doing penance on this earth. He also cured several persons, most of them dropsical.

November 18: Sun conjunct Mars

July 5, 29: Meeting Six Men, p. 300, vol. I

Jesus then went along the Sea of Galilee toward the north. He spoke very plainly of the Messiah. In many places, the possessed cried after him. Out of one man he drove a devil, and he taught in the schools.

Six men who were coming from the baptism of John met Jesus. Among them were Levi, known later as Matthew, and two sons of the widowed relatives of Elizabeth. They all knew Jesus, some through relationship, others by hearsay; and they strongly suspected, though they'd had no assurance of it, that he was the one of whom John had spoken. They spoke of John, of Lazarus and his sisters, and especially of Magdalene. They supposed she had a devil, for she was already living apart from her family in the castle of Magdala. These men accompanied Jesus, and were filled with astonishment at his discourse. The aspirants to baptism going from Galilee to John used to tell him all that they knew and heard of Jesus, while they that came from Ainon, where John baptized, used to tell Jesus all they knew of John.

November 27: Full Moon Scorpio

October 30, 30: Meeting with Elderly Relatives, pp. 94–95, vol. II

Early the next morning some inhabitants of Shunem came to Jesus at the inn earnestly begging him to go with them, for they had some children seriously sick whom they wished him to cure. Shunem was a couple of hours to the east of where Jesus then was. The poor people had long been vainly expecting Jesus' coming. But Jesus replied that he could not go then, because others were awaiting him, but that he would send his disciples to them. They rejoined that they had already had some of them in their town, but the cure of their children had not followed. They insisted upon his coming himself. Jesus exhorted them to patience, and they left him.

He now went with his disciples to Endor. On the road from Dothan to Endor were two wells of Jacob, to which his herds used to be led, and for which he often had to struggle with the Amorites.

Lazarus owned a field near Jezreel at some distance from Endor. Joachim and Anne owned another two hours to the northeast of Endor, and it was to it that the latter accompanied Mary on her journey to Bethlehem. It was from this field that the little she-ass, that ran on so gaily before the holy travelers, had been taken to be presented to Joseph. Joachim owned another field on the opposite side of the Jordan on the confines of the desert and forest of Ephron, and not far from Gaser. Thither had he retired to pray when he returned sad from the temple, and there, too, had he received the command to go to Jerusalem, where Anne would meet him under the Golden Gate.

Jesus paused at a row of houses outside of Endor and taught. At the earnest request of the people, he entered some of them and cured the sick, several of whom had been carried thither from Endor. Among the sufferers were some pagans, but they remained at a distance. One pagan however, a citizen of Endor, approached Jesus. He had with him a boy of seven years possessed of a mute devil, and he was often so violent that he could not be restrained. As the man drew near Jesus, the boy became quite unmanageable, broke loose from his father, and crept into a hole in the mountain. The father cast himself at Jesus' feet, bewailing his misery. Jesus went to the hole and commanded the boy to come forth before his Master. At these words, the boy came out meekly and fell on his knees before Jesus, who laid his hands upon him and commanded Satan to withdraw. The boy became unconscious for a few moments, while a dark vapor issued from him. Then he arose and ran full of talk to his father, who embraced him, and both went and fell on their knees before Jesus, giving thanks. Jesus addressed some words of admonition to the father, and commanded him to go to Ainon to be baptized. Jesus did not enter Endor.

The suburb in which he found himself had more beautiful edifices than the city itself. There was something about Endor that spoke of death. Part of the city was a waste, its walls in ruins, its streets overgrown with grass. Many of the inhabitants were pagans under the power of the Jews, and were obliged to labor at all kinds of public works. The few rich Jews found in Endor used to peep timidly out of their doors and quickly draw in their heads, as if they feared that someone was stealing their money behind their back.

From here Jesus went two hours to the northeast into a valley that ran from the Plain of Esdrelon to the Jordan, north of Mount Gilboa. In this valley lay on a hill, like an island, the city of Abez, a place of moderate grandeur surrounded by gardens and groves. A little river flowed before it, and eastward in the valley was a beautiful fountain, called Saul's well because Saul was once wounded there. Jesus did not go into the city, but to a row of houses on the northern declivity of Mount Gilboa between the gardens and fields, on the latter of which were high heaps of grain. Here he went into an inn in which a crowd of old men and women, his own relatives, were awaiting him. They washed his feet and showed him every mark of genuine confidence and reverence. They were in number about fifteen, nine men and six women, who had sent him word that they would meet him here. Several of them were accompanied by their servants and children. They were mostly very aged persons, relatives of Anne, Joachim, and Joseph. One was a young half-brother of Joseph, who dwelt in the valley of Zebulon. Another was the father of the bride of Cana. Anne's relatives from the region of Sepphoris, where at his last visit to Nazareth Jesus had restored sight to the blind boy, were among them. All had journeyed hither in a body and on asses in order to see and speak with Jesus. Their desire was that he would fix his abode somewhere and cease wandering about. They wanted him to seek a place where he could teach in peace and where there were no Pharisees. They set before him the great danger he ran, since the Pharisees and other sects were so embittered against him. "We are well aware," they said, "of the miracles and graces that proceed from thee. But we beg thee to have some settled home where thou canst quietly teach, that we may not be in constant anxiety on thy account." They even began to propose to him different places that they thought suitable.

These pious, simple-hearted people made this proposal to Jesus out of their great love for him. The bitter taunts uttered in their hearing against him by the evil-minded gave them pain. Jesus replied in affectionate, but vigorous terms, very different from those he was accustomed to use when addressing the multitude or the disciples. He spoke in plain words, explained the Promise, and showed them that it was his part to fulfill the will of his Father in heaven. He told them moreover that he had not come for rest, not for any particular persons, nor for his own relatives, but for all humankind. All indiscriminately were his brethren; all were his relatives. Love rests not. Whoever dreams of succoring misery, must seek out the poor. After the comforts of this life he did not aim, for his kingdom was not of this world. Jesus took a great deal of trouble with these good old people, who listened with ever increasing astonishment to his words, whose deep significance gradually unfolded to their understanding. Their earnestness and their love for Jesus grew at each moment. He took them separately for a walk on the shady part of the mountain, where he instructed and comforted them, each according to his or her special needs, and after that he spoke to them again all together. And so, the day

closed, and they took together a simple repast of bread, honey, and dried fruits that they had brought with them.

That evening the disciples presented to Jesus a young man from the environs of Endor, the son of a school master. He was a student preparing to hold a position similar to that of his father. He begged Jesus to receive him among his disciples. He had been informed, he said, that Jesus might perhaps have some need of him, that he might possibly give him some office. Jesus replied that he had no need of him, that the knowledge he came to bring upon earth was different from what he had acquired, that he was too attached to material things, and so he sent him away.

November 29: Venus opposite Node
November 10, 30: Valley of the Doves, pp. 136–39, vol. II

These pagans were at once baptized by Saturnin and Joseph Barsabbas. They stepped into a bathing cistern and bowed over a large basin in front of it that Jesus had blessed. The water was thrice poured over their head.

All were clothed in white. After the ceremony they presented to Jesus golden bracelets and earrings for the money box of the disciples. Those articles formed the principal part of their commerce. They were changed into money, which by Jesus' orders was distributed to the poor. Jesus taught again in the synagogue, cured the sick, and dined with the Levites.

After the meal, accompanied by several people, Jesus went a couple of hours farther on to the north to a little place named Azo, where were many people gathered for the celebration of a feast commemorative of Gideon's victory begun that evening. Jesus was received outside the city by the Levites. They washed his feet and offered him to eat, after which he went into the synagogue and taught.

In Jephthah's time, Azo was a fortified city, but was destroyed during the war that called him from the land of Tob. It was in Jesus' time a very clean little place, the houses in one long row. There were no pagans in it, and the inhabitants were singularly good, industrious, and well behaved. They had many olive trees skillfully planted on terraces outside the city that they carefully tended. Stuffs were also fabricated and embroidered here. The manner of living was the same as at Arga. The people of Azo looked upon themselves as Jews of exceptional purity, since they lived entirely apart from the pagans. Everything was very clean in Azo. The road led down through a gently sloping valley, in which lay the city flanked on the west by a mountain.

When Deborah ruled in Israel and Sisera was slain by Yahel, there lived for a long time at Mizpah a woman disguised as a man. She was descended from a woman who had survived the destruction of the tribe of Benjamin to which she belonged. This descendant assumed male attire and knew so well how to conceal her sex as to arouse the suspicion of no one. She had visions, she prophesied, and often served the Israelites in quality of spy. But whenever they employed her in that way, they met with defeat. The Midianites were encamped at that time near Azo, and that woman went out to them in the dress of a distinguished military officer. She called herself Abinoahm after one of the heroes present at the defeat of Sisera. She passed unperceived through several quarters of the camp, spying as she went. At last, she entered the general's tent and expressed her readiness to deliver all Israel into his hands. She had been accustomed to abstain from wine and to conduct herself with great reserve and circumspection. But upon this occasion she became intoxicated, and her sex was discovered. They nailed her hand and foot to a plank, and cast her into a pit with the words: "May even her name be here buried with her!"

It was from Azo that Gideon went out against the camp of the Midianites. Gideon was a very handsome, powerful man of the tribe of Manasseh. He dwelt with his father near Shiloh. Israel was in a critical condition at that time. The Midianites and other idolatrous tribes overran the country, laid waste the fields, and carried off the harvest. Gideon, a son of Joas the Ezrite, dwelling in Ephra, was very brave and liberal. He often threshed his wheat before his neighbors and generously divided it among the needy. I saw him going out at early morn before daybreak, while the dew still lay on the ground, to a very large tree with spreading branches under which his threshing floor lay concealed. The oak covered with its broad branches the wide rocky basin in which it stood. This basin was surrounded by a mound-like wall that reached to the branches of the tree, so that a person standing at the foot of the oak was as if in a large vaulted cave and could not be seen from without. The trunk was, as it were, formed of many single branches wound together. The soil was firm and rocky. Around in the walls were large cavities in which the grain was stored in casks of bark. The threshing was done with a cylinder that revolved on wheels around the tree, and on it were wooden hammers that fell upon the grain. High up in the tree was a seat from which one could see around. The Midianites pitched their tents from Basan down across the Jordan, and even to the very field of Esdrelon. The valley of the Jordan swarmed with grazing camels, which circumstance greatly served Gideon's purpose. He reconnoitered for several weeks, and with his three hundred men, moved slowly toward Azo. I saw him slipping unperceived into the camp of the Midianites, and listening to what was said in one of the tents. Just at that moment, a soldier exclaimed to one of his companions: "I have been dreaming that a loaf of bread fell down the mountain and crushed our tent." The other answered: "That is a bad omen! Gideon will certainly fall upon us with his Israelites." On the following night, Gideon and his handful of warriors, with lighted torches in one hand and the trumpets upon which they were blowing in the other, pressed into the camp. Other bands did the same from opposite sides. The enemy became panic-stricken. They turned their swords against one another, while being slain and routed on all sides by the children of Israel. The mountain from which the bread rolled down, as seen in the soldier's dream, was directly back of Azo and it was from there that Gideon made his attack in person.

DECEMBER 2023

December 10: Venus opposite Jupiter
October 4, 30: In Akrabis and Shiloh,
p. 71, vol. II

Next day Jesus made the rounds of the city, visited all the tabernacles, and gave instructions here and there. The people observed many customs peculiar to this festival; for instance, they took only a mouthful in the morning, the rest of the repast being reserved for the poor. Their employment during the day was interrupted by canticles and prayers, and instructions were given by the elders. These instructions were now delivered by Jesus. On his coming and going he was received and escorted by little boys and girls carrying around him garlands of flowers. This, too, was one of their customs. The residents of the different quarters sometimes went from their own tabernacles to those of their neighbors, either to listen to the instructions or to assist at an entertainment. On such occasions they went processionally, carrying garlands such as were borne by Jesus' escort.

The women were busied with all sorts of occupations in the tabernacles. Some were sitting embroidering flowers on long strips of stuff, others were making sandals out of the coarse, brown hair of goats and camels. They attached their work to their girdle as we do our knitting. The soles were furnished with a support like a heel both before and behind, also with sharp points, in order to aid in climbing the mountains. The people gave Jesus a very cordial reception, but the doctors of the Law were not so simple-hearted as their confreres at Ainon and Succoth. They were indeed courteous in their manner, but somewhat reserved.

From Akrabis Jesus went to Shiloh, distant only one hour in a direct line toward the southwest; but as the road winds first down into the valley and then over the mountain, it makes the distance a good two hours. The inhabitants of Shiloh, like those of Akrabis, were assembled in the tabernacles outside the gates of the city. They, too, knew of Jesus' coming and were waiting for him. They saw him and his companions from afar, climbing up the winding road that led to their city. When they perceived that he was not directing his steps to the gate nearest to Akrabis, but was going around the city more to the northwest, to what led from Samaria, they sent messengers to announce the fact to the people of that quarter. These latter received him into their tabernacles, washed his feet, and presented the customary refreshments. He went immediately to the central height of the city, where once the Ark of the Covenant had rested, and taught in the open air from a teacher's chair very beautifully wrought in stone. Here, too, were tabernacles and houses of entertainment, in which latter everything needed in the former was cooked in common. Men were performing this duty, but they appeared to me to be slaves and not real Jews.

December 12: New Moon Scorpio
November 13–14, 30: Raising of the Youth of Nain, pp. 141–143, vol. II

It was almost nine in the morning when Jesus and his companions drew near to Nain and encountered the funeral procession at the gate. A crowd of Jews enveloped in mourning mantles passed out of the city gate with the corpse. Four men were carrying the coffin, in which reposed the remains upon a kind of frame made of crossed poles curved in the middle. The coffin was in shape something like the human form, light like a woven basket, with a cover fastened to the top. Jesus passed through the disciples who, formed into two rows on either side of the road, advanced to meet the coming procession, and said: "Stand still!" Then as he laid his hand upon the coffin, he said: "Set the coffin down." The bearers obeyed, the crowd fell back, and the disciples ranged on either side. The mother of the dead youth, with several of her female friends, was following the corpse. They, too, paused just as they were passing out of the gate a few feet from where Jesus was standing. They were veiled and showed every sign of grief. The mother stood in front shedding silent tears. She may indeed have been thinking: "Ah, he has come too late!" Jesus said to her most kindly and earnestly: "Woman, weep not!" The grief of all present touched him, for the widow was much loved in the city on account of her great charity to orphans and the poor. Still there were many wicked and malignant people

SIDEREAL GEOCENTRIC LONGITUDES : DECEMBER 2023 Gregorian at 0 hours UT											
DAY	☉	☽	☊	☿	♀	♂	♃	♄	⛢	♆	♇
1 FR	13 ♏ 26	26 ♊ 41	28 ♓ 50R	4 ♐ 12	0 ♎ 30	9 ♏ 37	12 ♈ 2R	6 ♒ 3	25 ♈ 17R	29 ♒ 50R	3 ♑ 26
2 SA	14 27	9 ♋ 1	28 43	5 23	1 40	10 20	11 56	6 6	25 15	29 50	3 27
3 SU	15 28	21 6	28 38	6 32	2 50	11 3	11 51	6 9	25 13	29 49	3 28
4 MO	16 29	3 ♌ 2	28 35	7 37	4 0	11 47	11 45	6 12	25 10	29 49	3 30
5 TU	17 30	14 53	28 34	8 39	5 11	12 30	11 40	6 15	25 8	29 49	3 31
6 WE	18 30	26 43	28 34D	9 37	6 21	13 13	11 35	6 18	25 6	29 49	3 33
7 TH	19 31	8 ♍ 38	28 35	10 29	7 32	13 56	11 30	6 21	25 3	29 49D	3 34
8 FR	20 32	20 44	28 36	11 17	8 43	14 40	11 25	6 25	25 1	29 49	3 36
9 SA	21 33	3 ♎ 4	28 36R	11 58	9 54	15 23	11 21	6 28	24 59	29 49	3 37
10 SU	22 34	15 44	28 35	12 32	11 5	16 6	11 16	6 32	24 57	29 49	3 39
11 MO	23 35	28 45	28 31	12 59	12 16	16 50	11 12	6 35	24 55	29 50	3 40
12 TU	24 36	12 ♏ 8	28 24	13 16	13 28	17 33	11 8	6 39	24 53	29 50	3 42
13 WE	25 37	25 53	28 16	13 24	14 39	18 17	11 4	6 43	24 51	29 50	3 44
14 TH	26 38	9 ♐ 56	28 6	13 22R	15 51	19 1	11 1	6 47	24 49	29 50	3 45
15 FR	27 39	24 12	27 56	13 9	17 2	19 44	10 57	6 51	24 47	29 50	3 47
16 SA	28 40	8 ♑ 35	27 47	12 44	18 14	20 28	10 54	6 55	24 45	29 51	3 48
17 SU	29 41	22 59	27 39	12 8	19 26	21 12	10 51	6 59	24 43	29 51	3 50
18 MO	0 ♐ 42	7 ♒ 20	27 34	11 20	20 38	21 56	10 48	7 3	24 41	29 52	3 52
19 TU	1 44	21 34	27 32	10 22	21 50	22 40	10 46	7 7	24 39	29 52	3 54
20 WE	2 45	5 ♓ 39	27 32D	9 15	23 2	23 24	10 43	7 12	24 37	29 52	3 55
21 TH	3 46	19 34	27 32	8 0	24 14	24 7	10 41	7 16	24 36	29 53	3 57
22 FR	4 47	3 ♈ 19	27 32R	6 40	25 26	24 52	10 39	7 21	24 34	29 53	3 59
23 SA	5 48	16 55	27 31	5 17	26 38	25 36	10 37	7 25	24 32	29 54	4 0
24 SU	6 49	0 ♉ 21	27 27	3 55	27 51	26 20	10 36	7 30	24 30	29 55	4 2
25 MO	7 50	13 38	27 19	2 36	29 3	27 4	10 34	7 35	24 29	29 55	4 4
26 TU	8 51	26 43	27 9	1 22	0 ♏ 16	27 48	10 33	7 40	24 27	29 56	4 6
27 WE	9 52	9 ♊ 37	26 57	0 16	1 28	28 32	10 32	7 44	24 26	29 57	4 8
28 TH	10 53	22 17	26 43	29 ♏ 18	2 41	29 16	10 31	7 49	24 24	29 57	4 9
29 FR	11 55	4 ♋ 44	26 30	28 31	3 54	0 ♐ 1	10 31	7 55	24 23	29 58	4 11
30 SA	12 56	16 59	26 18	27 54	5 7	0 45	10 30	8 0	24 21	29 59	4 13
31 SU	13 57	29 1	26 8	27 28	6 19	1 30	10 30	8 5	24 20	0 ♓ 0	4 15

INGRESSES :

1 ☽ → ♋ 6:24	23 ☽ → ♉ 23:21
3 ☽ → ♌ 17:51	25 ♀ → ♏ 18:48
6 ☽ → ♍ 6:38	26 ☽ → ♊ 6: 4
8 ☽ → ♎ 18: 5	27 ☿ → ♏ 6:12
11 ☽ → ♏ 2:16	28 ☽ → ♋ 14:49
13 ☽ → ♐ 7: 5	♂ → ♐ 23:33
15 ☽ → ♑ 9:42	31 ☽ → ♌ 1:57
17 ☉ → ♐ 7:18	♆ → ♓ 10:48
☽ → ♒ 11:42	
19 ☽ → ♓ 14:20	
21 ☽ → ♈ 18:10	

ASPECTS & ECLIPSES :

1 ☽ N ☊ 4: 6	10 ♀ ☍ ♃ 3:33	☉ □ ☽ 18:38	28 ☿ ☌ ♂ 0:29
☽ ☍ ♇ 13: 5	☽ ☍ ⛢ 17: 1	21 ♀ ☍ ⛢ 7: 2	☽ N ☊ 8:21
2 ☉ □ Π 16:50	12 ☽ ☌ ♂ 10: 4	☽ ☌ ☊ 13:52	♂ □ ♆ 22:27
3 ♀ □ ♇ 13:24	☉ ☌ ☽ 23:30	22 ☽ ☌ ♃ 12:52	☽ ☍ ♇ 22:55
4 ☽ ☍ ♄ 6:25	14 ☽ ☌ ☿ 5:45	☉ ☌ ☿ 18:52	31 ☽ ☍ ♄ 18:22
☽ ☌ A 18:16	15 ☽ S ☊ 6:10	23 ☽ ☌ ⛢ 13:32	
5 ☉ □ ☽ 5:48	☽ ☌ ♇ 16: 2	☽ ☍ ♀ 19: 2	
6 ☽ ☍ ♆ 6:16	16 ☽ ☌ P 18:37	26 ☽ ☍ ♂ 2: 7	
8 ☽ ☌ ☋ 15:23	17 ☉ □ ♆ 3:51	☽ ☍ ☿ 7:54	
9 ☽ ☌ ♀ 14:22	☽ ☌ ♄ 23:30	27 ☉ ☍ ☽ 0:32	
☽ ☍ ♃ 15:40	19 ☽ ☌ ♆ 14: 6	☿ □ ♆ 7:31	

SIDEREAL HELIOCENTRIC LONGITUDES : DECEMBER 2023 Gregorian at 0 hours UT											
DAY	Sid. Time	☿	♀	⊕	♂	♃	♄	⛢	♆	♇	Vernal Point
1 FR	4:38:23	8 ♒ 33	21 ♋ 3	13 ♉ 27	7 ♏ 9	17 ♈ 57	11 ♒ 49	26 ♈ 11	1 ♓ 39	4 ♑ 40	4 ♓ 55'35"
2 SA	4:42:20	12 34	22 41	14 28	7 41	18 3	11 51	26 11	1 39	4 41	4 ♓ 55'34"
3 SU	4:46:17	16 43	24 18	15 28	8 12	18 8	11 53	26 12	1 39	4 41	4 ♓ 55'34"
4 MO	4:50:13	20 58	25 56	16 29	8 44	18 14	11 55	26 13	1 40	4 41	4 ♓ 55'34"
5 TU	4:54:10	25 22	27 33	17 30	9 15	18 19	11 57	26 13	1 40	4 42	4 ♓ 55'34"
6 WE	4:58: 6	29 53	29 11	18 31	9 47	18 24	11 59	26 14	1 40	4 42	4 ♓ 55'34"
7 TH	5: 2: 3	4 ♓ 33	0 ♌ 48	19 32	10 19	18 30	12 1	26 15	1 41	4 42	4 ♓ 55'34"
8 FR	5: 5:59	9 22	2 26	20 33	10 50	18 35	12 3	26 16	1 41	4 42	4 ♓ 55'34"
9 SA	5: 9:56	14 20	4 3	21 34	11 22	18 41	12 5	26 16	1 42	4 43	4 ♓ 55'34"
10 SU	5:13:52	19 27	5 41	22 35	11 54	18 46	12 6	26 17	1 42	4 43	4 ♓ 55'33"
11 MO	5:17:49	24 43	7 18	23 36	12 26	18 52	12 8	26 18	1 42	4 43	4 ♓ 55'33"
12 TU	5:21:46	0 ♈ 8	8 56	24 37	12 58	18 57	12 10	26 18	1 43	4 44	4 ♓ 55'33"
13 WE	5:25:42	5 42	10 33	25 38	13 30	19 3	12 12	26 19	1 43	4 44	4 ♓ 55'33"
14 TH	5:29:39	11 24	12 11	26 39	14 2	19 8	12 14	26 20	1 43	4 44	4 ♓ 55'33"
15 FR	5:33:35	17 15	13 48	27 40	14 34	19 13	12 16	26 20	1 44	4 44	4 ♓ 55'33"
16 SA	5:37:32	23 13	15 26	28 41	15 7	19 19	12 18	26 21	1 44	4 45	4 ♓ 55'33"
17 SU	5:41:28	29 18	17 3	29 42	15 39	19 24	12 20	26 22	1 44	4 45	4 ♓ 55'32"
18 MO	5:45:25	5 ♉ 28	18 40	0 ♊ 43	16 11	19 30	12 22	26 22	1 45	4 45	4 ♓ 55'32"
19 TU	5:49:21	11 42	20 18	1 44	16 43	19 35	12 24	26 23	1 45	4 46	4 ♓ 55'32"
20 WE	5:53:18	18 0	21 55	2 45	17 16	19 41	12 26	26 24	1 46	4 46	4 ♓ 55'32"
21 TH	5:57:15	24 19	23 33	3 46	17 48	19 46	12 28	26 24	1 46	4 46	4 ♓ 55'32"
22 FR	6: 1:11	0 ♊ 38	25 10	4 47	18 21	19 51	12 30	26 25	1 46	4 46	4 ♓ 55'32"
23 SA	6: 5: 8	6 56	26 47	5 48	18 54	19 57	12 31	26 26	1 47	4 47	4 ♓ 55'32"
24 SU	6: 9: 4	13 11	28 25	6 49	19 26	20 2	12 33	26 26	1 47	4 47	4 ♓ 55'31"
25 MO	6:13: 1	19 21	0 ♍ 2	7 51	19 59	20 8	12 35	26 27	1 47	4 47	4 ♓ 55'31"
26 TU	6:16:57	25 26	1 39	8 52	20 32	20 13	12 37	26 28	1 48	4 48	4 ♓ 55'31"
27 WE	6:20:54	1 ♋ 24	3 16	9 53	21 5	20 19	12 39	26 28	1 48	4 48	4 ♓ 55'31"
28 TH	6:24:50	7 15	4 53	10 54	21 37	20 24	12 41	26 29	1 48	4 48	4 ♓ 55'31"
29 FR	6:28:47	12 57	6 31	11 55	22 10	20 29	12 43	26 30	1 49	4 48	4 ♓ 55'31"
30 SA	6:32:44	18 30	8 8	12 56	22 43	20 35	12 45	26 30	1 49	4 49	4 ♓ 55'31"
31 SU	6:36:40	23 54	9 45	13 57	23 16	20 40	12 47	26 31	1 50	4 49	4 ♓ 55'30"

INGRESSES :

6 ☿ → ♓ 0:35
♀ → ♌ 12: 8
11 ☿ → ♈ 23:25
17 ☿ → ♉ 2:46
⊕ → ♊ 7: 8
21 ☿ → ♊ 21:36
24 ♀ → ♍ 23:33
26 ☿ → ♋ 18:18

ASPECTS (HELIOCENTRIC +MOON(TYCHONIC)) :

1 ☽ ☍ ♇ 15:30	☽ ☍ ☿ 10:29	15 ☿ ☌ ♃ 8: 6	19 ⊕ □ ♆ 0:28	☽ ☌ ⛢ 16:58	☽ □ ⛢ 18:58
☿ ☌ ♄ 19:41	9 ☽ □ ♇ 3: 9	♀ □ ♂ 16:59	☿ □ ♄ 2:40	24 ☽ □ ♄ 22: 6	☿ N ☊ 22:23
2 ☿ □ ⊕ 14:35	10 ☽ ☍ ♃ 5:42	☽ ☌ ♇ 17:36	☽ ☌ ♆ 17:20	25 ☽ ☍ ♂ 12: 6	31 ☿ □ ⛢ 11:56
☽ □ ♃ 18: 1	♂ □ ♄ 9:51	16 ☿ ☌ ☊ 1:17	☿ ☍ ♂ 20:58	26 ♀ ☍ ♆ 2: 9	
3 ☽ ☌ ♀ 7:24	☽ ☍ ⛢ 19:31	☿ ☌ ⛢ 12:26	♀ N ☊ 22:32	☽ □ ♆ 9:24	
☽ □ ⛢ 10:13	11 ☽ □ ♀ 17:32	☽ □ ♃ 17:59	20 ☿ ☌ P 18: 5	☽ □ ♀ 10:26	
4 ♀ □ ⛢ 4:16	12 ☽ □ ♄ 0: 4	17 ☽ □ ⛢ 5:37	☿ □ ♀ 20: 4	27 ☿ ☍ ♇ 13:52	
☽ □ ♂ 12: 3	☽ ☌ ♂ 1:31	☽ □ ☿ 18:26	22 ☽ □ ♇ 2:33	29 ☽ ☍ ♇ 0: 8	
☽ ☍ ♄ 18: 2	☿ □ ♇ 19:52	18 ☽ ☌ ♄ 8:28	☿ □ ♆ 4:20	30 ☽ ☌ ☿ 5:30	
6 ☿ ☌ ♆ 9:17	13 ☽ □ ♆ 10: 1	☽ □ ♂ 15:28	☿ ☌ ⊕ 18:52	☽ □ ♃ 7:11	
☽ ☍ ♆ 10: 1	14 ♀ ☍ ♄ 0:52	☽ ☍ ♀ 21:34	23 ☽ ☌ ♃ 5:25	☿ □ ♃ 9:18	

around, and numbers of others came flocking from the city. Jesus called for water and a little branch. Someone brought to a disciple, who handed them to Jesus, a little vessel of water and a twig of hyssop. Jesus took the water and said to the bearers: "Open the coffin and loosen the bands!" While this command was being executed, Jesus raised his eyes to heaven and said: "I confess to thee, O Father, Lord of heaven and earth, because thou hast hidden these things from the wise and prudent, and hast revealed them to little ones. Yea, Father, for so it hath seemed good in thy sight. All things are delivered to me by my Father, and not one knoweth the Son but the Father; neither doth anyone know the Father but the Son, and he to whom it shall please the Son to reveal him. Come to me, all you that labor and are burdened, and I will refresh you. Take up my yoke upon you, and learn of me, because I am meek and humble of heart, and you shall find rest to your souls, for my yoke is sweet and my burden light!" When the bearers removed the cover, I saw the body wrapped like a babe in swaddling clothes and lying in the coffin. Supporting it in their arms, they loosened the bands, drew them off, uncovered the face, unbound the hands, and left about it only one linen covering. Then Jesus blessed the water, dipped the little branch into it, and sprinkled the crowd. Thereupon I saw numbers of small, dark figures like insects, beetles, toads, snakes, and little black birds issuing from many of the bystanders. The crowd became purer and brighter. Jesus then sprinkled the dead youth with the little branch, and with his hand made the sign of the cross over him, upon which I beheld a murky, black, cloud-like figure issuing from the body. Jesus said to the youth, "Arise!" He arose to a sitting posture, and gazed around him in questioning astonishment. Then Jesus said: "Give him some clothing!" and they threw round him a mantle. The youth then rose to his feet and said: "What is all this? How came I here?" The attendants put sandals upon his feet and he stepped forth from the coffin. Jesus took him by the hand and led him to the arms of his mother, who was hastening toward him. As he restored him to her, he said: "Here, thou hast thy son back, but I shall demand him of thee when he shall have been regenerated in baptism." The mother was so transported with joy, amazement, and awe, that she uttered no thanks at the moment. Her feelings found vent only in tears and embraces. The procession accompanied her to her home, the people chanting a hymn of praise. Jesus followed with the disciples. He entered the widow's house, which was very large and surrounded by gardens and courts. Friends came crowding from all quarters, all pressing eagerly to see the youth. The attendants gave him a bath, and clothed him in a white tunic and girdle. They washed the feet of Jesus and the disciples, after which the usual refreshments were presented them. Now began at once a joyous and most abundant distribution of gifts to the poor, who had gathered around the house to offer congratulations. Clothing, linen, corn, bread, lambs, birds, and money were given out plentifully. Meanwhile Jesus instructed the crowds assembled in the courtyards of the widow.

Martialis, in his white tunic, was radiant with joy. He ran here and there, showing himself to the eager throng, and helping in the distribution of gifts. He was full of childish gaiety. It was amusing to see school children brought by their teachers into the courtyard and approaching him. Many of them hung back quite timidly as if they thought Martialis a spirit. He ran after them and they retreated before him. But others played the valiant and laughed at their companions' fears. They looked with disdain upon the cowardly and gave Martialis their hand, just as a large boy touches with the tips of his fingers a horse or other animal of which the little ones are afraid.

Tables were spread both in the house and courts, and at them all were feasted. Peter, as the widow's relative, for she was the daughter of his father-in-law's brother, was especially happy and at home in the house. He discharged in a certain degree the office of father of the family. Jesus frequently addressed questions and words of instruction to the resuscitated boy. He did this in the hearing of those present, who all appeared to be touched by what he said. His words implied that death, which had entered the world by sin, had bound him, had enchained him, and would have dealt him the mortal blow in the tomb; furthermore, that Martialis with eyes closed would have been cast into the darkness and later would have opened them where neither mercy nor help could be extended to him. But at the portals of the tomb the mercy of God, mindful of the piety of the boy's parents and of some of his ancestors, had broken his bonds. Now by baptism he was to free himself from the sickness of sin, in order not to fall into a still more frightful imprisonment. Then Jesus dilated upon the virtues of parents.

Their virtues profit their children in after years. It was in consideration of the righteousness of the patriarchs that almighty God, down to the present day, had protected and spared Israel; but now, enchained in sin and covered with the veil of mental blindness, they had become like unto this youth. They were standing on the brink of the grave, and for the last time was mercy extended to them. John had prepared the way and with a powerful voice had called upon their hearts to arise from the slumber of death. The heavenly Father had now, for the last time, pity upon them. He would open to life the eyes of those that did not obstinately keep them closed. Jesus compared the people in their blindness to the youth shut up in his coffin who, though near the tomb, though outside the gate of the city, had been met by salvation. "If," he said, "the bearers had not heeded my voice, if they had not set down the coffin, had not opened it, had not freed the body from its winding sheet, if they had obstinately hurried forward with their burden, the boy would have been buried—and how terrible that would have been!" Then Jesus likened to this picture he had drawn the false teachers, the Pharisees. They kept the poor people from the life of penance, they fettered them with the bonds of their arbitrary laws, they enclosed them in the coffin of their vain observances, and cast them thus into an eternal tomb. Jesus finished by imploring and conjuring his hearers to accept the proffered mercy of his heavenly Father, and hasten to life, to penance, to baptism!

It was remarkable that Jesus blessed on this occasion with holy water, in order to drive out the evil spirits that held sway over several of the bystanders. Some of the latter were scandalized, others were envious, and some again were full of a certain malicious joy at the thought that Jesus would certainly be unable to raise the youth from the dead. When Jesus blessed with the water, I saw a little cloud, composed of the figures or shadows of noxious vermin, arise from the youth's body and disappear in the earth. At the raising of others from the dead, Jesus called back the soul of the deceased, which was separated from the body and in the abode assigned it according to its deeds. It came at the call of Jesus, hovered over the dead body, finally sank into it, and the dead arose. But with the youth of Nain, it was as if death—like a suffocating weight—had been taken away from his body.

The meal over, Jesus went with the disciples to the beautiful garden of the widow Maroni at the southern end of the city. The maimed and sick lined his whole route, and he cured them all. The streets were alive with excitement. It was already growing dark when Jesus entered the garden where Maroni with her relatives and domestics, several doctors of the Law, Martialis, and some other boys were gathered. There were several summer houses in the garden. Before one more beautiful than the others, whose roof was supported on pillars, and that might be shut in by movable screens, was a torch placed high under the palm trees. Its flames lighted up the whole hall, and glistened beautifully on the long, green leaves. Near the trees, on which fruit was still hanging, one could see as distinctly and clearly by the light of the torch as by day. At first Jesus taught and explained walking around; afterward, he entered the summer house. He often spoke to Martialis in the hearing of others. It was a wonderfully beautiful evening in that garden. The night was advanced when Jesus and his followers returned to Maroni's house, in whose side buildings all found lodgings.

December 21: Venus opposite Uranus
March 12, 30: Last Visit with Eliud,
p. 414, vol. I

In the course of the day, Jesus returned to Nazareth, where he celebrated the sabbath. During the night from Sunday to Monday, he made his last visit to the home of the old Essene Eliud, who was close to death.

December 22: Inferior Conjunction Sun and Mercury

November 23, 31: Healing of the Man Born Blind—see Robert Powell's article, "The Healing of the Man Born Blind and the Central Sun" in the *Journal for Star Wisdom 2016*.

December 27: Full Moon Gemini

November 28, 30: Sermon on the Mount, pp. 162–63, vol. II

Jesus rowed with several of the disciples over the lake and landed one hour to the north of Matthew's. Already many pagans, as well as those whom Jesus had cured and the newly baptized, had repaired to the mountain east of Bethsaida-Julias where Jesus was to teach. All around stood the camps of the pagans. The disciples who had been fishing on the night of the miraculous draught asked Jesus whether they, too, should go with him, for their recent success had freed them from anxiety upon the score of provisions, and they felt that all was in his hands. Jesus replied that they should baptize those that were still in Capernaum, and after that employ their time at their accustomed occupations, as the immense number of strangers then in and around the city rendered extra supplies necessary.

Before crossing the lake, Jesus delivered to his disciples a comprehensive instruction. In it he gave them an idea of the whole plan of the discourses upon which he intended to dwell for a long time. He told them that they (the disciples) were the salt of the earth destined to vivify and preserve others, consequently that they themselves must not lose their savor. Jesus explained all this to them at full length, making use of numerous examples and parables. After that he rowed across the lake.

The disciples (the fishermen) and Saturnin began their work of baptizing in the valley of Capernaum. The son of the widow of Nain was here baptized and named Martialis, Saturnin imposing hands upon him. The holy women did not follow Jesus to the instructions, but remained behind to celebrate with the widow of Nain the baptismal feast of her son.

There were with Jesus, Joseph of Arimathea's nephews, who had come from Jerusalem; Nathaniel; Manahem of Coreae; and many other disciples. In these last days I saw about thirty of them gathered together in Capernaum.

On landing at the east side of the lake just below the mouth of the Jordan, the traveler ascended the mountain to the east and then, turning westward, went on to the spot upon which the instruction was to be given. Another way could be taken, namely, that over the Jordan bridge to the north of the lake. But this latter way, on account of the wild character of the country and its numerous ravines, was rather a difficult road to the mountain. Bethsaida-Julias was situated on the eastern bank of the mouth of the Jordan, the river there forming a bend. The western shore was high, and to it ran a road.

There was no teacher's chair on the mountain, only an eminence surrounded by a mound of earth and covered by an awning. The view from the west and southwest extended over the lake and to the opposite mountains. One could even descry Mount Tabor. Crowds of people, most of them pagans that had received baptism, were encamped around. There were Jews also present. Separation between them was not so rigorously observed here, since communication between the Jews and Gentiles was greater in these parts, and on this side of the lake the latter enjoyed certain privileges.

Jesus began by enumerating the eight beatitudes, and then went on to explain the first: "Blessed are the poor in spirit, for theirs is the kingdom of heaven." He related examples and parables, spoke of the Messiah, and especially of the conversion of the Gentiles. Now was accomplished what the prophet foretold of the Desired of Nations: "And I will move all nations. And the Desired of all nations shall come, and I will fill this house with glory, saith the Lord of hosts." There was no curing on this day, for the sick had been healed on the preceding days. The Pharisees had come over in one of their own boats and they listened to Jesus' words with chagrin and jealousy. The people had brought with them food, which they ate during the pauses of the instruction. Jesus and the disciples had fish, bread, and honey, also little flasks of some kind of juice, or balm, a few drops of which were mixed with the water they drank.

Toward evening the people from Capernaum, Bethsaida, and other neighboring places returned to their homes in the boats that awaited them on the lake. Jesus and his disciples went down toward the valley of the Jordan and into a shepherd inn, where they passed the night. Jesus still continued to teach the disciples, thus to prepare them for their future mission.

Jesus devoted fourteen days to instructions on the eight beatitudes, and spent the intervening sabbath in Capernaum.

December 28: Mercury conjunct Mars
    June 18, 31: On the Sea of Galilee, p. 403, vol. II (see commentary for October 29 above)

THE TWELVE MOODS: ZODIACAL MEDITATIONS

"This has nothing to do with imitating modern astrologers, whose methods surpass all materialism, simply adding ignorant superstition to materialist ignorance. Rather, we are concerned here with introducing the lawful relationships of a spiritual world that manifest equally in the universe and in the human being. True spiritual science does not try to find human laws from the constellations of the stars, but to find both human and natural laws from the spiritual world."

—RUDOLF STEINER
(Eurythmy performance remarks, 1915)

GLOSSARY

This glossary of entries relating to Esoteric Christianity lists only some of the specialized terms used in the articles and commentaries of *Star Wisdom*. Owing to limited space, the entries are very brief, and the reader is encouraged to study the foundational works of Rudolf Steiner for a more complete understanding of these terms.

Ahriman: An adversarial being identified by the great prophet Zarathustra during the ancient Persian cultural epoch (5067–2907 BC) as an opponent to the Sun God *Ahura Mazda* (obs.; "Aura of the Sun"). Also called Satan, Ahriman represents one aspect of the Dragon. Ahriman's influence leads to materialistic thinking devoid of feeling, empathy, and moral conscience. Ahriman helps inspire science and technology, and works through forces of sub-nature such as gravity, electricity, magnetism, radioactivity—forces that are antithetical to life. The influence of Ahriman's activity upon the human being limits human cognition to what is derived from sense perception, hardens thinking (materialistic thoughts), attacks the etheric body by way of modern technology (electromagnetic radiation, etc.), and hardens hearts (cold and calculating).

ahrimanic beings: Spiritual beings who have become agents of Ahriman's influences.

Angel Jesus: A pure immaculate Angelic being who sacrifices himself so that the Christ may work through him. This Angelic being is actually of the status of an Archangel, who has descended to work on the Angelic level to be closer to human beings and to assist them on the path of confrontation with evil.

Ascension: An unfathomable process at the start of which, on May 14 AD 33, Christ united with the etheric realm that surrounds and permeates the Earth with Cosmic Life. Thus began his cosmic ascent to the realm of the heavenly Father, with the goal of elevating the Earth spiritually and opening pathways between the Earth and the spiritual world for the future.

astral body: Part of the human being that is the bearer of consciousness, passion, and desires, as well as idealism and the longing for perfection.

Asuras: Fallen Archai (Time Spirits) from the time of Old Saturn, whose opposition to human evolution comes to expression through promoting debauched sexuality and senseless violence among human beings. So low is the regard that the Asuras have for the sacredness of human life, that as well as promoting extreme violence and debauchery (for example, through the film industry), they do not hold back from the destruction of the physical body of human beings. In particular, the activity of the Asuras retards the development of the consciousness soul.

bodhisattva: On the human level a bodhisattva is a human being far advanced on the spiritual path, a human being belonging to the circle of twelve great teachers surrounding the Cosmic Christ. One who incarnates periodically to further the evolution of the Earth and humanity, working on the level of an angelic, archangelic, or higher being in relation to the rest of humanity. Every 5,000 years, one of these great teachers from the circle of bodhisattvas takes on a special mission, incarnating repeatedly to awake a new human faculty and capacity. Once that capacity has been imparted through its human bearer, this bodhisattva then incarnates upon the Earth for the last time, ascending to the level of a Buddha to serve humankind from spirit realms. See also Maitreya Bodhisattva.

Central Sun: Heart of the Milky Way, also called the Galactic Center. Our Sun orbits this Central

Sun over a period of approximately 225 million years.

chakra: One of seven astral organs of perception through which human beings develop higher levels of cognition such as clairvoyance, telepathy, and so on.

Christ: The eternal being who is the second member of the Trinity. Also called the "Divine 'I AM,'" the Son of God, the Cosmic Christ, and the Logos–Word. Christ began to fully unite with the human vessel (Jesus) at the Baptism in the Jordan, and for 3½ years penetrated as the *Divine I AM* successively into the astral body, etheric body, and physical body of Jesus, spiritualizing each member. Through the Mystery of Golgotha Christ united with the Earth, kindling the spark of Christ consciousness (*Not I, but Christ in me*) in all human beings.

consciousness soul: The portion of the human soul in which "I" consciousness is awaking not only to its own sense of individuality and to the individualities of others, but also to its higher self—spirit self (Sanskrit: *manas*). Within the consciousness soul, the "I" perceives truth, beauty, and goodness; within the spirit self, the "I" becomes truth, beauty, and goodness.

crossing the threshold: a term applicable to our time, as human beings are increasingly encountering the spiritual world—in so doing, crossing the threshold between the sense-perceptible realm and non-physical realms of existence. To the extent that spiritual capacities have not been cultivated, this encounter with non-physical realms beyond the sense world signifies a descent into the subconscious (for example, through drugs) rather than an ascent to knowledge of higher worlds through the awaking of higher levels of consciousness.

decan: The zodiac of 360° is divided into twelve signs, each of 30°. A decan is 10°, thus one third of one sign or ¹/36 of the zodiac.

devil: Another term for Lucifer.

dragon: As used in the Apocalypse of John, there are different appearances of the dragon, each one representing an adversarial being opposed to Michael, Christ, and Sophia. For example, the great red dragon of chapter 12 opposes Sophia, the woman clothed with the Sun (Sophia is the pure Divine-Cosmic Feminine Soul of the World). The imagery from chapter 12 of Revelation depicts the woman clothed with the Sun as pregnant and that the great red dragon attempts to devour her child as soon as it is born. The child coming to birth from the woman clothed with the Sun represents the Divine-Cosmic "I AM" born through the assistance of the pure Divine Feminine Soul of the World. The dragon is cast down from the heavenly realm by the mighty Archangel Michael. Cast down to the Earth, the dragon continues with attempts to devour the cosmic child (the Divine-Cosmic "I AM") coming to birth among humankind.

ego: The soul sheath through which the "I" begins to incarnate and to experience life on Earth (to be distinguished from the term *ego* used in Freudian and Jungian psychology). The terms *"I,"* and *soul* are sometimes used interchangeably in Spiritual Science. The ego maintains threads of integrity and continuity through memory, while experiencing new sensations and perceptions through observation and thinking, feeling, and willing. The ego is capable of moral discernment and also experiences temptation. Thus, it is often stated that the "I" comprises both a higher nature and the lower nature ("ego").

Emmerich, Anne Catherine (also "Sister Emmerich"): A Catholic stigmatist (1774–1824) whose visions depicted the daily life of Jesus, beginning some weeks before the event of the descent of Christ into the body of Jesus at the Baptism in the River Jordan and extending for a period of several weeks after the Crucifixion.

Ephesus: The area in Asia Minor (now Turkey) to which the Apostle John (also called John Zebedee, the brother of James the Greater) accompanied the Virgin Mary approximately three years after the death of Jesus Christ. Ephesus was a very significant ancient mystery center where cosmic mysteries of the East found their way into the West. Initiates at Ephesus were devoted to the goddess Artemis, known as "Artemis of Ephesus," whose qualities are more those of a Mother goddess than is the case with the Greek goddess Artemis, although there is a certain degree of overlap between Artemis and Artemis of Ephesus with regard to many of their respective characteristics. A magnificent Ionic mystery temple was built in honor of Artemis of Ephesus at a location close to the Aegean Sea. Mary's house, built by John, was located high up above, on the nearby hill known as Mount Nightingale, about six miles from the temple of Artemis at Ephesus.

etheric body: The body of life forces permeating and animating the physical body. The etheric body was formed during ancient Sun evolution. The etheric body's activity is expressed in the seven life processes permeating the seven vital organs. The etheric body is related to the movements of the seven visible planets.

Fall, The: A fall from oneness with spiritual worlds. The Fall, which took place during the Lemurian period of Earth evolution, was a time of dramatic transition in human evolution when the soul descended from "Paradise" into earthly existence. Through the Fall the human soul began to incarnate into a physical body upon the Earth and experience the world from "within" the body, perceiving through the senses.

Fifth Gospel: The writings and lectures of Rudolf Steiner based on new spiritual perceptions and insights into the mysteries of Christ's life on Earth, including the Second Coming of Christ—his appearance in the etheric realm in our time, beginning in the twentieth century.

Golgotha, Mystery of: Rudolf Steiner's designation for the entire mystery of the coming of Christ to the Earth. Sometimes this term is used more specifically to refer to the events surrounding the Crucifixion and Resurrection. In particular, the Crucifixion—the sacrifice on the cross—marked the birth of Christ's union with the Earth. Also referred to as the "Turning Point of Time," whereby at the Crucifixion Christ descended from the sphere of the Sun and became the "Spirit of the Earth."

Grail: An etheric chalice into which Christ can work to transform earthly substance into spiritual substance. The term *Grail* has many deep levels of meaning and refers on the one hand to a spiritual stream in service of Christ, and on the other hand to the means by which the human "I" penetrates and transforms evil into good. The power of transubstantiation expresses something of this process of transformation of evil into good.

Grail Knights: Those trained to confront evil and transform it into something good, in service of Christ. Members of a spiritual stream that existed in the past and continues to exist—albeit in metamorphosed form—in the present. Every human being striving for the good can potentially become a Grail Knight.

I AM: One's true individuality, that—with few exceptions—never fully incarnates but works into the developing "I" and its lower bodies (astral, etheric, and physical). The **Cosmic I AM** is the "I AM" of Christ, through which—on account of the Mystery of Golgotha—we are all graced with the possibility of receiving a divine spark therefrom.

Jesus (see Nathan Jesus and Solomon Jesus): The pure human being who received the Christ at the Baptism in the River Jordan.

Jesus Christ: The Divine-Human being; the God-Man; the union of the Divine with the Human. The presence of the Cosmic Christ in the physical body of the human being called the Nathan Jesus during the 3½ years of the ministry.

Jesus of Nazareth: The name of the human being whose birth is celebrated in the Gospel of Luke, also referred to as the Nathan Jesus. When Jesus of Nazareth reached the age of twelve, the spirit of the Solomon Jesus (Gospel of Matthew) united with the body and sheaths of the pure Nathan Jesus. This union lasted for about 18 years, until the Baptism in the River Jordan. During these eighteen years, Jesus of Nazareth was a composite being comprising the Nathan Jesus and the spirit ("I") of the Solomon Jesus. Just before the Baptism, the spirit of the Solomon Jesus withdrew, and at the Baptism Jesus became known as "Jesus Christ" through the union of Christ with the sheaths of Jesus.

Jezebel: Wife of King Ahab, approximately 900 BC, who worked through the powers of black magic against the prophet Elijah.

Kali Yuga: Yugas are ages of influence referred to in Hindu cosmography, each yuga lasting a certain numbers of years in length (always a multiple of 2,500). The Kali Yuga is also known as the Dark Age, which began with the death of Krishna in 3102 BC (-3101). Kali Yuga lasted 5,000 years and ended in AD 1899.

Kingly Stream: Biblically, the line of heredity from King David into which the Solomon Jesus (Gospel of Matthew) was born. The kings (the three magi) were initiates who sought to bring the cosmic will of the heavenly Father to expression on the Earth through spiritual forces working from spiritual beings dwelling in the stars. The minds of the wise kings were enlightened by the coming of Jesus Christ.

Krishna: A cosmic-human being, the sister soul of Adam that over-lighted Arjuna as described in the Bhagavad Gita. The over-lighting by Krishna of Arjuna could be described as an incorporation of Krishna into Arjuna. An incorporation is a partial incarnation. The cosmic-human being known as Krishna later fully incarnated as Jesus of Nazareth (Nathan Jesus—Gospel of Luke).

Lazarus: The elder brother of Mary Magdalene, Martha, and Silent Mary. At his raising from the dead, Lazarus became the first human being to be fully initiated by Christ (see Lazarus–John).

Lazarus–John: At the raising of Lazarus from the dead by Christ, the spiritual being of John the Baptist united with Lazarus. The higher spiritual members of John (spirit body, life spirit, spirit self) entered into the members of Lazarus, which were developed to the level of the consciousness soul.

Lucifer: The name of a fallen spiritual being, also called the Light-Bearer, who acts as a retarding force within the human astral body and also in the sentient soul. Lucifer inflames egoism and pride within the human being, often inspiring genius and supreme artistry. Arrogance and self-importance are stimulated, without humility or sacrificial love. Lucifer stirs up forces of rebellion, but cannot deliver true freedom—just its illusion.

luciferic beings: Spiritual beings who have become agents of Lucifer's influences.

magi: Initiates in the mystery school of Zarathustra, the Bodhisattva who incarnated as Zoroaster (Zaratas, Nazaratos) in the sixth century BC and who, after he came to Babylon, became a teacher of the Chaldean priesthood. At the time of Jesus, the magi were still continuing the star-gazing tradition of the school of Zoroaster. The task of the magi was to recognize when their master would reincarnate. With their visit to the newborn Jesus child in Bethlehem (Gospel of Matthew), to this child who was the reincarnated Zarathustra–Zoroaster, they fulfilled their mission. The three magi are the "priest kings from the East" referred to in the Gospel of Matthew.

Maitreya Bodhisattva: The bodhisattva individuality that is preparing to become the successor of Gautama Buddha and will be known as the Bringer of the Good. This bodhisattva was incarnated in the second century BC as Jeshu ben Pandira, the teacher of the Essenes, who died about 100 BC. Rudolf Steiner indicated that Jeshu ben Pandira reincarnated at the beginning of the twentieth century as a great bodhisattva individuality to fulfill the lofty mission of proclaiming Christ's coming in the etheric realm, beginning around 1933: "He will be the actual herald of Christ in his etheric form" (lecture about Jeshu ben Pandira held in Leipzig on November 4, 1911). There are differing points of view as to who this individuality actually was in his twentieth century incarnation.

manas: Also called the spirit self; the purified astral body, lifted into full communion with truth and goodness by becoming the true and the good within the essence of the higher self of the human being. Manas is the spiritual source of the "I," and as it is the eternal part of the human being that goes from life to life, manas bears the human being's true "eternal name" through its union with the Holy Spirit. The "eternal name" expresses the human being's true mission from life to life.

Mani: The name of a lofty initiate who lived in Babylon in the third century AD. The founder of the Manichean stream, whose mission is the transformation of evil into goodness through compassion and love. Mani reincarnated as Parzival in the ninth century AD. Mani–Parzival is one of the leading initiates of our present age—the age of the consciousness soul (AD 1414–3574). One of the highest beings ever to incarnate upon the Earth, he will become the future Manu beginning in the astrological Age of Sagittarius. This future Manu will oversee the spiritual evolution of a sequence of seven ages, comprising the seven cultural epochs of the Sixth Great Age of Earth evolution from the Age of Sagittarius to the Age of Gemini—lasting a total of 7 x 2,160 years (15,120 years), since each zodiacal age lasts 2,160 years.

Manu: Like the word Buddha, the word Manu is a title. A Manu has the task of spiritually overseeing one Great Age of Earth evolution, comprising seven astrological ages (seven cultural epochs)—lasting a total of 7 x 2,160 years (15,120 years), since each zodiacal age lasts 2,160 years. The present Age of Pisces (AD 215–2375)—with its corresponding cultural epoch (AD 1414–3574)—is the fifth epoch during the Fifth Great Age of Earth evolution. (Lemuria was the Third Great Age, Atlantis the Fourth Great Age, and since the great flood that destroyed Atlantis, we are now in the Fifth Great Age.) The present Manu is the exalted Sun-initiate who guided humanity out of Atlantis during the ancient flooding that destroyed the continent of Atlantis formerly in the region of the Atlantic Ocean—the Flood referred to in the Bible in connection with Noah. He is the overseer of the seven cultural epochs corresponding to the seven astrological ages from the Age of Cancer to the Age of Capricorn, following the sequence: Cancer, Gemini, Taurus, Aries, Pisces, Aquarius, Capricorn. The present Manu was the teacher of the Seven Holy Rishis who were the founders of the ancient Indian cultural epoch (7227–5067 BC) during the Age of Cancer. He is known in the Bible as Noah, and in the Flood story belonging to the Gilgamesh epic he is called Utnapishtim. Subsequently this Manu appeared to Abraham as Melchizedek and offered Abraham an agape ("love feast") of bread and wine. Jesus "was designated by God to be high priest in the order of Melchizedek" (Heb. 5:10).

Mary: Rudolf Steiner distinguishes between the Nathan Mary and the Solomon Mary (see corresponding entries). The expression "Virgin Mary" refers to the Solomon Mary, the mother of the child Jesus whose birth is described in the Gospel of Matthew.

Mary Magdalene: Sister of Lazarus, whose soul was transformed and purified as Christ cast out seven demons who had taken possession of her. Christ thus initiated Mary Magdalene. Later, she anointed Jesus Christ. And she was the first to behold the Risen Christ in the Garden of the Holy Sepulcher on the morning of his resurrection.

megastar: Stars with a luminosity greater than 10,000 times that of our Sun.

Nain, Youth of: Referred to in the Gospel of Luke as the son of the widow of Nain. The Youth of Nain—at the time he was twelve years old—was raised from the dead by Jesus. The Youth of Nain later reincarnated as the Prophet Mani (third century AD) and subsequently as the Grail King Parzival (ninth century AD).

Nathan Jesus: From the priestly line of David, as described in the Gospel of Luke. An immaculate and pure soul whose one and only physical incarnation was as Jesus of Nazareth (Nathan Jesus).

Nathan Mary: A pure being who was the mother of the Nathan Jesus. The Nathan Mary died in AD 12, but her spirit united with the Solomon Mary at the time of the Baptism of Jesus in the River Jordan. From this time on, the Solomon Mary—spiritually united with the Nathan Mary—was known as the Virgin Mary.

New Jerusalem: A spiritual condition denoting humanity's future existence that will come into being as human beings free themselves from the *maya* of the material world and work together to bring about a spiritualized Earth.

Osiris: *Osiris* and *Isis* are names given by the Egyptians to the preincarnatory forms of the spiritual beings who are now known as Christ and Sophia.

Parzival: Son of Gahmuret and Herzeloyde in the epic *Parzival* by Wolfram von Eschenbach.

Although written in the thirteenth century, this work refers to actual people and events in the ninth century AD, one of whom (the central figure) bore the name Parzival. After living a life of dullness and doubt, Parzival's mission was to seek the Castle of the Grail and to ask the question "What ails thee?" of the Grail King, Anfortas—moreover, to ask the question without being bidden to do so. Parzival eventually became the new Grail King, the successor of Anfortas. Parzival was the reincarnated prophet Mani. In the incarnation preceding that of Mani, he was incarnated as the Youth of Nain (Luke 7:11–15). Parzival is a great initiate responsible for guiding humanity during the Age of Pisces, which has given birth to the cultural epoch of the development of the consciousness soul (AD 1414–3574).

Pentecost: Descent of the Holy Spirit fifty days after Easter, whereby the cosmic "I AM" was birthed among the disciples and those individuals close to Christ. They received the capacity to develop manas, or spirit self, within the community of striving human individuals, whereby the birth of the spirit self is facilitated through the soul of the Virgin Mary. See also World Pentecost.

phantom body: The pure spiritual form of the human physical body, unhindered by matter. The far-distant future state of the human physical body when it has become purified and spiritualized into a body of transformed divine will.

Presbyter John: Refers to Lazarus–John who moved to Ephesus about twenty years after the Virgin Mary had died there. In Ephesus he became a bishop. He is the author of the book of Revelation, the Gospel of St. John, and the Letters of John.

Risen One: The initial appearance of Christ in his phantom body (resurrection body), beginning with his appearance to Mary Magdalene on Easter Sunday morning. Christ frequently appeared to the disciples in his phantom body during the forty days leading from Easter to Ascension.

Satan: The traditional Christian name for Ahriman.

Serpent: Another name for Lucifer, but sometimes naming a combination of Lucifer and Ahriman: "The great dragon was hurled down—that ancient serpent called the devil, or Satan, who leads the whole world astray" (Rev. 12:9).

Shepherd Stream: Biblically, the genealogical line from David the shepherd through his son Nathan. It was into this line that the Nathan Jesus was born, whose birth is described in the Gospel of Luke. Rudolf Steiner describes the shepherds, who—according to Luke—came to pay homage to the newborn child, as those servants of pure heart who perceive the goodwill streaming up from Mother Earth. The hearts of the shepherds were kindled with the fire of Divine Love by the coming of the Christ. The shepherds can be regarded as precursors of the heart stream of humanity that now intuits the being of Christ as the spirit of the Earth.

Solomon Jesus: Descended from the genealogical line from David through his son Solomon. This line of descent is described in the Gospel of Matthew. The Solomon Jesus was a reincarnation of Zoroaster (sixth century BC). In turn, Zoroaster was a reincarnation of Zarathustra (6000 BC), the great prophet and founder of the ancient Persian religion of Zoroastrianism. He was a bodhisattva who, as the founder of this new religion that focused on the Sun Spirit Ahura Mazda, helped prepare humanity for the subsequent descent into incarnation of Ahura Mazda, the cosmic Sun Spirit, as Christ.

Solomon Mary: The wise mother of the Solomon Jesus, who adopted the Nathan Jesus after the death of the Nathan Mary. At the time of the Baptism of Jesus in the River Jordan, the spirit of the Nathan Mary united with the Solomon Mary. Usually referred to as the Virgin Mary or Mother Mary, the Solomon Mary bore witness at the foot of the cross to the Mystery of Golgotha. She died in Ephesus eleven years after Christ's Ascension.

Sophia: Part of the Divine Feminine Trinity comprising the Mother (counterpart of the Father), the Daughter (counterpart of the Son), and the Holy Soul (counterpart of the Holy Spirit). Sophia, also known as the Bride of the Lamb, is the Daughter aspect of the threefold Divine Feminine Trinity. To the Egyptians Sophia was known as Isis, who was seen as belonging to the starry realm surrounding the Earth. In the

Book of Proverbs, attributed to King Solomon, Sophia's temple has seven pillars (Proverbs 9:1). The seven pillars in Sophia's temple represent the seven great stages of Earth evolution (from ancient Saturn to future Vulcan).

Sorath: The great enemy of Christ who works against the "I" in the human being. Sorath is identified with the two-horned beast that rises up from the depths of Earth, as described in the book of Revelation. Sorath is the Sun Demon, and is identified by Rudolf Steiner as the Antichrist. According to the book of Revelation, his number is 666.

Sun Demon: Another name for Sorath.

Transfiguration: The event on Mt. Tabor where Jesus Christ was illumined with Divine Light raying forth from the purified etheric body of Jesus, which the Divine "I AM" of Christ had penetrated. The Gospels of Matthew and Luke describe the Transfiguration. The Sun-like radiance that shone forth from Jesus Christ on Mt. Tabor was an expression of the purified etheric body that had its origin during the Old Sun period of Earth evolution.

Transubstantiation: Sacramental transformation of physical substance—for example, the transubstantiation of bread and wine during the Mass to become the body and blood of Christ. During the Holy Eucharist the bread and wine are transformed in such a way that the substances of bread and wine are infused with the life force (body) and light (blood) of Christ. Thereby the bread and wine are reunited with their divine archetypes and are no longer "merely" physical substances, but are bearers on the physical level of a spiritual reality.

Turning Point of Time: Transition between involution and evolution, as marked by the Mystery of Golgotha. The descending stream of involution culminated with the Mystery of Golgotha. With the descent of the Cosmic Christ into earthly evolution, through his sacrifice on Golgotha an ascending stream of evolution began. This sacrifice of Christ was followed by the events of his Resurrection and Ascension, which were followed

in turn by Whitsun (Pentecost)—all expressing the ascending stream of evolution. This path of ascent was also opened up to all human beings by way of the power of the divine "I AM" bestowed—at least, potentially—on all humanity by Christ through his sacrifice on the cross.

Union in the Temple: The event of the union of the spirit of the Solomon Jesus with the twelve-year-old Nathan Jesus. This union of the two Jesus children signified the uniting of the priestly (Nathan) line and the kingly (Solomon) line—both lines descended from King David.

Whitsun: "White Sunday"; Pentecost.

World Pentecost is the gradual event of cosmic revelation becoming human revelation as a signature of the end of the Dark Age (Kali Yuga). Anthroposophy (Spiritual Science) is a language of spiritual truth that could awake a community of striving human beings to the presence of the Holy Spirit and the founding of the New Jerusalem.

Zarathustra: The great teacher of the ancient Persians in the sixth millennium BC (around 6000 BC). In the sixth century BC, Zarathustra reincarnated as Zoroaster. He then reincarnated as the Solomon Jesus (6 BC–AD 12), whose birth is described in the Gospel of Matthew.

Zoroaster: An incarnation of Zarathustra. Zarathustra–Zoroaster was a Bodhisattva. Zoroaster lived in the sixth century BC. He was a master of wisdom. Among his communications as a teacher of wisdom was his specification as to how the zodiac of living beings in the heavens comes to expression in relation to the stars comprising the twelve zodiacal constellations. Zoroaster subsequently incarnated as the Solomon Jesus, whose birth is described in the Gospel of Matthew, to whom the three magi came from the East bearing gifts of gold, frankincense, and myrrh.

CITED WORKS AND RELATED READING

See "Literature" on page 10 for an annotated list of books on Astrosophy.

Addey, John. *Harmonics in Astrology: An Introductory Textbook to the New Understanding of an Old Science.* London: Eyebright Books, 2009.

Andreev, Daniel. *The Rose of the World.* Hudson, NY: Lindisfarne Books, 1997.

Anonymous. *Meditations on the Tarot: A Journey into Christian Hermeticism.* New York: Putnam, 2002.

Bidez, Joseph. *La vie de l'empereur Julien.* Paris: Les Belles Lettres, 1930.

de la Bléterie, Jean-Philippe-René. *Vie de l'empereur Julien.* Paris: Savoye, 1775.

Dorsan, Jacques. *The Clockwise House System: A True Foundation for Sidereal and Tropical Astrology.* Great Barrington, MA: Lindisfarne Books, 2011.

Dreyer, John Louis Emil. *Tycho Brahe: A Picture of Scientific Life and Work in the Sixteenth Century.* Edinburgh: Adam and Charles Black, 1890.

Douno, Beinsa. *Paneurhythmy: Supreme Cosmic Rhythm.* Sofia, Bulgaria: Bialo Bratstvo, 2004.

Emmerich, Anne Catherine. *The Visions of Anne Catherine Emmerich* (3 vols.). Kettering, OH: Angelico Press, 2015.

Fox, W. Sherwood, and R. E. K. Pemberton. *Passages in Greek and Latin Literature relating to Zoroaster and Zoroastrianism.* Bombay: D. B. Taraporevale Sons, 1928.

Gauquelin, Michael. *Cosmic Influences on Human Behavior: The Planetary Factors in Personality.* London: Garnstone, 1973.

Gershom, Yonassan. *Beyond the Ashes: Cases of Reincarnation from the Holocaust.* Virginia Beach, VA: A.R.E. Press, 1992.

Greub, Werner. *Wolfram von Eschenbach und die Wirklichkeit des Grals.* Philosophisch-Anthroposophischer Verlag, 1974.

Hartmann, Steffen. *The Michael Prophecy and the Years 2012–2033: Rudolf Steiner and the Culmination of Anthroposophy.* Forest Row, UK: Temple Lodge, 2020.

Isaacson, Estelle. *Through the Eyes of Mary Magdalene,* 3 vols. Taos, NM: LogoSophia, 2012–2015.

Kimpfler, Anton. *Okkulte Umweltfragen. Zur Urteilsbildung gegenüber der Unternatur und den untersinnlichen Kräften* (Occult environmental issues. Forming judgments on sub-nature and subsensory forces). Wies, Germany: Anders-Leben, 1982.

Kuhn, Thomas. *The Copernican Revolution: Planetary Astronomy in the Development of Western Thought.* Cambridge, MA: Harvard, 1992.

Langdon, S., and J. K. Fotherinham. *The Venus Tablets of Ammizaduga: A Solution of Babylonian Chronology by Means of the Venus Observations of the First Dynasty.* Oxford, UK: Oxford University, 1928.

McLaren Lainson, Claudia. *The Circle of Twelve and the Legacy of Valentin Tomberg.* Boulder: Windrose Academy, 2015.

Powell, Robert A. *The Christ Mystery.* Fair Oaks, CA: Rudolf Steiner College, 1999.

——. *Christian Hermetic Astrology: The Star of the Magi and the Life of Christ.* Great Barrington, MA: Lindisfarne Books, 2009.

——. *Chronicle of the Living Christ: The Life and Ministry of Jesus Christ: Foundations of Cosmic Christianity.* Hudson, NY: Anthroposophic Press, 1996.

——. *Cultivating Inner Radiance and the Body of Immortality: Awakening the Soul through Modern Etheric Movement.* Great Barrington, MA: Lindisfarne Books, 2012.

——. *Elijah Come Again: A Prophet for Our Time: A Scientific Approach to Reincarnation.* Great Barrington, MA: Lindisfarne Books, 2009.

——. *Hermetic Astrology,* vols. 1 and 2. San Rafael, CA: Sophia Foundation Press, 2006.

——. *History of the Zodiac.* San Rafael, CA: Sophia Academic Press, 2007.

——. *The Most Holy Trinosophia: The New Revelation of the Divine Feminine.* Great Barrington, MA: SteinerBooks, 2000.

——. *The Mystery, Biography, and Destiny of Mary Magdalene: Sister of Lazarus–John and Spiritual Sister of Jesus.* Great Barrington, MA: Lindisfarne Books, 2008.

——. *Prophecy Phenomena Hope: The Real Meaning of 2012: Christ and the Maya Calendar, an Update.* Great Barrington, MA: SteinerBooks, 2011.

——. *The Sign of the Son of Man in Heaven*. San Rafael, CA: Sophia Foundation, 2007.

——. *The Sophia Teachings: The Emergence of the Divine Feminine in Our Time*. Great Barrington, MA: Lindisfarne Books, 2007.

Powell, Robert A., and David Bowden. *Astrogeographia: Correspondences between the Stars and Earthly Locations: Earth Chakras and the Bible of Astrology*. Great Barrington, MA: SteinerBooks, 2012.

Powell, Robert A., and Kevin Dann. *The Astrological Revolution: Unveiling the Science of the Stars as a Science of Reincarnation and Karma*. Great Barrington, MA: SteinerBooks, 2010.

——. *Christ and the Maya Calendar: 2012 and the Coming of the Antichrist*. Great Barrington, MA: SteinerBooks, 2009.

Powell, Robert A., and Estelle Isaacson. *Gautama Buddha's Successor: A Force for Good in our Time*. Great Barrington, MA: SteinerBooks, 2013.

——. *The Mystery of Sophia: Bearer of the New Culture: The Rose of the World*. Great Barrington, MA: SteinerBooks, 2014.

Powell, Robert A., and Lacquanna Paul. *Cosmic Dances of the Planets*. San Rafael, CA: Sophia Foundation Press, 2006.

Powell, Robert A., and Peter Treadgold. *The Sidereal Zodiac*. Tempe, AZ: AFA, 1985.

Prokofieff, Sergei O. *May Human Beings Hear It! The Mystery of the Christmas Conference*. Forest Row, UK: Temple Lodge, 2014.

Renold, Maria. *Intervals, Scales, Tones: And the Concert Pitch c = 128 Hz*. Forest Row, UK: Temple Lodge, 2015.

Rudhyar, Dane. *The Lunation Cycle: A Key to the Understanding of Personality*. Santa Fe: Aurora, 1967.

Selg, Peter. *Das Wesen und die Zukunft der Anthroposophischen Gesellschaft* (The nature and future of the Anthroposophical Society). Stuttgart: Verlag des Ita Wegman Instituts, 2013.

Selg, Peter, and Marc Desaules (eds.). *The Anthroposophical Society: The Understanding and Continued Activity of the Christmas Conference*. Great Barrington, MA: SteinerBooks, 2018.

Steiner, Rudolf. *According to Matthew: The Gospel of Christ's Humanity* (CW 123). Great Barrington, MA: Anthroposophic Press, 2002.

——. *Anthroposophical Leading Thoughts: Anthroposophy as a Path of Knowledge: The Michael Mystery* (CW 26). London: Rudolf Steiner Press, 1973.

——. *Approaching the Mystery of Golgotha* (CW 152). Great Barrington, MA: SteinerBooks, 2018.

——. *The Arts and Their Mission* (CW 276). Hudson, NY: Anthroposophic Press, 1986.

——. *Astronomy and Astrology: Finding a Relationship to the Cosmos*. Forest Row, UK: Rudolf Steiner Press, 2009.

——. *Autobiography: Chapters in the Course of my Life, 1861–1907* (CW 28). Great Barrington, MA: SteinerBooks, 2000.

——. *Calendar of the Soul* (CW 40). Hudson, NY: Anthroposophic Press, 1988.

——. *Christ and the Spiritual World and the Search for the Holy Grail* (CW 149). Forest Row, UK: Rudolf Steiner Press, 1963.

——. *The Christmas Conference for the Foundation of the General Anthroposophical Society 1923/1924: The Laying of the Foundation Stone, Lectures and Addresses, Discussions of the Statutes* (CW 260). Hudson, NY: Anthroposophic Press, 1990/2020.

——. *Concerning the Astral World and Devachan* (CW 88). Great Barrington, MA: SteinerBooks, 2018.

——. *Concerning the History and Content of the Higher Degrees of the Esoteric School, 1904–1914* (CW 264). Ft. Collins, CO: Etheric Dimensions, 2005.

——. *Constitution of the School of Spiritual Science: An Introductory Guide* (CW 37/260). Forest Row, UK: Rudolf Steiner Press, 2013.

——. *Et Incarnatus Est: The Time Cycle in Historic Events* (CW 180). Spring Valley, NY: Mercury Press, 2006.

——. *The Fall of the Spirits of Darkness* (CW 177). Forest Row, UK: Rudolf Steiner Press, 1993.

——. *The Festivals and Their Meaning*. Forest Row, UK: Rudolf Steiner Press, 1996.

——. *From Jesus to Christ* (CW 131). Forest Row, UK: Rudolf Steiner Press, 2005.

——. *The Foundation Stone / The Life, Nature, and Cultivation of Anthroposophy* (CW 260/260a). London: Rudolf Steiner Press, 1996.

——. *Freemasonry and Ritual Work: The Misraim Service* (CW 265). Great Barrington, MA: SteinerBooks, 2007.

——. *Human and Cosmic Thought* (CW 151). Forest Row, UK: Rudolf Steiner Press, 2015.

——. *Inner Experiences of Evolution* (CW 132). Great Barrington, MA: SteinerBooks, 2006.

——. *Interdisciplinary Astronomy: Third Scientific Course* (CW 323). Great Barrington, MA: SteinerBooks, 2003.

——. *Karmic Relationships: Esoteric Studies,* 8 vols. (CW 240). Forest Row, UK: Rudolf Steiner Press, 1982–2017.

——. *Man and the World of Stars. The Spiritual Communion of Mankind* (CW 219). New York: Anthroposophic Press, 1982.

——. *Mysterienwahrheiten und Weihnachtsimpulse. Alte Mythen und ihre Bedeutung. Geistige Wesen und Ihre Wirkung* Band IV (Mystery truths and Christmas impulses. Ancient myths and their meaning. Spiritual beings and their effect, vol. 4 [CW 180]). Basel: Rudolf Steiner Verlag, 2017.

——. *Mystery of the Universe: The Human Being, Image of Creation* (CW 201). Forest Row, UK: Rudolf Steiner Press, 2001.

——. *An Outline of Esoteric Science* (CW 13). Hudson, NY: Anthroposophic Press, 1997.

——. *The Reappearance of Christ in the Etheric: A Collection of Lectures on the Second Coming of Christ.* Great Barrington, MA: SteinerBooks, 2022.

——. *The Riddle of Man* (CW 170). Spring Valley, NY: Mercury Press, 1990.

——. *Secret Brotherhoods and the Mystery of the Human Double* (CW 178). Forest Row, UK: Rudolf Steiner Press, 2004.

——. *Spiritual Beings in the Heavenly Bodies and in the Kingdoms of Nature* (CW 136). Great Barrington, MA: SteinerBooks, 2011.

——. *The Spiritual Guidance of the Individual and Humanity: Some Results of Spiritual-Scientific Research into Human History and Development* (CW 15). Hudson, NY: Anthroposophic Press, 1992.

——. *Theosophy: An Introduction to the Spiritual Processes in Human Life and in the Cosmos* (CW 9). Hudson, NY: Anthroposophic Press, 1994.

——. *Toward Imagination: Culture and the Individual* (CW 169). Hudson, NY: Anthroposophic Press, 1990.

——. *True Knowledge of the Christ: Theosophy and Rosicrucianism—the Gospel of John* (CW 100). Forest Row, UK: Rudolf Steiner Press, 2015.

——. *The True Nature of the Second Coming.* London: Rudolf Steiner Press, 1971.

Steiner, Rudolf, and Édouard Schuré. *The East in the Light of the West / Children of Lucifer: A Drama* (CW 113). Blauvelt, NY: Garber, 1986.

Strauss, William, and Neil Howe. *The Fourth Turning: An American Prophecy: What the Cycles of History Tell Us about America's Next Rendezvous with Destiny.* New York: Three Rivers Press, 1997.

Sucher, Willi. *Cosmic Christianity and the Changing Countenance of Cosmology: An Introduction to Astrosophy: A New Wisdom of the Stars.* Hudson, NY: Anthroposophic Press, 1993.

——. *The Drama of the Universe.* Larkfield, UK: Landvidi Research Centre, 1958.

——. *Isis Sophia I: Introducing Astrosophy.* Meadow Vista, CA: Astrosophy Research Center, 1999.

——. *Isis Sophia II: An Outline of a New Star Wisdom.* Meadow Vista, CA: Astrosophy Research Center, 1985.

——. *Star Journals II: Toward a New Astrosophy.* Meadow Vista, CA: Astrosophy Research Center, 2006.

Thoresen, Are. *Encounters with Vidar: Communications from the Outer Etheric Realm: From Clairvoyance to Clairaudience.* Forest Row, UK: Temple Lodge, 2022.

——. *Travels on the Northern Path of Initiation: Vidar and Baldur, the Three Elemental Realms and the Inner and Outer Etheric Worlds.* Forest Row, UK: Temple Lodge, 2022.

Tidball, Charles S., with Robert Powell. *Jesus, Lazarus, and the Messiah: Unveiling Three Christian Mysteries.* Great Barrington, MA: SteinerBooks, 2005.

Tomberg, Valentin. *The Art of the Good: On the Regeneration of Fallen Justice.* Brooklyn, NY: Angelico Press, 2021.

——. *Christ and Sophia: Anthroposophic Meditations on the Old Testament, New Testament, and Apocalypse.* Great Barrington, MA: SteinerBooks, 2006.

——. *Inner Development: Seven Lectures.* Hudson, NY: Anthroposophic Press, 1992.

——. *Lazarus, Come Forth! Meditations of a Christian Esotericist on the Mysteries of the Raising of Lazarus, the Ten Commandments, the Three Kingdoms & the Breath of Life.* Great Barrington, MA: Lindisfarne Books, 2006.

——. *Studies on the Foundation Stone Meditation.* San Rafael, CA: LogoSophia, 2010.

von Eschenbach, Wolfram. *Parzival: A Romance of the Middle Ages.* New York: Vintage Classics, 1961.

Vreede, Elisabeth. *Astronomy and Spiritual Science: The Astronomical Letters of Elisabeth Vreede.* Great Barrington, MA: SteinerBooks, 2007.

ABOUT THE CONTRIBUTORS

KRISZTINA CSERI graduated as an economist and worked in the production and financial controlling field at various companies for twelve years. She started to work with astrology in 2002 and attended a course from 2004 until 2007. She became a student of Anthroposophy at Pentecost 2009, when a friend invited her to the anniversary celebration of Rudolf Steiner's "Budapest-lectures." Owing to the impact of that event, she soon left her financial career. She first encountered the work of Willi Sucher and Robert Powell in 2010. In 2012, with her husband she founded the Hungarian Sophia Foundation (www.szofia-magyarorszag.hu). They have a small publishing company and translate and distribute books on spiritual themes. Krisztina translated six books written by Robert Powell (and Kevin Dann) into Hungarian and finished translating *Meditations on the Tarot* into Hungarian in 2020. She is a mother of two little children and lives with her family in a village near Budapest.

NORM D. FEATHER — Norm is a private individual and known by only a few. Simultaneously, and paradoxically, he is a different man to different people and moves in many circles. He is at times a jazz pianist, at others a tour guide, a Thoreou enthusiast, and a farmer. He is at all times a Fool, a Christian Hermeticist, and above all a Musketeer. *Tous pour un et un pour tous!*

NATALIA HAARAHILTUNEN studied singing and Anthroposophy at Snellman College from 1999 to 2003. She invited Robert Powell to Finland in both 2012 and 2013. She was the editor of *Starlight* from 2019 to 2021. In recent years, Natalia has been collaborating with Joel Park to develop the Footwashing service. Her interest toward Star Wisdom has been growing year by year, and lately she has been working with Krisztina Cseri. **She welcomes emails at nataliah@olen.to.**

STEFFEN HARTMANN was born in 1976 in Freiburg, Germany. He studied piano in Hamburg and participated as accompanist in master classes with Elisabeth Schwarzkopf and Dietrich Fischer-Dieskau, and has worked closely with the soprano Marret Winger. In 2007, with Matthias Bölts, he founded the MenschMusik Institute in Hamburg, a leading innovator in the field of contemporary music education. He has followed an inner meditative path based on Anthroposophy since 1997 and has been a teacher of meditation for several years. Hartmann writes essays on salient topics connected to anthroposophic Spiritual Science, meditation, and music. With Torben Maiwald, he founded the publishing house Edition Widar and is the author of several books in German, of which one has been translated into English: *The Michael Prophecy and the Years 2012–2033: Rudolf Steiner and the Culmination of Anthroposophy* (Temple Lodge Puglishing, 2020), a chapter from which is republished in this volume. He has led the Rudolf Steiner Haus Hamburg branch of the Anthroposophical Society since 2012, in addition to lecturing internationally and leading seminar and concert activities in Germany, Switzerland, Austria, Finland, Greece, and Brazil.

JOEL MATTHEW PARK is a husband, father, and Christian Hermeticist based in Copake, New York. From 2011 to 2019 he was a life-sharing coworker at Plowshare Farm (a Camphill affiliate), farming and candle-making with people from a variety of countries, ages, and developmental backgrounds. During this time, he earned a certification in Social Therapy from the School of Spiritual Science through the Camphill Academy. He has been living and working in Camphill Village Copake since 2019. After a time devoted to elder care, he has become increasingly involved in teaching in the Camphill Academy, on topics such as Stargazing, the Karma of Vocation, Theosophy, the Human Soul, the Festival Year, and Philosophical Perspectives. Joel has been a student of Anthroposophy since 2008 and a Christian

Hermeticist since 2010. In 2014, he met Phillip Malone; together, the two of them have been investigating the *Tarot of Marseilles* since 2016. Since then, Joel has led two retreats on "Tarot and the Art of Hermetic Conversation" (2017 and 2019). The fruits of Joel and Phillip's collaboration in this realm can be found at www.the-unknown-friends.com. In 2015, he joined the Grail Knighthood, a group-spiritual practice offered through the Sophia Foundation. Through this, he met Robert Powell, whose work he had been studying since 2009. Since then, Joel has been working actively with him to continue the karma research Robert began in 1977 and exemplifies in works such as *Hermetic Astrology,* volumes I and II, and *Elijah, Come Again.* Joel's first contribution was to the *Journal for Star Wisdom* 2018, after which he became editor for the journal's continuation, the Star Wisdom series. The first volume of this series was published in November 2018. A selection of Joel's writings can be found on his website, Tree-House: www.treehouse.live.

ROBERT POWELL, PhD, is an internationally known lecturer, author, eurythmist, and movement therapist. He is founder of the Choreocosmos School of Cosmic and Sacred Dance, and cofounder of the Sophia Foundation of North America. He received his doctorate for his thesis *The History of the Zodiac,* available as a book from Sophia Academic Press. His published works include *The Sophia Teachings,* a six-tape series (Sounds True Recordings), as well as *Elijah Come Again: A Prophet for Our Time; The Mystery, Biography, and Destiny of Mary Madgalene; Divine Sophia—Holy Wisdom; The Most Holy Trinosophia and the New Revelation of the Divine Feminine; Chronicle of the Living Christ; Christian Hermetic Astrology; The Christ Mystery; The Sign of the Son of Man in the Heavens; Cultivating Inner Radiance and the Body of Immortality;* and the yearly *Journal for Star Wisdom* (previously *Christian Star Calendar*). He translated the spiritual classic *Meditations on the Tarot* and co-translated Valentin Tomberg's *Lazarus, Come Forth!* Robert is coauthor with David Bowden of *Astrogeographia: Correspondences between the Stars and Earthly Locations* and coauthor with Estelle Isaacson of *Gautama Buddha's Successor* and *The Mystery of Sophia.* Robert is also coauthor with Kevin Dann of *The Astrological*

Revolution: Unveiling the Science of the Stars as a Science of Reincarnation and Karma and *Christ and the Maya Calendar: 2012 and the Coming of the Antichrist;* and coauthor with Lacquanna Paul of *Cosmic Dances of the Zodiac* and *Cosmic Dances of the Planets.* He teaches a gentle form of healing movement: the sacred dance of eurythmy, as well as the Cosmic Dances of the Planets and signs of the zodiac. Through the Sophia Grail Circle, Robert facilitates sacred celebrations dedicated to the Divine Feminine. He offers workshops in Europe and Australia, and with Karen Rivers, cofounder of the Sophia Foundation, leads pilgrimages to the world's sacred sites: Turkey, 1996; the Holy Land, 1997; France, 1998; Britain, 2000; Italy, 2002; Greece, 2004; Egypt, 2006; India, 2008; Turkey, 2009; the Grand Canyon, 2010; South Africa, 2012; Peru, 2014; the Holy Land, 2016; and Bali, 2018. Visit www.sophiafoundation.org and www.astrogeographia.org.

WILLI O. SUCHER (1902–1985) worked for more than sixty-five years to understand humanity's new relationships to the stars. His work was inspired by Anthroposophy, his long study and path of spiritual development. The "lightning-bolt" that galvanized his intense interest in developing a vision of the human being's new relationship to the stars was a statement by Rudolf Steiner that the asterogram at one's death is more significant than a birth chart for understanding the significance of an individual life as it affects that person's further development. Sucher combined meticulous mathematical calculations and a fully scientific approach with a personal path of meditation and spiritual development to bring a high level of intuition and inspiration to his work.

ASCLEPIAS is Zizia: Jarrod Fowler and Amber Wolfe. Fowler is a horticulturist, entomologist, and percussionist/rhythmist. He samples sounds from terrestrial habitats. Wolfe is a teacher, astrologer, and singer/multi-instrumentalist. She composes scores from celestial maps. Together they create experimental music with collaborators. Zizia has performed across the United States and released cassettes, CDs, and seed bombs. Pisaura (Michael Pisaro-Liu / Zizia), Asteraceae was published by Sedimental Recordings in 2020. Visit online at https://zizia.xyz.

"When we look up to the Sun, to the planetary system—*and the same applies to the rest of the starry heavens,* for they are connected in a very real way with the human being—we can witness how human karma takes shape in the cosmos. The Moon, the planets Venus and Jupiter—truly, these heavenly bodies are not as physical astronomy describes them. In their constellations, in their mutual relationships, in their radiance, in their whole existence, they are the builders and shapers of human destinies; they are the cosmic timepiece according to which we live out our karma."

—RUDOLF STEINER, *Karmic Relationships,* vol. 7, pp. 169–170;
(translation revised and italics added by R. Powell)

VISIONS OF THE ZODIAC:
DRAWN FROM ANCIENT SUMERIAN WISDOM
by Sophia Montefiore

Beautifully written and illustrated in full colour, this multifaceted book is as delightful to look at as it is enlightening to read. The author and artist Sophia Montefiore explores the symbolism, mythology, and history of the Zodiac as it emerged within ancient Sumerian civilization. At the centre of the book are a series of twelve original paintings of the signs of the Zodiac, with the artist's reflections on their symbolism and archetypal significance. The book also includes sections on Zarathustra, Gilgamesh and Enkidu, archaeo-astronomy and a helpful explanation on the precession of the equinoxes and their associated cultural epochs.

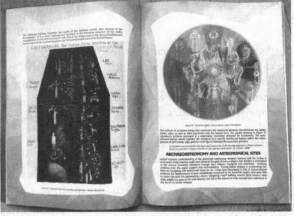

It is both wonderful and precious to imagine preindustrial times when humans kept company with the stars and planets each night, when the exquisite patterns of the constellations across the sky were familiar and accessible to all without the distractions of electric lights, pollution, air traffic, or satellites. Did people feel closer to this starry realm, which now, from our modern perspective, is separated from us by at least 40 trillion kilometres? (extract)

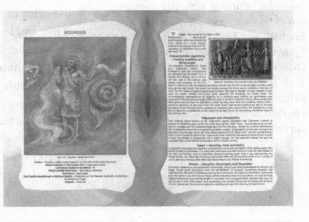

THE CLOCKWISE HOUSE SYSTEM

A True Foundation for Sidereal and Tropical Astrology

Jacques Dorsan

Edited by Wain Farrants
Translated by Lesley Spring

JACQUES DORSAN was born December 22, 1912, in Orléans, France. In 1936, he moved to Côte d'Ivoire, West Africa, where he drew his first horoscope with his index finger on the sand at Grand Bassam beach a little before sunrise, when the planet Mercury was visible. It took him more than seven years before he began to do consultations. Fourteen years later, after intense practice in Brazil and before returning to France, he had become convinced that the houses actually move in the direction opposite the zodiacal signs. He put his idea to the test for more than twenty years before publishing the original version of his book *Le véritable sens des maisons astrologiques* (1984), published in English as *The Clockwise House System* (Lindisfarne Books, 2011). Dorsan also lived in Morocco, New York City, Monaco, Luxembourg, Belgium, Zaire, and New Caledonia. He died September 8, 2005, in Nice, survived by his wife.

Jacques Dorsan was the leading pioneer of sidereal astrology in France. Using more than eighty sidereal horoscopes, this book illustrates Dorsan's clockwise house system. Most of the charts are from the original French edition, with many more added in this edition. The book embodies one of the most important astrological discoveries of twentieth and twenty-first centuries. Astrology normally views the twelve houses in astrology in a counterclockwise direction, the direction of the zodiac signs. According to Jacques Dorsan, however, we should view them in a clockwise direction.

Traditionally, Western astrologers have interpreted the houses as though they rotate in the same, counterclockwise direction as the zodiac signs. According to Jacques Dorsan, however, the houses are enumerated in a clockwise direction, following the daily diurnal motion of the Sun, for example. By using the clockwise house system together with the sidereal zodiac, everything suddenly falls into place astrologically when looking at a horoscope. This key unlocks the mystery of the horoscope.

Thanks to Jacques Dorsan, we finally have access to a true form of astrology—based on the sidereal zodiac and utilizing the clockwise house system—enabling a giant leap forward in the practice of astrology. It allows us to recover the original astrology. This is possible today because of Rudolf Steiner's indications, as well as the research of the French statistician Michel Gauquelin, who investigated hundreds of thousands of horoscopes and confirmed that the astrological houses run in a clockwise direction.

This English translation includes more than eighty charts, both those in the Jacques Dorsan's original work in French and more added by the editor of this edition. The clockwise house system is applied in this book using sidereal horoscopes. It can just as easily be applied using tropical horoscopes.

The Clockwise House System is an invaluable addition to the literature of modern astrology, allowing open-minded readers a unique and profound look at the new and limitless possibilities of this powerful tool of spiritual growth and understanding.

ISBN 9781584200956 | pbk. 6 x 9 in. 330 pp.

CHRIST AND SOPHIA

Anthroposophic Meditations on the Old Testament, New Testament, and Apocalypse

Valentin Tomberg

Introduction by Christopher Bamford
Translated by R. H. Bruce

"All of this work has a unique power, a fiery, adamantine, brilliant quality, stemming from the being of the author who, working within and for Anthroposophy, is always doing new work. Inspired by Rudolf Steiner, thoroughly immersed in Steiner's work, and following Steiner's meditative spiritual scientific method of research—while always acting in the service of Christ, whom he called 'The Master'—there is never a sense of mere commentary or exposition in his writings. We always feel the author speaking from his own experience and making it new....

"Christ and Sophia run throughout these 'meditations.' No 'abstract concept or merely pious mystical state,' Sophia is an actual transcendent being, acting in the cosmos as an archangel and communicating 'Unity'—the unity of the Trinity, of the cosmos, of humanity with all. It is she, close relative of the Holy Spirit and grace, who gives meaning to cognition, for she is true wisdom, cosmic intelligence, the 'plan of the temple.' Everywhere in Tomberg's work, she who is the servant of all is above all the servant of the master, Christ"

— **Christopher Bamford** (from the introduction).

I n these astounding meditations on the true Christian nature of the scriptures, Tomberg shows how the central story of entire Bible is really a history of the Christ being. He describes the cosmic and earthly preparations for the Mystery of Golgotha, its significance and results for humanity and the world as a whole, and the central role of the Sophia being and her relationship to the Christ, the Holy Spirit, the Disciples and Pentecost, and all of humanity. He also imagines the Grail nature of the Christ's involvement in earthly history.

Christ and Sophia contains all of Valentin Tomberg's essential anthroposophic works on the scriptures, providing an invaluable resource for anyone who wishes to gain a deeper understanding of Rudolf Steiner's spiritual scientific approach to esoteric Christianity, as revealed by a close, meditative reading of the Bible—from Genesis to John's Revelation.

VALENTIN TOMBERG (1900–1973) was drawn to the hermetic Martinism of G.O.Mebes as an adolescent, as well as to Theosophy and the mysticism of Eastern Orthodoxy. Later, he was strongly influenced by Vladimir Soloviev and had an inner experience of the Sophia at a cathedral in Holland. In 1925, he joined the Anthroposophical Society, under whose auspices he lectured in Holland and England and wrote on his understanding of the Bible, Anthroposophy, and esoteric Christianity. During World War II, he left the Anthroposophical Society and its internal struggles and converted to Catholicism. In 1948 in England, he became a translator for the BBC and monitored Soviet broadcasts during the Cold War, while continuing his devotion to meditation practice and further writing on his esoteric insights. In 1960, he retired to Reading near the River Thames and died while vacationing in Majorca.

ISBN 9780880107358 | pbk. 7 X 10 in. 472 pp.

GAUTAMA BUDDHA'S SUCCESSOR

A Force for Good in Our Time

Robert A. Powell, PhD
and Estelle Isaacson

ROBERT POWELL (please see page 225 of this volume).

ESTELLE ISAACSON is a contemporary mystic and seer, whose first books were published by LogoSophia in 2012: *Through the Eyes of Mary Magdalene: Early Years and Soul Awakening*. In volume 1 in her trilogy on the life of Mary Magdalene, Estelle Isaacson presents her visions of the life of Christ as seen through Magdalene's own eyes. Volume 2, *Through the Eyes of Mary Magdalene: From Initiation to the Passion,* enters the profound mysteries of Christ's Passion, culminating in the Resurrection. Estelle is also coauthor with Robert Powell of and *The Mystery of Sophia: Bearer of the New Culture: The Rose of the World* (2014).

"The Bodhisattva who took the place of Gautama when he became Buddha will come in the form of the Maitreya Buddha.... He will be the greatest of the proclaimers of the Christ Impulse."
— RUDOLF STEINER (April 13, 1910)

The year 2014 has a special significance that is addressed in this book by Robert Powell and Estelle Isaacson. Dr. Robert Powell is a spiritual researcher who in this short work—and in many other books—brings the results of his own research investigations. Estelle Isaacson is a contemporary seer who is gifted with a remarkable ability to perceive new streams of revelation. Both have been blessed in an extraordinary way by virtue of accessing the realm wherein Christ is presently to be found.

Powell makes the critical point that the year 2014 not only denotes the beginning of a new 600-year cultural wave in history but also that there is an ancient prophecy applying to this very same year, 2014, which can be interpreted as pointing to the onset of the twenty-first-century incarnation of the Bodhisattva who will become the future Maitreya Buddha, the successor to Gautama Buddha. Powell also makes the crucial point that the Maitreya Buddha awaited in Buddhism is the same as the Kalki Avatar expected in Hinduism.

Robert Powell's contribution serves as an introduction to Estelle Isaacson's offering, comprising a series of six visions relating to the future Maitreya Buddha. The visions are highly inspirational, communicating something of the profound spirituality, peace, radiance, and, above all, goodness of this Bodhisattva who is Gautama Buddha's successor. His title, Maitreya, means "bearer of the good," and in Isaacson's visions he emerges as a remarkable force for good in our time.

Also included in this book are two appendices: "A Survey of Rudolf Steiner's Indications Concerning the Maitreya Buddha" and "The Kalki Avatar and Valentin Tomberg's Indications Concerning the Coming Buddha-Avatar, Maitreya-Kalki." The third appendix discusses the significance of Rudolf Steiner's Foundation Stone of Love meditation as a herald of Christ's Second Coming.

ISBN 9781584201618 | pbk. 6 x 9 in. 158 pp.

EVENING MEDITATION

In the evening, meditate on the Earth as a great radiant green star shining out into the cosmos, and allow your heart to speak:

May this prayer from my warm heart unite

With the Earth's Light that reveres the Christ-Sun,

That I may find Spirit in the Light of the Spirit,

Breath of the Soul in the World's Breath,

Human Strength in the Life of the Earth.

Given by Rudolf Steiner to Maud B. Monges of Spring Valley, New York, March 9, 1924 (translated by Robert Powell)